# ALL FOR THE EMPIRE

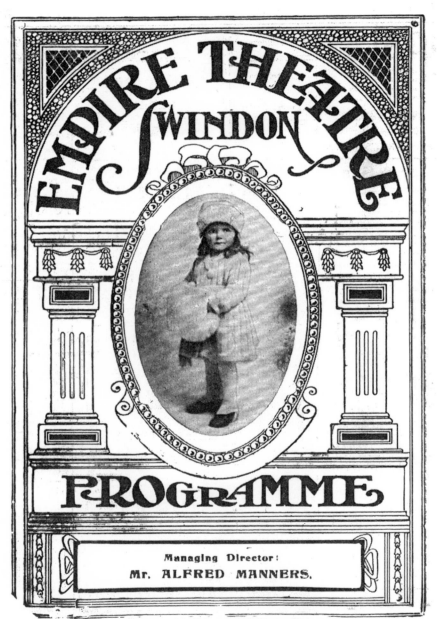

# EMPIRE THEATRE
## SWINDON

# PROGRAMME

Managing Director:
Mr. ALFRED MANNERS.

PRINTED AT THE "ADVERTISER" OFFICES, SWINDON.

# ALL FOR THE EMPIRE

## The history of Swindon's historic theatre

ROGER TRAYHURN
& MARK CHILD

First published in the United Kingdom in 2013
by The Hobnob Press, PO Box 1838, East Knoyle, Salisbury, SP3 6FA
www.hobnobpress.co.uk

British Library Cataloguing in Publication Data
A catalogue record for this book is available from the British Library

ISBN 978-1-906978-27-3

Typeset in Minion Pro 12/16 pt. Typesetting and origination by John Chandler
Printed by Lightning Source

# Contents

# *Introduction*

ROGER TRAYHURN WAS eight years old when the Empire Theatre closed in 1955. He sang lustily at its pantomimes, and shouted 'He's behind you', as appropriate. These experiences, the bright lights, and the happy laughing people made him yearn for the theatrical scene. He became a very accomplished amateur actor, and his interest in the Empire developed partly out of his personal love of theatre per se, and partly through the questions he was asked about the building during more than four decades as a reference and local studies librarian in Swindon. The Empire's history had never been documented; information about it was slight and was difficult to come by. Roger determined to become an authority on the theatre, and to give it a documented place in Swindon's history.

He trawled through more than half a century of local daily and weekly newspapers, and recorded every production that played at the theatre since it opened in 1898: some 2,400 in total. He also sourced their authors (many were quite obscure and had to be found independently), and listed the main players, or the main acts in the variety shows. He amassed an archive of programmes, posters and illustrations, now numbering over 350 items, and he interviewed people who had personal memories of the place. These included former employees, performers, and members of audiences. He also collected references to the theatre and its shows that appeared in the local press and theatrical publications. Roger gives illustrated talks on the subject of his research, and would like to hear, through the publishers of this book, from any readers who can contribute information or memorabilia to his archive collection of Empire Theatre material.

MARK CHILD IS a writer on architecture, history and topography, whose books include *The Towns and Villages of the Windrush Valley, Downton and the Tanning Industry, Discovering Church Architecture, Discovering Churches and Churchyards, English Church Architecture: A Visual Guide,* and *Abbey House and Gardens, Malmesbury.* Since 1960, he has also written books and monographs on Swindon's history. Amongst his Swindon books are *Aspects of Swindon History, Swindon: An Illustrated History, Swindon Old Town Through Time, Swindon Central Through Time* and, for children, *Hometown History Swindon.*

His great-grandfather was a professional musical hall entertainer. He has vivid memories of the Empire Theatre, where he quickly learnt to loathe pantomimes, and love everything else. He watched the theatre being pulled down during the year in which he started his working life in reference librarianship and local history research in Swindon. When Mark left the profession in 1967, Roger Trayhurn took over in the reference library. Roger concentrated on researching performance details at the Empire, carrying out interviews and amassing a collection of Empire Theatre ephemera. Mark ordered this archive of material, carried out additional research, and wrote All for the Empire, adding a final chapter on his own personal experiences of the one-time Swindon theatre.

# *Acknowledgements*

SPECIAL THANKS ARE due to Allyson Jordan, Head of Service, Swindon Libraries and to the staff of the Local Studies Library – Darryl Moody, Dawn Osborne, Liz Phoenix, Alison Swann, Katherine Cole, Rhonda Dempsie, and Tom Blake for their help and patience. Other organisations and people who gave valuable assistance include Claire Skinner and the staff at the Wiltshire and Swindon History Centre, Chippenham; the Swindon Advertiser; the staff of the University of Bristol Theatre Collection; John Bultitude of the Theatre Royal, Norwich, and the archivist Maria Andrews; the Norfolk & Norwich Millennium Library, and the Theatre Royal, Bristol.

The following people donated material, shared their memories, and allowed their printed memorabilia to be copied: Marlene Adams, Fran Bevan, Andy Binks, Rod Bridle, Amos Brown, Ron Burchell, Brian Carter, Graham Carter, James Carter, Pat Chapman, Ivor Chesterman, Owen Clarke, Doug Davis, Dulcie Dunne, Diane Everett, Geraldine Fernandez, Colin Finch, Harry and Jill Fleetwood, Barbara Fuller, C. (Napper) Gould, J. A. Gould, Jan Flanagan, Janet French, Cedric Green, Gill Greenaway, Joan Greenshields, Rose Haddon, Joan Hamilton, Mark Harris, Barrie Hudson, Josie Humerick, Jackie Hussey, Glenys Johnson, Carol Lee, Bob Lewis, Peter Long, Philip Loveday, Doug Martin, Rosa Matheson, Bryn Mayl, Albert Morgan, the late Arthur New, Barry New, Joan Saunders, Bet Simmonds, Roy Simmons, Cilla Slipper, Gordon Staples, Mark Sutton, Mollie Tanner, Barry Telling, Peter Timms, Bob Townsend, Monica Tovey, Graeme Trim, Chris Viveash, David Wainwright, Frances Wateley, Paul Williams, Shirley Wills, and Andrew Witts. Lorraine Child filtered and proofed the narrative.

# 1

# From the middle class to sinners and back-sliders

ERNEST CARPENTER'S DECISION to build a theatre at Swindon in the closing years of the 19th century was opportunistic and speculative. At that time, the population of the Wiltshire town was 43,000. The largest employer was the Great Western Railway Company, whose huge combined locomotive, carriage and wagon works accounted for 11,000 men. The focus for their recreation, culture and self-improvement was a mechanics' institution. This was formed in the town's railway works in 1843 as a society for personal improvement, the same year that the New Swindon Improvement Company was established to provide premises in which these ideals might be realised. Its building, the Mechanics' Institute, was opened near the railway works in 1855.

From the outset, the Mechanics' Institute included a large hall, with a stage at one end, which was used for lectures, concerts and theatrical productions. Over the next forty years, popular plays, musicals, concerts and pantomimes were performed there, and also at other venues in the town, such as the Corn Exchange and the swimming baths. Most of these venues were used on an ad hoc basis, and none of them was large enough to attract first-class theatrical companies of the kind experienced at the Theatre Royal, King Street, Bristol, where Carpenter was the lessee.

The decision to build at Swindon was taken on the crest of a wave of unprecedented new theatre building that gathered momentum early in the 1880s and lasted until it crashed on the inhospitable beach of World War I. Carpenter's dichotomy was whether the people of Swindon would patronise the sort of productions he proposed in sufficient numbers needed to fill a theatre of the size he had in mind. There were no local precedents on which he could base his deliberations. Hitherto, theatre in Swindon had been uncoordinated, and was largely amateur in nature. Production runs rarely lasted longer than two or three days. There was no tradition of music hall in the town, although there had been an experiment. In 1874, the Unitarians moved out of their barrel-shaped 'iron church' in Regent Street, close by the Wilts & Berks Canal, and sold the building. Almost immediately, it was turned into a venue for music hall, when it rapidly became the lowest of its type, presenting entertainment of the bawdiest kind to the rowdiest of audiences, amongst whom passed the town's prostitutes in the hope of securing trade.

There was considerable opposition in Swindon to the nature of the entertainments, for the doubtful reputation of music hall elsewhere had preceded its opening, and its critics' worst fears were now being realised. Yet dissension was not a factor in the early demise of the iron church music hall; it was simply that the project was financially unsuccessful and consequently closed after a relatively short period of time. The building went on to have several more lives (one of which was as a store for beer barrels), and it was relocated to other areas of the town; but music hall was not again presented in Swindon.

The town's social demography of the 1890s was not a particularly promising one for live theatre, as Swindon was then mainly populated by low-paid manual workers and their families. It has to be said that Carpenter's experiences in Bristol were of a predominantly quite different social class. There, as in London and other large centres of population, aspirational, late Victorian, middle-class audiences were rescuing the generic playhouse from the improper reputation it still had amongst their parents' generation. Indeed, by the mid-1880s, the middle-class clientele was about to elevate the theatre to its social apogee, where it would remain for the next forty years. Elsewhere, the theatre was beginning to be the place in which to be seen, and there were plays to which one simply had to go. Would it work in Swindon?

Although the town had a number of middle-class families, their theatrical preferences were largely unknown. Carpenter did have the prospect of attracting audiences from a wider and potentially more lucrative catchment area, facilitated by the Great Western Railway's line that ran east to west, and by the north to south-running line of the Midland & South West Junction Railway. Both lines stopped at Swindon. Of course, the GWR conferred on Swindon another advantage, namely that the town was well placed to take touring shows from London, whose cast and scenery could be conveniently conveyed by rail to within a very short distance of the proposed theatre site.

Carpenter was born in 1868 in Islington, London, the son of Frederick Carpenter, a fine art publisher. Ernest was attracted to the stage from an early age. At fourteen, he was employed as a clerk in a London office and earned extra money by acting three or four times a week in the working men's clubs around the East End. 'My parts were studied at all times and seasons,' he said, 'commonly as I went to and from the office, but occasionally they were put inside my desk and I learnt the words surreptitiously when my chief's back was turned.' In one of the plays, *The Lady of Lyons* by Claude Melnotte, he was required to play the part of an old man. This was revived by another company in 1884, when, because of his previous experience, he was 'called upon at two days' notice', to take another part. He always said that it was *The Lady of Lyons* that encouraged him to take up acting rather more seriously.

At seventeen years of age, he turned professional, joining touring companies playing provincial theatres. Soon he was able to style himself 'theatrical manager', being in charge of the touring companies. These were tough, impecunious times. He told of the day when, having just sixpence-halfpenny left after paying the bill for his lodgings at the completion of an engagement at Harwich, he was required to get himself to the Theatre Royal, Colchester, where he was scheduled to open next day in a new part. The lack of funds meant that he had to walk all the way, carrying his few belongings in a bag, and learning the part as he walked.

Sometimes, the company played six different venues in as many days; then, for two years, he acted exclusively in *The Middleman* by Henry Arthur Jones, a play for which he became well known. It was during the tour of *The Middleman* that Carpenter fell in love with Jessie Beatrice Lord from Manchester, whose father, John Buckley Lord had been head of the Transfer Department of the Lancashire & Yorkshire Railway. She was an actress, part of Carpenter's company, and just prior to their marriage the two were lodging, together with the rest of the company, at The Marquis of Granby, Butchery Street, St Swithin's, Lincoln. Ernest and Jessie married on 14 July, 1891 at Haslingden, Lancashire, and the couple had a daughter, Marjory Lord, in 1897.

Eventually, he met J. Pitt Hardacre (sometime owner of the Queen's Theatre and the Gaiety Theatre, Manchester) who was then of a mind to lease his almost derelict little theatre above a post office and some shops at Darwen in Lancashire. This venue had been offering 'the worst kind of provincial melodrama'. Carpenter took an impulsive gamble; he had the place cleaned, renovated, and restored, and he improved the quality of the programming. After eighteen months at Darwen, he sold the lease and took on that of the Theatre Royal, Bristol, for which he wrote his first pantomime, *Babes in the Wood*. Two years later, he had the chance to buy the old Empire Palace at

Hanley in the Potteries, an establishment in worse condition than that at Darwen had been, and a place into which 'hardly a soul would go'. Hanley took the entrepreneur to its heart and onto the town council. (Carpenter would also become a member of the town council in both Swindon and Brighton, where at the latter, for a short period of time, he owned the Grand Theatre.) Eighteen months after buying the Empire Palace, Carpenter sold it for double his purchase price; it had been thoroughly renovated and had become a profitable music hall. It was, according to Carpenter, the first place to put Wilkie Bard at the top of the bill, paying him and his wife, who also performed, eight pounds a week.

The proposal to build a theatre in Swindon also had the backing of those local businessmen who felt that Swindon's robust rate of industrial and residential expansion during the 1870s and 1880s was indicative of the venture's potential viability. And Carpenter might also gamble on the 'new Swindonians'. These were immigrants and their families who, attracted by the possibility of better employment in the emerging and expanding town, were relocating from the north of England and the Midlands where they might previously have been more exposed to music hall and theatre. If Swindon's population continued to grow at the projected rate (and if the widely expected amalgamation of Old Swindon and New Town came about – as it did in 1900), what some lacked in artistic appreciation might be more than compensated for by sheer volume of numbers. He had a lot to consider but, on balance, much of it was in favour of going ahead.

On 1 May, 1897, the *Swindon Advertiser* announced Carpenter's intention to build a theatre in Swindon. 'The theatre will accommodate about 1600 persons. Three sides of the building will be on public streets. It will be well provided with dressing room and bar accommodation, and will be heated with hot water. The height of the auditorium from the pit stalls to the sun burner is 40 feet.

The proscenium opening, boxes and internal decoration generally will be Italian Renaissance, very artistically treated. Ample means of ventilation are provided. Externally the theatre will be, like nearly all public buildings in Swindon, of brick and freestone. It is to be called the Queen's Theatre, not inappropriate seeing that it is to be built in this Queen's Diamond Jubilee Year.' The piece concluded: 'It is expected that the theatre will be opened about the beginning of October by Mr F. R. Benson's Shakespearean Company.'

R. Milverton Drake and John M. Pizey, architects of Bank Chambers, Baldwin Street, Bristol, designed the Swindon theatre in Renaissance style. Their plans were dated 27 July, 1896, which showed that the intention to build in Swindon predated the public announcement by at least a year. Charles Williams, builder of Regent Street, Swindon, and his men took just thirty weeks to construct it in brick with freestone dressings, on a site measuring 115 feet x 90 feet on the corner of Clarence Street and Groundwell Road. The designers gave the place an Italian-influenced interior, painted in cream and gold, with what were said to be 'temporary' gold and blue hangings on the boxes. The ceiling over the 1,600-seat ventilated auditorium featured a richly plastered dome, forty feet in diameter, from which hung a large sun burner for lighting purposes. The interior comprised orchestra stalls and a circle. Nine fire exits led from the auditorium and three exited from the stage. This had a width of fifty-five feet, a depth of thirty-five feet, and a proscenium opening that was twenty-nine feet wide and twenty-six feet high. There was also a stage loft, some eighty feet high. *The Stage* (founded 1880 as a theatre trade paper) noted that such a configuration would enable the Swindon theatre to accommodate shows then being produced at the leading theatres in London. It would also enable the original scenery to be used, and this could be raised perpendicularly, 'thereby enabling a manager to produce pieces with startling effects'.

Jack Gladwin, whom the *Swindon Advertiser* described as combining 'experience and energy and a key eye to the popular taste in matters of amusement', was put in charge of the theatre. Gladwin's experience to date had mostly been in Ireland where he acquired considerable business acumen and was primarily involved in fit-ups, a theatrical term meaning getting together the hardware and scenery, mostly in such a way that it can be accommodated by touring productions to fit different venues. It seems likely that his appointment at the New Queen's was temporary from the outset, for he was installed as 'acting manager', and did not stay for long.

The theatre was officially named New Queen's Theatre, and even though this is how the title appeared on its posters, it became known almost at once as The Queen's, and was thereafter referred to as such in the press and in its advertisements. Although the building was not entirely ready, it opened on 8 February 1898. On opening night, Ernest Carpenter presented each theatregoer in the stalls, and each occupant of the boxes, with a souvenir programme, printed on satin. In his inaugural address, he said how heartened he was by the welcome his enterprise had received, and he apologised for the difficulties that had to be overcome. It was such a sizeable project that the theatre was not finished, but he hoped that this would not interfere with the comfort of its patrons. He assured them that when the theatre closed for its summer recess, the outstanding work would be completed.

There was no box office inside the New Queen's Theatre, although there was a small vestibule facing Groundwell Road, at each end of which was a 'shop', and from where the manager's office could be gained. Tickets had to be bought from Milsom & Son, a music shop in Fleet Street. A box could be had for 21/-; reserved seats in the orchestra stalls cost 3/- each, and 2/- each in the pit stalls; seats in the pit were 6d each; and theatregoers in the grand circle parted with 1/-. The doors opened at 7 p.m., although for an extra 6d an 'early doors' policy allowed patrons to enter half an hour before this, and the shows began at 7.30 p.m. Latecomers arriving after 9 p.m. were allowed in at half price, except for the pit.

The lack of music hall in Swindon in a generic sense and the failure of the one-off experiment in particular are important if we are to understand why the town arrived at the type of theatre programming that it did. In business terms, Carpenter had to create a hybrid. His programming needed to attract an audience that comprised those who were socially more suited to the music hall model, even if it had been largely eschewed in the town, and the middle-class clientele from the catchment area who required a higher level of entertainment. Both elements had in common that they wanted to be taken out of themselves, entertained, and sent home without having been intellectually challenged. But whereas much of the typical music hall patter and songs derived from working-class hardships, social situations and day-to-day minutiae, the middle class preferred to leave all of that at home when they went to the theatre. The answer for Swindon was to stage variety, generically as a varied mix of plays and, more specifically, the multi-turn variety shows that were to become the staple diet of the New Queen's.

The opening production was not the anticipated *Shakespeare*, but the George Phillips Company's pantomime *Dick Whittington*, with a cast of forty that included acrobats and dancers. *The Stage* commented that 'there was a large and appreciative audience, comprising the elite of the neighbourhood' and 'the performance was evidently to the taste of those present since the encores were numerous'. The patrons of the New Queen's Theatre were always very vocal in their appreciation. When *In the Ranks* was presented in August 1898, they 'cheered the stirring episodes until they were hoarse, and vigorously applauded those loaded with pathos'. The villain received 'little mercy at the hands of the virtue-loving denizens of the pit and gallery'.

With such vocal responses very much the norm, audiences thought a little alcoholic libation might not be unreasonable. On the 24 February 1898 the more thirsty members of the audience discovered that they were unable to obtain alcoholic refreshment during the interval of the play *Between the Lights*. They returned to the auditorium, and protested. Ernest Carpenter appeared on stage and explained that although he had the appropriate dramatic licence from Wiltshire County Council, certain people, probably teetotallers, had objected to a drinks licence in the New Queen's, despite the fact that almost all theatres at the time were able to provide alcoholic refreshment.

Carpenter promised to sort out the matter, and on 3 March he successfully challenged the objections before the licensing committee, backing up his words with a three-thousand-signature petition. The New Queen's was granted a full theatrical licence, free of any restrictions, and within a couple of days Ernest Carpenter had stocked the refreshment bars with beer, and opened them to welcoming and appreciative customers. The New Queen's was off the wagon, and its customers were in the bar.

*Dick Whittington* ran for two weeks and was followed mainly by popular touring plays and musical comedies. Many of the shows returned regularly, although not always with the same producers or casts. Many plays, as well as musical entertainments, visited the theatre on several occasions. Opera was presented there from the outset. Between 1898 and 1902, Rouseby's Grand Opera Company, the D'Oyly Carte Company, and the Neilson Grand English Opera Company were regular visitors.

Ernest Carpenter took a risk when he booked Arthur Rouseby's Grand Opera Company to play a week at the newly opened theatre in March 1898. There was no precedent to suggest that the people of Swindon would patronise grand opera, so he was perhaps staking the success of the experiment on its novelty value. Yet he left nothing to chance in the pre-season advertising. 'The greatest musical event in the annals of Wiltshire' trumpeted the publicity; and for once the publicity was undoubtedly correct. 'Full chorus and ballet! Augmented orchestra!' The latter even came with its own Director of Music, Signor Valenza, whose name must have sounded to the people of Swindon as if it had been composed musically. Carpenter explained that 'notwithstanding the enormous expense', prices would only be raised to a small extent. A seat in the orchestra stalls cost 3/6d; 2/6d in the pit stalls; the grand circle set back patrons by 1/6d, or 6d for the pit at the rear. Arrangements with the two railway companies servicing Swindon meant that cheap tickets for the performances could be had from all stations between Didcot and Swindon, and also from Malmesbury, Somerford, Dauntsey and Wootton Bassett on the Great Western Railway Company's lines; and from Cirencester, Cerney, Cricklade, Chiseldon, Ogbourne, and Marlborough stations on trains run by the Midland & South West Junction railway.

The operas chosen were popular ones, beginning with Gounod's *Faust* of which the *Advertiser* reported: '… it has been hailed with delight by all true lovers of good music'. Verdi's *Il trovatore* followed, but it was noted that the house was not as large as might have been expected. Then came Balfe's *Bohemian Girl*, which 'attracted a splendid attendance, so much so that one was almost inclined to retrieve the foreboding that Swindon was less musical than it has been given credit for'. The newspaper praised the quality of the singers and the orchestra of Wagner's *Tannhäuser*, adding that 'the famous overture was a pure and unadulterated triumph, and the crowded and appreciative audience naturally applauded it'. *Cavalleria rusticana* and *I Pagliacci* followed on, and the short season also included *Maritana* by William Vincent Wallace. Opera had been so successfully received in Swindon that Carpenter presented the D'Oyly Carte Opera Company in October, and three more companies the following year. In all, twenty-one weeks of opera were successfully presented between then and 1931.

One of the earliest shows at the New Queen's, John Isham's company of black comedians, singers and dancers, came from New York in 1898 with *Oriental America*. This was a variety entertainment, described in ways that would not be acceptable today, but in which nothing then was considered to be derogatory. 'Shorty May, a darkie, receives rounds of applause for his clever dancing' set the tone. 'The evening's entertainment concludes with the Coon Cake Walk, which is a genuine representation of negro cake walking, a custom which dates back to the dark days of negro bondage', wrote the reviewer, 'The Coon Cake Walk is a peculiar walk or prancing natural to the darkies. A cake is awarded to the best couple, and the audiences are the judges – by their applause.' The whole entertainment was apparently one of innocent amusement.

During 1898, the fortunes of Carpenter's rival variety theatre in Bristol, the Empire, between Old Market Street and Carey's Lane, reached an all-time low. Despite his heavy involvement at Swindon, he pounced on the opportunity to buy the lease of the Bristol Empire, briefly closed it for refurbishment, and reopened with a long variety show. Even though some nationally applauded, top-of-the-bill artistes were presented over the next few months, Bristol theatregoers remained unimpressed with their Empire. In 1900, less than two years after he had acquired the place, Ernest Carpenter sold on the lease, thereafter concentrating his efforts on the Theatre Royal in Bristol and the New Queen's in Swindon.

On 18 September in its opening year, the New Queen's hosted a Sunday of Salvation, with three meetings during the day conducted by General William Booth of the Salvation Army. These were held at 11 a.m., 3 p.m. and 6.30 p.m.; crowds thronged the theatre to catch a glimpse of the great man; admission was one penny, no children were allowed, and the houses were full.

If there was one person whose stock remained high in the affections of Swindon's theatregoers, it was Ernest Carpenter. On the 27 December 1898, less than a year after the theatre opened, the venue staged a benefit variety show in honour of the work he had done in establishing and managing the enterprise. Local and professional artistes took part. During the interval, Carpenter addressed the audience amidst cheers, and thanked them for the way they had supported him and for the many kindnesses they had shown. He said that only ten months ago there had been many people who said that he would never make a theatre pay in Swindon. He was proud to find that the people of the town understood how a well-conducted theatre was an institution which could enhance the well-being of the town. The first season at Swindon had been so successful, he believed that, in a very short time, the New Queen's could be the best paying concern he had. It all showed, he said, how appreciated were his endeavours to provide good entertainment in Swindon.

Drama was also a great hit with Swindon audiences. When *The Streets of London* was performed in October 1899, 'the various actors were loudly applauded for every bit of sentiment that awoke a responsive echo in (the audience's) hearts. They hissed the villain with hearty goodwill, gave audible token of their sympathy with the hero and heroine in the time of their distress, and when vice was vanquished and the villain safe in the hands of the law, they applauded vociferously'. Most years there were two or three pantomimes but they were not always during the Christmas period. For example, in 1899, *Aladdin* was presented from 6 February, and *Cinderella* followed at the end of the month.

Swindon's theatregoers were certainly appreciative of patriotism and spectacle. In April 1899, Milton Rode's company produced *Tommy Atkins* by Arthur Shirley and Ben Landeck, a play in four acts and fifteen scenes that ranged between the interior of an English village church and a battleground in Egypt. It called for a cast of seventy, more than five tons of scenery, a brass band (composed of Swindon musicians) and a detachment of local army volunteers for the church parade and battle scenes. The audience loved it.

Joseph Poole's *Myriorama or Sights of the World* made its first visit to the New Queen's Theatre for two weeks commencing 10 April 1899. These were moving panoramas, often by way of travelogues or depictions of events of some moment, and were the wonder of an age before actual moving pictures. They had been presented at the Corn Exchange in Old Swindon for around thirty years, and had always been very popular, showing scenes as diverse as the Sudan War, including the great Battle of Omdurman, the bombardment of Santiago, the Indian frontier rising, Derby Day and Queen Victoria's Diamond Jubilee celebrations.

Publicly exhibited panoramas had been around since the end of the 18th century, and the Poole family had been associated with them since early in the 19th century. It is they who coined the term 'Myriorama' principally to disassociate their product with an early competitor's style of panoramas on which they originally worked before branching out on their own. Joseph Poole claimed to have established his show in 1837, and advertised it as 'Time Tested in the Crucible of Public Opinion'. Included in the programme at the New Queen's was a variety show which featured 'The Marvellous Saletos', continental gymnasts and acrobats, and an orchestral concert by the combined bands of Joseph Poole's Myriorama and the Queen's Theatre Orchestra. This entertainment played to large and enthusiastic audiences.

Two performances of the drama *A London Mystery* by William Bourne had to be cancelled in 1899 when, on opening night, one of the leading actors, Herbert Kirke, suffered an attack of giddiness at his lodgings and cracked his head on a wash basin, causing a wound on the side of his head. As it was the start of the tour of the play, there was no understudy, so the audience were refunded the price of their tickets and 'dispersed peacefully'. Walter Kellson proved to be a more than capable substitute, opening after only two days' rehearsal, when the play went well.

Jack Gladwin's first benefit (he had another the following year) was held in 1899. Ernest Carpenter's Grand Variety Company performed to a packed house, and Carpenter took part, as did his wife Jessie. Several local musicians, singers and dancers took their turn with the professionals, and the orchestra was under the direction of Herr Klee, its first musical director. The Carpenters appeared in the 'pretty comedietta' *My Mother's Bill* by G.W. Godfrey, a piece that was currently playing at the Court Theatre in London. At one point, a phonograph was brought on to the stage, and the audience listened attentively to the selections from comic operas that were played on it. In all, there were seventeen items at the benefit, including multi-instrumentalist Gertrude the Musical Minim, and Herr Klee played a violin solo. Presentations to Gladwin included one from the orchestra, a 'beautiful bicycle' subscribed by 'friends', a watch and chain from Carpenter, and a cigarette case from the Swindon Billposting Company.

Also in 1899, 'Popular Services for the People' were inaugurated at the theatre, free of charge but with a collection for expenses. They consisted of solos by special singers, and a full orchestral band, and Revd F. J. Murrell spoke on topics with titles such as 'A Woman's Treachery', 'Thought Reading' or 'The Man Who Missed His Mark'. Religion continued to be a Sunday theme at the theatre. General Booth returned on 12 November 1899, when there were also three meetings at a penny entrance fee; this time, however, a few selected seats cost sixpence, and those wishing to make a day of it could pay one shilling. Once again, children were not admitted. This time, General Booth was greeted less enthusiastically, and the congregation at the morning service was not large. Each of his services finished with a 'Penitents Forum', an invitation to 'sinners and back-sliders', of which many came forward in Swindon.

Back in 1896, a theatre in London had first introduced a cinema show into its programme. It was done as a kind of entr'acte, but soon 'bioscope' became the buzz word of the day, and was soon common enough even in the provinces. Theatre managers saw film as an added attraction to their main programmes of on-stage entertainment. They did not dream that what they were harbouring was a fledgling cuckoo in the nest, and that within a few years it would have flown into a life of its own, seriously affecting the profits of the industry that nurtured it. Jack Gladwin had noticed the public's interest in moving pictures and he wanted his establishment to be at the cutting edge of entertainment technology. He brought in an Edisonograph, Thomas Edison's first device for showing moving pictures, and introduced it during a run of *Cinderella* in February 1900.

It showed images of the Boer War that were uncompromising and vivid. In one, a Boer climbs out of a trench up the side of a sandpit to look for the British; he turns to give the alarm and falls back with a bullet in him. The British rush in, bayoneting one man and pursuing the remainder down the hill. The audience responded with loud and prolonged applause. This was an important moment for the theatre, the realisation that there might be profit in showing moving pictures, and something on which it would later capitalise.

In August 1900, the melodrama *A Dark Secret* was staged at the New Queen's; it required a river of water on the stage (in which, at one point, one of the characters was drowned). The scenes were designed by William Thompson Hemsley. He was a native of Newcastle who came early in life to Swindon, when his father obtained employment at the Great Western Railway Company's Works in the town. There too, Hemsley served an apprenticeship, and took up evening classes in art at the Mechanics' Institute, for whose theatrical productions he also painted scenery. This was the beginning of a career during which he would become one of the foremost scenic artists of his day, working at Covent Garden, the

Theatre Royal, Haymarket, His Majesty's, and at Drury Lane, as well as many other London theatres. Other plays with scenes designed by Hemsley that played the New Queen's between 1901 and 1903 were *Hearts are Trumps, In Old Madrid, Judy: a Child of the Streets* and *The Fatal Wedding*. He died in London on February 1918 aged 68, leaving a son Harry, the well- known comedian and children's mimic, who was born in Swindon.

Jack Gladwin left the New Queen's on the 25 August 1900 to join the Clarence Sonnes organisation that had theatres in Aldershot, Birmingham, the London provinces, and Newport. The *Evening Advertiser* sounded a strange note: 'It would not be rash to prophesy his return in a greater and more important role than he has yet occupied'. Within two months, Gladwin had become acting manager of The Theatre Royal, Aldershot. Some years later, he would be back, but for the moment his replacement as acting manager was Claude Jullion, 'the genial Mr Jullion' as he was frequently referred to by the *Evening Advertiser*.

On the second night of the revue *Frivolity* in September 1900, Henry Thomas Day of Cley-next-the-Sea, Norfolk, a member of the acrobatic troupe 'The Leopolds', was turning a double somersault when he fell on the back of his neck, severely injuring his spine, and lost consciousness. He was admitted to Swindon's Victoria Hospital where he died five days later, with his wife at his side. He was just twenty-three years old, had been with 'The Leopolds' for one year and nine months, and had one child of eighteen months and one three-week old. At the inquest held the next day at the Frome Hotel, Ernest Carpenter said that the accident occurred when the deceased did a single turn, and in attempting to do a double somersault, made a mistake and came down on his head in the middle of the table. He did not strike the side of the table at all, but was rendered insensible. Mr Carpenter advanced his opinion that the feat did not appear to be at all dangerous, and no precaution, which could have been taken, would have prevented it. A verdict of accidental death was returned, and the funeral service for Henry Day took place on 3 October at St Paul's Church, Swindon. He was buried in Radnor Street Cemetery, and Mr Carpenter and the entire theatre staff attended the service and the burial.

Tragedies were not confined to the stage. On the day of the inquest into Henry Day's death, just before the curtain rose on Walter Melville's Edwardian melodrama *The Worst Woman in London*, one of the occupants of the circle appeared to be taken ill, and expired before assistance could be summoned. The body was removed to Carpenter's office, where the doctor pronounced that life was extinct, and the man was identified as George Bragg, aged about thirty-five, and living at 17 Graham Street. The body was taken away on a stretcher. Enquiries revealed that Bragg had received a serious blow on his head during the Mafeking relief celebration procession that passed through Regent Circus in May 1899. Then, in early August 1900, he was involved in a very bad accident whilst riding a bicycle down Church Hill, Swindon. Through no fault of his own, he ran into a little child and was thrown from his machine, knocked unconscious, broke his collar bone, and was severely shaken. This was revealed at the inquest at the County Ground Hotel on 3 October, when a verdict was passed in accordance with medical evidence presented.

Sometimes the audience was badly behaved. In February 1901, the *Swindon Advertiser*, reviewing *The Second Mrs Tanqueray*, reported on 'the ill-behaviour of certain denizens of the pit', who 'hissed, coughed and whistled throughout despite exceedingly commendable efforts by others of their company to quell them'. Swindon was reverting to type. Arthur Wing Pinero's play that raised social questions about marriage to a woman with a sexual past, which had shot Mrs Patrick Campbell to fame as an actress barely eight years before, was just too much for the narrow-minded, working-class Victorians of the town.

The *Swindon Advertiser* called it 'a masterpiece', and commented that 'the working man who pays his sixpence week in and week out and takes his place in the pit should surely have gained sufficient experience to recognise what is and what is not a good play'. It ranted: 'let those whose comprehensive powers are so limited that they cannot grasp the language and the drift of the piece, choose the more manly alternative of leaving the place rather than interrupting with such frequency as to prevent those who would from enjoying the play'. Swindon, it seems, was not altogether ready for meaningful theatre that asked social questions.

They were, however, happy to watch children performing in ways more usually associated with adults, and adults pretending to be children. Little Miss Marjorie Murray scored a great hit in 1901, aged twelve, as Cissy in *The Silver King*. She was as much praised for her stamina in achieving 700 performances without a break, her tireless readings in schools, her recitations at afternoon charity bazaars, and her fund-raising – to date one hundred pounds for a fund for soldiers' widows. All that to carry out, whilst presumably also attending to her own formal education! Then there was Elre Salambo who, at the age of seven, invited the audience to test her ability to employ a system of mnemonics by which she could answer 10,000 historical questions. 'When will King Edward be crowned?' asked some wag. 'You tell me, and I'll tell you,' she retorted, apparently 'sending the house into a roar of laughter'. A few weeks later, 'the audience simply rocked in their seats, so convulsed were they with laughter' when Cyrus Dare imitated a child of five playing the piano to an elderly relative, and crying in the night-time for 'a drink of water, 'cause am firsty''. The audience of simple souls fell about.

One might suppose that variety in Swindon at the time operated in a vacuum, its naïve audiences willing to accept the most banal of performances, and sometimes to receive them warmly. How they marvelled when Salambo of Salambo and Olivette's New Wonder

Company (of which the above-mentioned, precocious child was a part) seemed to ignite a sheet of paper with his breath; and when one of The Medoras sang whilst the other rapidly made colourful sketches, there was no end of enjoyment. But even in Swindon there was a limit to mediocrity. Within a few years, the extent to which artistes at the Swindon theatre failed to live up to their pre-programme publicity was to become a topic for open discussion, as were the effects of such dubious blandishments on the houses for those whom they correctly described. The theatre would learn that there was a negative payback to its particular style of crying wolf.

Fallen women of a different kind to that of *The Second Mrs Tanqueray* came to the theatre in 1902, when Claude Jullion engaged Miss Bradford of Liverpool, 'champion lady wrestler of the world', and her troupe, direct from their success at the Royal Music Hall, London. The participants comprised: 'Miss Rosita, Spain's champion; Miss O'Connor, Ireland's champion; and Miss Noake, Germany's champion'. The *Swindon Advertiser* reported that they: 'Gave a grand performance of the art of wrestling, a sport very rarely witnessed in Swindon. In the first place, Miss O'Connor met Miss Noake, and after some very pretty work, Miss O'Connor won in the time of 4 minutes 22 seconds. Miss Bradford then wrestled with Miss Rosita, the former winning in the time of 10 minutes 19 seconds. Both these latter ladies were particularly smart and their work brought forth unstinted applause. The style of wrestling shown was the Greek and Roman.'

Amateur productions were featured at the New Queen's from early 1904. The first of these was *The Idol of Kano* or *The Crocodile and the Bride*, which played for five performances. It was written by W. F. Hewer, composed by T. Pope Arkell and performed by 'Local Ladies and Gentlemen'. 'For the first time on any stage, the entirely new and original comic opera in two acts', trumpeted the publicity. The proceeds were divided between the town's Victoria Hospital and the Royal Agricultural Benevolent Institution. Just before Christmas

1905, the Cirencester Cricket Club Dramatic Society staged *That Brute Simmons* by Arthur Morrison and Herbert C. Sargeant, and *The Duke of Kilkrankie*, a farcical romance by Robert Marshall, with proceeds going to the Wiltshire County Cricket Club. Both pieces were produced by Arthur Chesney of the Garrick Theatre, London.

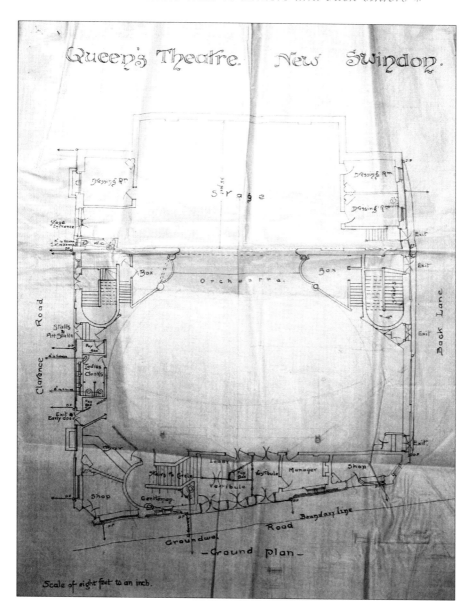

Bristol architects Drake & Pizey drew up the original plans for a theatre in Swindon in 1896, a year before Ernest Carpenter's intention was announced in the Swindon press. The plans were rather ambiguous, confirming only that all walls 'were to be built in accordance with the local bye-laws'. (continued overleaf)

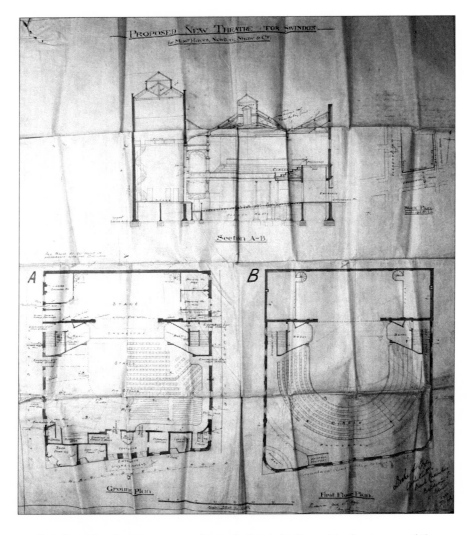

*Just three dressing rooms were planned, situated adjacent to the stage, and the administrative offices and two shops occupied much of the ground floor front of the building. (Plans by permission of the Wiltshire and Swindon History Centre)*

The theatre's builder was Charles Williams, who by 1888 was working in the town as a small-time builder. His workmen managed to have the theatre ready for opening in just thirty weeks. This drawing of Williams was published in 1898 in the North Wilts Herald, when his premises were in Princes Street.

Another drawing of 1898 depicted Jack Gladwin, brought in as temporary 'acting manager' whose previous experience had involved getting together the scenery for touring shows, mostly in Ireland. He did not stay long, but would eventually return to become the long-time owner of the building.

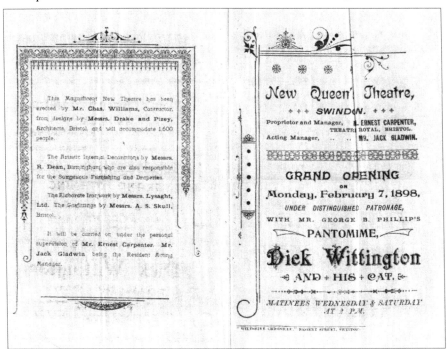

For Six Nhts and Two Matinees.

MR. GEO. PHILLIPS' SPECTACULAR

# PANTOMIME,

ENTITLED:

## DICK WITTINGTON

AND HIS CAT.

### MORTALS.

| | |
|---|---|
| Dick | Miss JENNIE ARMSTRONG |
| Tommy (the faithful Cat) | Mr. GEO. DANVERS, Jun. |
| Alderman Fitzwarren | Mr. ALBERT JAMES |
| Alice (his only Daughter) | Miss BEATIE KENT |
| Biddy Macarthy | Mr. GEO. BOLTON |
| Jack Dole | Mr. OSCAR SCHALLER |
| Sally Slut | Miss CISSY TRENT |
| Polly Pert | Miss JENNIE BONEHILL |
| Captain Spankin of the "Saucy Sally" | Mr. A. KAYE |
| Tommy Tucker | Miss EVA WILLOUGHBY |
| Jack Mainbrace | Miss FLORRIE BONEHILL |
| Stevedore | Mr. T. MACKNEY |
| Emperor of Japan | Miss G. MONTROSE |
| Ko-Ko Ti (his Prime Minister) | Mr. H. ARTHUR |
| Princess Ko-Ko Tina | Miss KITTY GOULDSTONE |

### IMMORTALS.

| | |
|---|---|
| King Rat | Mr. A. RICHARDS |
| Fairy Bow-Bell | Miss CLARA BRADSHAW |

Other Characters by Mesdames KIRBY, POOLE, SECTON, SECTON, BERVOR, &c.

### SYNOPSIS OF SCENERY.

Scene 1.—Goblin Belfry of Bow Bells—The abode of King Rat.

Scene 2.—Olde Cheapside — Exterior of Fitzwarren Eporium.

Scene 3.—Fitzwarren's Counting House.

Scene 4.—Street near London Docks.

Scene 5.—The Summit of Highgate Hill Pastoral Ballet.
In this Scene THE ELLIOTT TROUPE will appear.

Scene 6.—Wapping Old Stairs.

Scene 7.—The Open Sea—The Raft—The Calm.

Scene 8.—A Japanese Landscape.

Scene 9.—The Emperor's Palace Gardens—Japanese Ballet.

Scene 10.—The Guildhall, London.

#### GRAND TRANSFORMATION
The Butterflies Home.

#### HARLIQUINADE

Scene 1.—A Well Known Spot.

Scene 2.—Somewhere in Particular

*The New Queen's Theatre opened early in 1898 with a production of Dick Wittington, although the building was not completely finished. The opening programme (see also preceding page) pointed out that 'artistic internal decorations and sumptuous furnishings and draperies' were by Dean of Birmingham; Lysaught provided the 'elaborate ironwork', and the gas fittings were the work of A.S. Skull of Bristol.*

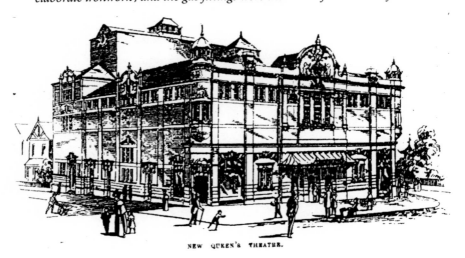

NEW QUEEN'S THEATRE.

The newly-built theatre, pictured c1900, is advertising the Fred Karno Company. Karno was the business name of the music hall impresario Frederick John Westcott (1866-1941), one-time owner of Tagg's Island in the River Thames, and an associate of the great theatre designer Frank Matcham. His name was associated with a chaotic style of knockabout theatre, and he organised several shows that played Swindon's theatre in its early days. The association did not stop at his death; a revue called Fred Karno's Army was performed at the Empire in 1951 and 1953.

(opposite) This line drawing of 1898 shows the south and west elevations of the theatre. The house behind the theatre in Clarence Street was soon to be demolished, and the terraces of Groundwell Road had not yet reached the site of the New Queen's, although it was this part of Swindon that was rapidly expanding at the time.

This William Hooper picture of the interior, taken in 1902, shows that the theatre originally had only stalls and circle. The stalls were divided into 'orchestra stalls' which occupied the half of the auditorium nearest the stage, and the 'pit stalls' behind them; at the back of the circle was 'the promenade'. Historically, this was an area of a theatre set aside for members of the audience to walk about whilst watching the performance. In Tudor times it was the part of the theatre most likely to be associated with prostitutes; the term 'promenade theatre' today defines a performance area without a stage where there is a degree of interactivity between the performers and the audience.

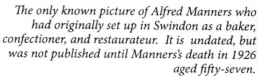

The only known picture of Alfred Manners who had originally set up in Swindon as a baker, confectioner, and restaurateur. It is undated, but was not published until Manners's death in 1926 aged fifty-seven.

> QUEEN'S THEATRE, SWINDON
>
> PROPRIETOR & MANAGER - MR. R. CARPENTER
>
> EXTRA SPECIAL ATTRACTION FOR THIS WEEK.
> MONDAY, DEC. 15, & DURING THE WEEK,
> FIRST TIME OUT OF LONDON.
> THE ORIGINAL TROUPE OF
>
> # LADY WRESTLERS.
>
> Including Miss BRADFORD (Champion Lady Wrestler of the World).
>
> Seats can now be booked at Milsom & Son's, Flea Street, Swindon. Times and Prices as usual. [188

From the day the New Queen's opened, it offered pantomimes, comedies, straight plays and melodramas, operas, and musicals. The arrival of the 'Lady Wrestlers' at the end of 1902 must have been a spectacle the likes of which had never previously been seen in Swindon. By wrestling 'in Greek and Roman styles', they were at least able to preserve a degree of classical theatre.

This photograph, taken c1902, shows how retail Swindon was gradually creeping towards the theatre. The house on the end of the terrace was destined to become a sheet music shop, then a cutler, and a tobacconist and newsagent in the 1920s. Today it is an Indian restaurant.

For a while, the theatre occasionally issued picture postcards as part of the publicity for the show that was on that week. This one, from October 1904, shows a scene from the melodrama The Midnight Mail by Arthur Shirley.

The show being advertised in this picture is The Bells of Haslemere, which dates it to October 1904, just one month after Swindon's tram service was inaugurated. The picture shows how close to the theatre the trams passed on their journeys between Old Swindon and New Swindon. The tram service proved to be a means of transporting the theatre's patrons to the Midland & South-west Junction railway station in the old town, and to the Great Western Railway Company's station in the new town whenever special trains were arranged for their convenience.

This picture was taken between 1903 and 1906, and can be dated by A. W. Seaton's Coronation Music Stores, part of whose premises is just visible to the left of the picture, and which existed only during that time. The conversion of the last house in the terrace was no doubt done to take advantage of a growing local market for sheet music of the songs being heard at the theatre.

This picture can be dated to early 1904, because scaffolding is being erected immediately to the north of the theatre, behind which the county court building would soon be erected in Clarence Street.

*The New Queen's Theatre was built in Swindon almost halfway through what was, nationally, they heyday of great theatre building, driven by an explosion in the urban population with theatre-going potential. The great theatre designer Frank Matcham was putting much ornamentation into his work, and although Swindon's theatre was not quite in his class, this 1905 view from the stalls shows how the style was emulated.*

*Also taken in 1905, this view by William Hooper from the centre of the circle shows the full extent of the decorative plasterwork. It also shows that posters for forthcoming attractions were put up on the walls of the stalls.*

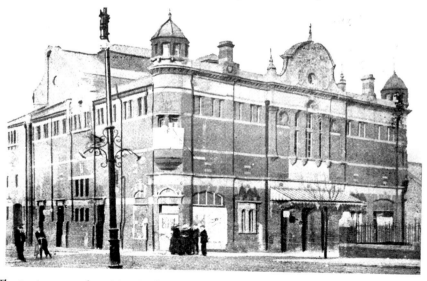

*The posters are advertising Dick Wittington which was presented at the theatre three times between 1900 and 1908. This picture could have been taken at any of them, and nothing is known of H.E. Newsome, stationer of Wellington Street.*

"The Sleeping Beauty."

WEE GEORGE WOOD. BOY COMEDIAN AND MIMIC. THE SMALLEST ARTISTE ON THE STAGE.

*In 1907 Alfred Manners left the theatre under circumstances that were never explained, although 'artistic differences' may be the likely explanation, caused by his adherence to styles of programming and standards of quality that did not accord with the theatre owners' preference for more popular, down-market entertainment. Much was made of the benefit night that marked his leaving, wrapped around the drama The Lights of London, which was playing the theatre that week.*

*Wee Georgie Wood first came to Swindon in 1906, and would return several times during his long career, four of them by 1912. This publicity piece is from the 1907 appearance of the 'boy comedian and mimic … the smallest artiste on the stage' in The Sleeping Beauty. That production included Stanley Jefferson, later to become better known as Stan Laurel.*

*Beauty and the Barge, a love story featuring a civic official's daughter and a bargee, by W.W. Jacobs and Louis N. Parker came first to Swindon in 1905. This postcard was issued for its second appearance at the theatre, in 1907. Both productions featured the actor Maitland Marler, whose leading ladies were respectively Lillian Hallows and Hilda Vaughan.*

*Arthur Wimperis and Lionel Monckton's musical The Arcadians was another fixture in the early years; it came four times between 1910 and 1918 (when much of the cast were substantially the same players), and altogether was performed at the Empire nine times.*

*The musical comedy Peggy, by Leslie Stuart (best known for Florodora) and George Grossmith Jnr., was performed at the theatre in 1912. The stars were Harry Phydora who went on to make recordings and to have a career in Australia and New Zealand, and Lula Evans.*

# 2

# *Alfred Manners and the Theatre of Variety*

At the end of the 1903-04 season, Ernest Carpenter leased the New Queen's Theatre to Alfred James Manners. Born in Kensington, London, in 1870, Manners as a young man travelled extensively, and was in China at the time of the Boxer rising. He also visited America and several other countries. In 1892, at St Pancras, London, he married Ellen Eliza from Longparish, Andover, Hampshire, where their first child was born a year later. The family came to Swindon in 1900, where Manners immediately set up a bakery, confectioners, and dining rooms in their home at 104 Victoria Road. At the time, they had two children, Esther, born Longparish, Hampshire in 1893, who was to play a very significant part in her father's work in Swindon during the First World War, and Alfred James (born Paddington, London) the year the family moved to Swindon. They would have three more children, all born in Swindon, but none of whom would play any part in the Empire: Winifred (b.1901), Elsie (b.1902), and Reginald Charles (b.1906).

On the last night of Carpenter's general management, at the end of May, E. Hoggan-Armadale, a leading actor of the day whose company was presenting *The Lyons Mail*, introduced the new man to the audience, and thanked resident manager Claude Jullion, who was presented with a cheque for five guineas.

Manners expressed the hope that Swindon's theatregoing public would give Jullion a good send-off, then he set out his intentions: during the summer shut-down he would redecorate the theatre and install electric lights throughout (which met with great applause); and he would book good companies for the future. Harry J. Snelson was appointed to the position of resident manager in the place of Claude Jullion, working under Manners. The Swindon theatre also lost John J. Gale, the conductor of the pit orchestra, who had succeeded Herr Klee; and its popular percussionist, G.H. Benge, also left the company. Ernest Carpenter immediately took over the lease and the management of the Eden Theatre, Brighton, which he closed for the summer vacation, renamed it and reopened as the Grand Theatre.

How or why the New Queen's Theatre was invested in a Swindon retailer with no apparent experience in the profession has never been established. It is clear that Alfred Manners had a strong sense of the quality of entertainment needed to maintain an air of respectability in the concept of theatre. His approach to maintaining what he believed to be the required standards would, as we shall see later, almost cost him the job. Twenty-one years into the future, the local newspaper would refer to his policy of 'providing Swindon with the best of theatrical fare', but would also point out that 'one is bound to say that it has not always been the best that has received the most liberal patronage'. Swindon's reputation as a town that has never properly appreciated culture goes back a long way, and it is even today occasionally accused of such a failure.

Although Manners was not an actor-manager, he seems to have modelled himself on the typical attributes by which those of the 'legitimate theatre' of the later Victorian period gained supremacy and a following: notably his degree of personal involvement in all aspects of the theatre, and in his willingness to be available for his audiences. Over the years, Manners's appearances before the footlights were so many that he might indeed have passed for an actor-manager. The audience 'knew' that the omnipresent Manners would always be on hand, not remote but safely tucked away in the wings, and willing to appear if they called for him or whenever a problem needed to be explained. All of this, and his work in the community, brought Alfred Manners into intimate contact with Swindon's theatregoing public, and over the years it translated into a deep affection for the man who was to manage the theatre until the mid-1920s.

The auditorium underwent a programme of re-fitting and redecoration during the summer vacation of 1904. The interior of the dome was painted in cream, picked out in green and gold; the proscenium was highlighted in cream, green, pink, old gold, and gold leaf; gold paper went up on the walls of the boxes, which were painted in green and terracotta; the front of the circle was decoratively carved; and pictures including the arms of the Borough of Swindon were placed around the walls of the stalls. Two innovations were included for the first time: one, the electric light; the other, a public telephone, which was installed in a private area so that 'patrons called up at the theatre may transact their business of the moment in the adjoining room and return to the pleasures of the evening'.

The Era (newspaper 1838-1939, noted for its theatre coverage) wrote that Manners had used the summer holiday to make the Swindon theatre into 'one of the prettiest playhouses in the provinces'. It enthused about the tone and delightful taste of the colouring, especially of the ceiling and proscenium, and the way in which it had been embellished throughout by a clever arrangement of electric lighting which provided a very pleasing effect when turned on at full. Such a novelty! The tasteful placing throughout of cooling palms and ferns, and nicely framed pictures and pier-glasses in the private boxes and stalls, caught the attention of the reviewer. He noted that the stalls had been re-fitted with newly upholstered drop-seats, and the warm carpets much enhanced the prevailing comfort. Further striking improvements that *The Era* wished to bring to the attention of its readers included a beautifully designed entrance hall to the higher priced seats, and the rearrangement of the refreshment rooms.

In all, Manners had spent £1,000 in a programme of rejuvenation that also included 'overhauling the sanitary arrangements' – additional lavatory accommodation and ladies' cloakrooms had been provided. Presumably, the appointment of Snelson had not gone according to plan, for Manners appointed H. B. Astin as acting manager, and pianist Fred H. Lucas as the theatre's musical director.

Alfred Manners's first offering, at a grand reopening for the 1904-05 season on 1 August, was Laurence Brough's company's production of *The Lady of Ostend*, in the presence of the mayor, Alderman James Hinton, who performed the opening ceremony. The play was a hilarious farce by Sir Francis Cowley Burnand, who was editor of *Punch* from 1880 to 1906. During the interval, Brough presented Manners with a floral horseshoe as an emblem of good luck. Booking could now be done at Milson's in New Swindon, and at 5 Bath Road, Old Swindon, where W. Summers Morris had his booksellers and stationers shop.

Patrons were further facilitated following the inauguration of Swindon's tramways services in September 1904, which passed the theatre and 'met patrons at fall of curtain for Gorse Hill, Old Town and Rodbourne every evening'. In addition, Manners told the press that 'special cheap trains will run from Marlborough, Cirencester, Cerney, Cricklade, Wootton Bassett, Faringdon, Highworth, Tidworth, Ludgershall, and intermediate stations'.

The Swindon audiences were still not that easy to please and they readily showed their displeasure whenever a production was sub-standard. In June 1905, *A Gay Girl* opened, billed as a farcical musical by Charles Russell. In fact, it was written by Edgar Dereve, lessee-manager of the Maidenhead Theatre, and occasional playwright, in which capacity he achieved no lasting success. The audience quickly became disenchanted with the standard of the piece, and there was a disturbance during the first act when some object was thrown on to the stage in protest. By the middle of the second act, the hostilities had reached such a pitch that Manners appeared on the stage and ordered the curtain to be dropped. He told the audience that he had engaged a reputable company, but they had experienced previous problems unbeknown to him. There were to be no further performances of *A Gay Girl*. Manners thanked the audience for their support over the preceding twelve months and said that by way of compensation he would give free tickets for a variety show the following Wednesday evening. He closed the theatre until then, when he mounted a mixture of local acts and artistes engaged from London, and organised a collection for the relief of the *Gay Girl* performers who had found themselves stranded in Swindon without funds.

The provincial theatre generally was, by this time, going through a period of recession, as indicated by the problems with the company of *A Gay Girl*. Manners had taken on the New Queen's at the start of what had proved to be, in his own words, the worst season known to the profession for upwards of a quarter of a century. Business being done was so bad that the majority of the best touring companies had been taken off the road, making it increasingly difficult for managers of those theatres that were still viable to provide an acceptable play, week-on-week, for its patrons.

In the winter, the New Queen's Theatre could be very cold. It was said that 'cold blasts swept almost the entire front of the theatre' and there were complaints from the audience and the acts. At the end of the 1904-05 season, Manners installed a powerful boiler in the basement, from which pipes ran around the dressing rooms and along the back of the stage. Two radiators were placed on the proscenium, and six rows of pipes were fitted in the stalls – a row under each line of seats. A coil of piping was laid in front of the orchestra, and in other parts 'excellent arrangements' were made 'to secure a fair and comfortable distribution of warmth'. The work was carried out by

Edwards, Bays and Rye, of the Castle Works, Swindon, under the supervision of T. M. Barrington.

By 1905, moves were afoot to mark Alfred Manners's first year at the theatre with a 'grand complimentary benefit'. The suggestion had come from Louis R. Rydill, a bookseller of 8 Regent Street, and it was taken up by the local authority. A committee was formed of town councillors, and Lord Edmond Fitzmaurice, Fitzroy Pleydell Goddard (lord of the manor of Swindon) and the mayor, Alderman William Reynolds, were the scheme's patrons. The services of well-known local artistes were engaged, as were a couple of professionals from London. In the event, the show lasted for nearly four hours, during which time the Great Western Railway Mechanics' Institute Operatic and Dramatic Society performed an original 'laughable comedietta' called *Our Borough*, set in the Bagliete Tavern in Swindon. It was written by a Swindon man, Charles Richens, whose wife performed in the production. It 'bristled with pungent criticisms of the borough council', who were now perhaps wondering whether their enthusiastic patronage had been quite such a good thing. The event was a case of the honour being more important than the result, for all Manners got out of it was a silver cruet.

Manners had done his sums, and wanted to use the event to gain more patronage of, and through, the town's business community. 'I have often thought,' he said to the assembly, 'if any of you fully realise, especially the tradesmen in the town, the benefit the town derives from having such a theatre in your midst. I have carefully calculated the sum of money that is circulated in the town by the running of the house. It amounts to no less a sum than upwards of £6,000. In getting those figures I have taken a fair average amount the artistes expend during their visits here. I know by careful enquiry that four-fifths of the amount paid by me to the companies is left in the town.' He wanted support for the New Queen's to be doubled or trebled, pointing out that only in that way would he be able to ensure Swindon benefitted from quality London productions that subsequently went on tour. What did not help was the way in which audiences drifted in during the performance; reports regularly mentioned how relatively few seats might be taken up at the start of a performance, that the theatre might be half-full by the time of the interval, but 'much better attended' during the second half!

Immediately after Manners's benefit, the theatre closed for two months. When it reopened, the *Evening Advertiser* welcomed 'the local attractive temple of Thespis … for another run of legitimate business, and, we may hope, good luck'. Its opening show was put on by the Fred Harcourt Vaudeville Company, featuring Babs Lloyd 'the baby coon', and the Casino Girls from Paris. 'Music and girls go together like strawberries and cream', declared the reviewer.

In 1906, public confidence was severely shaken in the Swindon tramway system, on which so many patrons had been conveyed to and from the theatre for the previous couple of years. On 1 June, the brakes failed on tramcar No.11 (Swindon had thirteen trams that ran until 1929) as it descended Victoria Road, heavily laden with visitors coming away from the Bath & West and Southern Counties Show being held at Broome Manor. As it gathered speed, it swayed and lurched, and was eventually derailed at the points and crashed on to its side. Five people died and some thirty were injured. Alfred Manners, who was standing at the entrance to the stalls when this happened, later described the incident thus: 'The car came down the hill at a great speed. On reaching the points it jumped, and went on to the wrong line of the rail and suddenly turned over. The scene that followed was most heart-rending. The car came over with a terrific crash and the passengers were laid in a heap all more or less badly hurt – some in their bewilderment, doing themselves serious injury amongst the broken glass. The cries were terrible.'

At the inquest, Manners testified that he was looking up Victoria Road when he saw a car coming down the hill at what seemed to him a fast pace, although no faster than others he had seen on the same stretch of road. Even so, he admitted that the speed was such that he could not have crossed the road in front of the tram, adding that he would not have attempted to cross the road unless the car had been stationary. He said that his attention was called to this tram, at a point where it had reached the technical schools (the old Swindon College in Victoria Road) because someone was shouting. When it reached the foot of the hill it seemed to take to the outer lane, gave a jump and then turned over. He observed the driver was at his wheel, but could not say whether or not he seemed alarmed just before the accident, or whether the brakes were on or off. Mr Manners said he did not think the tram was over-crowded; this was an odd statement, since it is known that all seating was taken up and passengers were standing inside the car and along the open top.

One week after the inquest into the tram disaster, the Empire Theatrescope and Vaudeville Company paid its first visit to Swindon. The Company brought to the theatre a programme of short films including travelogues, newsreels, and fiction. Here was 'the very latest in animated photography' producing 'some very remarkable and up to date effects'. The features included *Winter Sports in Other Lands*, *Victims of the Storm*, *The Detective* ('about as exciting a picture as one could wish to see'), and *The Invisible Men* ('the very latest in animated photography'). 'Many of the pictures are distinctly funny and create roars of laughter,' said the publicity, 'others are highly interesting and instructive, at the same time being projected on the screen with striking distinctiveness.' Swindon, still reeling from the tram disaster, was not impressed, and the showing was poorly attended.

These were the years when opera and Shakespeare proved very popular. In 1904, the Elster-Grime Grand Opera Company (with a cast of forty-five) made its first appearance at the New Queen's. This short-lived company had been formed in 1900 by singers Marie Elster (real name Mary Violetta Larnach) and Edward Grime. At Swindon, they performed the usual repertoire that had become the staple diet at this theatre. The (Fanny) Moody (Charles) Manners Grand Opera Company, founded by the husband and wife team in the year the Swindon theatre was opened, made their first appearance there in 1905. Opera fell out of fashion at Swindon in 1907. Shakespeare remained popular, however, mostly in the hands of Osmond Tearle's Shakespearean [sic] Company. Tearle was an old Shakespearian actor who had turned his back on the London stage, preferring to play the country theatres and thereby earning his epithet 'the Irving of the Provinces'. His company came several times to the New Queen's in its early years, and was always rewarded with good houses.

The type of female headwear that was fashionable in the Edwardian era nonetheless caused a problem for theatregoers. Early in the 1906-07 season, a plea appeared in the *Swindon Advertiser* to 'certain of the gentler sex who occupy the stalls at the New Queen's Theatre. Large hats are all very well on such as church parades', wrote the correspondent, 'but in the stalls at the theatre they are distinctly irritating to those sitting immediately behind them, and should either be removed or left at home.' The writer went on to point out that ladies who consider it 'a dream of an idea to join the no-hat brigade nonetheless attend the theatre in creations which suggest a cross between a parasol and a shower bonnet'.

Alfred Manners soon proved himself to be an able and popular manager of the New Queen's Theatre, and its patrons were concerned to learn that he suffered a serious accident on Bonfire Night in 1906. A Roman candle, which had apparently failed to ignite, exploded in his face when Manners went to investigate the cause, thereby causing burns and a serious injury to his eye. A doctor dressed the wounds but was unable to tell whether the damage to the eye would be permanent. Manners was very highly regarded, to the extent that this information was announced to the audience that evening, during the interval of the play *The Trumpet Calls*. The injured man returned to work a few days later, went on stage just before the finale of *Florodora*, and was cheered by the audience, who were relieved to hear that his disability was not permanent.

Pantomimes did not take place at Christmas in the early years of the New Queen's Theatre. The first yuletide extravaganza of this nature was presented on Boxing Day 1906, when *Sinbad the Sailor* took to the stage, a pantomime in three acts and three tableaux written by Alfred Manners and Newman Maurice, and produced in-house by Samuel James. The mayor, Francis Stook Coleman, attended the crowded first night, and so did the *Swindon Evening Advertiser* (the paper slightly altered its name in 1906), who thought that the production was too long. Nonetheless, it ran until 12 January 1907.

Alfred Manners had proved to be very popular with the New Queen's Theatre audiences, and he was a generous supporter of charities, and a sponsor of sport in the town. The first indication that he was leaving came as a considerable surprise. It appeared, in a very subtle way, in an advertisement placed in the *Swindon Evening Advertiser* on 29 February 1907 for the play *The Shulamite*. 'Support your townsman in the last two weeks of his management', it said. This was followed up a week later with the enjoinder 'do not fail to visit the Queen's tomorrow (9 March) for the Complimentary [*sic*] benefit to Alfred Manners upon the last night of his management'. Swindon took it to their hearts; it was a record house, packed out from wall to wall, and the takings grossed £9 more than the sum taken since the theatre was opened.

During the interval, Alfred Manners went onstage and received a gift from Alderman J. Brewer, who spoke of the theatre manager's many attributes. Manners addressed the house as 'my old friends' and explained that he was severing his connection with the theatre and – to cries of 'No! No!' – was handing it over to 'a better man'. He said that his employers wanted a lighter form of entertainment than he had been able to put before the public and that this could be better provided by his successor, George Dance. He also said he was very greatly indebted to his staff of fifty-five, and that during his period at the theatre there had only been two staff changes. As regards the plays, they had been of the very best and he thanked his patrons most heartily for their support, which he hoped would continue if ever he came back to Swindon. Later, at the close of the performance, Manners again appeared before the footlights and once more wished every success to Mr Dance. Yet these valedictory speeches would prove to be premature.

The circumstances of Alfred Manners's leaving remain a mystery, but an even greater mystery was that of the negotiations that must have taken place over the next few months. The theatre remained closed until August 1907, and there were no further newspaper or trade press reports about it or its personnel; absolute silence reigned, and George Dance did not appear. Then, on 20 August, the *Swindon Evening Advertiser* announced that the theatre was about to reopen and that 'certain arrangements have been made whereby Mr Alfred Manners will resume control, though this does not imply that the unfortunate dispute between himself and Mr George Dance has been settled'. The next day the paper reported that barring any unforeseen difficulties, the theatre would reopen on the 26 August with the play *The White Carnation*. It went on to explain that 'the dispute had still not been settled but after a good deal of engineering, certain arrangements had been made whereby Mr Manners would resume control at the theatre'. There had been widespread sympathy for him, according to the newspaper, in consequence of the 'trying and anxious time he has had to face'. 'When the theatre reopens', said the Swindon Advertiser, 'it is hoped the public will give practical expression to that sympathy by extending to him a liberal measure of support to compensate for the many weeks of strain and mental worry.'

The return of Alfred Manners (now designated General and Business Manager), and the reopening of the New Queen's Theatre was treated as a major event in the town. The *Swindon Evening Advertiser* reported: 'At last, after nearly six months of patient waiting, of rumours, promises, contradictions, possibilities, probabilities, the New Queen's Theatre has at last reopened. Mr Alfred Manners, who, taking things all round, has had a fairly rough time of it, has resumed control, and looks for such degree of support from his numerous patrons, indeed from the whole theatre-going public in Swindon and district, as will to some extent compensate him for the strain, worry and anxiety of the past five or six months.'

The opening night, 26 August 1907, certainly supplied every possible reason for encouragement. There was a procession from the County Ground to the theatre, accompanied by the Swindon Borough Prize Military Band under the direction of F.G. Davis, and by a banner calling upon people to 'support your townsman'. The theatre was virtually full; the noisy element were at strength, with ear-piercing yells from those in the pit; and 'the buzz of excitement and impatience sometimes broke out into a shrill shout and then the whistling'. The 'elite of Swindon' were out in force; and in the pit stalls was the town's football team (described as 'the hopes of Swindon's future success and distinction in the First Division of the Southern League'). When at length the curtain rose to reveal Mr Davis and the Borough Band, the house 'roared its satisfaction'. They played a selection of tunes from *The Mikado*, then Mary Jarvis Finn sang the National Anthem, and the first show proper got under way. It was a musical play, in which many of the songs alluded to the town, to the Swindon football team, the Wilts & Berks Canal, and even to Alfred Manners himself. At the conclusion, Manners appeared on stage and thanked the audience for supporting himself and the performance so splendidly. His hope that he would merit their continued approbation was met with hearty cheers.

H. B. Levy and J. E Cardwell's Celebrated Juvenile Pantomime Company visited the New Queen's Theatre in October 1907, with the pantomime *The Sleeping Beauty*. Leading the company was Wee Georgie Wood who, as a significant star, would visit the theatre many times in later years. Tucked away in the cast playing 'Ebeneezer (Golliwog 2)' was 'Master Stanley Jefferson, aged 17', who had made his professional stage debut in Glasgow the previous year, and in Swindon 'supplied some first class business' according to the newspaper review. This Jefferson was born to a theatrical family in Ulverston, Lancashire on 16 June 1890; thirty-one years later he would change his name to Stan Laurel, and become one of the world's biggest film stars. Young Stan Jefferson returned to the New Queen's with the same company in 1909, with the pantomime *The House That Jack Built*. He played the part of Percy, and was described as 'a hard worker'. (In 1921, Stan Laurel was paired for the first time in a film with Oliver Hardy, and in 1947 the pair visited Swindon as part of a nationwide tour. All Stan could recall of Swindon at that time was that 'it was winter, and as we were kids we played snow balls'.)

In November 1907, Alfred Manners announced that the New Queen's Theatre, universally known for nearly a decade as the Queen's Theatre, if never officially acknowledged as such, was to be renamed The Empire. It closed on 30 November after the final performance of Frederick Melville's 1904 melodrama *The Ugliest Woman on Earth*, and reopened with its new name and a variety show on Boxing Day. In the intervening month, much had taken place. The auditorium was re-seated, re-upholstered, redecorated, and draught-proofed ('to stop the draughts that used to haunt the building like icy spectres'). The heating system was augmented, especially around the pit area; and electric lighting was installed. The stage underwent a 'complete transformation', including a new drop curtain. All of this, said the local newspaper, 'imparted a refinement and better tone to the interior' and facilitated scenes that would 'give proper effect to the better class of entertainment that will be provided'. There was, for the first time, a box office inside the theatre, and Alfred Manners had become the managing director. The Empire was described as now being one of the cosiest theatres in the provinces. If the promoters of the change in name thought that there could no longer be any ambiguity in the matter, they must have been disappointed when the press called it Swindon's 'Empire Theatre of Varieties'.

The theatre was opened on Boxing Day 1907 by Major Fitzroy Pleydell Goddard, High Sheriff, and last of the males of that ancient family line to live in the town and to be lord of the manor of Swindon. The occasion turned into yet another testimonial for Alfred Manners when Goddard presented him with a silver plate, subscribed by the townspeople, and an illuminated address of thanks for his charitable work. The citation ran: 'To Mr Alfred Manners. We beg your acceptance of this address and the accompanying articles of silver plate to mark our appreciation of the way you have conducted the Queen's Theatre during your management, and to signalise the many kindnesses to the (Victoria) hospital, sports and other institutions by organising entertainments, and granting the use of this theatre, etc. which resulted in considerable amounts being added to the funds of the above objects. With our best wishes for your future success. Signed on behalf of the subscribers by F. P. Goddard, December 26th 1907.'

One of the opening acts epitomised the type of variety artiste for which the theatre became well known. This was Mlle Ampere, 'The Human Battery'. She used high-tension electrical currents, said to be never less than 20,000 volts; lit electric lamps, caused handkerchiefs to catch fire at a distance, using 'wireless electricity' from her body; and lit gas jets with pieces of ice. She also used bananas and hats in her performance.

There had been only occasional variety (or vaudeville) at the New Queen's in the very early days and it did not become a regular part of the programming until the end of 1907, after the theatre had been renamed the Empire Theatre (of Variety). Variety, which grew out of the music hall, although it was less rowdy, consisted of singers, dancers, comedians, comediennes, jugglers, equilibrists (balancing acts), acrobats, animal acts, strong men, sportsmen (and women), magicians, illusionists, and male and female impersonators. Comediennes were very popular and there were very few weeks of variety without acts such as Maggie Rimmer, Mollie Augarde, Ida Brophy, Alice Lingard and Flo Melville.

There were also many quite bizarre acts. One such was Unthan, top of the bill for a week in February 1908, who was described as 'an armless wonder who could be seen driving a carriage and pair through the streets of Swindon during his stay'. Born without arms, he played violin and cornet with his legs and feet; similarly he shuffled, cut and played cards; dined; and used his feet to take a cigar case from his pocket, take out the cigar, clip off its end, and smoke it. His act ended when he loaded a rifle and fired it, hitting the cork from the top of a bottle. Other unusual acts included Cambo, the musical monkey; Judge's Marvellously Trained Cockatoos; Billy, the educated horse; and Argo, the Farmyard Mimic.

Female baritones often appeared at the Empire. For example, Mlle de Rose came in August 1908, when she was rapturously applauded for her rendition of 'Where are the boys of the Old Brigade'. In April 1909, her powerful baritone voice was heard in a novel drawing-room entertainment, assisted by the soprano Hilda Claremont. Marie Dreams, who came to the theatre in June 1909, was also described as a young lady with a powerful baritone voice, and an encore was demanded for her interpretation of *Come back to Erin*. Also in 1908, Manners executed something of a coup in bringing to the town Seymour Hicks and Zena Dare in a flying matinée of *Gay Gordons*.

The Chinese illusionist Chung Ling Soo, one of the most famous and inventive variety acts of the day, made his first appearance at the Empire in 1908, and played to full houses. His was a long act; it was said that he brought with him an amazing amount of props, and one would have to watch his act many times to see all of his tricks. These involved turning a tub of sawdust into a can of rich milk with a flash of lightning, conjuring a large shower of coins out of thin air, and expelling smoke and flames from his mouth. At the climax of his act, three men shot at Soo from the body of the house, using ordinary rifles, and he caught the bullets in a plate. He played the Empire again in December 1912.

It was a variation of the shooting act that went wrong and killed Soo during a performance at the Wood Green Empire on the 24 March 1918, when he was discovered to be, in fact, an American named William Ellsworth Robinson. Soo's real identity mattered little; the audiences at Swindon, as elsewhere, had loved his illusions.

By now, the theatre's patrons had become wise to the fact that pre-programme superlatives were not necessarily lived up to by the acts they purported to describe. 'There is a limit', warned the *Swindon Evening Advertiser*, 'to the gullibility of the public.' In a telling editorial, it described how 'on many occasions the building has been packed to its utmost limits, with eager and expectant audiences, and on some of those occasions the attraction which has called forth so much rush and crush has not been worth it. At other times there have been good things provided of a distinctly superior order when the audiences have been meagre in the extreme'. It laid the blame for this firmly at the door of advertising 'carried too far, or beyond the bounds of discretion'. The piece implied that the promoters of shows at the Empire had been guilty of proclaiming entertainment that was 'vastly superior to anything ever seen at the principal places of amusement in the Metropolis, the Continent, or anywhere else for that matter', and then providing entertainment that 'the people would not care to go and see if the doors of the playhouse were opened free'. The promoters stood accused of announcing performances the like of which no-one living had yet seen, only to provide, in the event, something 'as old as the hills'.

It was a damning piece, whose anonymous author cited 'by methods of this sort the prospects for the future are often seriously affected'. It was too easy, he said, to blame shortage of money when the fare is good but the audiences are poor; rather it is suspicion and fear of deception that keep people away. Rather strangely, these words appeared in the late summer of 1908, following a week when the theatre had broken all audience records to date for a variety show. Clearly, though, the question of audience numbers was at the time a hot topic, and one in which the management of the Empire had a considerable interest, if possibly a different view. The writer of the *Swindon Evening Advertiser* piece was not to be put off the stroke of his vituperative pen by such a one-off success.

The weekly programme at the theatre included 'Empire Pictures'. A private box now cost 10/6d. Other seats cost 1/6d in the orchestra stalls, 1/- in the stalls, 6d in the circle, and 3d in the pit (those who wanted to arrive half an hour early could now access all of these for 1/9d, 1/3d, 8d and 4d respectively). Much was made of the fact whenever officers of the Borough of Swindon attended. 'The second house appeared to be an unusually large one too, and the appearance of two aldermen and at least four town councillors and at least two ex-councillors in the stalls would suggest that the Empire is coming into more than ordinary favour.' It had become quite common, at each house, for Alfred Manners to impart late news of some moment to the audience, and such was frequently met with cheers. An example of this occurred when, in 1908, Lloyd-George negotiated a provisional agreement at the Board of Trade with representatives of the parties in the engineering dispute on the north-east coast. The telegram confirming the settlement, having been received by the *Swindon Evening Advertiser* after its last edition had gone to press, was immediately passed on to Manners by the editor.

In November 1908, Manners announced that henceforth, programming would revert to a single house per night, showing a mixture of musical comedy, drama and variety. Owen Hall & Leslie Stuart's great musical comedy *Florodora* was to be one of the immediate highlights, no doubt taking advantage of the new facilities for a 'better class of entertainment', as would the Philip Michael Faraday & Frederick Fenn's comic opera *Amasis*, about the pharaoh of old Egypt.

The success of the previous two or three seasons at Swindon brought out the entrepreneur in Alfred Manners. It occurred to him that a theatre might be opened to entertain military personnel stationed in the army accommodation at Tidworth and Ludgershall, in south Wiltshire. The War Office agreed, and financed, at a cost of some £6,000, the intimate, but adequate, building at Tidworth: a hall with a gallery at the rear, internally boarded throughout, having cushioned tip-up seats, and with an orchestra pit. The auditorium was lit by gas, and the stage was illuminated by electricity. The theatre was leased to Manners on the understanding that he would provide entertainment there on the first three nights of the week, and opened as The Garrison Theatre on 14 June 1909. The opening production was *Bluebeard* by Charles Constant's company, which had played at the Swindon Empire the previous week. So packed was The Garrison Theatre that the curtain was half an hour late going up, and the play was greeted with such enthusiasm from the start and so frequently delayed by unscheduled audience participation that the final curtain did not come down for three and a half hours.

# 3
# *Silver screens to battle fronts*

IN 1908, AN open air café set up a screen in Regent Circus, put on a programme of short films, and pulled in the crowds. This was Swindon's version of the 'electric theatres' that were soon to be found going up elsewhere; tent-like structures that promised, around their canvas entrances and awnings, 'the latest in life-sized moving pictures' suitable for all the family. Soon afterwards, permanent picture houses began to open in Swindon, inside which audiences could experience black and white moving pictures. At about the same time, the Empire Theatre introduced newsreels during its variety shows. For theatre manager Alfred Manners, flickering films presaged a developing trend in entertainment that had the potential to threaten his share of local disposable income. The developing popularity of the silver screen was an early indication that here was an art form that had more than novelty value, and its continued patronage would soon engender a watershed in entertainment in the town.

On 23 December 1909, Ernest Carpenter, the man who had built the first professional theatre in Swindon, died at 2 Dorset Square, London, although his home was 4 Gordon Mansions, Bloomsbury. He was forty-one years of age. Carpenter left Swindon in 1904 for the Eden Theatre, Brighton; in 1907, he took over The Lyceum Theatre in London with his business partner, Henry R. Smith. There he was phenomenally successful, and is credited as the man who brought 'legitimate theatre' back to that establishment, mostly by way of melodramas, Shakespeare and pantomimes. The last named he wrote himself, and it was during a performance of one such production, *Aladdin*, that he died. He had felt unwell during the final rehearsals for the show, in which his daughter Marjory Lord Carpenter was to star, and believed the trouble to be indigestion. When this failed to settle, his wife persuaded him to leave the theatre, thus missing his daughter's performance, and he died soon afterwards of what was described as a particularly dangerous hernia.

Carpenter left just £382. 5s 6d, and a number of creditors, including Carpenters' Theatres Limited, who made a claim in the Court of Chancery against Jessie, his widow and sole executrix. Marjory performed as part of a company brought together at the Lyceum Theatre on 4 October 1910 in a 'complimentary matinée for the benefit of Mrs Ernest Carpenter'. There were fifty-four artistes on the stage, of the calibre of, and including, Wilkie Bard, Sir Herbert Beerbohm Tree, Little Tich, Fanny Brough, Lily Elsie, Sir Harry Lauder and Bransby Williams. At the Lyceum on that day in 1910 was a cast so star-studded, to raise funds for the beloved late manager's wife, that it would have done credit to the first Royal Command Performance, then two years in the future. Thereafter, Marjory continued her career as an actress, and Jessie lived until 1926.

In Swindon, within two years of the screen at the open air café, the Luton Electric Pavilion Company bought a site in Regent Street. Two of its directors, W.R. Rooper and a Mr Aulton, designed a seven-hundred-seat picture house, and the building contract was given to Swindon firm H. & C. Spackman, of Hunt Street. The new picture house measured ninety feet by thirty-six feet, and seated 700 people; an additional forty feet of space was secured at the rear, and this could be utilised, at some future date, to accommodate a further five hundred patrons. The building was heated for use in the winter, and a sliding roof was installed for ventilation in the summer.

This new venture was called The County Electric, and was opened by the mayor of Swindon, Alderman William Henry Lawson, on 10 February 1910. The inaugural programme went for humour: *A Late Guest, Foolshead Steals a Carpet* and *Mr Poorluck Gets Married*, and were 'all greeted with gales of laughter'. Swindonians flocked to the moving pictures from the outset, and another venture, The Picture House, set up in Regent Circus at almost the same time as The County Electric. The management of the Empire Theatre now realised that recreational films posed a serious threat to live theatre, but it was one that might be turned into an opportunity. For the moment, Manners continued to hedge his bets on the newsreels, which he probably felt appealed to a better class of patrons. In the years to come, he would state time and again that his intentions were always to provide the very best in entertainment for the most discerning of audiences; he just had to decide the level of that discernment. This was as difficult for Manners to answer as had been the considerations that originally confronted Ernest Carpenter when he set up the theatre in Swindon.

Meanwhile, The Empire continued its association with amateur theatre. In 1910, it staged Charles McEvoy's *The Village Wedding*, performed by a company of villagers from Aldbourne, a nearby downland village. McEvoy, who lived there at the Old Malt House, was one of the playwrights to take advantage of The Stage Society's policy of producing private performances of new, avant-garde and experimental plays at established theatres, many of which were in London. This it continued to do from 1899 until the outbreak of the Second World War. McEvoy formed the Albourne Village Players, and established the Aldbourne Village Theatre, who performed in his Malt House Barn in South Street. It was there that his play was first produced, and later the same year went on at the Empire, with the Aldbourne Silver Band providing the music, and George Bernard Shaw (another writer to be produced by The Stage Society) in the audience. *The Village Wedding* went on a national tour, and its performance at The Empire, in the presence of the author, attracted a large and enthusiastic audience.

Twenty-eight members of the theatre's staff went on a firm's outing in 1910. In draughty February, they embarked at Swindon train station at 5.30 a.m. for Weymouth, arriving in time for a substantial breakfast at the Crown Hotel. The weather was fine, and the occasion was further enlivened when the company visited John Grove & Son's brewery, where they all sampled the Weymouth Ales. Dinner was taken at 2 p.m. in The Crown; tea was had there at 6 p.m., and the company caught the scheduled 10.30 p.m. train service back to Swindon. In case anyone was still feeling peckish, the 'Outings Committee' had thoughtfully provided sandwiches and light refreshments for what proved to be 'a merry journey home' into the small hours of the morning.

Just before Christmas 1910, thieves broke open the till in the theatre bar. Finding it empty, they helped themselves instead to brandies and sodas, and made off with some cigarettes. Another merry journey home, no doubt.

Between 1910 and 1919, musical comedies such as *The Arcadians*, *The Merry Widow* and *Our Miss Gibbs* played the Empire, and some of them returned many times. Playwrights whose works were performed there included Wilson Barrett, actor-manager and playwright, whose long career on the boards in the provinces during the 19th century was characterised by a heavy diet of tragedy and melodrama. Walter Howard, Frederick Melville, Walter Melville, G. Carlton Wallace, Arthur Shirley and Hall Caine were also well-known playwrights of their day whose work was featured at the Empire.

More serious fare during this period included that provided by such as the Alexander Marsh Company, which appeared regularly with a repertoire of Shakespeare. In the same vein, the great latter-day

Shakespearian actor-manager Henry Baynton brought his relatively short-lived company (1917-1930) to Swindon. The H. Armitage and Arthur Leigh's Company performed straight plays at the Empire, as did the Harrison Frewin Company, and the F. B. Wolfe players. The Joseph O'Mara Travelling Opera Company, formed by the Italian-trained Irish tenor in 1912, was one of the operatic successes to play Swindon, as was the Carl Rosa Opera Company, formed in 1873 and still in existence today. Amongst the other opera companies that found favour with the Empire's audiences and returned on several occasions were the Moody Manners Opera Company and the Arlington Charsley Grand Opera Company. The work of Gilbert & Sullivan was regularly presented.

Manners had always been mindful of the Empire's potential for charitable works that would benefit the local community, and he occasionally mounted events over the next couple of years aimed at obtaining funds for good causes. One of these, particularly dear to his heart, was Swindon's Victoria Hospital, which had been financed by public subscription, opened in 1888, and was always in need of funds. In 1911, he enabled Alexander Marsh, Carrie Baillie and the company to perform a matinée of Sheridan's *The School for Scandal* in aid of the hospital. A well-attended matinée performance of *His Excellency the Governor*, an amateur production of Robert Marshall's play directed by Orlando Barnett at the Empire in 1912, raised over £200, which benefited the Victoria Hospital, as well as the Wiltshire Nursing Home in Old Town.

The Victoria Hospital again benefited in 1912 when an aeroplane made its first appearance in the town. Piloted by the French pioneer aviator Henri Salmet, and as part of a tour sponsored by the *Daily Mail* newspaper, the Bleriot monoplane landed on a field beside the road to Coate, where its occupant was greeted by civic dignitaries. He gave onlookers a 'fascinating flying acrobatic exhibition', before being whisked away to delight an audience at the Empire with a lighthearted presentation on the possibilities for the future of flying. The money raised was donated to the Victoria Hospital.

G.H. Elliott ('The Chocolate Coloured Coon') and his Company made an appearance in 1912. He was a true black and white minstrel, in the sense that he blacked up his face, but wore a white suit and a white top hat. Child acts were also well received at the Empire; we read of much approbation for the child comedienne named 'My Sister'; how the audience warmed to Madame Holt's Juvenile Follies; how they agreed that Babie Beattie was truly a 'child marvel'; and of Wee Dot and Doris, who went down well as 'juvenile entertainers'.

Pantomimes usually came to the Empire two or three times a year. Two members of the cast of *Babes in the Wood*, which played there in March 1912, were Charlie Naughton and Jimmy Gold, who first teamed up together in 1908. In 1931, almost twenty years after their first visit to the Empire, they would be billed with a pair of former acrobatic dancers and jugglers named Jimmy Nervo and Teddy Knox; and all four would come together, just six years later, as 'The Crazy Gang', with Bud Flanagan, Chesney Allen, and sometimes 'Monsewer' Eddie Gray (who also played the Swindon Empire as a solo act).

In April 1912, the world was shocked when 1,517 people were killed in the *Titanic* disaster. In Swindon, the mayor, Alderman George Brooks, set up a fund to aid the victims' families, and, under the auspices of this, Manners immediately arranged a concert at the Empire, which consisted almost entirely of local talent, and for which he bore all the expenses. The concert raised £55, of which £10 was collected by 'Miss Dolly Manners'. Esther Dolly Manners was Alfred Manners and his wife Ellen's first child, and now, at nineteen years of age, was poised to become a principal fund-raiser for her father's favourite causes. In the 1911 census, she was designated as assistant to her father's position as theatrical manager. When the First World War broke out, she would find herself working hard to finance food parcels for troops at the Front.

Manners also favoured charities for the armed forces, and in 1913 he held a benefit night for the local Territorial Benefit Fund. The house was full for the production of *The Catch of the Season*, an Edwardian musical comedy by Seymour Hicks and Cosmo Hamilton, and Manners handed over half of the evening's takings. Within a year, the First World War broke out, and thereafter Alfred Manners and Dolly would be very much involved in fund-raising.

During the 1912 summer break, the theatre was again redecorated. Whenever possible, Manners preferred to use local labour, so the work was carried out under the direction of Tom Finn of Finn Brothers, plumbers and painters, 23 Devizes Road, Old Town. The thirty men who were engaged to carry out the work took sixteen days to complete the refurbishment. They brought into bold relief the elegant figures of the fresco work in the gallery by giving them a background of carmine and gold, and coating them with antique silver. They transformed the proscenium, applying a beautiful rose tint on a cream background, and studded the panelled ceiling above it in mother-of-pearl. The fine floral work was enhanced on the Georgian-style boxes, their cream-coloured marble columns were picked out in Siena marble effect, and the figure-work, draped in pink with gold enrichments, was repainted. The handsome dome above the auditorium was given a blend of shades from sienna to cream, and from carmine to the palest of pink. Beneath this, the interior was painted rose-pink, and otherwise papered to blend with the colour scheme, with new effects on the panels of the entrance screen to the stalls. The vestibule was treated in silver and crimson. New carpets were laid and additional lighting was installed.

In October, Alfred Manners announced that heavy plush curtains had been added to the entrance doors, making them practically draught-proof. Extra 'heating apparatus' had also been put in place, which made the theatre most cosy and comfortable. The following February, a box office was opened at the Empire, and notices were placed in the *Swindon*

*Evening Advertiser* to the effect that it was open between 6 p.m. and 10 p.m., whilst from 10 a.m. to 6 p.m. the booking agent was still Milsom's, the music sellers in Fleet Street.

At his curtain call at the end of the 1913 summer season, Alfred Manners reported that, in the ten years since he had taken over the running of the theatre from Ernest Carpenter, the nightly receipts had increased fourfold. On that night, a decade ago, there was no picture house in the town to affect receipts, yet the average weekly returns at the theatre had been just £93. That average, over the last four years, had been £203 per week. It was, he told his audience, a wonderful record of success, and thanked them all for their 'hearty support'. It did not matter how able and successful a manager may be, Manners told the assembled patrons, if he does not receive the hearty support of the general public. He trusted that when the theatre reopened after a break of two weeks, the patrons would continue to give such support. The assembly were much heartened, and there was considerable applause.

By now, it was clear that moving pictures were rather more than a passing fancy. In 1913, Alfred Manners bought The Picture House in Regent Circus, and renamed it The Ideal Picture House. The first film there under Manners's management, screened on 20 October, was *The Red Duke*, which played for three nights, and was followed by *The Invaders*. The new owner said that he intended to provide the finest and most exclusive cinema in Swindon. He also wanted to show programmes of highly educational value, aimed at making his investment 'a social meeting place with families and parties particularly catered for'. Later that year, Fred Stone became the leader of the Empire's pit orchestra, although this seems to have been a part-time appointment as many of the musical shows brought their own musical directors, if not their own touring orchestras. Otherwise, local musicians were called upon by the management of the Empire, as and when required.

On the day before war broke out in 1914, a revue called *Wait and See* was playing the Empire Theatre. On its opening night, Alfred Manners appeared with the whole company on stage before curtain-up, and led the audience in the National Anthem and 'Rule Britannia', before calling for 'three cheers' for England in the time of crisis. Back on stage during the interval, Manners read the latest war news that had been received by telegraph and telephone at the *Swindon Evening Advertiser* office.

War was officially declared the following day. There was great excitement in the town, and at 7.49 p.m. on 4 August, the pre-arranged signal of ten blasts on the Great Western Railway Company's Swindon Works hooter called the town's Territorials to mobilise. The streets were crowded as men assembled outside the drill halls in New Swindon and Old Town. Suddenly, thousands more men were on the move to either venue: men who had been told to hold themselves ready, and not to leave the town. The Swindon contingent of the Royal Army Medical Corps paraded at the New Swindon drill hall at 6.30 a.m. on 5 August; the advance guard of the Royal Engineers left Swindon at 9 a.m. from the GWR Station; and the Swindon Squadron of the Royal Wilts Imperial Yeomanry paraded at 10 a.m. at the Vale of the White Horse Repository. At 6 p.m. on 6 August, the main body of the local Territorials embarked on trains at the Midland and South Western Junction Railway station in Old Town. The mayor of Swindon, Alderman Charles Hill, in the company of other members of the Council, gave a stirring speech that was much applauded, and the troops departed. Swindon was now at war.

Revue was a relatively new form of theatre that met wartime audience's need for something more frivolous than what had hitherto been the usual bill of fare. The Edwardian melodramas and serious plays were not sufficiently divorced from real life to provide the kind of escapism that those patrons needed, who were constantly in fear of receiving the news that they dreaded of their loved ones at the Front.

Even those people who had no family circumstances to affect them in that way were daily exposed to the most disheartening newspaper reports. A brief sojourn in a theatre seat, assailed by laughter and music, provided a tonic, at least for the duration. The revue was entertainment at its least profound; frothy dance numbers and catchy tunes linked humorous sketches and slapstick comedy, and this became staple fare at the Empire during the war. One such production, *Wait and See*, was playing the theatre when war was declared, and thereafter they came thick and fast. Revues with titles like *S'Nice, I'm Sorry, Oh! You Must, Good Evening*, and *Smile Please* must have been virtually indistinguishable one from the other in content, style and running order. Yet they were so much of their time, and they played to packed houses twice nightly.

Thousands of soldiers were billeted in Swindon during the second week of August 1914, and the town's Territorials were mobilised. They all left Swindon on 16 August, during the day, and that evening Manners mounted a hastily compiled programme of patriotic music and song at the Empire in aid of the Prince of Wales's National Relief Fund; this would give financial aid to the families of men who were killed in action. Some of the professionals who were working at the theatre that week took part; otherwise, the artistes and bands were local and amateur. Everyone gave their services free of charge, and Manners also made a personal contribution to the fund. Thus began the manager's charity work for the forces and their dependants, which would extend throughout and beyond the First World War. He announced on 16 August that he had arranged for a series of concerts to be given at the theatre on Sunday evenings, when the takings would go towards national relief funds. The audience gave a hearty reception to every artiste on the first night, and in the spirit of fervent patriotism and optimism that blinded the truths at the start of the Great War, it augured well for theatre audiences throughout the duration.

Under Manners's control, the Empire Theatre had always supported various good causes, and the focus of his fund-raising now became the war effort and the requirements of local troops, on a rising tide of patriotism. When the Mayor's Relief Fund was launched in mid-August, he pledged five pounds, and thereafter, throughout hostilities, he and his daughter Dolly both raised a great deal of money for the local soldiers. He also tried to provide for their entertainment, building a picture house at Draycott Road, Chiseldon, on a military camp just a few miles south of Swindon. On 1 December 1914, just a few months after it opened, this picture house was completely destroyed in a severe gale.

On 16 August, the company of *All the Nice Girls*, which had been playing at the Empire that week, gave their services free of charge in the first of a series of Sunday concerts (always held 'strictly in accordance with the regulations for Sunday evening concerts'), which continued until 23 September, in aid of the Prince of Wales's National Benefit Fund. These performances attracted large audiences, and the professionals were augmented by local entertainers such as the Swindon Orpheus Male Voice Choir, the Gorse Hill Prize Band, Hilda D'Arcy and Gordon James. To ensure that fund-raising concerts for troops held in the town did not clash, he arranged for organisers to set a programme that could be mutually agreed upon week by week. He also encouraged local bands in the town to give their services free of charge, and reduced his theatre seat prices for the fund-raising events held at the Empire. A seat in the pit cost 2d; it was 4d in the circle; and the stalls sold at 6d each. Programme selling was in the hands of Dolly Manners, and a group of volunteers.

In 1914, a week of opera by the O'Mara Grand Opera Company Ltd was held at the Empire. The *Swindon Evening Advertiser* reported that this company, with the exceptions of 'a brave little Belgian and a sturdy Russian', was composed entirely of British artistes. The operas were sung in English, with the exception of the German *Tannhäuser* by Richard Wagner.

In May 1915, Alfred Manners was summoned to appear before Swindon Magistrate's Court (next door to the theatre in Clarence Street), charged with allowing intoxicating liquor to be consumed at the Empire Theatre after nine o'clock in the evening. This was in contravention of an Order made by the Licensing Justices under the Intoxicating Liquor (Temporary) Restriction Act, 1914. Superintendent Moore made the allegation, to which Manners pleaded guilty, and was fined £20 with £5 costs.

The Dolly Manners' Soldiers' and Sailors' Christmas Gift Fund (initially called the Christmas Pudding Fund) was established in October 1915, when female cast members of *A Pair of Silk Stockings*, then playing at the Empire, made a collection which brought in over £90. Two months later, the local newspaper reported that the response to date had yielded over £200 towards the fund, including more than £40 from the theatre, and one guinea from the Gorse Hill Working Men's Club. Manners and Dolly received many letters of thanks from Swindon men fighting for their country, including one from F. C. Frampton, 49th Mess, HMS Orion, c/o GPO, London, dated 10 December 1915:

'My dear Miss Manners. Just a few lines, thanking you for your gift, which you have been kind enough to send me, also for the card and the beautiful words which are on it. I shall appreciate it very much, knowing that it came from the people of Swindon, and knowing that they are thinking of us while we are away doing our duty for our King and Country. It lightens our hearts when we know our friends at home are thinking about us. So will you kindly thank the people of Swindon for me for their kindness in assisting you to send us these beautiful gifts, which kindness will always live in our memory. Again thanking you for your kindness and wishing you and Mr and Mrs Manners and the people of Swindon a bright and merry Christmas and a most prosperous and peaceful new year.'

This was one of numerous letters that the Manners family received from serving soldiers throughout the war, not only thanking them for the contents of the parcels, but also for the encouraging and inspiring words they wrote on the accompanying cards, which the recipients said helped to boost their morale. The first card, sent in time for Christmas 1914 by Manners and his daughter to Swindon men serving in France, was printed on stiff card, measuring four inches by two inches; on the front were photographs of the allied national flags, printed in colour, and the words 'From Mr, Mrs, and Dolly Manners and Swindon Friends'. The British flag was reproduced in colour on page four. The inside verso page read: 'God bless the gallant defenders of England, God save the men who were true to the call; Tell them the love of the nation is mingled, With honour and prayers for their safety through all'. The recto bore the words 'Dear Friend, in enclosing you this little reminder of Yule-Tide from Father, Mother, Self and Friends in Swindon, we do so with our hearts beating true to you for the services you are rendering to our King and Country. We know that God and the Right is with you while you are away. We shall doubly welcome you on your return. Dolly Manners. Empire Theatre, Swindon.'

According to the *Swindon Evening Advertiser* , this type of war support work was unique to Swindon. Nor were the wives and children of the town's fighting men forgotten. Throughout the war, free entertainments and refreshments were laid on for them at the Empire, courtesy of Alderman (James E.) 'Raggie' Powell. Born into poverty in 1849, and unable to read or write before he came to Swindon in 1890, Powell was a rag and bone man, a dealer in rabbit skins, and trader in furniture and works of art. He was also a generous benefactor over four decades in his adopted town, and was made a Freeman of the Borough in 1920, partly for his charitable work during hostilities.

In 1916, Alfred Manners and Dolly received a letter from a Major Dawson, the officer commanding a contingent of the Royal Engineers stationed at Weymouth, who had under his command sapper William Blake of Swindon, who played the cornet. There were two more cornet players in the contingent, and Dawson discovered that in all he had twenty-six men who could play musical instruments; he at once decided to form a band. The three cornet players were given a special pass to see how many instruments they could borrow or otherwise 'obtain' over a weekend. Despite having some success, they were still several instruments short, so Major Dawson dashed off a line to the theatre manager and his daughter. The Manners set up a fund, the people of Swindon responded, and a new set of instruments was obtained. A few weeks later, the Royal Engineers came to the town, played a game of football at the County Ground, and the next day gave a band concert to a packed audience at the Empire Theatre. One of the pieces was 'Asleep in the Deep', played as a trombone solo by William Blake.

At the end of September 1916, Dolly Manner announced that she was about to open the third fund for the provision of Christmas gifts for the Swindon soldiers and sailors, and that she would be pleased to receive subscriptions, in addition to money collected at the Theatre. Collecting cards were issued to 'responsible applicants' and her parents undertook to add ten shillings to every sovereign subscribed. In order to comply with the War Charities Act, a committee consisting of well-known local businessmen and gentry had been formed, and Dolly acted as the honorary secretary. In November 1916, the revue It's a Bargain came to the Empire. Its cast included a virtual unknown named Gracie Fields, who nonetheless received ecstatic reviews. She would return six years later, a star in the ascendant, when her appearance would be eagerly anticipated.

On Christmas Eve 1916, the mayor of Swindon, Alderman Albert John Gilbert, attended a concert at the theatre, aimed at augmenting the money for providing parcels to be sent to the Front, under the auspices of Dolly Manners' Soldiers' and Sailors' Christmas Gift Fund.

So it went on, with the Empire very much part of the Swindon war effort: keeping patriotism on the boil, raising funds for the provision of gift parcels to the Front, and keeping up the spirits of Swindon theatregoers with fine entertainment at the theatre. In 1917, collections at the Empire Theatre meant that Manners was able to contribute £767 8s 2d to the Mayor's Appeal for funds needed to buy the contents of the parcels being sent to British prisoners of war held abroad. Extra money was needed because prices of the goods enclosed were increasing, as were the number of interned military personnel.

A matinée of the American play *Kick In* was given by the Armitage and Leigh's Company. It was well received by a crowded house and the proceeds went to the Mayor of Swindon's Wiltshire Regiment Prisoners of War Fund, with Alfred Manners defraying all the expenses. Manners also defrayed the expenses, the same year, at a concert in aid of the St Mary's Hostel for Women War Workers, which was opened under the auspices of the Swindon Girls' Club Union. There were nearly four thousand women war workers in Swindon at that time, and many of them needed support from the local community. The concert consisted of members of the *Tina* company, who were appearing at the Empire Theatre, and the Band of the Orchestral Society from Chiseldon camp.

Also in 1917, Esther Dolly Manners married Adrian Noel Kendal in Swindon. The Christmas card that year was printed on pink card, and bore the borough coat of arms on its front page amidst floral decorative motifs. It was from 'Mr and Mrs Manners and Dolly Kendal née Manners and Swindon Friends' and was inscribed 'God bless the gallant defenders of England, God save the men who were true to their call, Tell them the love of the nation is mingled, With honour and prayers for their safety through all'. The text on the next page read: 'Empire Theatre, Swindon. Dear Friend, Once again it gives my Mother, Father, and Self the greatest pleasure in sending you this little parcel and Season's Greetings. We had hoped to have given you a welcome home this Christmas but please God the day is drawing near when Victory will be yours. Be assured once more our hearts beat true to you for your continued safety and a happy return in the near future to your homes. God Bless You. Dolly Kendal née Manners'.

It was not all plain sailing at Tidworth, however, where Manners was manager and lessee of the Garrison Theatre, and against whom, in 1917, Gwendoline Smith of 9 The Grove, Camberwell, brought an action for damages for breach of contract before Mr Justice Ridley and a jury at Salisbury. Miss Smith was the proprietress of a touring company, whose revue *Keep Fit* had been contracted by Manners to appear at the theatre the previous year. She was to supply the artistes in return for fifty-five per cent of the gross takings; Manners was contracted to provide gas, the usual band, and to produce the piece according to the resources of the theatre. The usual band at Tidworth comprised some nine musicians, which Miss Smith considered to be quite suitable for her musical accompaniment. On the opening night, the orchestra failed to include a drummer, whose various sound effects were crucial to the success of *Keep Fit* generally, and for the comedian's turn in particular. She maintained that the drummer's absence on opening night accounted for an inferior house and therefore poor takings on the second night, when the orchestra had also been further reduced to two violin players and a trombone. The audience thought it amusing, but some of them left. On the fourth night, there were no musicians at all. As a result of the poor houses, the expected takings of between £300 and £400 had been reduced to £191, of which her share was about £100.

The whole cased devolved on what was meant by 'the usual band'. Manners pointed out that the Garrison Theatre belonged to the War Office, and he operated it on behalf of a military committee who answered to the military authorities. It was a condition of his agreement with them that the theatre's orchestra be made up of military musicians. This meant that any military duties for which they might be required, musical or otherwise, and no matter at how short a notice, had to come first. This included playing in the officers' mess. Manners argued that everyone at Tidworth appreciated this possibility, so the reduction in musicians, or even their complete absence, would not have been a determining factor for the audience.

He also gave details of the financial arrangements at the Garrison Theatre. Each performing company agreed with Manners to receive a percentage of the gross takings for the length of their residency; the military authorities took one-third of the remaining amount. The judge decided that 'the usual band' meant 'the usual band at Tidworth', which clearly included an acceptance of the conditions under which it was contracted to play. Mindful of this, he found in the theatre manager's favour, and the jury returned that the plaintiff had suffered no damages.

The play being performed at the Empire on Armistice night was *Betty*, a musical comedy by Frederick Lonsdale and Gladys Unger, which had been first performed just after war broke out four years earlier. Alfred Manners invited the whole of the available officers, non-commissioned officers, soldiers from Chiseldon and other camps in the area, and men billeted in Swindon to attend the performance to commemorate the signing of the Armistice. The theatre was packed; the majority of the men present wore khaki, and an unprecedented number of them were wounded. This led to seating difficulties, and Manners apologised to the able-bodied members of the audience who expected to be seated, but felt sure they would, in that instance, be happy to give up their seats to the injured troops. To underline this, the orchestra were brought in early to play patriotic tunes, including the British national anthem and those of the allied countries. The performance of the musical that followed 'sparkled with fun and merriment and was greatly appreciated by the audience'.

During the interval, there processed onto the stage three colonels of the Worcestershire Regiment, trailing Alfred Manners. Colonel

Prince publicly thanked the theatre manager for all he had done since the beginning of the war. Colonel Archer spoke of the extremely good work that Manners had undertaken with the wounded at Chiseldon, Tidworth and elsewhere. Colonel Stewart remarked at length on what the Manners family had done for soldiers and sailors overseas by way of Christmas parcels, and the great deal of money they raised. There were great cheers and much applause for the Manners family.

Yet if anyone thought the end of hostilities and this public appreciation might mark the end of Alfred Manners's fund-raising on behalf of the military, they were mistaken. It was estimated that less than five per cent of British troops would be home for Christmas, so money was still needed. His target was £1,100, and of the £541 raised so far, £99 had been contributed by Alfred and Ellen Manners; Thomas Arkell, the brewer of Kingsdown, had added £25. Before the company of *Betty* went on their way, they played a thanksgiving matinée, and the money raised was added to Dolly's Sailors' and Soldiers' Christmas Parcel Fund. In December 1918, an auction of surplus Christmas puddings was held during the second interval of *Searchlights*, the play then being presented, and the auctioneer was Louis Hector, its leading actor. It proved great fun, with Hector in fine form, and raised a further £19. Bidding for the puddings started at 2s 6d, and they all sold at prices ranging from 10s to 30s, but one was resold and fetched 37s 6d.

The pantomime immediately following the end of the war was *Dick Whittington*, which opened on Christmas Eve 1918. A private box cost £1 5s, and was limited to four people; pre-booked or early doors stalls were priced at 3s 6d; 3s was the ordinary doors price. Early doors in the circle cost 1/10d, or 1/6d for ordinary doors; the orchestra pit and the general pit were 1/3d and 9d respectively. Children under twelve years of age were accommodated in all parts of the theatre at half price, including early doors in the pit for matinées. The last play of the year was the patriotic *The Luck of the Navy*, a brand new comedy espionage thriller by the novelist and playwright Mrs Clifford Mills.

This naval theme continued, and in 1919 a number of patriotic films that had recently been shown at the Queen's Hall in London made their way onto a screen at the Empire Theatre. Collectively, they were called 'The Deeds of War', and included *The surrender of the German Fleet and U Boats, Views of the American Fleet 400 miles Out at Sea*, and *The Giant Handley Page Aeroplane*. Harrison Hill, the famous London entertainer, sang humorous songs and told amusing naval stories, as well as describing the pictures as they appeared on the screen.

The Soldiers' and Sailors' Christmas Gift Fund, latterly known as the Christmas Parcel Fund, was closed at the beginning of March 1919. It had been very much a co-operative effort. Dolly had organised it, Manners and his wife had contributed substantially, the staff at the Empire had provided volunteer labour in its cause, and other local businesspeople had helped. These included Henry George English, a grocer with premises in Fleet Street and Bath Road, who supplied goods at cost price; Clifford Cunningham, who ran the Central Cinema, and his wife; and James Smith Protheroe, an income tax inspector of Victoria Road, who acted as the fund's treasurer. Not only did monies raised pay for parcels, a substantial surplus amount went to the treasurer of Swindon's Victoria Hospital, and to the treasurer of the Navy Vegetables Fund.

In a letter addressed to 'My Friends and Patrons', which appeared in the *Swindon Evening Advertiser* on 23 June 1919, Alfred Manners wrote:

'...we can all be justly proud of the good work which has been accomplished through the medium of my theatre; not only has every soldier and sailor received a Christmas parcel and a cheering card each Christmas, but through your practical assistance some thousands of parcels have been sent to our late prisoners of war. Hundreds of pounds have been raised for the British and other Red Cross Funds, for our Blinded Heroes and for our local charities, totalling an aggregate that has never been excelled by any other single private enterprise, and would not have been attained were it not for your continued generous assistance'.

The Treaty of Versailles that ended the First World War was signed on Saturday, 28 June 1919. As Swindon celebrated, Alfred Manners opened the Empire Theatre to children. In the morning, around 2,300 of them 'lustily sang the National Anthem' and settled down to a free two-hour programme of films. Some 2,000 boys and girls turned up for the afternoon session, when Alderman Samuel Edward Walters, mayor of Swindon, gave a stirring speech, and the headmaster of Lethbridge Road School, Mr Anderson, led the National Anthem. That evening, Manners opened up the theatre to service men, ex-servicemen, their wives and lady friends, and, after he welcomed them all, the audience were treated to a variety show with 'a patriotic flavour'. Among those appearing were comedian Fred Dunstan, soprano singer Joan Dolaro, Fraser and French with their black and white comedy act, and a 'speciality comedy duo' named Robbins and Collier. During the interval, Alderman Walters made his second appearance of the day, singling out Manners, servicemen and ex-servicemen for honorary mention. At the end of the evening, the roof was again raised with a rousing National Anthem.

Manners thought it scandalous that, immediately after the First World War, so many thousands of men in the town were out of work. He decided that every place he was interested in should undergo repair and re-decoration by local workmen. The Empire Theatre underwent extensive refurbishment, carried out by E.W. Beard, a local firm of builders. The 'plastic enrichments' of the interior were repainted a cream colour on a background of old gold. The dome above the auditorium was picked out in rose colour, blended with two shades of gold, and the eight panels within it were blended with sky-blue, darkened at the bottom and shaded lighter at the top. The panels were labelled in crimson with 'May our memories be always green in honour of our fallen heroes' as a tribute to those from Swindon who lost their lives in the war. The front elevations of the circle and the boxes were cleaned up and painted, and the proscenium arch and sides were given cream enrichments, picked out with gold leaf. By the time the Empire opened, with Jack Cromo's comedy revue *Strawberries and Cream* in July 1919, after its summer break, it had been extensively refurbished and redecorated.

Various memorials to the men of Swindon who were killed in hostilities had been erected in the town since 1916, but none had been considered suitable, and at least two had been burnt down. At the end of the war, it was decided to build a public hall as a lasting commemoration, at a cost of between £30,000 and £40,000, to be raised by public subscription. Alfred Manners, and Major Fitzroy Pleydell Goddard, (lord of the manor of Swindon) headed the list with generous sums of money; but soon afterwards, the donations dried up and the fund was far short of the amount required. Amongst the alternative options was a cenotaph at an estimated cost of £1,000, to be erected in Regent Circus. Even this amount proved difficult to raise, and eventually the *Swindon Evening Advertiser* came up with an idea for a 'Shilling Fund'. Manners, Goddard, and Sir Frederick W. Young (who was the town's Conservative MP 1918-22) gave generously. In just two weeks, 10,882 shillings (almost half the required amount) had been raised. The cenotaph was finally opened on 30 October 1920.

(THE DOLL).
By Maurice Ordonneau and Arthur Sturgess.
Music by Edmond Audran.
FULL CHORUS & AUGMETED ORCHESTRA

NEXT WEEK—

"WOMAN AND WINE."
By Ben Landeck and Arthur Shirley.

## THE IDEAL PICTURE HOUSE

(Opposite the Town Hall)
Under the control of Alfred Manners.
RE-OPENS MONDAY NEXT, October 20th
PRICES AS USUAL.
The Exclusive Programme for the Re-opening
is as follows :—
MONDAY, TUESDAY, WEDNESDAY,
THE RED DUKE,
A Story of Adventure—and many others.
THURSDAY, FRIDAY & SATURDAY,
THE INVADERS,
A Charming Picture Play—and numerous others

## DANCING.

CLASSES and ASSEMBLIES EVERY
WEDNESDAY.
NEXT CINDERELLA—Oct. 22nd
Latest Novelties, "Georgian Gavotte," "Le
Tortis," and "Tango." Private Lessons.
Prospectus—

In 1913 Alfred Manners bought The Picture House that had opened in a one-time Sunday School in Regent Circus in 1910. He renamed it 'The Ideal Picture House', and opened in October with The Red Duke, a silent picture.

(opposite page)
Each year during World War 1, the Manners family sent patriotic-style and encouraging Christmas cards to Swindon residents who were serving abroad with the forces. This one is from 1915.

## PUBLIC NOTICES.

## EMPIRE THEATRE, SWINDON.

**6-50.** TWICE NIGHTLY.
MONDAY, AUG 3RD 1914 **9.**
AND DURING THE WEEK.

MATINEE, MONDAY, AT 2-30.

Tom Vernon's successful West-End Revue,

# WAIT AND SEE.

THE "UNITED CLEFTS,"
World-Renowned Vocal Quartette

Next Week—That most successful Farcical Comedy

## "Baby Mine,"

Wait and See with Harry Monkhouse and Emmie King was the revue playing at the Empire Theatre when war was declared in 1914. That evening, patriotic songs were sung before curtain up, and Alfred Manners read the war news during the interval.

From

Mr., Mrs. & Dolly Manners

and

Swindon Friends.

God bless the gallant defenders of
England,
God save the men who were true
to their call,
Tell them the love of the Nation
is mingled,
With honour and prayers, for
their safety through all.

Dear Friend,

In enclosing you this little
reminder of Yule-Tide, from Father,
Mother, Self and Friends in Swindon,
we do so with our hearts beating
true to you for the services you are
rendering to our King and Country.

We know that God and the
Right is with you while you are
away.

We shall doubly welcome you
on your return.

DOLLY MANNERS.

Empire Theatre,
Swindon.

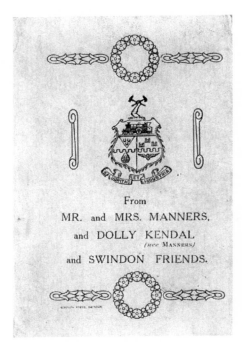

From
MR. and MRS. MANNERS,
and DOLLY KENDAL
*(nee* MANNERS*)*
and SWINDON FRIENDS.

*By Christmas 1916, Dolly Manners had married, but she continued to be the driving force behind the yule-tide cards for servicemen and the fund-raising events through which they were supplied with food parcels.*

God bless the gallant defenders of
  England,
God save the men who were true
  to their call ;
Tell them the love of the Nation is
  mingled
With honour and prayers for their
  safety through all.

Empire Theatre, Swindon.

Dear Friend,
    Once again it gives my Mother, Father, & Self the greatest pleasure in sending you this little Parcel and Season's Greeting.

    We had hoped to have given you a welcome home this Xmas, but please God the day is drawing near when Victory will be yours.

    Be assured once more our hearts beat true to you for your continued safety and a happy return in the near future to your homes.
    God Bless You.
                DOLLY KENDAL.
                  *(nee* MANNERS*)*.

(above) James E. 'Raggy' Powell was an illiterate Swindon rag and bone man and slaughterhouse keeper, born into abject poverty, but who became a patron of the arts in the town and was one of its greatest benefactors. During the First World War he organised free shows at the Empire for families of the town's servicemen, and this picture was taken on such an occasion in 1916.

(right) This postcard was issued for the 1917 production of Aladdin, then the fifth of what would be twelve outings for the pantomime in the Empire's history. Ironically, its scheduled thirteenth appearance was for 1955, when it was 'the show that never came'.

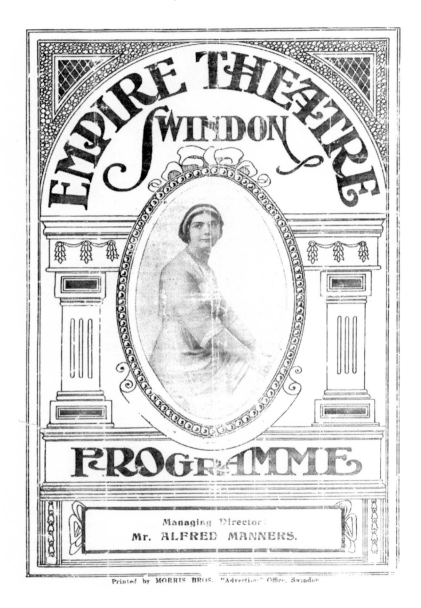

The theatre's printed programmes were now arguably at their most attractive, certainly their most decorative. By 1917, they featured portraits of young women, a different sitter on each. Perhaps the management thought they might find their way to France, where they would be a cheery reminder to the troops of what was waiting for them back home.

The musical comedy Betty by Frederick Lonsdale, Gladys Unger, Adrian Ross and Paul Reubens came to the Empire in 1917, the first of three visits. It is the story of a kitchen maid who responds sufficiently to her marriage of convenience into the aristocracy to be accepted by society and win the heart of her formerly profligate husband. Its story had so many elements that would appeal to Edwardian audiences.

**EMPIRE THEATRE, SWINDON.**

MONDAY, Nov. 11th, and Each Evening during the week.

ONCE NIGHTLY, at 7.30

FREE LIST ENTIRELY SUSPENDED.

WELCOME RETURN VISIT.

Messrs. MACDONALD and YOUNG present

**"BETTY."**

A NEW MUSICAL PLAY.

AUGMENTED ORCHESTRA under the direction of Jack Robertson.

Next Week. Once Nightly at 7 30—

**"FRAGMENTS,"**

*A wet day in July 1918 has put a stop to road repairs beside the Golden Lion public house in Bridge Street. However, the hoarding on the side of the pub clearly shows some lovely posters for revue Entre Nous, the current attraction at the Empire which starred Cora Lingard and W.L. Rowland.*

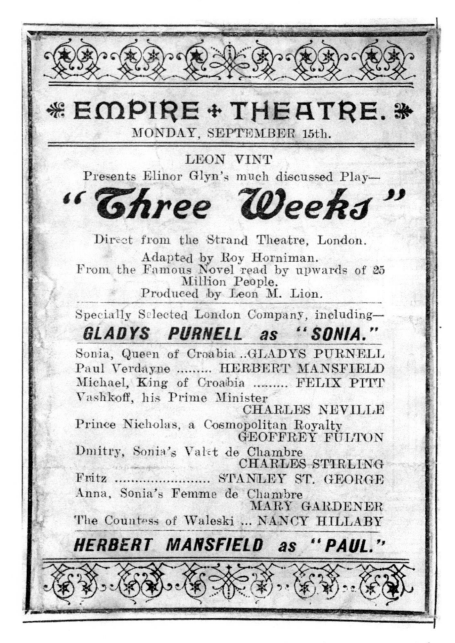

## ❋ EMPIRE ✦ THEATRE. ❋

### MONDAY, SEPTEMBER 15th.

LEON VINT
Presents Elinor Glyn's much discussed Play—

# "*Three Weeks*"

Direct from the Strand Theatre, London.
Adapted by Roy Horniman.
From the Famous Novel read by upwards of 25
Million People.
Produced by Leon M. Lion.

Specially Selected London Company, including—

### GLADYS PURNELL as "SONIA."

Sonia, Queen of Croabia ..GLADYS PURNELL
Paul Verdayne ......... HERBERT MANSFIELD
Michael, King of Croabia ......... FELIX PITT
Vashkoff, his Prime Minister
                        CHARLES NEVILLE
Prince Nicholas, a Cosmopolitan Royalty
                        GEOFFREY FULTON
Dmitry, Sonia's Valet de Chambre
                        CHARLES STIRLING
Fritz ..................... STANLEY ST. GEORGE
Anna, Sonia's Femme de Chambre
                        MARY GARDENER
The Countess of Waleski ... NANCY HILLABY

### HERBERT MANSFIELD as "PAUL."

*Three Weeks, the sensational story by novelist Elinor Glyn about an aristocratic love affair came to the Empire in 1920. The cast included Gladys Purnell (a beauty in her time) and Herbert Mansfield.*

*(left and below) Not stills from one of the Empire's productions; here were two groups of the theatre's usherettes, having appropriated costumes and props, pictured in 1920.*

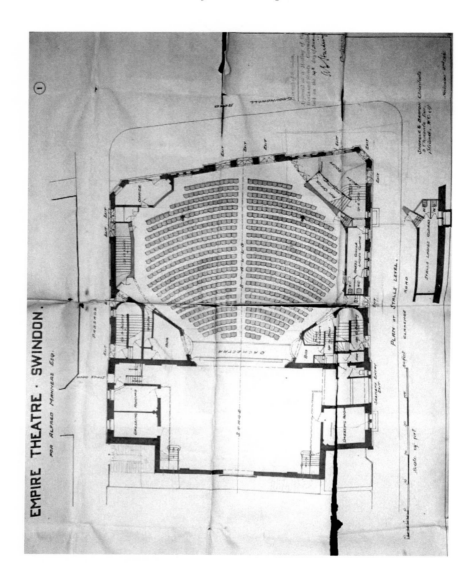

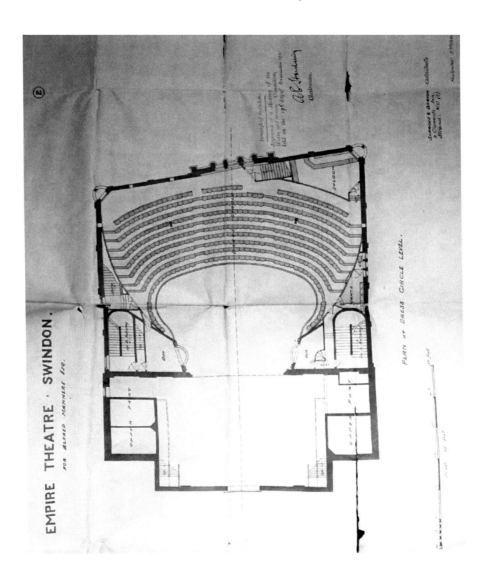

*(opposite page and above) Architects Sprague & Barton of 2, Clements Inn, London, were commissioned by Alfred Manners to submit plans for a remodelling of the Empire's interior in 1921. These plans show changes to the stalls and the dress circle.*

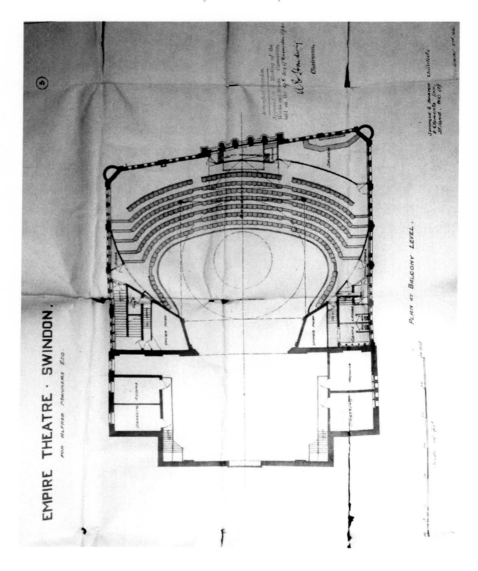

*Sprague & Barton redesigned the dress circle, and inserted an upper circle above it.*

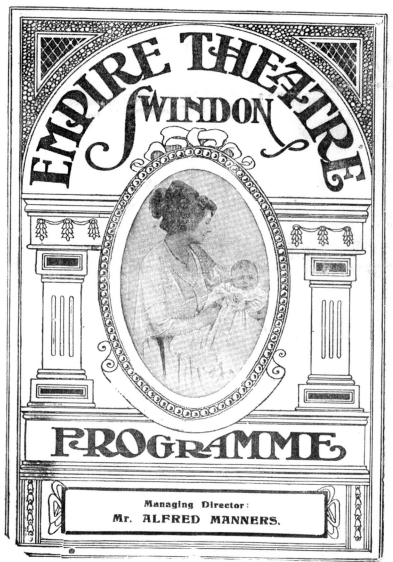

The covers of the theatre's printed programmes still featured portraits. This one, printed in 1921, clearly emphasised 'motherhood', a theme that the theatre began in 1919. These covers still had rather more of an Edwardian 'feel' about them than might an illustration that was more in keeping with the developing spirit of the new post-war age. Between 1922 and 1924, the illustration was of a little girl with a muff.

The musical A Night Out was being performed at the Empire when this picture was taken in October 1921. By now, all of the houses in the terrace opposite the theatre were in trade at street level, and have since remained so.

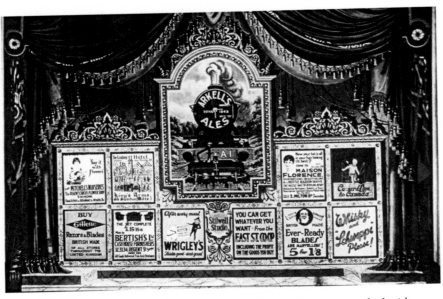

The Empire had a succession of safety curtains, each of them packed with advertisements. This one was in use during the 1920s. Note that Swindon's own Arkells Ales were 'on sale at this theatre'.

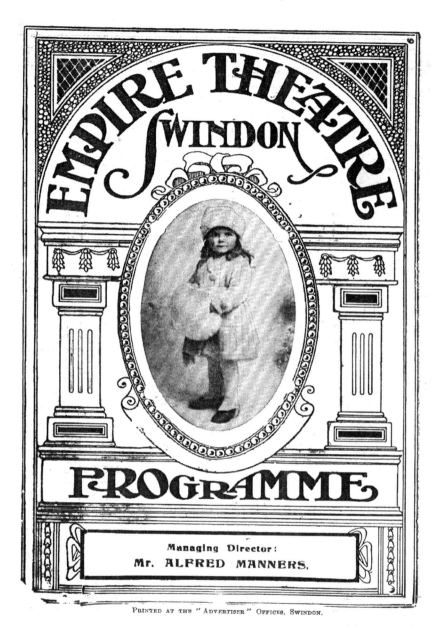

*By 1924, the pictures on the front of the printed programmes depicted what the management felt to be appealing children.*

*The Nine O'clock Revue was playing the Empire when this picture was taken in November 1924. It featured M.Klit Gaarde whose career was mainly conducted in Scotland, Hugh Rene, and Gola Betti.*

### NEW THEATRE PROPRIETORS.

Mr. Jack Gladwin and Mr. Joe Collins, the new proprietors of the Empire theatre, Swindon. They take over the control of the theatre at the end of the present month.

*Jack Gladwin, who was acting manager of the theatre when it opened in 1898, and his business partner Joe Collins, took over the Empire in August 1925.*

*Howard Flynn's Symphonic Band is the star attraction in this picture from 1926. As Howard Flynn and his Orchestra, this band of session musicians went on to make typical jazz-style dance band recordings for Edison Bell in the 1930s.*

Millie:—"Sure! I've been teaching her the splits——one of these."

*Few postcards were issued that showed an actual scene from a play; this one depicts a moment in The Best People by David Grey, which came to the Empire in 1928. Its stars were Mary Byron and Amy Elstob.*

*(above)  At the time of this 1928 picture, The Wrecker by Arnold Ridley (1896-1984) was exciting audiences at the Empire. Ridley was the author of the better-known The Ghost Train, which had played the Empire the previous year, and would much later become a household name as Private Charles Godfrey in the television programme Dad's Army.*

*(opposite page)  Charley's Aunt, the famous farce by Brandon Thomas that was first performed in 1892 in Bury St Edmunds, came to Swindon six years later when it was the first play to be performed at the New Queen's Theatre. Charley's Aunt returned on five subsequent occasions. This is the poster from 1928.*

# 4
# *Lighter entertainment*

REVUES WERE POPULAR entertainments at the Empire just before the First World War, and during hostilities, but were less attractive to the audiences of the early 1920s. Then, patrons preferred comedies, and light operettas such as *The Belle of New York*, *The Quaker Girl* and *The Maid of the Mountains*. Each of these included elements of the downtrodden emerging triumphant. Respectively, the shows mentioned featured a Salvation Army girl engendering virtue and finding love; a young, conservatively garbed Quaker girl, banished for breaking the family's moral code, whose clothes become high fashion; and a bandit's moll who finds love through tortuous adversity. Their musical numbers lifted the audiences' spirits, but their structure of initial innocence, followed by complexity and anxiety, ultimately ending in success, at the same time echoed the course of the late Great War. For many who saw them, it was also reminiscent of their own lives carried on in straitened or reduced circumstances, and they could use these theatrical productions to speculate on how their own lives might evolve more happily. There were also echoes of the war, of espionage, and of soldiers of fortune, in the romantic military dramas and spy stories of Walter Howard, perhaps the most successful writer in this genre of the period. His work such as *Seven Days Leave*, *Why Men Love Women* and *Her Love against the World* became the staple fare at the Empire. Associated with Walter Howard was the actress Ruby Kimberley, who also wrote plays and musicals such as *The Home of the Fairies, Eastern Nights*, and *One Night of Folly*, which each played the Empire. Before the war, she had been part of Walter Howard's No. 1 Company, and then performed her own plays under the name of Mr & Mrs F.G. Kimberley's All-Star Company. She became a very prolific writer.

Oswald Bentley, born Dewsbury, Yorkshire, the son of a carpet weaver, took over the baton at the Empire from Fred Stone in 1920. Bentley started his working life as a factory hand, but had become a 'musician and pianoforte player' by his early twenties, by which time he was living in Stockton-on-Tees. There, he led the theatre's orchestra from 1904 until his relocation to Swindon. *The Home of the Fairies* was a great success at Swindon in the early 1920s. Billed as 'a musical pantomime play of fairyland', it included Madame Walker's little fairies 'in their great specialities, songs, dances, fairy scenes, etc'. The professional little fairies were augmented by fifteen local children when the production returned two years later.

The established order of touring companies also continued to perform at the Empire. The Henry Baynton Company and the Charles Doran Company staged Shakespeare. The latter made their first visit to the Empire in 1921, performing seven of the Bard's plays in six days. Amongst the players on that occasion was Donald Wolfit. The Hamilton Deane Company, the H. Armitage and Arthur Leigh Company, and the actor/producer Harry Foxwell's Company offered twice-nightly repertory theatre. This arrangement suited Swindon, even if it meant hard work for the actors; just a few minutes after the final curtain had fallen on the first house about 8.40 in the evening, it was raised on the second house, and the cast had to perform all over again to a fresh audience, who were eager, lively, and expectant. The Royal Carl Rosa Opera Company, the D'Oyly Carte Opera Company and the Frederick G. Lloyd Opera Company provided opera on two-week-long engagements. It was not unusual for touring companies to present a different play each night for the week of their engagement, and sometimes to add another by way of a Wednesday matinée. The actors in Harry Foxwell's Company, for example, performed six quite different plays in as many days.

Lectures by eminent persons also found favour at the Empire in the 1920s. Sir Johnston Forbes Robertson, one of the most distinguished actors of his day, took to the stage on the afternoon of Friday, 21 January 1921 to expound on Shakespeare's plays. He divided his lecture into two parts: the first dealt with the early historical plays, and the second with four great tragedies. Forbes Robertson performed several speeches from these plays, and the gratifyingly large and delighted audience, which included groups of schoolchildren, was much taken with his 'To be or not to be' soliloquy from *Hamlet*. In July, the explorer Sir Ernest Shackleton gave two lectures on his recent Polar expedition, illustrated by lantern slides, and spoke of his hopes for his next big adventure. Proceeds from these lectures went to the Victoria Hospital.

Alfred Manners decided that he needed to boost trade, particularly the size of the audiences for the second houses, and did so by cutting ticket prices; a seat could then be reserved for two shillings, and it would be possible to gain admission for just fivepence. 'Swindon Empire theatre has this week entered upon a noteworthy enterprise', reported the local press, 'with excellent prospects of success.' It pointed out that 'Such a departure cannot fail to be appreciated and rewarded by those who take delight in stage studies: but its abiding success must largely depend upon the nature of the plays presented.' *The Knave of Diamonds* was chosen for this experiment, a play from the novel by Ethel M. Dell, which opened at the Empire in March 1922. It featured Josset Ellis and Frank Pettingell (later to make his name as a film character-actor) who were 'each responsible for splendid studies' in a 'thoroughly convincing production that should prove a popular booking'. A performer whose name was already firmly established by his association with the Henry Irving Company was Sir John Martin-

Harvey who, in 1922, arrived at the Empire for a 'flying matinée' of *The Burgomaster of Stilemonde* by Maurice Maeterlinck. This was an important theatrical event – a relatively new play (1918) by a modish author, enacted by a theatrical great. Manners capitalised on the sense of occasion by advising his patrons to book early.

Also in 1922, an amateur company, the Swindon Musical and Dramatic Society, was formed 'to give operatic, dramatic and orchestral performances in Swindon and district'. Proceeds from its productions would go to charity, including Manners's favourite Victoria Hospital fund. Its first production, Gilbert and Sullivan's *Iolanthe* was held at the Empire in April 1923. It was followed in 1924 by *The Rose of Persia*, and thereafter annually until 1939 when the Society disbanded after performing *Miss Hook of Holland*.

In October 1922, Gracie Fields starred at the Empire alongside her manager Archie Pitt (who that year became her first husband) in the musical comedy revue *Mr Tower of London*. Then on the brink of huge stardom, she won the hearts of the audience and scored 'a complete personal triumph' with her comedy acting and staccato singing.

In the same month, a revue, *The Circus Queen*, played the Empire; it was billed as 'G. and J. Kirby's circus musical comedy' and featured the 'comedy flying effects invented and arranged by the Kirbys' (later to be known as 'Kirby's Flying Circus'). The revue's leading comedian was Swindon-born Charlie Jones, who confessed to being nervous whenever he played his home town. The family had come to Swindon c1887 from Swansea, and his father, William Jones, worked in the blacksmith's shop allied to the carriage and wagon department in the GWR Works. The family lived in Medgbury Road. Charlie was educated at Sanford Street School, where he excelled in football, and he played for Swindon Town Juniors before embarking on a theatrical career. On the stage, he toured in various revues and pantomimes, and also developed a solo comic act. His career included a very successful sixteen-performance run at the London Palladium, deputising in the part of Widow Twankey for the well-loved comedian Charles Austin, and receiving enthusiastic acclaim. In *The Circus Queen*, he played the part of the village policeman, which afforded him ample opportunities to display his comic talents. The following year, Charlie Jones was back at the Empire in *Jingles*, another revue, when he scored a similar success. Appearing with him in this was a young comedienne named Hylda Baker, who went on to achieve television fame in the 1950s and 1960s.

There must have been many times when the management of the Empire Theatre, various companies of actors, and even the local newspaper despaired of Swindon's attitude towards quality theatre. This was brought into sharp focus in February 1923 when the great Irish actor-manager Hamilton Deane brought his company of West End players to the town, presenting twelve plays. It was 'A Two Weeks Season of Leading Dramatic Plays, presented with that fine interpretation and completeness seldom seen in the Provinces'; and for once the publicity was spot on. Hamilton Deane had cut his acting teeth from 1899 with the Henry Irving Company and could hardly have arrived with a better provenance or reputation in the theatre. The selection of plays was excellent and included the extremely popular *A Message From Mars*, which had just been filmed for the third time. Deane had recently formed his own touring company and was writing his famous stage interpretation of *Dracula*, which was performed for the first time the following year. Swindon, perhaps simply ignorant of the giant in its midst, or maybe disinterested in live theatre, failed to respond, and at the start of week two the town was rebuked by the local newspaper.

'The poor support that has been extended to Mr Hamilton Deane and his excellent company at the Empire Theatre prompts one to ask 'what does Swindon want?'. Dramatic fare of the quality that was served up last week would have filled a theatre in any other town, and in many places money would have had to be turned away, but not once at the Empire last week was the house entirely full, and more often than not, it was more than half empty. A poor reward surely for the efforts that Mr Manners, in the face of great difficulties, has been making to give Swindon the best that the provinces can provide in the way of theatrical entertainment.' It was becoming clear that respectable actors, significant plays, and quality acting, on which Manners had built his reputation and which he steadfastly maintained as being his theatrical aim, did not necessarily accord with the preferences, insofar as there were any, of his audiences. Swindon generally had never really been comfortable with classic theatre; those who enjoyed it were now in the minority, and the majority were looking towards a loosening of the entertainment stays. It was, after all, the 1920s.

Artistically, Alfred Manners stuck to his guns. He pulled off what was, in terms of provincial theatre, a successful master stroke when he booked Seymour Hicks, the world-famous actor, author and producer, to make a personal appearance in November 1923. Hicks (who would be knighted in 1935 for his services to the theatre) came with the entire West End company of the English version of Sacha Guitry's daring farce *Sleeping Partners*, comprising himself, Mabel Green, Stanley Turnball and Frederick Wills. It was an expensive production, but Manners maintained normal seat prices, and the performance was a triumph.

By the middle of the 1920s, Swindon had caught the backlash to austerity that was asserting itself across the country: the changes in fashion, music and morals that characterised the new freedom of the Jazz Age, the Art Deco era. Suddenly, stage revues were back in fashion. Swindon's audiences wanted frivolity, the kind of slapstick that they saw on the cinema screens, and they looked for silver sirens on the stage. In 1925, the Empire put on twenty revues with titles like *April Showers, Around the Town* and *Attaboy*. Another one was *London-Day and Night*, with Charlie Jones. The *Swindon Evening*

*Advertiser* noted that he had 'filled out considerably' since his previous appearances, but was well received by his audience, which included some men who, as boys, had been at school with him.

Not all the stage revues were appreciated by the local newspaper. Their critic of *What ho!*, which played a week at the beginning of 1926, decided that it was not done in the best of taste. He was particularly scathing of Mark Rivers, comedian, who 'would be well advised to cut out many of the alleged jokes because they were not funny and did not have the saving grace of being clean and wholesome'. The prudish reviewer went on to write of the 'bare-legged and bare-backed chorus', whose singing and dancing he nonetheless enjoyed, and of other acts that he found agreeable; but one nonetheless has a vision of a provincial, lemon-lipped reviewer who had not moved with the times.

Someone who *was* thinking of moving was Alfred Manners. The Empire Theatre had been built in a slightly isolated position a little to the east of the town centre, but, by the 1920s, residential Swindon was also developing eastwards. This expansion devolved on Groundwell Road, on which was the Empire's main entrance. Yet during the opening years of the Twenties the theatre had not done as well as Alfred Manners had hoped; he had received several tempting offers for the Empire, and, after a period of soul searching, had decided the time might have come to move on. The Royal Antediluvian Order of Buffaloes, of which Manners was a Brother, determined that they would mark the occasion of his leaving and also his charitable work by presenting him with an RAOB medal. It was arranged that this should take place on 20 September 1920 between the second and third acts of the play *The Master of the House*. The assemblage of luminary Buffaloes, wearing the chains of their order, duly appeared at the prescribed time, and Manners was given his medal. In his speech, the popular manager made it clear that he had decided to stay on, to the following January at least. In the event, it was to be five more years before he gave up the job.

Two factors had made him reconsider. Manners was anxious that the Empire should not be converted into a 'super picture house', which was what he thought would become of the building in other hands. Also, both of his sons had shown a keen interest in the management side of the business and he dared to hope that they would follow in his footsteps. Alfie, the elder of the two, had shouldered much of the burden of management since his father met with his unfortunate accident, and had shown great aptitude for the work. He was well known to the audiences of the Empire Theatre, and to most of the residents of the town. At the age of fifteen, he left public school to join the Colours, and during the Great War he saw active service. He was a strong swimmer, a good rifle shot, and played for Swindon Rugby Team.

An act that played the Empire in 1923 was the Elliott Savonas, who came, spectacularly garbed, with their *Garden of Harmony*. Their other famed production, along similar horticultural lines, was *The Garden of Orpheus*, in which they wore equally flamboyant costumes and performed against intricately painted backdrops. They were a seven-member, family musical ensemble who sometimes appeared as trick cyclists The Cycling Elliotts, and would, in a long career, eventually become Hazel Elliott and her Candies, and The Seven Musical Elliotts. They made their first appearance at the Swindon theatre in 1909, and for the return engagement brought their 'big spectacular act' with which 'they have not only appeared in all the principal dramatic theatres in England but have also made a world tour on four separate occasions'. They dressed eccentrically, the females with feathered headdresses and the men in Georgian-style costumes, and they played some fifty instruments, including the harmoniously humming 'spinning seashells'. Nor did they come alone. On the same bill were G.H. Carlisle ('The King of Ragtime') at the piano; Chas and Carrie Kasrac, who provided 'Merry Moments'; the singer and danseuse Eileen Lilley; Ara and Zeta who were trick and comedy cyclists; Jimmy Hughes, the 'character comedian'; Miller and Phlora, who gave 'vaudeville cameos'; and Dick Rawson, who was inexplicably billed as 'The Blob'. This show was particularly significant; when Manners was having difficulties with the licensing authorities the following year, he singled out the Elliot Savonas' touring production as the kind of high-class variety entertainment that he wanted to attract regularly to the Empire.

Although Manners had decided in 1920 not to leave the theatre, doubts about any prolonged tenure lingered on. A decision that he made in 1923 was spectacular, and one that would put an end to the rumours of his intention to retire from theatrical management. Not only would he stay, but he drew up plans to build a new palace of variety, which would occupy the same island site, between the Empire and the nearby County Court building in Clarence Street. 'I am confident that the tide is turning', he said, 'and that better times for everybody and years of real prosperity are surely dawning.' He was an optimist.

'I have come to the conclusion', he explained, 'that the only thing to do is to bring one's methods up to date. It is useless to remain in business and stand still, just as surely as it is impossible to run a business successfully if you do not advertise. Hence it is that I have decided to go on with the reconstruction of the Empire Theatre, and also to erect a first-class palace of varieties.' This new building would be similar in height to the Empire; it would have stalls, pit stalls, a grand circle and an upper circle; there would be tip-up seats throughout for not less than 1,600 patrons; there would be ten dressing rooms and a sliding roof. It was optimism too far.

Meanwhile, the planned reconstruction of the Empire promised to be comprehensive and expensive. It was put into the hands of theatre designers W.G.R. Sprague and W.H. Barton of London. They proposed demolishing the existing pillars and entirely rebuilding the interior of the building. There would be a new entrance to the stalls and the grand circle, located on the corner of Clarence Street and Groundwell Road, where previously this part of the elevation had been used for posting playbills and theatre posters.

Plans for revamping the Empire were sufficiently advanced by the end of the year for Manners to be more specific about his intentions. The theatre's existing auditorium was to be demolished, as would be the obstructive columns. From then on, all patrons would have 'a clear and uninterrupted view of the stage'. Two new circles, made of concrete and steel, were to be put in, increasing the seating accommodation in the two circles to 1,000. This would turn it into 'one of the most commodious and largest-capacity theatres in the provinces'. Everyone could sit on 'the latest comfortable tip-up seats', enjoying a new ventilation system that would give equable conditions all year round. He planned an entirely new scheme of decoration for the auditorium and other parts, in what he called 'free Renaissance style', and in a soft French grey colour with Rose Du Barri draperies, and carpets ('heavy carpeting everywhere'). Electric lighting was part of his general scheme, and a new system of low-pressure hot water heating would be installed. Easy access was to be provided between the auditorium and the refreshment rooms, and new 'retiring and cloak rooms would be provided in all parts of the house'. Manners also planned a room with two film projectors and a separate re-winding room adjacent, out of view behind the auditorium. He would also address the problem of draughts on the stage and in the dressing room areas, although nothing that was done in this regard ever managed to eliminate what appeared to be a built-in difficulty with draughts during the whole of the theatre's existence.

Manners also paid attention to the exterior elevation of the theatre at ground level and the entrance area. He intended to build a 'fine entrance crush room' at the corner of Clarence Street and Groundwell Road, from where there would be easy and direct access to the stalls, the dress circle or grand circle (he had not yet decided what to call it) and the boxes. This entrance would have mosaic marble floors, with a marble staircase leading off. The booking office was to be constructed of Honduras mahogany, and other elaborate and brass furnishings would work in harmony with the general scheme of redecoration. Those wishing to access what Manners called 'the family circle' would do so through a pay box and entrance adjoining the main stage door in Clarence Street. There would also be a handsome iron and glass shelter, wrapped around the main entrance, and extending outwards to the kerb in Groundwell Road.

Lloyds Bank agreed to advance the cost of the rebuild. Manners expected to close the theatre immediately after Easter week in 1924. He estimated that the work, which he had insisted on giving to the local building firm of A.J. Colbourne, would take ten weeks, and would provide employment for between eighty and one hundred men. The theatre would reopen on August Bank Holiday Monday.

Just as plans were being finalised for the new work, Manners lost his musical director, Oswald Bentley, who, in February 1924, decided to take up a similar appointment at the Hippodrome, Ipswich. He left having been presented with a box of cigars, a well-stocked tobacco pouch, and a new wallet containing an unspecified number of banknotes.

The Empire Theatre had a liquor licence for stage plays only, a condition being that no intoxicants would be served during music hall or variety performances. The patrons of these were considered by the magistrates to be potentially quite rowdy enough, without the addition of alcohol, but its absence undoubtedly led to smaller audiences than would otherwise have been the case. On 5 February 1924, Alfred Manners applied to the Swindon Licensing Sessions, through his solicitor F.J. Tucker, for the renewal of his liquor licence for the Empire Theatre, with its restrictions removed.

Tucker argued that revues and variety were now being put on at the Empire as a commercial response to the public's desire for a lighter form of entertainment, but patrons of these also expected a supply of alcoholic refreshment. The question arose as to whether 'lighter entertainment' was of equal quality to stage plays. Were revues and variety attracting the same people who hitherto would have gone to stage plays and who now simply wanted something different, or were its patrons still likely to be a lower level of society, not to be trusted with alcohol? Certainly, some of the revues had been of doubtful content and quality, but Manners now proposed to engage only first-rate variety artistes, and at the same time be able to provide his audiences with alcoholic refreshment.

Alfred Ernest Withy, who was the magistrates' clerk, (and also a solicitor of the firm Wiltons & Withy, formerly of Albion Buildings, Bridge Street, Swindon) questioned Manners closely on the effects of alcohol sales on audience numbers. The manager said that during variety dates, with no sale of liquor, returns at the theatre were down by forty per cent.

Withy observed that this restriction did not affect the type of entertainment that Manners could supply. Manners countered by bringing the Church into the proceedings, by way of the Venerable Reginald Thomas Talbot, DD, Archdeacon of Swindon and Canon of Bristol Cathedral, who lived in Bath Road, Old Town and who clearly liked a chuckle and a tipple. The archdeacon agreed with Withy, but explained that the current licensing restrictions did affect attendances at the theatre, and that the public saw them as a kind of tyranny, and asked for freedom. The Swindon and District Free Church Council were opposed to any greater facilities for drinking being granted, and the magistrates decided to refer the application to the licensing sessions to be held in March.

By the time this came around, Manners had gone deeper into the financial implications and was having second thoughts. He had been made aware that a new licence fee, if granted under the extended terms, would mean he had to pay £1,800 to the Inland Revenue; it would increase the fee tenfold. He told the justices that theatres in other parts of the country did not have such restrictions imposed on them, withdrew his application for a universal licence, and re-applied under the previous terms.

The curmudgeonly magistrates decided to take the opportunity to give Manners a hard time. They reminded him that a circus was currently performing at the theatre, and the manager had failed to give the clerk to the justices the required seven days' notice that the premises were going to be used under the music and dancing licence for other than stage plays, but had opened the theatre's bars. Discussions and arguments ensued on points of the law; then A.E. Withy dropped a bombshell. He had information, which had been given openly during another court case, that someone had gone into the theatre's bar without going into the theatre. Manners countered that it would be extremely difficult to ensure that this did not happen, given the nature of a theatre and the volume of patrons moving about it during intervals. Furthermore, he pointed out, such a situation would not matter had his original licensing application been granted. Begrudgingly, the magistrates decided to renew the Empire's liquor licence on the same conditions as the previous year.

The whole process, and in particular A.E. Withy's observations, had left Alfred Manners once more considering his future. In a way, he felt that he was letting down his patrons by not obtaining a full liquor licence, and perhaps the time had come to pass on the theatre to someone who felt less personally involved than himself. He discussed the matter with his family, and decided that he could not carry on. In March 1924, he wrote in the *Swindon Evening Advertiser* that he was thinking about disposing of the theatre, for which he had received several offers, and leaving the town.

Manners completely disagreed with A.E. Withy's interpretation of what constituted 'a stage play entertainment licence' as defined by the Theatres Act 1843. This piece of legislation had attempted to sort out a melting pot of theatrical entertainment of one sort or another that then pertained amongst 'legitimate' theatres, music halls, saloons, pub concerts, supper rooms and the grey areas in between, and to set out parameters and restrictions for operating each. One of the latter was that theatres would thereafter not be allowed to sell alcohol, a trade-off for relaxing the ban on spoken drama outside the theatre, in places more readily associated with musical entertainment. This created a restriction that caused proprietors to choose the category in which they preferred to operate, and caused problems for those who had hitherto depended on the sale of drink. The Act also devolved more autonomy in these matters on the local authority.

Manners said that the licence he held from the Swindon Borough Council carried with it the right to serve a glass of beer to such patrons who required it during the performances. He had read the 1843 Act many times since he returned home from the hearing, and the more often he read it, the more he was convinced that it covered the kind of family entertainment he was currently presenting. He wrote: 'But even though a legal mind is able to interpret a different meaning into the 1843 Act, and advise the magistrates accordingly, may I, in all honesty, suggest to the licensing justices and to Mr Withy that we have to adapt ourselves to the requirements of 1924.' There was even a suggestion that he might abort his plans for redesigning the theatre, even at the eleventh hour with financial and building contracts in place. 'The observations of the Bench, through the Borough Magistrates' Clerk, have convinced me I haven't the confidence I feel I ought to have if I am to proceed with my one aim – to make my theatre a place that everybody can point to with pride.'

Manners felt that 'an obsolete Act of Parliament', such as 'no other body of men or women in any other town would dream of raising against a man who has worked very hard for the position he has attained, and who has done so much for the town', had scuppered his chances of turning the Empire into a first-class theatre. 'I am being restricted', he wrote, 'into putting on third-class and even worse plays, simply because of a technicality.' Yet, if he gave up, he said, it would hurt his family and himself; it would be a serious blow for the town; employment would suffer, and so would other areas for 'seventy-five per cent of the money taken at the doors is actually re-spent in the town'. It was a calculated, if heart-felt plea. Manners knew that the people of Swindon, who regarded him well for himself, and for the years of charity work he had undertaken, would be firmly on his side. They would think that the law was being stupidly applied by officials who were quite out of touch with what was expected by theatre audiences in 1924.

Perhaps because of Manners's letter, the long arm of the law was not about to give up. On Easter Monday 1924, it materialised at the Empire Theatre in the shapes of the Deputy Chief Constable, Superintendent Brooks, and a police constable, who kept observation. Between 10.35 p.m. and 10.45 p.m., whilst the performance was still in progress, they saw two men enter the theatre, and others leave. From this they deduced that illegal drinking might be taking place, so thirteen minutes later they entered the theatre and made their way to the bar. There, doubtless to their great delight, they observed five persons around a table on which were beer bottles and glasses, one of which was half-full of liquor, whilst the others were wet with froth. Two men were standing at the bar, one of whom had a glass in front of him containing whiskey, and the other had a glass with him that seemed to contain beer. Manners was summoned to appear in court on 12 June 1924, charged with supplying intoxicating liquor after permitted hours. He was not in court because he had just undergone an operation as a result of his recent accident, but after a long hearing the bench convicted in his absence and fined him £30, plus five guineas in costs. The arm of the law had flexed its muscles.

After all these problems, and a lot more soul searching, Alfred Manners dropped his plans to sell the Empire, but also axed his previously stated intention to build a new theatre adjacent. For the moment, however, he would not leave, and would press on with his remodelling of the Empire. Even so, it is likely that Manners had at this point decided to give up the Empire in the not-too-distant future; others continued to express an interest in taking it over. He was still suffering from the effects of the accident of three years earlier, when he slipped and fractured his thigh while alighting from his car. The injury troubled him considerably, and he intended to go into hospital for another operation to relieve the pain. He had no faith in the licensing authorities, and he felt that the police were watching his every move. He must also have felt that he could press ahead with his plans for upgrading the theatre to ultimately greater financial advantage, and that an improved venue would attract more potential buyers and allow him to place a premium on what he had for sale.

The last week before closure was a huge success. The programme, entitled *The Musical Romance*, featured the world's largest stage organ. It had five keyboards, seventy-five stops, 2,303 pipes, and weighed nearly five tons. The organist, F. Rowland- Tims, played excerpts from *The Mikado*, but the big success was the spirited rendition of a composition of his own, which musically evoked a storm, complete with thunder and lightning. At the end of both performances on the Saturday night, Mr Rowland-Tims read a letter from Manners, thanking the audience for their support, and describing the plans for the big refurbishment over the summer break. He apologised for not being able to attend, but he had never properly recovered from his accident, was constantly in pain, and was expecting to go into hospital for another operation, quite soon. On the following day, Sunday, 27 April 1924, two crowded concerts were given at the Empire by The Musical Romance Company, with Mr Rowland-Tims on the organ, given in aid of the Victoria Hospital. Then the theatre closed down for three months.

In July 1924, the *Swindon Evening Advertiser* reported 'a great push in process at the Empire Theatre'. It spoke of drastic alterations, and more or less repeated the description that Manners had given for the work, at the end of the previous year. A reporter, who had just been taken inside, noted there was still a great deal of scaffolding about: decorators were busy on the ceiling; others were completing the decorative devices of the front of the circle; and labourers were busy mixing cement on the floor beneath. It seemed unlikely that it would all be finished by August Bank Holiday. But Manners was buoyant, and had a new slogan for the theatre: 'No early doors, and every seat bookable'.

'Swindon's theatre. Most comfortable in the west', reported the *North Wilts Herald* of 8 August 1924, adding that the place was expected to open towards the end of the following week. They repeated the general description, but were then in a position to add further information. A four-tier chandelier with sixty electric lights had been hung from the dome of the theatre, where there was also a huge electric fan, with another one on each side of the building, near the roof. The floors of the grand circle, orchestra stalls and stalls were carpeted in grey; the circle floor was covered in cork linoleum. The seats throughout were upholstered in velvet, had recoil springs so that they rose automatically when not in use, and mahogany arm rests. In order to solve the problem of draughts, corners had been rounded, and an ingenious system of boarding was employed to minimise draughts from the stage. The theatre box office telephone number was Swindon 96.

The strain of carrying out the rebuilding had adversely affected Manners's health. He also felt severely let down by the authorities, who appeared to be more intent on discovering breaches of the law at the theatre than understanding what he was trying to do for the people of Swindon. He genuinely wanted to give the town's theatregoers top quality entertainment in a venue commensurate with his high standards. Many family and business discussions took place behind the scenes whilst the Empire was being remodelled.

Following its remodelling, the Empire reopened on 16 August 1924. The ceremony was carried out by the mayor of Swindon, Alderman Thomas Charles Newman, and was attended by civic dignitaries and prominent townspeople. There followed two performances of *Hey Presto*, a revue featuring Clive Maskelyn, Frederick Culpitt, Stephanie Stephens and Tom Heathfield. Private boxes for four persons cost 15/- ; it was 2s 4d to sit in the grand circle or the orchestra stalls; the ordinary stalls cost 1/3; and a seat in the circle was sixpence, or 8d if booked in advance.

On 24 October 1924, one of the Empire's bar attendants, Sidney James Maidment, of 2 Rolleston Street, collapsed and died at his place of work. The body was found by Reg Manners, son of the manager, who noticed that the electric lights had not been switched on in the bar, and went to investigate. Maidment, who was born in 1859, was at one time a member of the Swindon fire brigade when the fire engine was drawn by horses. He was later employed as a driver of steam rollers by Swindon Corporation, and had also been an evening bar attendant at the theatre since 1902.

On 11 August 1925, Alfred Manners announced that he had disposed of his interest in the Empire Theatre. The new owners were Jack Gladwin and Joe Collins, who would retain the existing staff, and the new team would take over at the end of the month. Manners retired to 'The Gables' in County Road, Swindon, but was to suffer a devastating blow when, on 7 March 1926, his son Alfie, on route to Rhodesia to take up tobacco growing, fell overboard from the ship *Gaika* and was drowned. He was twenty-seven-years old. Manners never came to terms with this, and it seems likely that the presence of the Empire Theatre, now in the hands of others, was also almost too much to bear. The family relocated to Corner Crest, Friar's Road, Christchurch, and it was there that Alfred Manners died, aged 57, on

10 December 1926. He was survived by his widow Ellen Eliza; his son Reggie, who was living in New Zealand; and three daughters, Dolly (Mrs Kendal), Winifred and Elsie. His mother was also alive. Probate was granted to his widow, and he left £29,562 14s 6d.

Gladwin had managed the Empire Theatre at Swindon for its first three years, under Ernest Carpenter. Since then, he and Collins had gone into theatre ownership, and were associated (c1915-1930) with the Hippodrome at Aldershot, and, (c1919-1930) with the Kingston Empire at Kingston-upon-Thames. The first show put on at Swindon after Gladwin and Collins took over was a revue entitled *Spasms*, which played to large audiences on the first night. The pair installed Cecil Rand Collinson as manager, formerly general manager of the Aquarium Theatre and Theatre Royal, Great Yarmouth. He had also worked as manager of the principal company of the Royal Carl Rosa Opera Company, regulars at the Empire Theatre, who coincidentally were booked to appear there for four nights commencing in October 1925. Collinson's management was short-lived; in February 1926, he was replaced by Harry W. Briden, who had worked with Gladwin and Collins for some years. This was also the year in which Gladwin and Collins took on the lease of the Theatre Royal, Norwich.

Jose Collins, the original *Maid of the Mountains* and *Southern Maid*, visited the Empire in July 1926, when she was joined in some numbers by baritone Trevor Watkins. One of the big stars of the day, Collins delighted enthusiastic, full houses with her repertoire, incomparable style, and glorious voice.

The revue *Here's to You* ran at the Empire in September 1926, bringing to Swindon the incomparable Florrie Forde, in a range of magnificent dresses. She delighted the audiences with songs like 'Hold your hand out, naughty boy', 'The old Bull and Bush', 'She's a lassie from Lancashire', 'Flanagan', and 'Pack up your troubles in your old kit bag'. Two up and coming comics who joined her in this revue were Bud Flanagan and Chesney Allen, although they were not yet a double act. All three returned in December 1927 for the pantomime *Babes in the Wood*, when Florrie was Robin Hood and Flanagan and Allen were the robbers. The following year, they were back again in *Jack and Jill*, with Florrie as principal boy, Bud Flanagan as Sammy Oatcake the village idiot, and Chesney Allen as the wicked baron.

The famous 'Royal Illusionist', Horace Goldin made his first appearance at the Empire in September 1926. He specialised in sawing a woman in half (a trick for which he is generally credited, but probably incorrectly, as the inventor), pulling the two halves apart and moving between them, and in the Indian rope trick, during which he made a boy disappear while suspended from a rope in the centre of the stage. He also appeared again in October 1927 when he presented 'Blown to Atoms', billed as 'an oriental execution', and 'A wonder from Bombay', in which he apparently bored a hole through a human being.

*Tom Jones* was performed at the Empire Theatre in 1928, and was the first production there by Great Western (Swindon) Amateur Theatrical Society, a group whose origins lay in the Great Western Railway workshops in Swindon in the 1850s. This society, which also had a flourishing musical section, had hitherto been associated with the Mechanics' Institution in the town where, in 1904, they had opened under that name with a performance of *Trial By Jury*. They were to continue using the Empire for the next decade, finishing with *The New Moon* in 1938.

The world-famous comedian George Robey, known as 'The Prime Minister of Mirth', appeared at the Empire in November 1930, and scored a great success. The newspaper's critic said that he was a true professional; his jokes were subtle and funny, and he knew just how to tell them to be successful every time.

'BEYOND THE BLAZE OF THE BRILLIANT FOOTLIGHTS' read the title of the article that appeared in what was then called the *Evening Advertiser*, on 1 May 1930. The paper's reporter took readers on a backstage tour of the Empire during an actual performance. It began with the call boy, making his pre-curtain-up round of the dressing rooms and reminding the cast of 'five minutes please', and the performers collecting in the 'friendly semi-darkness of the evening'; once the show had got under way, this worthy member of theatre staff dutifully reminded the performers when they were next on stage. Above him, the reporter saw nearly fifty lots of hanging scenery, operated by an innumerable mass of ropes in the flies, and explained how, to get to them, one had to climb several flights of stairs to a height of about seventy feet. He pointed out that each stage hand, numbering between six and thirty depending upon the nature of the production, had their own particular job to do under the supervision of the stage manager. He wrote of the chief electrician who operated the switchboard that controlled all the lamps, and who supervised the people operating the follow spots.

Viewed from the wings, said the reporter, 'the play itself has an artificial atmosphere; from the front one can believe it, from the wings it is shorn of reality. These stage players are truly remarkable people', he enthuses, 'the moment they step into the wings they are a different people, and I have known instances of 'stage lovers' who cut each other dead off the stage.' As for the modern chorus girl, she is 'an independent little person, well educated and well paid'. There was a time when actors or actresses were unmistakable 'half a mile away'; but not in the 1930s. 'The chorus girl is very little different in appearance from the woman clerk.'

This piece described the arrangement of the dressing rooms at the Empire. The star of the show was accommodated nearest to the stage, where the room was said to be nicely furnished and very cosy. The main supporting acts dressed next door, but the rest of the performers were required to find their dressing rooms 'by threading their way through stacks and stacks of scenery and hard-working stage hands who are ever on the alert', and going ever higher into the building, depending upon their importance. Despite several attempts over many years to improve the dressing rooms at the theatre, they always had the reputation of being cold, draughty and third-rate.

Betty Clelland, a young Swindon-born soprano, appeared at the Empire Theatre in August 1930 in the show *The Novelty Box*, when she delighted the audience with her singing of 'My Hero' from *The Chocolate Soldier* and 'Carmina'. Betty was born in Birch Street, Swindon, and was educated at Queenstown School, where she took part in school plays and showed an aptitude for entertaining. Her father was employed in the railway works, and the family relocated to Newcastle when Betty was nine years old. She had previously appeared at the Empire in the 1928 revue *The Showcase*. During the run of *The Novelty Box*, she stayed with friends in Swindon.

The *Evening Advertiser* reported in September 1930 that attendances at the theatre during the previous few weeks had been poor, in spite of the high quality of the shows being presented. *Fine Feathers* , the revue then playing, was considered to be excellent entertainment, and the reporter warned that if the theatre did not receive the support it deserved, the people of Swindon would have only themselves to blame if it went over to becoming a cinema. He added that this was not improbable. Either he was prophetic or he had heard a strong whisper and wanted to make sure that he could declare at a later date, 'you heard it here first'. Less than four months later, on 29 December 1930, Jack Gladwin and Joe Collins leased the Empire Theatre to Swindon Entertainments Limited, of which M. Dent of Birmingham was managing director. Joe Collins remained on the board of the new company.

This came just five days after a fire occurred, thought to have been caused by an electrical fault, at the Mechanics' Institute on the night of Christmas Eve 1930. Three fire brigades fought the blaze; by the time it was under control, the whole central section of the building had been gutted, including the theatre and stage. This meant that for the moment, Swindon was without a venue dedicated to live theatre. If the new owners of the Empire Theatre ever considered taking advantage of this situation, they took no steps to put it into practice. The Regent Cinema had opened in Regent Circus in 1929, just a few hundred yards from the Empire, and the two were about to go into celluloid competition.

With Swindon Entertainments Limited came the change at the Empire that Alfred Manners had long feared. All members of the permanent staff, and the gentlemen of the orchestra, were given their notice. The leader and violinist at the time was Thomas 'Tim' Coxon, who contemplated forming a dance band, utilising the talents of some of the other musicians in the Empire's orchestra, but as most of them also had daytime jobs, this did not materialise. The theatre was to be converted into a cinema; in place of the safety curtain, there would be a silver screen, and the three-dimensional interaction on the stage would give way to the two-dimensional 'talkies' on the silver screen. This measured twenty feet by fourteen and a half feet, was made of a rubber composition, cost £80, and was erected twelve feet behind the footlights, so that people in the front seats would be at least twenty to twenty-four feet from the moving pictures. Some £5,000-worth of Western Electric Talkie Apparatus was installed directly behind the screen to ensure 'perfect reproduction of sound'. The box office was altered to allow the latest automatic six-way ticket machine to be installed.

By retaining the necessary licence to mount theatrical productions and variety shows the new company hedged its bets on the prospect of future live theatre. The last live show, the revue *The Singing Clown*, was presented on 19 January 1931.The review in the paper said it was 'the last flesh and blood performance to be presented at the Empire Theatre before the showing of talking pictures'. Immediately it finished, an army of men took over the Empire to complete the installations before talking pictures began the following week. On the 26 January 1931, the Empire became a cinema.

Gladwin and Collins bought the Theatre Royal, Norwich in 1928, after leasing it for two years; Jack Gladwin moved to Norwich and became fully occupied with the theatre there. Joe Collins remained on the board of Swindon Entertainments Limited to represent the interests of the Empire Theatre's owners in Swindon, but only for a short period of time. He died in 1931, whereupon his half-share in all of the theatres the pair owned jointly passed straight to Jack Gladwin. He became the sole owner of the Empire Theatre, Swindon, and remained as such for the next quarter of a century.

# 5
# *The celluloid years*

THE EMPIRE OPENED as a cinema, managed by Stanley C. Mills, who was also designated musical director, on 26 January 1931. Immediately prior to the post in Swindon, he had been manager and musical director at the New Theatre, Cardiff. There was no inaugural celebration for the new picture house at Swindon, but an advertisement that declared: '*Go first to the Empire Perfect Talkie Theatre: the voice of action*'. It went on to mention that this establishment was the only Western Electric installation in the area, a piece of brevity that must have been quite meaningless to the general public. In fact, it referred to the New York-based Western Electric Manufacturing Company's horn cinema speaker system, which the venue had installed, and which was capable of blasting the audience with sound. The first film to be shown there was *All Quiet on the Western Front*, the 1930 epic war film directed by Lewis Milestone, from the book of the same name by Erich Maria Remarque. Thereafter, except for pantomimes, concerts, some amateur musicals, an occasional play, and with the single exception of 1937 when the venue reverted to live shows for much of the year, the Empire remained a picture house until 1947.

As a cinema, the Empire had strong competition from the outset. *All Quiet on the Western Front* played at the same time as *On Approval* with Tom Walls and Yvonne Arnaud was showing at the nearby Regent. The Rink in Old Town had Maurice Chevalier in *Love Parade*; Mary Astor was at The Palace in Gorse Hill in *The Runaway*

*Bride*; The Arcadia in Regent Street had *The Wild Party* with Clara Bow; and Lilian Davies was running in *Just for a Song* at the Palladium in Rodbourne. The Empire began its matinées at 2.30 p.m., and the weekday evening performances played continuously from 6 p.m. There were two separate programmes at 6.15 p.m. and 8.40 p.m. on Saturdays and during holidays. At that time, all of the town's cinemas were closed on Sunday.

Swindonians who wanted to experience live professional theatre now had to travel to Bristol or Oxford. Otherwise, they might patronise the local amateur groups who occasionally performed at the Empire until the outbreak of the Second World War. These groups included the Swindon Amateur Musical and Dramatic Society, which staged *The Student Prince* at the Empire in 1931; and the GWR Mechanics' Institution Amateur Theatrical Society, which the same year performed *Princess Charming*.

Meanwhile, work had gone on apace to rebuild and refurbish the Mechanics' Institute, where the opportunity was taken to upgrade the performance area from a hall with a stage to a properly designed and dedicated theatre that might attract professional companies. In went a much-improved stage, and a new fly tower; dressing rooms were added high up in the wings; a new proscenium appeared with Art Deco mouldings; and a raked auditorium was laid out to seat 623 people. The venue opened on 3 September 1932 with twice-nightly performances of Leon Gordon's adult play *White Cargo*, which centred on a man's infatuation with a sexy but savage African native girl, who turned out to be possessive of him and full of murderous intent. It was not the sort of play that the people of Swindon had been used to, and it marked the Mechanics' Institute's intention to present itself as a major force for live theatre in the town.

Swindon Entertainments Limited gave the Empire a strapline – 'Where Everybody Goes'. It did not exactly say why they should do so, or for what purpose, and was, of course, quite untrue. Very occasionally, live performances were presented on stage between programmes of films. These included children's Saturday matinée variety performances that featured a yo-yo competition, and the appearance of Revd A.R. Smart, who spoke from the stage during the run of *The Man I Killed*, which starred Lionel Barrymore and was billed as the film 'all Swindon is flocking to see'. Another production, called *A Musical Interlude*, was presented by Reg Thomas and Doris Staniforth for one night in March 1932 when *Street Scene* was being screened. Stanley C. Mills and his Embassy Broadcast Band (most probably a local ensemble, but given an aspirational name) played three times a day, live on stage during the following week. Thereafter, the Embassy Broadcast Band continued to play daily during the intervals between each cinema house.

During the summer of 1932, the theatre experimented with composite cinema and stage offerings. This was called Non-Stop Cine Variety, and was billed as a 'super new type of entertainment'. There were a number of reasons for this. Mills clearly saw himself as a musical entertainer, and his tenure of the Empire had come at a difficult time. Many people felt that another cinema in Swindon was unnecessary; some missed live theatre; others believed that the Empire deserved still to be offering what it had been custom-built to provide – it was simply too good a building to be turned into a cinema. The local press was at best ambivalent, waiting on nuances of public opinion, but seemingly happy to pick up any opportunity to refer to the return of regular stage performances, mention the lack of them, and indicate that the matter was really in the hands of the theatregoing public. Or, in Swindon's case, the apparent lack of a viable audience.

During the cine-variety experiment, there were two houses of films daily, except for one day during the run when the film supporting the main feature was dropped and replaced by an hour's worth of live programme based around Mills and his Embassy Broadcast Band. Delores Costello in the film *Expensive Women* was sacrificed in favour of *Vaudeville*, 'One Hour of Music and Mirth' in which the band was joined on stage by baritone George Taylor, soprano Hilda Bickham, comedian Stan Platt, xylophone player Les Lewis, violinist Ernest Lewis, and The Famous Australian Male Voice Quartette. On another occasion, several of the same musicians turned out again in the company of trombonist Alex Dawson, comedian Percy North, and the North Wilts Highland Pipe Band for the *Evening Advertiser Variety Hour* in aid of the 'Poor Kiddies' Outing'.

'Here we are again, happy as can be', chimed the publicity for Mills and his ensemble. And so they were, playing for the *Evening Advertiser Hidden Talent Competition*, held in August. On came tenor H. Shepherd, piano duettists Davidge & Timbury, clarinet player H.C. Welch, comedian Bert Rice, baritone Mervyn Harper, whistler H. Voake, and vocalist Winifred Blackford. The last of these experiments took place in September 1932 when, between the on-screen showing of Stanley Lupino in *Love Lies*, an hour of *Cabaret* hit the stage, with Mills and his band providing the music for Boyd & Dane, and Grant & Faber, which were principally dance acts. In his spare time, Stanley Mills also took on the job of honorary conductor with the Great Western Railway Silver Prize Band.

As 1932 drew towards its close, so did Stanley C. Mills's incumbency at the Empire Theatre. In November, he returned to the New Theatre, Cardiff, (having been presented with a cigarette lighter in the shape of a knight in armour) and his place in Swindon was taken by E. Wilmot-Carlton, who had taken over Mills's job in Cardiff when the latter moved to Swindon two years earlier. Wilmot-Carlton's experience in the business also included three years at the Winter Gardens, Cheltenham; six years at the King's Hall, Birmingham; and as manager of the Palais de Danse, Hammersmith, with similar positions in Birmingham, Edinburgh and Glasgow. He had also managed the Jubilee Hall Cinema at Weymouth and The Elite Cinema at Nottingham. 'Under Entirely New Management' roared the Empire Theatre's posters, as Wilmot-Carlton took the helm at the end of 1932.

Pantomimes continued, the first of which, *Robinson Crusoe*, was staged in eleven scenes in January 1933. This three-hour show was especially designed and produced for the Empire by Harry Benet, a specialist pantomime and revue impresario who had offices in Soho, London. It featured Renee Roy, Florrie Lenner, and 'a cast of 40 London Artistes'. The *Evening Advertiser* found the comedy to be 'clean and wholesome', although 'inclined to drag a bit in the opening scenes'. In effect, this was a variety show hung loosely on the concept and principal characters of this well-known pantomime. Louis Roberts did a spot as a comedian; the Flying Potters performed their trapeze act; the Mirabelles danced; and it is now anybody's guess as to the nature of Madame Wall's Twenty Dancing Demons.

The same year, *The Good Companions* by J. B. Priestley came with a cast of seventy, and seems to have been the only professional performance of a drama at the Empire during its first period as a cinema. Its publicity trumpeted: 'The Greatest Stage Achievement of all times', and the production came from His Majesty's Theatre, London. The *Evening Advertiser* took the opportunity to highlight the lack of professional theatre in Swindon. 'It is admittedly not the kind of thing Swindon playgoers have been accustomed to, and the measure of support given to it this week will go some way towards supplying the answer to the question 'What does Swindon really want?'. Last night's audience was not big, but it was friendly.' It was a conservative notice that did not seem to augur well for a positive answer to the question. The newspaper also took the opportunity to moralise: 'There are good lessons to be learned from *The Good Companions*, which we should all be the better for learning, and one of these is that a kind word and a cheery smile go a long way towards smoothing life's pathway.'

A touring production of Noel Coward's operetta *Bitter Sweet* came to the Empire in October 1933, with a company of sixty artistes and its own orchestra. The production that arrived at Swindon had been doing a round of the provinces for some time, following its inaugural two-year run at His Majesty's Theatre, London, where it opened in 1929. It did not, however, have any of the original star cast (although the scenery and dresses were said to have been those used in the London production) of 'the most beautiful musical play ever staged'.

The following December, *Goody Two Shoes* played for two weeks. Roy Limbert and Harry Russell's production was billed as 'the most costly, magnificent, and spectacular pantomime ever staged in Swindon'. This one lasted for three and a half hours, and featured Hilda Campbell-Russell, then of the Malvern Players. She was a former pupil of the Italia Conti Stage School, and a some-time model, who was to have a seventy-year career in theatre, films and television. In the 1930s and 1940s, she specialised in pantomime, and this was one of the very best. The *Evening Advertiser* raved: 'I have never seen a show so rich in comedy. The moth-eaten jokes could easily be counted on the fingers of one hand, and there are few gags with whiskers on. In handing out bouquets, it is difficult to know where to begin.' The audiences were especially appreciative of the juveniles – Lily Bell's Dainty Dots and Goody Goody Girls – in the chorus, who were also clever little acrobats, and of the 'sensational aerial acrobatic novelty athletes', The Four Lagringlos, who 'looped the loop in the air'. The production featured a fearsome-looking dragon that, 'at the touch of a fairy wand, transformed into a dazzling array of fairies'.

Sundays concerts held at the Empire during 1934 included Raye Noualla and his Tango Band with G.H. Carlyle at the piano, and Julia Johns. Leonardo and his Milano Accordion Band turned out with 'musical stars' Wee Vivian and Little Dolly. Alan Selby and his Murray's Club Dance Orchestra came with Marie Schappelle ('and a microphone') and 'the celebrated soprano' Doreen Bristoll. Any artiste, no matter how obscure, who had ever been heard on the wireless, even fleetingly, was trumpeted on the Empire's playbill as the 'BBC Star' or even, if national fame had so far eluded them, 'from the Regional Station'. The pantomime in 1934 was *Babes in the Wood*. 'Fresh and vigorous, with a rare breeziness', wrote the newspaper critic, who also noted the 'amazingly lithe maidens whose performance is a show in itself'. The show included The London Rodney Hudson Girls and the Full London Chorus & Ballet, but its principal artistes were almost entirely unknown to the Swindon audiences.

The building changed hands in June 1935 when Swindon Cinemas Limited acquired the lease. The Watch & Pleasure Grounds Committee of Swindon Corporation granted an application from Henry Gilbert McGill, 'the actual and responsible manager' (of the Empire Theatre) for a licence for the public performance of stage plays. A surprising and stark notice appeared in the Evening Advertiser on 1 July announcing: 'This theatre is now under entirely new proprietorship and is closed for re-seating and redecorating throughout. Watch for the opening date of Swindon's new super-cinema.'

The two sets of boxes on each side of the stage, and the plastic decorations which were above the stage, were swept away and replaced by an Art Deco-style proscenium in silver. It was hailed as 'modernistic'. Brilliant green upholstery contrasted with the peach coloured walls, and a new multi-coloured lighting system was installed in the auditorium. The front of the stage was reduced, but a larger screen was installed. The refurbished Empire had become a 'Super Cinema', and reopened on 5 August with a continuous programme from 2 p.m. to 11 p.m. Its reopening blockbuster was *The Scarlet Pimpernel* starring Leslie Howard and Merle Oberon, and the musical film *The Cockeyed Cavaliers*, which was a vehicle for the much-loved comedy duo of Bert Wheeler and Robert Woolsey.

The reopening coincided with a series of Sunday variety concerts, organised by James David Norval, a theatrical agent of 9

Great Newport Street, London. The agent pocketed sixty per cent of the takings, and the remaining forty per cent went to the licensee of the Empire. These concerts were not well attended, and Norval had the idea of filling the theatre by giving away free seats to the following week's show. This was a precedent that had been set by certain London theatres. He thought that more people would attend if they knew that they had the chance of winning free entry, and implemented this by numbering the programmes (which were each priced at twopence); holders of programmes bearing the numbers called out during the evening won free entry the following week. On one occasion, the numbering system broke down, and Norval stamped the winning programmes with 'Empire Swindon'.

This led to an appearance in the police court in late 1935 when Norval was charged with 'selling a chance on a lottery depending on the sale of programmes bearing numbers at the Empire Theatre'. The prosecution alleged that by selling the numbered programmes, the theatrical agent had indeed carried out a lottery; it maintained that since every person in the house was a prospective winner, the defendant was distributing the prizes by means of chance. Part of the problem was that Norval told the audience that he hoped they would all buy programmes to get the chance of a free ticket in the future, left the stage for five minutes for more programmes to be sold, and then returned and called out the numbers of the winners. Norval maintained that no lottery had taken place; he contended that the winners were quite simply his guests, and he was entitled to invite whomever he liked to see the show, free of charge. Furthermore, the means by which he chose to invite them was up to him. It was an arrogance too far for the Swindon magistrates, who found him guilty of running a lottery, and fined him ten pounds.

No pantomime was presented during 1935, and by the end of the following year, it was clear that there were too many cinemas in the town. Swindon Cinemas Limited decided to try a revival of live theatre from the following spring. Meanwhile, Olga May and George Bolton came with *Mother Goose* in December 1936. For unspecified reasons 'beyond the control of the theatre's management', curtain up on *Mother Goose* was not until eight o'clock in the evening, so the performance would not finish until at least 11 p.m. This meant that an application had to be made to the town's Education Committee for an extension for the twelve local children taking part. One councillor said that children should not be kept out so late, and this was supported by another 'for the children's sake'. The committee agreed, and recommended by seven votes to six that the licences be extended to enable the children to appear on the stage until 10.30 p.m., and 'be clear of the theatre premises not later than ten forty-five'. It meant that the youngest performers could not take part in the finale.

Also *The Last of Mrs Cheyney* was presented, a comedy by Frederick Lonsdale, which played for five nights in the hands of the Swindon Amateur Musical & Dramatic Society. This heralded a period of live theatre, intermittent at first, which began in January and continued throughout 1937. The Great Western (Swindon) Amateur Theatrical Society presented the musical comedy *Virginia*, and, thereafter, mostly professional entertainment became the order of the day.

A number of adverse factors affected the fortunes of the live theatres in the early 1930s, particularly those in the provinces, and although by effectively becoming a cinema the Empire at Swindon was not troubled by these, their legacy would come back to haunt the place in 1937. At the time the Empire became a picture house, variety bills were struggling to survive in the face of increasingly polished styles of entertainment, carried out by sophisticated entertainers, and this was being beamed into homes everywhere across the airwaves. Magazines of the day depicted younger, much more stylish performers and styles of entertainment, a lot of which devolved on the dance bands of the day, their singers, and their comedy numbers. These were being broadcast nightly by the BBC, either from Broadcasting House or from posh hotels in London where the bands had residencies.

These bands soon began to tour the country, taking full shows to the provincial theatres and playing a week at a time to packed houses. Of course, ordinary people had previously bought the gramophone records they made, but the real catalyst for change was the radio. Now, those ordinary people could see the bands and the faceless radio stars in the flesh; the hitherto inaccessible, formerly the remote province of the better- off elements of society, had come to town. As long as the Empire remained as a cinema, it failed to capitalise on the financial potential of presenting the radio band shows to an appreciative audience. For other provincial theatres, it was a new lease of life.

The Empire did not learn this lesson because it never really experienced the problems that beset music hall in the early 1930s, which had then been re-launched relatively unsuccessfully as variety. Some of its former stars who had long ago made their name, and would still be a considerable draw, had largely priced themselves outside the financial means of the provincial theatres. Also, these luminaries were disinclined to subject themselves to the rigours of weeks on the road, when they might find themselves presented as the only possible excuse for the unattractive bill of supporting artistes. In addition, many of those music hall acts that had successfully integrated into variety bills were ageing. They had survived the savage chapter of history that was the First World War, but they were not of the twentieth century. Nor were they a product of the euphoria of the 1920s; they were old hat, and the theatre-going public wanted more contemporary, energetic and professional entertainment, in keeping with the more relaxed mood of the time. The old music hall stars found themselves slipping lower down the variety bill, increasingly relying on reprising their decades-old' triumphs simply for their nostalgia value.

When the Swindon Empire's management back-tracked in 1937, encouraged by the crescendo of local calls for the re-establishment of live professional theatre at the venue, they also tried to turn back the clock. Along came the supporting acts of old, clinging to the wreckage of variety: seven or eight of them each time, mediocre in their offerings (and most quite rightly never heard of again), with a radio star at the top of the bill, and sometimes a former music hall artiste somewhere near the bottom.

The style of presentation had not changed; the light boxes on each side of the Empire's stage flickered and flashed, sometimes illuminating the number of the turn according to the programme, sometimes failing to indicate anything at all. And on they trooped: the speciality acts and novelty acts, red-nosed comics and dour comedians, ventriloquists, tap dancers and adagio dancers, jugglers, magicians, performing doves and performing seals; many were examples of the two-a-penny daughters (and sons) of numerous Mrs Worthingtons who should never have been allowed to take to the stage.

Of course, those who did appear were sometimes in need of help off-stage. Very little has been written about life behind the scenes at the Empire, but we do have some notes by Sydney Snook, who described himself as a general factotum at the theatre during the 1930s. The apparently rather accident-prone Sydney's job included 'repairing broken seats, manipulating curtains and scenery backstage, providing special effects, acting as usher', and, on one occasion, taking over the role of commissionaire from the one who was sacked on the spot for being drunk on duty. In 1932, Arthur le Clerq wrote the song 'He Played His Ukelele As The Ship Went Down', which was an immediate hit for Leslie Sarony, and which quickly became a favourite with the theatre's pit orchestra. Sidney's job, when the musicians set sail, was to simulate thunder, which he achieved by attacking a piece of corrugated tin suspended by a rope high up in the flies. On one first night, the rope snapped and the flying piece of tin almost decapitated a stage hand who was manipulating the lights.

One Christmas, Sidney was required to fill a sack with tiny scraps of paper, put this and a young stage hand inside a large basket, and swing it out over the stage during a woodland glade scene featuring carol singers, so that the lad could distribute 'snow' as the contraption swung from side to side. The rope caught on a hook, the basket tilted, the terrified stage hand hung on to the rope, and the sack thudded down on the hapless carol singers 'bowling them over like ninepins'. Sidney wrote that the audience clapped and cheered, and he had to bring down the curtain to restore order. On another occasion, he brought down the heavy house curtains when the manager was on the stage, addressing the audience. 'He was swept right off his feet, and howls of laughter followed him as he made an undignified exit stage left on his hands and knees.'

A week-long talent contest was held at the Empire in March 1937, with a Phillips radio and £4 in cash as the prize, and the promise of a week's engagement in a forthcoming variety show starring Nellie Wallace for those hopefuls who came first and second. Some forty-five amateur acts took to the stage and were each judged by the audience. The winner was a whistler and bird impersonator named Reg Bullock from Calne. Second place went to sixteen-year-old Dulcie Dunne from Swindon, who was later to conduct her own choir, the Lansdown Singers. G.A. Frayley, sword swinger of Commercial Road, Swindon, took third prize, but was not to swing his swords on Miss Wallace's bill. The mayor, Alderman Lewis James Newman gave the prizes, and his wife was presented with a bouquet of red carnations. Newman took the opportunity to suggest to H.G. McGill, and the directors of Swindon Entertainments Limited present, that more live theatre might be a good idea. He was given a guarded reply. 'It would be the policy of the Empire to secure at all times the best possible variety artistes and musical shows for the entertainment of the Swindon and district public', said Leonard Gold, the company director, adding that at the moment they were 'more or less in the experimental stage in order to see what suited Swindon best'. There were frustrating times ahead.

Of the talent contest, Dulcie recalled: 'I went along with my mother as chaperone. The stage seemed very large, and you could not see anything because of the bright lights. There were no microphones, so you had to sing right out to hit the back of the circle. All types of people were competing – magicians, musicians, singers, and sword swallowers. I thoroughly enjoyed it but don't remember mixing with any of the professionals. The same year I had a role in the *Yeoman of the Guard* and sang in a quartet. I remember the sets for this production being very spectacular.'

The 1937 season began in earnest in April, with a week of variety featuring Nat Gonella and his Georgians, on a bill with Harry Tate and his son Ronnie, who presented their 'On the Road' burlesque sketch. There were the usual speciality acts, and a pair of 'elegant steppers' with 'a touch of strip-tease', the first time this had been mentioned on a variety bill at the Empire. Thereafter, variety shows, musical comedy, and revues were staged week after week. Beryl Orde ('radio's most famous mimic'), Herschel Henlere ('the mirthful music master'), and Tommy Coram and his doll Jerry Fisher ('the world's most famous ventriloquist') starred in one of these. This show marked the first appearance on stage of the Empire pit orchestra, named, for the purpose, as Ivan Barry and his Empire Melody Makers. They would become regulars on the stage during variety shows, starting a trend that would continue under several subsequent directors of music, and several different names of orchestra.

The 1930s was also the time when artistes (or their agents) used the most embarrassing puns in their publicity: skipping speciality act The Shamvas, 'we're (r)oping you'll like us' is an example; another is '(w)hoops daisy' for Stylo & Sonny. Then there were those descriptions that people today would consider to be downright inexplicable: 'Penny Soc-her Pools' came to the Empire 'in twelve magnificent scenes – see how 'Josser' wins £40,000 for twelve results'. And this, on a variety bill (called a 'new musical melange of new ideas, new dresses, new dances, new scenes, new songs, new artistes') with Ernie Lotinga: 'Britain's ever-popular up-to-the-minute comedian'. It was all too reminiscent of desperation rather than publicity, and that is probably what it was. Ernest Lotinga (1876-1951) married eighteen-year-old Winifred Emms at Lambeth in 1901; by then, she had already worked the halls for a dozen years as a singer and entertainer named Hetty King. She was to be a frequent visitor to the Empire. Lotinga was a music hall comedian turned comedy actor, who achieved considerable popularity in the 1920s and 1930s for his character 'Jimmy Josser', whom he played on stage and in short films. Yet he, and his creation, failed to make the transition between live performer and nostalgia to be kept alive, and both are today remembered only by students of the entertainment genre.

It is often said that the Empire Theatre's audiences were rarely treated to the very best artistes and, perhaps a little unkindly, that they only got what they deserved. Both of these statements hide half truths; contemporary computer technology has made it possible to see short films of many of these supporting acts, only to wonder how on earth they were ever thought to have had any talent, or entertainment value. But there were occasions when great stars of the music hall did shine brightly, if briefly, from the other side of the footlights as top of a variety bill.

One of these, the great Billy Bennett, came in 1937 when he was fifty years old and at the height of his success. Bennett was the supreme performer of comic songs (some of which he wrote himself) and parodies of well-known dramatic monologues, but his act derived much of its appeal from the performer's eccentric appearance and erratic manner of delivery. A distinguished soldier during the First World War (for which he had been awarded several military honours), Bennett's stage persona was embellished by a 'sergeant-major-style' military moustache and a strange quiff of hair that the army would never have allowed. (He also had a stage act – named 'Alexander and Mose' – with Albert Whelan, another favourite of the audiences at Swindon's Empire Theatre.) Bennett dressed in a dinner suit with an intractable roller blind of a shirt front, and trousers that did not reach the army boots he wore on his feet. The ensemble was completed by a red silk pocket handkerchief, which was permanently employed in mopping his brow. He was a truly original comic talent who entertained huge audiences. He died in 1942.

Bennett was followed at the Empire by Horace Goldin, on a return engagement, only this time the illusionist was not simply part of a miscellaneous variety bill: the whole show was built around him. Goldin said that he had been searching India for eighteen years, sparing no expense in trying to trace the origin or the theory of the Indian rope trick or an actual performer. He had been 'following up clues here and there' until one of these led to 'the disciples of a yogi in Rangoon'. Goldin claimed that he was 'the only white man in the world to discover the secret of the most discussed and challenged mystery of the century'. He had perfected it, as had been his lifelong ambition, and it had cost him more than £1,000 to do so. Now he could perform the trick in the open, as well as on the stage.

'Here at Last!' yelled the publicity, 'First Time Out of India'; and it had become 'the most discussed and challenged trick in the universe'. And here was Goldin, about to present the Indian rope trick as performed by Yogi Caram Dumbila, whom he now impersonated by wearing a turban and a cloak over his ubiquitous dress suit. The *Evening Advertiser* described the event: 'Slowly, against a black background, one sees the rope rearing its head in serpentine fashion, until we believe that it is standing rigid and unsupported. An Indian boy then climbs the rope, and when fired at vanishes into thin air.' It sounds as if there was a huge build-up to something of an anti-climax. Clearly you can't hang a whole show on a single disappearing boy.

Goldin knew this; he also had a 'Strip Tease Auction' up the sleeves of his dinner jacket.

This was only the second time the words 'strip tease' had been mentioned in conjunction with the Empire, although it would be far from the last. The auction, over which the press drew a discreet veil, was said to have been invented and written by Goldin, and was 'the latest American novelty'. He famously worked with a number of attractive young women who appeared and disappeared, handing props to the magician, removing them from him at the end of a trick, and sometimes taking part themselves, whilst he wandered about the stage performing 'fifty tricks in as many minutes'. Doubtless, the same young women were pressed into the service of the striptease auction, removing articles of clothing as requested, and the newspaper's silence in the matter was to avoid calling attention to any rowdiness this might have generated. On the night, Goldin also made a woman appear inside a huge balloon that was blown up on stage, caused an assistant to apparently walk through plate glass, and, of course, sawed a woman in half. The other acts that were hung loosely about Goldin's blandishments were three novelty dancers billed as 'a peach and a green pair', performers of 'graceful and grotesque carnival capers', musicians who were 'almost a musical act', and a 'merry burlesque' of a group. In 1937, they certainly knew how to take the banal and the third-rate, and to make it all sound even worse than it probably was. One realises that what really killed variety was that it had settled for mediocrity, at best, for far too long.

Coronation week in May was marked by the appearance of Nellie Wallace (1870-1948), in whose show the soprano Dulcie Dunne performed. By then, Nellie Wallace had long been one of the great music hall stars of her day. She was also an actress, comedienne, dancer and songwriter, and was known as 'the essence of eccentricity'. Her grotesque appearance, enhanced by her ability to produce incredible facial expressions, made her very popular as a pantomime dame, and her stage act devolved on extremely tight dresses and a whole catalogue of songs with saucy, if not downright ribald, lyrics. 'Under the Bed', Let's Have a Tiddly at the Milk Bar' and 'Three Cheers for the Red, White and Blue' were amongst her major hits.

She brought to Swindon her *Grand Coronation Carnival and Cabaret* variety show of 'antics and anecdotes'. Reg Bullock, the talent show winner, was then presented as a 'siffleur' (French for whistler, which perhaps sounded more exotic), who doubtless found himself overwhelmed by the thirty-strong, singing and dancing Corona Babes (and one boy) who were on the same variety bill. There were two comedians, Norman Carroll and Len Clifford, and the theatre orchestra – Ivan Barry and his Empire Melody Makers – had a spot to themselves, 'dressed in patriotic costumes'. There must have been something very incongruous about this band, so loyally attired but playing the Slavonic Rhapsody, which was apparently the great hit of their set.

The May Bank Holiday was illuminated by the appearance of Flotsam & Jetsam, 'the famous radio and vaudeville stars'. Their programme from the stage of the Empire Theatre was broadcast over the Western wavelength of the wireless, in the presence of the town clerk, W. H. Bentley, and the mayor and mayoress of Swindon, Alderman and Mrs Lewis James Newman. Fifty-eight-year-old Ella Shields, the American male impersonator, by then almost a forgotten and obscure figure of the music hall, was also on the same bill; she was clearly there to reprise her most famous song 'Burlington Bertie from Bow' as written by her husband. Shields was hardly mentioned in the press report, upstaged by Terina the female paper tearer, who endeared herself to the local press by incorporating the words *Evening Advertiser* into her act; the whirlwind skaters that were the Desardo Duo; and Los Cottrillos, the Mexican counter-balancers. Another variety bill that year at the Empire featured Murray (Walters) the Escapologist, an Australian who is sometimes credited with coining the term; and Kitty Masters, who was a well-known vocalist with Henry Hall's BBC Dance Orchestra. This one-year experiment in reviving this kind of show at Swindon did nothing to enhance the waning reputation of variety in general, or that of entertainment in Swindon in particular.

The general schedule for 1937 allowed few alternatives to variety. One of these was the musical comedy review *Going Places* in nine scenes, which starred Fred Kitchen Jr., Joan Edmondson ('who dances and sings with delightful abandon'), and a supporting cast of whom several had trodden the boards in the West End. The show came with its own orchestral director, so Ivan Barry was reduced to conducting only during the interval. There was also a version of the musical comedy called *Jill Darling!*, written by Desmond Carter, and Marriott Edgar (who wrote monologues for Stanley Holloway), and with music by Vivian Ellis. This had been such a hit for Frances Day when it opened at the Saville Theatre in London in late 1934, and in Swindon featured Fred Kitchen Jr., Jeffrey Piddock (who had been in the touring production of *The Good Companions*, and who, by the 1950s, was more often associated with nude reviews), and Joan Edmondson.

This was followed by a real oddity for Swindon, the all-male revue *Splinters of 1937*. The show was promoted as 'the famous wartime revue' with the rationale that 'some of the 1914-18 atmosphere is recaptured with 1937 modernisations'. It was 'the exact programme as played in France by Les Rouges et Noirs (the Reds and Blacks) and made the battle front rock with laughter'. The *Evening Advertiser* explained to its bemused readership that this style of entertainment came about when troops during the Great War made their own costumes and took the parts of women, for the enjoyment of their comrades. Several of the performers on stage at the Empire had first acted in these makeshift productions in France, and had sufficiently enjoyed the experience to afterwards tour with the concept as a professional company. *Splinters of 1937* featured Hal Jones ('the inimitable Lancashire comedian in his original role as he appeared in France'), the female impersonator George Ellisia ('The Perfect Lady'), and 'the most wonderful beauty chorus touring, in which every 'lady' is a gentleman'.

There was also a ten-week, mid-summer season of plays performed by the newly formed Swindon Repertory Company, which had twelve actors who were all experienced London performers. Ernest Pierce was chosen to run these, which consisted of popular dramas and comedies that had recently been successfully performed in the West End. Pierce directed Twelfth Night in 1933 at the open-air Minack Theatre overlooking Porthcurno Bay in Cornwall, and went on to be the founder and producer of the Cornish Shakespearean Festival, which in the 1930s took place at Nancealverne, near Penzance. In Swindon, a creative artist was retained to paint the scenery, which was made especially for the productions at the Empire. The season of ten plays started in May with *Distinguished Gathering* by James Parrish from St Martins, and finished with *The Man from Toronto* by Douglas Murray, which had been successful at The Royalty. The repertory season did not appeal to theatregoers of Swindon, and the directors of Swindon Cinemas Limited began to think about selling the theatre and the business. If there was too much cinema competition in Swindon, and insufficient interest in live plays, what could they do? In the short term, they reverted to variety shows.

In June, pupils of Swindon's Doris Keene's School of Dance performed *Matinée Dansante* at the Empire, in aid of the Victoria Hospital. A photograph taken of this production shows a young Diana Mary Fluck, entertaining with her 'balloon and muff dances'. This is one of the earliest public performances of a Swindon girl who would later become better known as Diana Dors.

During 1937, the people of Swindon were treated to a number of stars of stage and radio in the flesh at the Empire. One of these, Stanley Holloway (1890-1982), was then at the height of his fame as a reciter of comic monologues, in particular those about 'Sam Small' (his own creation), and Marriott Edgar's young 'Albert Ramsbottom', whose difficulties with a lion are still recited today. By the mid-1930s, Holloway had built up an act based on these characters and on his earlier career as a singer, which meant that he was in huge demand for pantomimes, variety, and theatrical revues. He went on to develop a career in stage and film, becoming one of the country's best-loved character actors.

Stanley Holloway appeared at Swindon in 1937, on a variety bill with (Terry) Bartlett & (Colin) Ross, arguably the most successful female impersonators (and pantomime dames) of their day. The same show included The Du-Roy Sisters, a 'boxing burlesque', billed as a 'comedy act with a punch'; and a contortionist-dancer named Brenda Carole. Comedy was provided by Devon ('the half-wit') and Wayne ('the nitwit'). Once again, Ivan Barry and his Empire Melody Makers took to the stage, and the audience's cries of 'Sam! Sam!' ensured that Holloway did not leave without reciting a monologue about the asked-for character.

British comedian and writer Tommy Handley (1892-1949) also came to the Empire in 1937, billed as 'the radio and variety star', although he was still a couple of years away from becoming nationally famous in the radio programme ITMA (It's That Man Again), which ran for ten years from 1939. When Handley appeared in Swindon, he had recently formed a comedy partnership with Ronald Frankau, working to great acclaim as 'Murgatroyd & Winterbottom'. He was said to have been particularly pleased with the warmth of the Empire's patrons' welcome. Handley was top of a variety bill that also featured Albert Whelan, the impersonator, singer and pianist, immaculate in his bow tie and tails; and 'The BBC entertainer' and recording artiste Florence Oldham, singer of comic songs and love songs, mostly to piano accompaniment. At Swindon, Handley performed the military musical piece 'The Disorderly Room', billed as his 'world-famous sketch'.

Empire Theatre audiences also saw Sid Field (1904-50), who came in 1937 with a variety show called *Red Hot and Blue Moments*. Field began his career as a child performer and, as an adult, toured the variety circuit for many years. When he came to Swindon with an act based on comedy characters and situations, his national fame as 'Slasher Green the Cockney spiv' was still some while off, as was his sudden capitulation as 'an overnight star' in the West End, and his rather less successful transfer onto celluloid. Field later scored great hits in the stage productions of *Strike a New Note*; *Strike it Again*, and *Piccadilly Hayride*.

Leslie Fuller, (1888-1948), 'Britain's comedy film star', otherwise known as 'the rubber-faced comedian', also made a personal appearance at the Empire. Although Fuller's time as a performer began before the First World War, and included wartime concert parties, he had been largely an east-coast local entertainer until his career took a national turn, c1930, largely through a series of short, self-made films that he made over about fifteen years. His appearance at Swindon in 1937 came about halfway through this period in his life, when he was at his most prolific and artistically successful. His relatively brief span of popularity is probably why he is today a forgotten talent. Interestingly, Fuller was the star of the 1932 film *Kiss Me Sergeant*, from a play of the same name by Syd Courtenay, who partnered Fuller in several projects. The play was performed at the Empire in October, billed as a military burlesque, with Tom Gamble in Fuller's part as 'Bill Biggles', a character who appeared in several of Courtenay's pieces.

*Red Hot and Blue Moments* had a cast of sixty, many of whom were accounted for by Henshaw's Beautiful Young Ladies, the exact nature of whose entertainment was not disclosed or commented upon in the press. The show included Ted Lewis and his Rhythm Band, The Six Kohlers, and The Bobs. The year of variety concluded in November 1937 with *Hip! Hip! Zoo-Ray!*, a circus revue. It must have meant a huge logistics headache for the theatre's management, which had to get groups of Royal Bengal tigers, forest-bred lions, black Himalayan bears, sea lions, ponies and elephants safely in and out of the building, and on and off the stage.

Then, as suddenly as it had begun, the ten-month experiment in live entertainment was over; the week following *Hip! Hip! Zoo-Ray!*, the Empire, with no preamble or explanation, once again became a cinema, showing Errol Flynn and Olivia de Havilland in *The Charge of the Light Brigade*. 'We revert to films', declared the publicity 'with the greatest film of the year'. The sad fact was that despite some very attractive stars, and a programme that included some good variety shows, revues, straight plays, and a repertory season, the year had not been a success. The directors of Swindon Cinemas Limited decided to sell the lease.

During the latter part of 1937, discussions took place between Swindon Cinemas Limited and B&J Theatres of Charing Cross Road, London, with a view to the latter buying the Empire Theatre. B&J Theatres, should the deal go ahead, were of a mind to occasionally mount variety performances, and were anxious that all the licences were in place that would enable them to do so. The management of the Empire held a theatre licence, an excise licence, a music and dancing licence, and a cinematographic licence. The theatre bars were allowed to open only when the Empire operated as a theatre; the bars would normally have to remain closed to the public when a variety show was the only offering, but Swindon Cinemas Limited had found a loophole. The theatre's patrons could imbibe in the bars if a sketch or play that had been licensed by the Lord Chamberlain was put on immediately after the interval during a variety show. As an extra incentive to negotiations, the prospective buyers were told that, when an amateur company was performing a stage play, the bars could be left open at all times, enabling friends of the performers to drink their way to a profitable contribution for the theatre. In fact, bar takings for the weeks of an amateur production could be double the amounts taken at other times. It all seemed set fair for a takeover by B&J Theatres. They would purchase the lease for £3,400, (Swindon Cinemas Limited had originally asked for £6,000), and would carry on the venue as a cinema until February 1938. In the meantime, Swindon Cinemas Limited would try to cancel any arrangements already made for films after that date.

In January 1938, a director of B&J Theatres arrived at the Empire, with an electrical contractor. The pair inspected the electrical arrangements at the rear of the stage, and the director said that he was taking over the theatre. It was an intention that was about to go awry. The directors of B&J Theatres identified what they alleged to be anomalies concerning the licences (some of them appeared to be missing), became unhappy about some of the information they had been given by Swindon Cinemas Limited, and were in two minds about the legality of putting on a legitimate play following the interval in order to keep open the bars. This led to an unseemly incident just as the purchase money was being banked, when, on the day earmarked for completion, one of B&J Theatre's directors snatched part of the purchase money from the hand of Leonard Gold, a director of Swindon Cinemas Limited, and refused, at the eleventh hour, to complete the contract. This led to a court case in November 1938, by which time Swindon Cinemas Limited had firmly re-established films at the Empire, and which they brought against B&J Theatres for breach of verbal contract. Mr Justice Crossman heard the case in the Chancery Division, which ended abruptly when B&J Theatres agreed out of court to pay £1,000 to Swindon Cinemas Limited, plus its costs to the value of £300. That association was at an end.

It was the exterior of the Empire Theatre at night that made such an impact on Ron Burchell, who knew the place from 1938. This was a time, wrote Ron, when Swindon's Regent Street had gone neon: individual shops were picked out in neon strips, some of which glowed steadily throughout the hours of darkness; others flashed individual letters in sequence; and as a result, rosy glows hung or changed shape in pockets around the shopping centre. One such vibrant glow edged the Empire Theatre, whose dull, daytime extremities were transformed at night by neon that picked out its whole outline, and by the word 'Empire', which was composed of light bulbs. In the eyes of the young Ron, advancing down Victoria Road to where the Empire stood on its corner with Groundwell Road, it was a spectacle of fairyland. But it was not one that would last; as the effects of war closed in on Swindon, so the lights outside the Empire went out, and would never come on again. The Empire was not damaged during the Second World War, although it was shaken during a performance in 1942 when bombs dropped a few hundred yards away in Drove Road.

Just before nine o'clock on the evening of 1 December 1939, two men in army uniform entered the vestibule of the Empire, where the female box office clerk was working alone. Outside, it was dark, but even more so than usual as the town was subjected to a wartime blackout. The clerk had just cashed up, and was putting the evening's takings of about £40 into a bag, which was sitting on her desk. The men asked about seats, turned as if to go towards the auditorium, and then swung round, grabbed the bag of money, and disappeared into the night. Their escape was aided by the blackout, which helped to conceal the direction they followed. The police were called, but even though they arrived within five minutes, they could do very little. The empty bag was later found in Old Town, near to the Midland & South West Junction Railway's station, off Newport Street.

There were no more pantomimes until December 1939, when Hamilton, Frances Hughes and Clifton Court performed in *Cinderella*. *Babes in the Wood* was presented in January 1944 with Harry Orchid and Maisie Weldon, followed by *Cinderella* featuring Anona Winn, and which began on Boxing Day 1944. The pantomime in December 1945 was *Aladdin*, which opened on Christmas Eve for four weeks and featured Wally Patch, Sylvia Kellaway, Tom Payne and

Bill Waddington. It was advertised as Swindon's first pantomime to be broadcast, and it went on air on 4 January 1946. *Mother Goose*, with Leonard Henry and Helen Clare, played a five-week season from Christmas Eve 1946.

*The film that opened the Empire's first period as a 'talkie theatre' in January 1931 was Lewis Milestone's 1930 production of Erich Maria Remarque's First World War drama All Quiet on the Western Front. It starred Louis Wolheim, Lew Ayres, John Wray, Arnold Lucy, and Ben Alexander.*

Empire Theatre and Groundwell Road, Swindon

(above) *The Empire Talkie Theatre wanted to point out that it had installed a 'Western Electric Sound System' for its patrons, as this 1931 picture shows. The film of the day was What a Night, directed by Monty Banks, and starring Leslie Fuller who appeared live at the theatre in 1937.*

(right) *Sometimes, the Empire hedged its bets, or perhaps wanted to see whether there might still be an audience for live theatre. This example, from 1932, shows how films were sometimes shown as the first house, to be followed by a stage show at the second. On such occasions, the Empire's house band also took to the stage under the baton of the theatre's musical manager.*

## EMPIRE
### SWINDON

**NOW!**

The Finest Programme for Many a Day—A Patron.

WALTER HUSTON    CHARLES (CHIC) SALE
in

## "THE STAR WITNESS."
COMEDY . THRILLS AND ABOVE ALL A GOOD STORY.

ON THE SAME PROGRAMME

DOLORES COSTELLO in
## "EXPENSIVE WOMEN."

ON THE STAGE.

## THE EMBASSY BROADCAST BAND
Directed by STANLEY C. MILLS.

| New Ideas. | New Novelties. | New Numbers. |

TO-NIGHT, 2nd HOUSE ONLY.
SPECIAL STAGE PRESENTATION
## "VAUDEVILLE"
ONE HOUR OF MUSIC AND MIRTH

Geo. Taylor (*Baritone*).    Hilda Bickham (*Soprano*).
Stan Platt (*Comedian*).
Les Lewis (*Xylophone*).    Ernest Lewis (*Violin*).
The Famous Australian Male Voice Quartette
and of course The Embassy Broadcast Band
directed by STANLEY C. MILLS.

*Special Notice*—"EXPENSIVE WOMEN" will NOT be shown 2nd house

- 151 -

*(right) The musical Florodora, written by Owen Hall, with lyrics by Ernest Boyd-Jones and Paul Rubens, and music by Leslie Stuart, first performed in London in 1899, came to Swindon in 1900 and then five more times in the next seven years. In all, it was performed nine times at the Empire, and this publicity shot of local actor Billy Richardson is from the 1932 show.*

# EMPIRE
## SWINDON

TWICE DAILY AT 2.30 & 7.30.

DOORS OPEN AT 2 & 7.    COME EARLY.
BOOK YOUR SEATS NOW, BOX OFFICE OPEN 10 to 9. Phone 96.
EXCELLENT UNRESERVED SEATS AVAILABLE AT DOORS.

ALL THIS WEEK.
ON THE STAGE.

STUPENDOUS SUCCESS!
JACK O'SHEA & GEORGE LAWRENCE present JULIAN WYLIE'S
PRODUCTION of

# "THE GOOD COMPANIONS"

FROM J. B. PRIESTLEY'S NOVEL.

## The Greatest Stage Achievement of all times

ADAPTED BY J. B. PRIESTLEY AND EDWARD KNOBLOCK.
MUSIC BY RICHARD ADDINSELL.

## PLAYED BY A COMPANY OF 70.

PRODUCED BY JULIAN WYLIE AT HIS MAJESTY'S THEATRE, LONDON.

PRICES OF ADMISSION (INCLUDING TAX):

|  | Matinees. | Evenings. |
|---|---|---|
| ORCHESTRA STALLS | 2/6 | 3/5 |
| CENTRE STALLS | 1/6 | 2/6 |
| BACK STALLS | 1/- | 1/6 |
| DRESS CIRCLE | 2/6 | 3/6 |
| CIRCLE | 1/3 | 1/10 |
| UPPER CIRCLE | 7d. | 9d. |

BOXES (to seat 4), 18/-.
SEATS AT 1/10 UPWARDS MAY BE RESERVED.
EXCELLENT UNRESERVED SEATS AVAILABLE AT DOORS.

*(left) The only professional on-stage drama at the Empire during its first period as a cinema was The Good Companions, a play with music based on J.B. Priestley's book. This 1932 production was remarkable for its cast of seventy, and for the high quality of their performance, but it did not attract the size of audience it disserved. Modestly supported houses re-ignited the debate about whether it was worth bringing this level of production to a largely unappreciative Swindon.*

(left) Jack Gladwin, looking every inch the profitable theatre owner that he had become by 1934.

(right) Local amateur theatrical societies used the stage at the Empire for live performances whilst it operated as a cinema. In 1934, the Great Western Amateur Theatrical Society mounted a production of Guy Bolton and Fred Thompson's 1927 musical Rio Rita.

The Great Western (Swindon) Amateur Theatrical Society present ————

RIO RITA

Empire Theatre, Swindon, April 9th——14th, 1934

The Swindon Amateur Musical & Dramatic Society brought Lorenz Hart and Richard Rogers's musical comedy *The Girl Friend* to the stage of the Empire in 1935. Its only other outing at the theatre was when performed by a professional company in 1929.

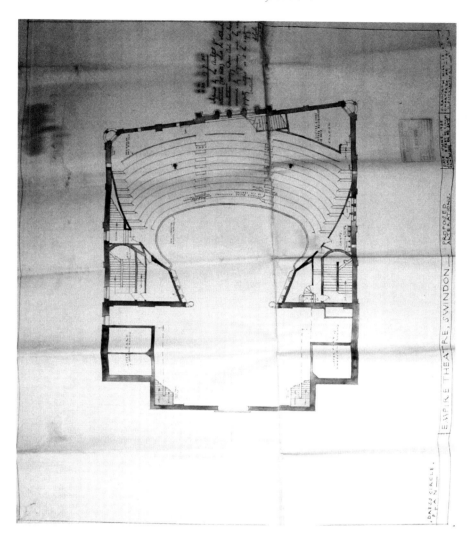

*(above and overleaf) In 1935 plans were drawn up to once again remodel and refurbish the interior of the Empire. The commission was given to J. Raworth Hill, architects of 11 Buckingham Gate, London, and the alterations heralded the relaunch of the building as a 'Super Cinema'.*

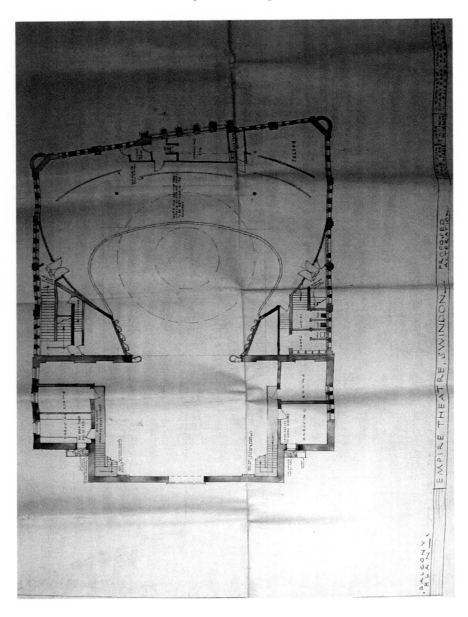

*(above, and above right: see caption on previous page)*

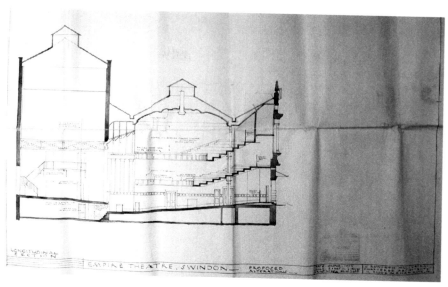

*August Bank Holiday Monday 1935 was when Swindon's 'Super Cinema' came into being. It opened with a showing of The Scarlet Pimpernel, directed by Alexander Korda and starring Leslie Howard, Raymond Massey and Merle Oberon.*

**"Balloon and Muffs Dances"** Selwood House School.
Peggy Peploe, Mary Tayler, Barbara Bailey (Balloons).
Marilyn Hyde, Peggy Miles, June Drury, Margaret Higgins,
Diana Fluck, Brenda Milton, Christine Huck.

*Page Five*

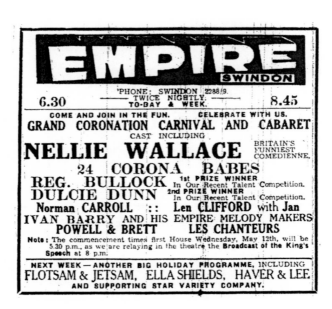

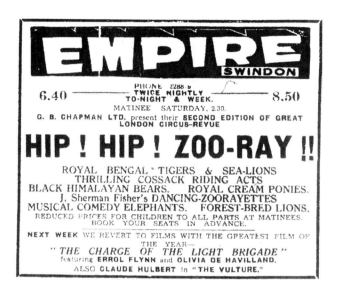

**EMPIRE** SWINDON

PHONE 2288-9
6.40 ——— TWICE NIGHTLY ——— 8.50
TO-NIGHT & WEEK.
MATINEE SATURDAY, 2.30.
G. B. CHAPMAN LTD. present their SECOND EDITION OF GREAT
LONDON CIRCUS-REVUE

# HIP ! HIP ! ZOO-RAY !!

ROYAL BENGAL ⁕ TIGERS & SEA-LIONS
THRILLING COSSACK RIDING ACTS
BLACK HIMALAYAN BEARS. ROYAL CREAM PONIES.
J. Sherman Fisher's DANCING-ZOORAYETTES
MUSICAL COMEDY ELEPHANTS. FOREST-BRED LIONS.
REDUCED PRICES FOR CHILDREN TO ALL PARTS AT MATINEES.
BOOK YOUR SEATS IN ADVANCE.

NEXT WEEK WE REVERT TO FILMS WITH THE GREATEST FILM OF
THE YEAR—
"*THE CHARGE OF THE LIGHT BRIGADE*"
featuring ERROL FLYNN and OLIVIA DE HAVILLAND.
ALSO CLAUDE HULBERT in "THE VULTURE."

*(opposite, above) In 1937, a group of children from the local Selwood House School performed a series of 'Balloon and Muffs Dances' on stage at the Empire. The girl on the left in the front row is Diana Mary Fluck, later to become better known as the actress Diana Dors.*

*(opposite, below) One of the high spots of 1937 was the Nellie Wallace company's variety show which gave the opportunity for amateur talent competition winners Reg Bullock and Dulcie Dunne to share the stage with professionals as acts in their own right.*

*(above) The Empire's year-long experiment with a return to live theatre came to an end in November 1937 with the circus-style Hip! Hip! Zoo-ray!! It was not that stage shows had proved to be unsuccessful per se, rather that films were cheaper to put on and held a much greater potential for larger audiences.*

*(right) Billy Richardson, who worked in the GWR railway workshops in Swindon and was a member of the Works' Male Voice Choir, was also a recording artiste of comic songs on the Regal Zonophone label, and a local charity worker. Here he is, in The Yeomen of the Guard.*

For decades, the covers of the Empire's programmes were printed in tints of red and blue, and the same design was used for years at a time. This one is from 1947, when it reverted to stage shows as 'the premier theatre of the west'.

The appearance of Koringa, 'the only female yogi in the world', struck fear into the hearts of theatre management everywhere, and filled pit orchestras with terror. They knew they would be in the front line if any of her reptiles slithered or crawled off the front of the stage. It happened at the Empire in 1947.

The variety shows at the Empire mainly comprised forgettable and forgotten acts, enlivened by a star name at the top of the bill. Here, in 1947, the latter were Laurel and Hardy. Thomas Coxon, director of the theatre's orchestra on that occasion, was by day a motor mechanic at the nearby Victoria Garage.

*Stan Laurel first appeared at Swindon's theatre in 1907 as a bit-part juvenile in a pantomime. Forty years later with his stage partner he signed this publicity card, for Joan Bobby, daughter of the Empire's manager.*

*Bill Bobby's wife Julia also had her admirers; here is a card signed to her by Elsie and Doris Waters, Gert and Daisy, in 1947.*

(right) The Swindon Musical Society mounted its first production at the Empire in 1947: Mlada by Rimsky-Korsakov. The Society staged nine more productions there before the theatre closed in 1955.

THE EMPIRE THEATRE · · SWINDON

Week Commencing Monday, March 17th, 1947
at 7.0 p.m.

OPERA-BALLET

# MLADA

(RIMSKY-KORSAKOV)

by the

### Swindon Musical Society
President: HIS WORSHIP THE MAYOR.

Musical Director: H. S. FAIRCLOUGH

Hon. Treasurer: B. L. MONAHAN.
Hon. Organising Sec.: EDITH A. WARD.
Hon. Secretary: THOS. S. MERRICK.

Page one

(below) Manager Bill Bobby relaxes in one of the theatre's bars with some friends in 1948. The theatre had recently staged Hit Parade of 1948 starring the singer Betty Driver who, years later, was to become famous in a bar of her own, as Betty Turpin of the Rover's Return in Coronation Street.

# Our Manager and Staff

**W.** S. BOBBY. First began his career in the entertainments business at the age of 20 as Assistant Manager at a small cinema just outside Chester. Joined Odeon Theatres, Ltd., in 1937 and managed theatres for that Company in Glasgow, Warrington, Chester and Oldham. Volunteered for the Royal Engineers in September, 1939, and served with the B.E.F. in France. Was discharged through injury after the evacuation of Dunkirk. Rejoined Odeon Theatres upon return to civil life and in 1943 resigned from that Company to join us. Has since managed Cinemas and Ballrooms for us in Cambridge and Folkestone.

Mr. Bobby cannot speak too highly of the many friends he has made in Swindon during the 3 years he has been resident at the EMPIRE, and now that the theatre has reverted to full time "live" shows he expresses his confidence that the people of Swindon will rally round and give this grand old theatre the support it deserves.

**W. S. BOBBY**
Licensee and Manager

**D. STUART-KELSO**
Assistant Manager

**HARRY JOSEPH**
Musical Director

**DICK HART**
Stage Manager

**GEORGE PRICE**
Chief Electrician

*The Empire marked its 5oth anniversary in 1948 by publishing a special brochure. This page pictured its senior staff at the time.*

*Aladdin played the Empire in 1948, when this picture was taken. However, it was not printed until after the theatre closed seven years later, ironically while it was waiting for another production of Aladdin to arrive.*

(above) Jane of the Daily Mirror, the saucy and morale-boosting strip cartoon turned into a stage production, arrived at the Empire in 1948. Risqué for the time, it nonetheless set the scene for the 'girly' shows that were soon to follow as the Empire's management, like that of very many provincial theatres throughout the country, tried desperately to boost dwindling audiences by presenting naked female flesh during the 1950s.

(right) The cover of this late 1940s programme retains more than a hint of cinema. Perhaps it was an intentional reminder to patrons that if they did not support live theatre they could once more lose it to the screen. Meanwhile, the Empire remained firmly in the grip of variety theatre.

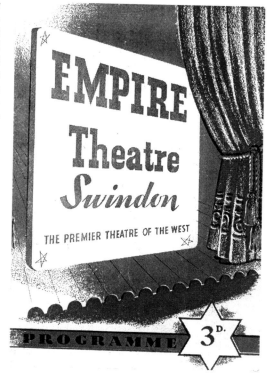

EMPIRE Theatre Swindon

THE PREMIER THEATRE OF THE WEST

PROGRAMME 3D.

## PROGRAMME

**Week Commencing 6th September, 1948**

### THE TRINDER SHOW
Produced by CHARLES HENRY

1. OVERTURE ..... By the Empire Theatre Orchestra
2. THE TRINDER SHOW arrives with—
   THE JOHN TILLER GIRLS, HAL COLLINS and TOMMY TRINDER
3. IT'S NOT IN THE PROGRAMME
4. BOB BEMAND with his PIGEONS
5. TRINDER Makes a Discovery
   with COLIN DUNNE and HARRY ARTHURS
6. WOODS and JARRETT Those Two Coloured Gentlemen
7. "THE WOOING OF HUN LUNG WO"
   A Chinese Melodrama   Introduced by HAL COLLINS
8. TRIO GROSSETTO   French Comedy Jugglers
9. INTERMISSION—A Selection of Irving Berlin's Songs
   arr. Zalved by the Empire Theatre Orchestra under the direction of   ALBERT DUNLOP
10. "BESIDE THE SEASIDE" The JOHN TILLER GIRLS
11. SAME BEACH——Further Along
    JUNE KUESTER, IRIS SHAND & TOMMY TRINDER

12. YOUTH MUST HAVE ITS SWING
    JERRY ALLEN ..... Organ
    JOE LEE ..... Piano
    LES SHANNON ..... Drums
    *Introducing—*
    JEAN BARRIE Sophisticated Singer of Sentimental Songs
    and THE JOHN TILLER GIRLS
13. HOLLYWOOD PERSONALITIES
    Brazilian Bombshell ..... TOMMY TRINDER
    Sonny Boy ..... LES SHANNON
    The Voice ..... TOMMY TRINDER
    Parade of the Stars :
    The Body ..... TOMMY TRINDER
14. THE GANJOU BROTHERS and JUANITA
    "A Romance in Porcelain"
15. TOMMY TRINDER ..... You Lucky People
16. FINALE ..... The Show Departs

Costumes by London Palladium Wardrobe. Sound Effects by Levy's Sound Studios. Tommy Trinder's Wigs and Make-up by Wig Creations Ltd. Scenery by Harry Delvin. Orchestrations by Jan Ralfini and Dave Raphael. Tommy Trinder's Suits by Bud Flanagan

| General Manager | For | Dan Draper |
| Musical Adviser | TOMMY | Bob Gibson |
| Stage Director | TRINDER | Gerry Barry |

## PROGRAMME

**Week commencing Sept. 13th 1948**

1. OVERTURE

2. ANITA and BILLY DENNIS
   Dancers Perfique.

3. BILLY DAY
   New Style Ventriloquist.

4. CYCLING ASTONS
   Thrills on Wheels.

5. TERRY O'NEIL
   Smile Awhile.

6. BOB and RITA REMA
   Novelty Perch Balancers.

7. INTERVAL
   by the Theatre Orchestra under the direction of Albert Dunlop. Fantasia, "MEMORIES OF THE BALLET" *arr. King Palmer.*

8. ANITA and BILLIE DENNIS
   To Dance again.

9. BUD CORDELL
   Crazy Cartoonist.

10. MARTHA RAYE with Frank Still at the Piano.
    The Famous Hollywood film Comedienne.

11. JOTHIA and JOAN
    A Juggling Cocktail.

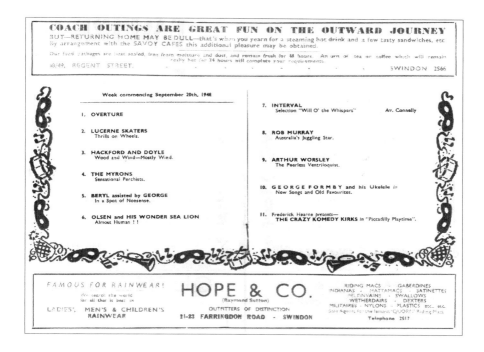

Week commencing September 20th, 1948

1. OVERTURE

2. LUCERNE SKATERS
   Thrills on Wheels.

3. HACKFORD AND DOYLE
   Wood and Wind—Mostly Wind.

4. THE MYRONS
   Sensational Perchists.

5. BERYL assisted by GEORGE
   In a Spot of Nonsense.

6. OLSEN and HIS WONDER SEA LION
   Almost Human ! !

7. INTERVAL
   Selection "Will O' the Whispers"          Arr. Connelly

8. ROB MURRAY
   Australia's Juggling Star.

9. ARTHUR WORSLEY
   The Peerless Ventriloquist.

10. GEORGE FORMBY and his Ukelele in
    New Songs and Old Favourites.

11. Frederick Hearne presents—
    THE CRAZY KOMEDY KIRKS in "Piccadilly Playtime".

*(opposite, above) Tommy Trinder was one of the top-of-the-bill radio stars to play the Empire. He came in 1948 with the famous Tiller Girls, the precision dance troupes that began in 1890 and continued for almost 120 years. However, the order of programme clearly shows the extent to which the proceedings were really just a vehicle for its star performer.*

*(opposite, below) Acts didn't come any more popular than Martha Raye, the American singer and comic performer who allegedly wore no underclothes and had to be zipped into the figure-revealing dresses in which she performed on stage.*

*(above) It turned out nice again for the Empire's patrons when George Formby and his wife Beryl arrived in 1948. A particularly strong company also included the droll but sensational Australian juggler Rob Murray, and Arthur Worsley, one of our best-ever ventriloquists.*

By arrangement with
the Management of the

**EMPIRE THEATRE
SWINDON**

the Swindon Branch of the
Royal Air Forces Association
present the Finale of their

**BATTLE OF BRITAIN
CELEBRATIONS
1949**

Programme 3d.

## In Remembrance and for Your Entertainment

1. **THE BAND OF THE ROYAL AIR FORCE STATION YATESBURY**
   GRAND MARCH—"Pomp & Circumstance No. 4" - *Elgar*
   CHARLES WILLIAMS' "Dream of Olwen" - *arr. Dennis Wright*
   HANDEL's "Largo"
   FANTASIA—"Golden Age" - *Greenwood*
   HYMN—"Deep Harmony" - *Handel Parker*

2. **BERYLDENE HUNT** - Elocutionist

3. **ST. AUGUSTINE'S BOYS' CHOIR** (Conductor, Clayton G. West, Esq.)
   "Rejoice Greatly" - *Handel*
   "Dream Angus" (Old Gaelic Air) - *Churchill*
   "A Tragic Story" - *Benjamin Britten*
   "A Lullaby" - *Clayton West*
   "Nymphs and Shepherds" - *Purcell*

4. **ARTHUR CARRON**
   "Take a Pair of Sparkling Eyes" (The Gondoliers) - *Sullivan*
   "On With the Motley" (Pagliacci) - *Leoncavallo*

   *INTERVAL*

5. **DUET BY ARTHUR CARRON & REGINALD V. HIPPERSON**
   "Watchman, What of the Night?" - *Sarjeant*

6. **MOLLY LEAPER**
   "Still is the Night" - *Karl Bohm*
   "Lullaby" - *Cyril Scott*
   "Softly Awakes My Heart" - *Saint Saëns*

7. **PETER SELLERS—Speaking for the Stars**
   The Radio Star of "Variety Bandbox", "Ray's a Laugh" and Seller's Market"

8. **REGINALD V. HIPPERSON**
   "The Song of the Flea" - *Moussorgsky*
   "Largo el Factotum" (Barber of Seville) - *Rossini*

9. **THE BAND OF THE ROYAL AIR FORCE STATION YATESBURY**
   "Land of Hope and Glory" - *Elgar*

   EPILOGUE
   Miss Beryldene Hunt

*Swindon's Battle of Britain commemorations in 1949 ended with a pro-am performance of remembrance staged at the theatre by the Swindon Branch of the Royal Air Forces Association. Well known locals taking part included Beryldene Hunt, opera singer Arthur Carron, and Reginald V. Hipperson. The programme also featured Peter Sellers 'speaking for the stars'.*

# 6
# Big names and gradual decline

IN 1943, THE Empire was taken over by an organisation called The Mayfair Circuit, and it traded from 1946 under the auspices of its associate company, Park Theatrical Productions. The company's chairman was Walter C. Elcock, who bought the leasehold of the theatre for £25,000; Walter Fellows was managing director; and William Stanley Bobby was installed as the manager and licensee. He was charged with overseeing the change back to live theatre.

Bobby was born in Northampton and began his career in the entertainment industry, at the age of twenty, as an assistant manager at a small cinema outside Chester. He joined Odeon Theatres Ltd in 1937 and managed their establishments in Glasgow, Warrington, Chester and Oldham. In September 1939, he volunteered for service with the Royal Engineers, served with the BEF in France, and was evacuated from Dunkirk in 1940. His was the last unit to get away from St Nazaire on the day the *Lancastria* was sunk by enemy aircraft. Discharged from service through injury, he re-joined Odeon Theatres, and in 1943 moved to Park Theatrical Productions, working in their cinemas and ballrooms in Cambridge and Folkestone.

His immediate superior in Cambridge and Folkestone was W. Fouldes, who was a director of Park Productions, and who was based at the Central Cinema, Folkestone before transferring to the

Empire Theatre at Swindon, sometime in 1944. Fouldes relocated to Manchester in 1945, and his position at the Empire was taken by James Webster, who was also a musician, general entertainer and compere. Webster's wife Marjorie was a BBC radio artiste, and he soon left the Empire to join her as a comedy double act with a piano. When Bill Bobby came to Swindon in early 1946, he shared the manager's office, just off the right-hand side of the auditorium, with assistant manager Derek Stuart-Kelso, and Dorothy Rice, who was the theatre manager's secretary.

In December 1946, Park Theatrical Productions, now under the name of Mayfair Circuit (Swindon) Ltd, mounted the pantomime *Mother Goose* with Tommy Godfrey and Leonard Henry, for a five-week season. But the venue was not free to revert entirely to stage shows. The *Wiltshire Herald and Advertiser* reported the hope 'that live shows would return to the theatre in the near future', but prior contracts meant that films continued to be shown until April 1947. January of that year saw a week of variety take to the stage, entitled *Yuletide Fantasy a feast of mystery, melody and mirth*. It featured 'The Great Benyon'; this was the world-famous master magician and quick-change artiste Edgar Wilson Benyon from New Zealand, who for decades toured the world with his own variety show based around his considerable accomplishments. He was followed the next week by a variety bill headed by Troise and his Mandoliers. Pascal Troise, an Italian who founded his ensemble in 1932 (they also appeared as Troise and his Banjoliers), were huge favourites in the 1930s and 1940s amongst those who liked the allegedly Latino-gypsy sounds of mandolins, piano, guitars, banjo, violins and accordion, and were regularly employed on the wireless, particularly in the mid-morning *Music While You Work* slot.

More films followed at the Empire until the middle of June, and thereafter full-time variety, revue and musical comedy became the prominent entertainment. The prices for tickets in April 1947 were front stalls, 4/; centre stalls, 3/-; back stalls, 2/6; dress circle, 4/-; circle, 3/-; and upper circle, 1/6. The management hoped to stage straight plays if theatregoers would support them. Meanwhile, Albert H. Dunlop became the conductor of the Empire pit orchestra.

The wild-eyed, wild-haired Koringa, known as 'the only female Yogi in the world', snake charmer and manipulator of reptiles, came to the Empire in 1947. (She came again in 1951.) Part of her act included rolling herself over a table covered in broken glass, treading with her bare feet on sharp swords, and having a rock on her chest broken by two hefty men wielding sledgehammers. However, she was best known for her work with snakes, alligators and crocodiles. One night, she let go of a young alligator as she pushed it towards the front of the stage, launching it into the Empire's orchestra pit. Jim Mason, one of the musicians, recalled: 'All hell was let loose; the alligator lashed its tail and gnashed its jaws. We didn't hang about. Sheet music went one way and music stands the other. The lady violinist lifted her skirt and cleared the front of the pit. Some of us shot through the trap door and the rest leapt after the violinist. The only exception was pianist Arthur Love, who in true theatre tradition bravely kept the music going until the stagehands managed to catch the alligator, with the aid of a large sack. For the rest of the week, the management ordered all musicians out of the pit during Koringa's act – except for the gallant pianist who played solo with one foot outside the pit, ready to take off.' It was said of Koringa that when on tour, she kept her alligator in a bath at her digs. There were seldom queues for the bathroom.

Rose Haddon was usherette at the Empire between 1948 and 1954. 'Our main jobs were to show people to their seats, sell programmes, and sell ice creams in the intervals. As the tickets in the gods were for unreserved seats and could be bought on the door, we also had to give the tickets out and take the money at the separate box office. This we did twice nightly (or three times on matinée days), and so generally had to be at the theatre between just before six o'clock and just after eleven.

'The seats were red, and the boxes were also decorated in red. Our uniforms were brown with gold buttons and made of heavy serge, which was very hot in the summer. One of the usherettes had a nephew who was a tailor, so she got him to make us some pink and black summer uniforms out of a light material. When the musical *Annie Get Your Gun* came, we usherettes all dressed up as cowgirls. When one of the ice shows played, the ice began to melt early during the last performance and so the orchestra, and their music and instruments got wet.

'Most of the stars gave us signed photographs; the only one who wouldn't was Frankie Howerd. I remember Max Miller, Tessie O'Shea, and Steve Conway, who had a lovely blue suit which he said cost £50. Allan Jones got so drunk on the Tuesday that he slurred his songs badly; his condition had not improved by the next night, so he was sacked, and pianist Winifred Atwell was moved up to top of the bill. Olive, one of the usherettes, volunteered to be hypnotised and duly went under. The next night she was on duty, and when the hypnotist got to that point in his act she went under again, on duty! The manager made her stay away from the auditorium area for the rest of the week. One of my nieces, Sylvia Jefferies, won a prize in the *Carroll Levis Discoveries* (which came to the Empire in 1950 and 1954). This gave her the chance to make a record, but her parents would not let her go to London.'

In 1949, Cedric Green came from Eastbourne, where he had been working for Park Productions as assistant manager at the Hippodrome Theatre, and was house manager at the Empire for a year. He recalled: 'My main duties were responsibility for the front of house staff (usherettes, commissionaires, cleaners, the box office (managed by Mr Todescue), and bar staff. I was responsible for collecting the wages in cash, on foot, from a bank in Regent Street, and for paying show company managers, who in turn paid their artistes. I looked after the visiting companies, billeting artistes from our list of local theatrical digs, checking they were happy with them and, if not find, arranging alternative accommodation. Most of the shows were twice-nightly, but big musicals played only one performance per night, which meant that ticket prices had to be doubled. The audience didn't like this at all.

'There was a circle bar, a stalls bar, which opened out on to Clarence Street and which was open to the public all day, and the artistes' bar, which was under the stage. The safety curtain had to be lowered once during each performance (during the interval). Just before I went there, the Empire acquired a haystack lantern, a glass section of roof that, when operated by a lever, opened at the sides and end so that any flames or smoke would go directly upwards and not engulf the stage.

'When Norman Wisdom came to the Empire, he didn't go into digs but had a caravan, which he parked on any piece of land he could find when touring. Harry Secombe appeared in a show called *Soldiers in Skirts*, but he claimed he didn't know it was a drag show until he started rehearsing it. When the Imperial Opera Company appeared, it required such a large orchestra that three rows of seats had to be taken out of the stalls, and the musicians also used the boxes.

'There were problems when we first mounted a touring ice show because their electrical equipment was not compatible with our power supply, which we did not find out until we had built the ice rink ready to open on the Monday night. The only solution seemed to be to lay a cable from the Whale Bridge sub-station, along the gutter the whole length of Princes Street, and up to the theatre. This work took so long to carry out that there was then insufficient time left to get the ice frozen and ready for the opening performance. In the event, we bought ice from the Swindon Ice Company to assist the freezing, but we had to cancel the Monday performance, let people know through the *Evening Advertiser* and relocate the tickets for the rest of the week.

'The biggest lion we had ever seen came with a circus production. It arrived through the stage door in its own wagon, and stayed in its cage in the theatre for the whole week, roaring and growling. To keep it quiet during the performances, the circus owner's wife sat by the cage, knitting, and stroking the lion's front paws, which were on her lap. One of the chorus girls in another show hung her flimsy costume so close to the very hot dressing room mirror lights that it caught fire. Smoke billowed through the dressing room window, and the fire brigade burst into the auditorium. I quickly ushered them out before there could be any panic in the audience, and redirected them to the alley at the side of the building, from where they rushed into the dressing room and put out the fire.

'Of course, we were always trying to attract larger audiences. We used to go to the surrounding villages and find some well-liked person in the community whom we persuaded to become the theatre's local agent. They sold tickets for the shows, and we arranged coaches to bring people to the theatre and take them home again.'

The late 1940s were the Empire's golden years, when many top artistes of the day came to the theatre, including Vera Lynn, Max Miller, Norman Wisdom, Frankie Howerd, Derek Roy, Bill Kerr and Issy Bonn. Many were radio stars and were publicised as such: Charlie Kunz, 'Radio's Wizard of the Piano', and Suzette Tarri, 'Radio's Comedy Queen', are examples. There were shows such as *Ignorance is Bliss*, featuring its stars Michael Moore, Harold Berens and Gladys Hay, which were all advertised on the strength of their radio success. Later on there were touring 'girlie' shows, which many social commentators believe to have been a cause of so many theatres closing in this period. Yet it was television that had the greatest adverse effect on live theatre. In 1949, some 126,000 were in use; as a result of the Coronation in 1953, the number of sets in the country increased almost overnight from 300,000 to more than three million, and the figure had topped 4,500,000 by 1955. Now that so many people could see moving pictures as well as sound in their own homes, and part of that programming was the very style of variety show being regularly put on at their local provincial theatre, why should they bother to go out for their entertainment?

For the moment, though, the Empire Theatre was forging ahead. Famous names to appear in 1947 were Elsie and Doris Waters (with their characters of 'Gert and Daisy'), Donald Peers, Henry Hall and his Band, Charlie Kunz, and three acts who were to return to the Empire time and time again – Sandy Powell, Harry Lester and his Hayseeds, and Big Bill Campbell.

Arguably the greatest names of all were Laurel and Hardy, who appeared at the Empire for a week's run in September 1947 as part of an extensive tour of the United Kingdom. They and their wives stayed at the Bear Hotel, Hungerford, because no Swindon hotel at the time could offer them en suite accommodation, and from where they were chauffeured to the Swindon theatre at not more than 25 mph, at the behest of Hardy. Hardy's wife was a big woman and she wore rather loud clothes, including a particularly unattractive tartan outfit. Contrary to his on-stage persona, Laurel was the boss of the act. When the pair were on stage, Laurel's wife stood on a side aisle in the auditorium, applauding wildly in order to encourage the audience to do likewise. He was happy to socialise, going afterwards to the artistes' bar in the hospitality suite beneath the stage, but Hardy, when not performing, kept to his dressing room.

Barbara Fuller (the daughter of theatre manager W.S. Bobby) recalled meeting Laurel and Hardy in hospitality, in what she described as 'a sumptuous room – all dark wood, brass fittings and red velvet, and which smelled of cigars'. Stan Laurel shook her hand and made a fuss of her. Hardy just 'harrumphed' and went into his dressing room. Between performances, they retired to their shared dressing room (a small space with just a couch and a large, mirrored dressing table). There they lay, each man with his head on his wife's lap, to enjoy a head massage. Both men were generous to the theatre staff, who were each given a ten shilling tip.

Hardy could sometimes be nice. Carol Rawlins, then aged sixteen, was cycling along Groundwell Road, when she saw the pair about to enter the stage door for a matinée performance, and seized the chance to get their autographs. She was wearing a brooch with her name on it, and Hardy said, 'Carol, that's a purty name', and was very charming about it. She treasured those autographs. Carol later became a member of Swindon Musical Society, appearing in the chorus of *Carmen* in 1950.

The *Evening Advertiser* reporter remarked that the famous duo fully lived up to their reputations as two of the finest comics the cinema screen had ever produced. 'From the first moment that the orchestra strikes up the squeaky little signature tune,' he wrote, 'the audience is in sympathy with the harmless, vacant little Laurel, who is always doing the wrong thing and being picked on by his ponderous chaperone. Here on the stage is that artistry which in the minds of millions all over the world has placed them as the most lovable pair of comedians on the screen. Their sketch, *Getting a Driving License*, in which they are ably assisted by Harry Moreny, provides full scope for their mimicry and will even further endear them to their fans.' This show was presented by Bernard Delfont, later Lord Delfont, who was to become the artistes' booking agent for the Empire, for a period from May 1948, and was one of the most respected theatrical producers of the twentieth century

Bill Bobby's daughter Barbara took her autograph book backstage with her, and has it still; it is dated mainly 1948 and includes the signature of 'Hutch', the pianist and entertainer Leslie Hutchinson, although she thought that her father would not have taken her to meet him had he known of the entertainer's rather disreputable, sexual reputation. In the book, too, are the signatures of the Jerry Allen Trio, Wally Patch, Peggy Cochran, Doug and Eddie Wilcox, Allan Jones, Joey Porter, Ernest Maxim, Ray Johnson, Betty Driver, Terry O'Neill, George Formby, Tommy Trinder and Big Bill Campbell.

Ron Burchell recalled the day in 1948 when Ralph Vaughan Williams attended the production of his opera *Hugh the Drover*, given by the Swindon Musical Society under the direction of H.S. Fairclough. Otherwise known as 'Love in the Stocks', the two-act production was set in the nearby Cotswolds, where the composer was born in the vicarage at Down Ampney. Ron also recounted a concert given at the Empire by the London Philharmonic Orchestra, under the baton of a 'demonstrative Italian conductor'. 'The man waited for complete silence from the large audience before raising his baton, then, as he did so, a latecomer arrived. Seats clattered into the upright position as people stood to allow free passage along the row. The furious conductor turned and glared at the embarrassed offender, and once more waited for complete silence before raising his baton again. We all wanted to roar with laughter.'

Pantomimes took a prominent place in the programming, and continued for the rest of the Empire's life. Each year, there was one home-produced show, starting in December and playing for four weeks, and then another one, playing for two to four weeks. During the run of *Cinderella* in 1950, a child's tricycle was given away at each performance to a three-year old plucked from the audience by Terry O'Neill, in the guise of Buttons. The child had to successfully 'blow out' Rudolph the red-nosed reindeer's electrically illuminated red nose. How the creature had strayed into Cinderella land is one of those idiosyncrasies known only to pantomime writers. That notwithstanding, each chosen child performed to hearty audience encouragement and was always, ultimately, successful.

Amateur productions began again in the post-war period. In 1951, a new society, the Swindon Amateur Light Operatic

Society, known as SALOS, was formed, and presented its first three productions at the Empire. These were *The Arcadians* in 1952, *The Desert Song* in 1953, and *The Vagabond King* in 1954. (This society moved to the Playhouse on the closure of the Empire, and then to the Wyvern Theatre on its opening in1971.)

David Wainwright was a founder member of SALOS. 'I was in the first three shows staged by the society. The Empire at the time was a rather dusty and dirty place, and was rather cramped backstage; in fact, there was less space backstage than at the Playhouse in the Mechanics' Institute. The dressing rooms were on the ground floor, stage left, and opened into the wings. The scenery was brought in stage right; it was not flown in, making it cramped in the wings. Concrete had been laid in the orchestra pit, thereby lifting the orchestra and making it sound very loud. Such were the acoustics, that persons sitting in the dress circle had the unsettling experience of hearing the trumpets, apparently detached from the rest of the orchestra, and coming from behind them. There were no microphones and so the performers really had to project their voices.

'In *The Desert Song*, I had to lead Vera (Vera Bennett, David's wife and leading lady) on to the stage whilst she was sitting on a donkey, which had been fed peppermints. The creature refused to move; other members of the cast tried pushing it, and some scenery got knocked over. The donkey was sacked and replaced by a horse, which behaved itself until the Saturday matinée, when it defecated onstage; Vera, unable to see this, nearly stood in the result. In *The Vagabond King*, Reg Hipperson was coming down the staircase, when part of the scenery began to collapse, and he gallantly sang the song 'Come all ye beggars of France' while holding up the scenery using his sword!'

In 1947, Swindon Musical Society performed *Mlada* by Rimsky-Korsakov at the Empire, the first of several Russian operas that the society performed there with great success. Between Mlada, and 1955, when the society ceased to operate, it staged nine more productions at the Empire: *Hugh the Drover* by Vaughan Williams in 1948; *Sadko* by Rimsky-Korsakov in 1949; Bizet's *Carmen*, and *The Mikado* by Gilbert & Sullivan in 1950; Stanford's *The Travelling Companion* in 1951; *Goyescas* by Granados, and Weill's *Down in the Valley* in 1952; *The Snow Maiden* by Rimsky-Korskov in 1953; and Massanet's *Cinderella* in 1954.

During this period, the Swindon Musical Society's chorus rehearsed in the Drove Road School's hall, and its gymnasium was taken over by the dancers. The soloists, chorus, dancers and orchestra came together for the first time in each case just two days before the show was scheduled to open at the Empire. Monica Trim, a member of the society during this period, recalls how each production was fraught from start to finish. 'Mr Fairclough was always late in informing us which productions were to be performed, which led to sudden, very intense rehearsals. Scenery came from professional suppliers, and our costumes from Sadler's Wells. Then, alterations to the routines were commonly made at the very last moment, when everyone got together. The audience on the opening night (Monday) was always made up of children from various schools, accompanied by their teachers, and this was regarded as the final dress rehearsal. Then we played the week to packed houses, and usually to the highest praise, even by critics from London.'

Suzette Tarri, Stanelli and Les Allen, stars of a variety show put on at the Empire in April 1947, were broadcast live between 7.30 p.m. and 8 p.m. one evening, from the studios at Bristol. A report in the *Evening Advertiser* described this event: 'At three o'clock in the afternoon, everyone assembled for the 'balancer test', fitting the ribbon microphones in position under the supervision of Roy Furneaux, the BBC engineer. The three stars are all experienced broadcasters and cooperated while Hamilton Kennedy, the producer, ruthlessly slashed minutes off of their scripts. The theatre was only lit by a few working lights during the hour this work took, but everyone was satisfied and the orchestra was fitted in. Meanwhile a GPO engineer had fitted the telephone lines direct to the Bristol studios to be tested thirty minutes before the broadcast began.

'The assembly broke up and Bill Bobby, the theatre manager, and his assistant worked on the programme which had to be broken into bits and pieces to fit the three stars acts into one half hour. Just before 7.30, Kennedy walked onto the stage and explained to the waiting audience the procedure for the evening and soon after the broadcast began and went smoothly and with perfect timing. The stars kept to their allotted time slots and finished right on time. Everyone was happy with the broadcast, but it was not known that Suzette Tarri had a bad throat and was not able to speak during the rehearsal as she was saving her voice for the broadcast. However the estimated timing of her act proved accurate and she finished her act right on time. She closed the show by singing 'Red Sails in the Sunset'.

Big names who trod the boards of the Empire in 1948 included Betty Driver, Tommy Trinder, Winifred Atwell, 'Hutch', George Formby, Wee Georgie Wood, Allan Jones, Martha Raye, and Arthur Lucan and Kitty McShane. The shows consisted of variety, revues, and musical comedies such as *Me and My Girl*; plays, including *Worms Eye View*; two drag show, *Soldiers in Skirts* and *Forces Showboat* (with a young Harry Secombe); and one circus.

The posters for Allan Jones described him as 'the world-famous singing star of stage, screen and radio … always remembered for his rendering of 'Donkey Serenade', direct from his successful appearance at the London Casino'. The *Evening Advertiser* critic reported: 'Topping the bill is Allan Jones, whose powerful tenor voice was enthusiastically acclaimed. He sang songs from his films, and included the famous 'Donkey Serenade'. The audiences were loath to let him go, and after giving a couple of encores the star gave a graceful speech of thanks and paid tribute to his accompanist, Len Edwards and the Empire Orchestra under Mr Albert Dunlop'.

Allan Jones did not go sober to the Empire, and the singer proved to be difficult. The local press reported the rumour that he had become 'unwell' before his performance, causing the manager to appear and inform the audience that Jones would be unable to take to the stage. According to the late Reg Cole, who was there at the time, Bill Bobby was so fed up with the intoxicated star that he decided to tell the truth. 'I won't tell any lies,' he informed the audience, 'but Allan Jones is back- stage, paralytic drunk and can't appear. Anyone who wants their money back, please go to the cash desk.' Reg could not remember anyone taking up this offer. Jones was taken out of the show for the rest of its run at the Empire. Bernard Delfont, who presented the singer on his English tour, described him as 'unreliable', and the pianist Winifred Atwell was advanced up the bill to take his place. 'Her repertoire,' said the press, 'is remarkable in its versatility,' adding that 'with flashing eyes and broad engaging smile, she played rhythm in the boogie-woogie style, and then received the tribute of complete silence while rendering Greig's Piano Concerto.' She became a great star on television, and returned to the Empire on several occasions.

Indeed, many of the stars who played the Empire, such as the attractive slapstick comedy artiste Martha Raye, liked to drink rather more alcohol than was good for them. Raye had a wonderful figure, wore no underclothes, and had to be zipped into her figure-hugging dresses. Another of her assets was her large mouth, which she emphasised in her work. Barbara Fuller recalled how Martha Raye arrived drunk at a party at the manager's house in Shrivenham Road, completely missed the sofa, and landed on the floor.

The giant Lofty was exhibited at the theatre in November 1948, in the revue *Would You Believe It*, hardly very different from the type of display shown at seaside freak shows. Lofty was 9ft 3½ inches tall, and the same bill included an armless man who 'uses his feet with greater dexterity than most people use their hands', mentioned the *Evening Advertiser*, 'and to crown it all a slip of a girl romps with a lion'. The paper wrote very conservatively, if at some length, of this production. 'From the first turn a bizarre atmosphere is set. Fredel, a man made up like a tailor's dummy, stalks the stage in such a rigid manner that it is hard to believe he is really alive. Elroy, the armless wonder, fires a rifle, plays a trumpet, and draws pictures, all with his feet. In appearance, Crochet looks, comparatively speaking, an ordinary person, but there is nothing ordinary in the way he plays seven different musical instruments. Bespaly describes his partner as an 'unbreakable doll'. He hurls her around the stage, and all through she retains the limpness of a rag doll. Pete Collins, the promoter, next parades Lofty for the customers' amazement. The giant, who weighs over 26 stones, mixes with the audience and standing in the stalls shakes hands with people in the circle. Pippi, a midget, is an excellent foil for the giant's height. Just when the imagination is becoming sluggish with all the unusual sights, Ellen Harvey, the young lion tamer, comes on to stagger it again.'

In 1949, Albert Dunlop left, and the baton of the Empire's pit orchestra was taken up by Thomas Coxon, known as 'Tim'. More stars appeared at the Empire that year, some of whom were Max Miller, Frankie Howerd, Norman Wisdom, Vera Lynn, Billy Cotton, Tessie O'Shea, Elsie and Doris Waters, and Vic Oliver. Several musical comedies were staged, including *The Dancing Years* and *No, No, Nanette*; a circus came, there was an ice show, and a week of opera was presented by the Imperial Opera Company, who performed five different productions. Phyllis Dixey, the well-known striptease artiste, appeared for the first time, and Hughie Green presented his *Opportunity Knocks* at the Empire.

One section of society who particularly appreciated Miss Dixey were the lads of the Royal Army Pay Corps, who were at the time undertaking their National Service, and stationed at Devizes. One of these lads was Albert Morgan, whose father had been (c1914-36) a devotee of Collins Music Hall in Islington, London, and in wartime at the Hackney Empire. Dixey's *Peek-a-Boo* of 1949 was Albert's one and only visit to the Empire Theatre in Swindon, and he remembered how information about her forthcoming appearance 'went round the camp faster than a rookie's response to a drill sergeant's order.' A couple of coaches were booked (each National Service soldier's pay at that time was four shillings per day), stalls tickets were bought, as was just one programme. This was put in possession of a lance corporal seated at the end of the row, who was charged with indicating when the femme fatale was about to appear. When she did, said Albert, she was 'sideways on, and looking like Britannia on the back of a penny, and about as microscopic'. He thought the fan dance was an anti-climax: 'the wafting and caressing only excited the multi-coloured fans.

'Soon the agony and the ecstasy were over and the virgin soldiers piled into the coaches. The sole topic of conversation on the journey back to Devizes was whether or not Phyllis had been wearing a body stocking. Back in the barrack room, it was all too much for the lance corporal, who wearily threw down the much-thumbed programme. 'Pass me *No Orchids for Miss Blandish*', he muttered.' The reference to this book is interesting. It was written by James Hadley Chase, and published in 1939; in the 1960s, it was described, citing 'unreliable authorities', as being the novel 'most appreciated by the troops' during the war. It has been said that, although slated by the critics, the book's popularity with servicemen and the public derived from the way it mirrored, on a more domestic scale, the widespread belief in the enemy's potential for atrocities. By 1942, Chase had adapted his own book for the stage (which was similarly harangued by the critics for its content), and a version of this had played at the Empire Theatre in March 1948, the same year as the first film version (also lambasted for its violence) was released.

The pantomime in December 1949 was *Mother Goose*, with Albert Grant. Marlene Adams, née Jones, recalled this show. 'I was about twelve years old, enjoyed dancing, and had some lessons with Yvonne Sutton, a local teacher, when I saw an advertisement in the *Evening Advertiser* for an open audition for pantomime dancers at the Empire Theatre. When I arrived late at a hall in Old Town, with my brother Stan for support, a lot of girls were there, all already dressed in dancing outfits. The two blonde women from London who were running the auditions told me to do a solo tap dance in my tap shoes, and another in my ballet shoes. I did have some ballet shoes, but no experience of dancing ballet, and so I just flitted from one side of the room to the other, wondering why I had bothered to come.

'At the end of the session, the ladies called out twelve names, of which mine was one. One of them put her hand on my head and said all the girls would have to have their hair cut in a fringe just like mine. Some of the mothers were a bit disgruntled but the choreographers said that anyone who didn't wish to comply with this plan should speak now and the girls would be replaced. No one did. They said they would provide red pleated skirts and yellow blouses for rehearsals, and we would also have to go to London for further rehearsals, wearing camel coats and red pillbox hats, with 'Graham Nelson Juveniles' printed on the hats, but we would have to pay for them. My mum bought a camel coat from Morse's department store in Regent Street, and paid for it weekly. I remember we earned one guinea per week for the run of the show and most of our rehearsals took place above the White House pub in Swindon. We were called the Twelve Little Sisters in the show. I can well remember going up some iron stairs to our dressing room. My family saw the show from a box that was hired by a friend of the family.

'After a month at the Empire, the show played Folkestone for another few weeks. At first my family did not want me to go, but relented after the choreographer assured them that there would be schooling and a chaperone. We stayed in a nice boarding house. I loved dancing and my time in the pantomime at the Empire. However it was the only real stage dancing I did because soon I met the young man I was to marry and together we developed a love for ballroom dancing and eventually taught Ballroom and Latin American for many years.'

Musical comedies featured heavily in the Empire's programme for 1950. These included *Careless Rapture*, *The Student Prince* and two weeks of *Annie get Your Gun* and *Bless the Bride*. Plays included *Charley's Aunt* and several that were termed 'adult' plays. *White Cargo* made another appearance in Swindon, as did *No Trees in the Street* and *A Woman Desired*. Variety stars included Max Miller and Old Mother Riley, and other productions included a midget show, *Midget Town Marvels* and Prince's International Circus. There were also several Sunday concerts at the end of the year. The Squadronaires came with Roy Edwards, The Quads and Firth Arthur; Ted Heath and His Band performed with Jack Parnell on drums, and featured singers Lita Rosa, Denis Lotis, and Dickie Valentine. Tito Burns and his Sextet with Terry Devon rounded off the year.

Seven novelty acts were put together in 1950 for *Seeing is Believing*, a 'show of surprises and sensations'. The star of the show was a twenty-four-year-old escapologist and magician named Alan Alan (who would later became one of the luminaries of the genre, have a long career in magic, and be honoured by the Magic Circle). Only the previous year, he had been lucky to escape with his life when his suspended burning rope trick went wrong, and he had also been in difficulties on another occasion when buried alive. At the Empire, Alan performed a variation of the rope trick when 'vivid wheals and bruises on his skin afterwards indicated that the chaining (by members of the audience) had been done in no half-hearted manner'. But this was all grist to the publicity machine that was Alan Alan, who revelled in the knowledge that his act was so potentially dangerous that he had 'twice recently been in hospital as the result of his exploits'.

On the same bill were the Knife Throwing Denvers, who were the first act of the type ever to appear on television when they took part in test programmes from Alexandra Palace in the 1930s. They excited the Empire's audience with their blazing hatchets routine. Prince Kari-Kari and his African company demonstrated fire eating and danced on broken glass; Ladd West performed as a contortionist; and Regina Maida juggled, using her feet. The American Spitfires rode their miniature-engined motor cycles 'in breathtaking speeds' around a tiny bowl-shaped, slatted track on the stage. *Seeing is Believing* also marked the return to the Empire of 'continental artiste' Fredel, the human dummy. Xylophone player Reggie Dennis, and comedian Al Marshall gave some lighter relief to this otherwise stressful show.

W.S. Bobby had suffered increasingly poor health since the war, and had contracted tuberculosis. He left the theatre in April 1949, when his place was taken by Handel P. Evans, who remained as manager until Thomas E. Casey took over in July 1950. Meanwhile, Bobby was being treated for the disease in the Winsley Sanatorium for Consumptives, near Bath, where he was admitted in June 1949. He had sufficiently recovered to resume his role at the theatre in November 1950, but was to be back for less than a year.

One notable production at the Empire in 1950 was the *Battle of Britain Week Festival*, compered by David Jacobs, and which starred the soprano Lena Walker, 'fresh from her American and Canadian tour'. 'Her voice', said the over-enthusiastic reviewer, 'was reminiscent of Gracie Fields at her zenith and with perhaps more power.' At one point, she sang 'It's A Lovely Day' with interim theatre manager Tom Casey. Mezzo-soprano Nellie Stanton and baritone Reg Hipperson (a prime talent on the amateur music scene in the town at the time) also sang, and most of the other performers were local amateurs. The British Rail Veterans' Choir were singled out for a rendition of 'Grandfather's Clock' which 'nearly brought the house down'; Donald Wood, stationed at RAF Yatesbury, but lately of the Yorkshire Boy's

Concert Choir, performed on the piano; and the RAF Yatesbury Military Band 'were in excellent form'.

Hal Monty was another radio and stage comedian who achieved modest success during the 1940s, made a couple of films, and appeared at the Empire in 1950. He had formerly operated as a variety double act with Bernard Delfont, before the latter turned impresario, and it was Delfont's agency that supplied many of the performers to the Empire in its later years. By the time he arrived at the Empire, Monty was very much a 'Workers' Playtime' radio comic, and although much was made of this association in his publicity, he was never a true top-of-the-bill act. Indeed, this was the kind of turn that gave the Empire the reputation of being on the 'B circuit', as far as performers were concerned. Monty's show at Swindon was *Skimpy Goes to Paris*, which was based around his character, Skimpy Carter, whom he reprised in his films. He also fleshed out his act by making animal shapes with balloons, and presenting these to a number of children who were invited on to the stage.

By the late 1940s, there were early indications that Park Productions was in financial trouble. There was little money to pay the artistes working at the Empire, and the standards of cleanliness were low. One eye-witness account described the time when people in the audience were stamping on the floor in time with the music during a concert by Tito Burns and his band on Christmas Eve 1950, and the dust was so bad that 'we could hardly see the stage'. The place was rapidly acquiring a reputation for dampness, and for unspecified but pungent smells. Cleaning staff were cut to a minimum, and Bill Bobby was reduced to going around the auditorium and spraying it with disinfectant and essence of gardenia.

Bobby also tried to compensate for the lack of money by mounting shows with fewer professional performers, and a good deal more audience participation. People were invited on to the stage to compete against each other, and some of the shows consisted entirely of amateur acts. Bill Bobby resigned his post at the Empire Theatre in October 1951, and was replaced by Albert J. Matthews. The following year, Bobby moved to Devizes, where he became manager of the Regal Cinema, and later the Palace Cinema. He retired in 1975 when the Palace became part-cinema, part-bingo hall, but he later returned to manage the venue on a part-time basis. He died in 1978, in Devizes.

# 7
# *Naked to the end*

A NUMBER OF SUPPORTING performers at the Empire were accommodated in the homes of Swindon residents. Two of these were Joan and Jeff Haynes, who lived at 40 Princes Street with their daughter. The family kept a visitors' book between July 1951 and November 1952 (although they continued to take theatrical lodgers after that), in which the boarders wrote comments about the food and accommodation. The daughter, Jackie Hussey, remembered that her family received complimentary tickets to see the shows from the gods, where the roof leaked to such a degree that those sitting there wore their raincoats when it rained. At the house, she recalled, 'The lodgers, usually two and sometimes three at a time, had the upstairs double bedroom and the front room, which was known as the sitting room. Mum gave them a late breakfast, and often supplied supper as well. The Snow family came quite regularly; Cyril Snow, his wife and daughter were in *Red Riding Hood* at the Empire in 1951. I remember the Indian Rubber Man, who brought some other members of the cast back for a party and entertained everyone with his act. When some dwarfs stayed, dad had to extend the toilet chain for them to reach.'

Puppeteers Paul and Peta Page stayed with the Haynes family, and wrote in the book: 'Thank you Mrs Haynes for a spotlessly clean and well-cooked week. Kindest regards'. Betty Lotinga, who played Dick in *Dick Whittington* in 1952, was more expansive. Her entry read: 'Mere words cannot express my gratitude to dear Joan and Jeff for all they have done for me and mine during the four happy weeks I have spent at no 40 Princes St., especially for the care and attention they have bestowed on my small son, Fabian, who was thrust on them at a moment's notice, and without any warning whatsoever. I hope we may all (Max included) have the pleasure of returning on some future occasion. Once again my heartfelt thanks (not forgetting wee Jacqueline), Joan and Jeff. And wishing you all the very best of luck always.'

Stars who played the Empire during 1951 included Reg Dixon, G.H. Elliott, Arthur English, Reg Varney, Charlie Chester and The Four Ramblers, who included Val Doonican. This was the year when the striptease or saucy girlie shows began to be regular bill of fare, with titles such as *Pardon my French*, *Strike a Nude Note*, *Ladies be Good* and *Why go to Paris*. Many of the other shows were variety and revues, but there were very few plays or musical comedies, and the Ambassador Ballet made the only appearance of its kind.

The 1951 pantomime was *Little Red Riding Hood*, which included the first appearance of Swindon's Mollie Tanner Dancers (then named the Tanwood Juveniles) on stage at the Empire in a professional show. Thus her Tanwood School of Dancing began performing there in pantomimes, later transferring to the Wyvern Theatre after it opened in Swindon in 1971. The dancing school also performed in other towns. The first Empire date came about when Harry Lester, who was directing *Little Red Riding Hood* and starring in it, asked for 'sixteen Swindon sweethearts' who could dance in the show that starred himself and his Hayseeds. Earlier that year, Mollie had hired the Empire to put on a dancing show to raise money for the families of the sailors who had died when the Royal Naval submarine 'Affray' had been sunk. The show made £53 for the cause, a considerable amount in those days, and Bill Bobby realised she and her girls would suit Harry Lester.

Early in 1952, Tim Coxon handed over the role of musical director at the Empire to Charlie Comley. After the Empire closed, Comley became the musical director for shows such as *The Quaker Girl*, *Carmen*, *The Merry Widow*, and *Showboat*, staged at the Playhouse.

The stars of 1952 included Max Wall, Billy Cotton, Arthur Lucan (Old Mother Riley), Elsie and Doris Waters, Anne Shelton, Dorothy Squires and Eddie Calvert. There were also some more girlie shows; a circus came, and so did a midget show. A young Julie Andrews appeared with Alfred Marks and Naunton Wayne in a revue entitled *Look In* during March 1952. The *Evening Advertiser* reporter noted '... she is a coloratura soprano of wide range and superb diction. It was an enchanting moment when this sweet, sixteen year old girl, so pretty in yellow taffeta, with a blue ribbon in her hair, brought a depth of feeling to Gounod's 'Ave Maria', adding prophetically, 'one felt she would become a great star'.

Chris Viveash (now a Jane Austen expert, and author of a book about her friend, *James Stanier Clarke, Librarian to the Prince Regent*), recalled his first lone visit to the Empire in the summer of 1952. 'I became aware that a touring company was about to present *The Maid of the Mountains*, and had heard it was a colourful show with bandits and gypsies and any amount of lovely songs. It was not the same as a pantomime, which was principally for children, but was a grown-up performance with a sensible story. We lived in Old Town, and the theatre was at the bottom of the main hill in New Swindon, but I assured my mother that this presented no problem to a nine-year-old boy who was perfectly capable of getting to the Wednesday matinée on his own. Mother scraped together the cost of the ticket, and I went down to the theatre to book one of the seats that were high up in the gods.

'Then, in my excitement, I inadvertently ripped the prized ticket! Mother calmly found a blank postcard and glued the Empire ticket (sadly jig-sawed with torn edges) and instructed me to present myself to the lady at the box office and explain what a foolish child I was. This I duly did, and the kind soul in her little window scrawled on it 'OK Bert', or some such indication to the man who was collecting tickets on the door.

'The auditorium seemed so high; the fire safety curtain with its painted advertisements for local firms emblazoned in bright hues made a fine glow beneath the level of the balcony. Eventually it was raised to reveal the house-curtains bathed in warm lighting, looking most glamorous. The small touring orchestra filtered into the pit, and the fiddles began to be tuned to the great wonder and suppressed delight of this small boy. Then, a blast of the overture from the musicians, and the curtain rose to reveal a rocky mountain-scape setting, peopled by handsome robbers and rather louche young women, all posed in brazen and suggestive ways with hands on hips, and fingering cigarellos.

'It was all vastly entertaining, and the songs so sensibly fitted the action, in contrast to the sing-along form of the pantomime, which I was more used to. One thing intrigued me, though; the rocks which the men bravely climbed with their ill-gotten contraband were in fact steps with painted cut-outs nailed on to imitate natural rocks. This worried me because I could see it, but wondered whether patrons in the stalls would think they were real rocks and perhaps be misled. Such were the thoughts of a boy who had never thought through the principles of stage design. The show was most absorbing, and was to my mind a great improvement on anything I had seen before. I felt that I had somehow grown up by attending an adult show all on my own.'

L. Durban-Long became the theatre manager at the Empire in June 1952, just before the theatre closed for several weeks in the summer. In early autumn, an advertisement appeared in the *Evening Advertiser* for the production of *Godiva Goes Gay*, which stated, 'The theatre is now under new control'. According to the *Wiltshire Herald and Advertiser*, the theatre was again under the direct control of the Mayfair Circuit, the lessees since 1943 and the organisation that had run it as a cinema until 1947 when Park Theatrical Productions took over the lease for the presentation of live shows. The transfer took place just as Park Theatrical Productions gave up their lease on the Pleasure Gardens, Folkestone, which had also returned to the direct control of its lessees, South Coast Pleasure Gardens Ltd, an associate company of the Mayfair Circuit. Walter Elcock, who was chairman of the Mayfair Circuit and the South Coast Pleasure Gardens Ltd, was also chairman of Park Theatrical Productions until he resigned on the transfer of these two theatres back to his control. A. J. Matthews continued as general manager of the Empire Theatre at Swindon. The paper reported that the registered office of the Mayfair Circuit, which had been at 140 Park Lane, London, the same address as the office of Park Theatrical Productions, was in the process of being registered at the Empire Theatre in Swindon. A spokesman for Park Theatrical Productions explained that the transfer of the Empire was 'not a financial transaction' and said that it did not indicate any change of policy in regard to the venue, which would continue as a live theatre.

The programmes of this period remained silent on exactly who owned the theatre. By Christmas, Matthews was listed as Licensee and General Manager, and he wrote in the back of the programme asking for the audience's support. 'Our bookings in the future will be of a very high-class nature,' he informed the public, 'but I ask your support to enable me to continue booking good shows. A monthly programme will be posted to you every month if you will please leave your name and address with any of my usherettes.' The pantomime at the Empire in 1952 again included Mollie Tanner's Juveniles. It was notable for the waterfall in Jimmy Currie's Amazing Aquatic Spectacle, which flooded the orchestra pit.

Ralph Birch Productions, which ran the Pleasure Gardens at Folkestone, took over the management of the Empire at the beginning of 1953. The company told the *Evening Advertiser* that it intended to make the Swindon theatre a number one touring date. Birch aimed to confine the Empire's bookings to pre-London productions, and immediate post-London successes with their original West End casts. He added that if he could not get first-class productions, he would produce them himself, and to this end he had bought several new plays. His policy was to intersperse straight plays with occasional first-class musicals and bring the biggest theatrical names to Swindon. But that, he warned, would depend on the support of Swindon theatregoers. The first programme with Ralph Birch's name on was *Fred Karno's Army*.

L. Durban-Long was made supervisor of Ralph Birch Entertainments Ltd, whose portfolio included the Empire at Swindon; he left the town and was succeeded at the Empire by C. Hamiliton Doak, who came to Swindon from Wimbledon. Sunday night concerts in the summer brought Sid Phillips and his Band with Denny Dennis and Jill Allen; and Billy Daniels with Cab Kaye & his Famous Coloured Orchestra.

Towards the end of 1953, eleven straight plays were presented, including *The Housemaster*, *The Dominant Sex* and *Worms Eye View*. Well-known actors who appeared in them included William Kendall, Frank Lawton, Jack Hulbert and Jimmy Hanley. There were musical comedies such as *Oklahoma* and *King's Rhapsody*; and concerts were given by Nat Gonella and his Georgians, the Western Brothers, 'Wee' Georgie Wood, Diana Dors and Rose Murphy (the Brr Brr girl). There were also some more 'girlie' shows, including *Naughty, Naughty, The Sauciest Girls of 1953* and *Front Page Lovelies of 1953*.

By now, the Empire was limping towards its end; so too, was the Playhouse in the Mechanics' Institute. It had been run professionally by the Swindon Repertory Company Limited, who leased the theatre.

By 1953, work needed to be carried out on the fixtures and fittings, but there were insufficient funds. Publicity had been restricted for months, and the company relied on volunteers to operate its front of house. Goodwill was waning. The directors needed to raise £1,000 immediately to avoid closure, and applied for an Arts Council grant. The Arts Council made it a condition of its interest that the company had the support of the local authority. Early in 1954, Swindon Corporation landed the killer punch on the Playhouse: it refused to grant any aid from the rates. The Swindon Repertory Company mounted its last production at the Mechanics' Institute at the end of January, and went into voluntary liquidation. Most of the professional actors and actresses returned to London.

This blow came at a time when several of the long-standing services at the Mechanics' Institute, such as the library and the reading room facilities, were also in decline. Revenues had fallen, and the Institute could not afford to let its theatre remain idle; it advertised the Playhouse for lease in the theatrical press, but had no takers.

The Council of the Mechanics' Institute held talks with F. L. Parker, licensee and general manager of the Majestic Ballroom, a rather pompous name for the public swimming baths on those intermittent occasions when they were covered over and made available for dances. He was not interested in operating a theatre, but was prepared to hold dances there. The Mechanics' Institute paid £548 to remove the sloping floor of the auditorium, expose the original floor beneath, and make it suitable for dancing. That done, Parker took on the tenancy of the Playhouse for three years, to operate the venue as a ballroom. Its name was changed to The Regal, and it opened in 1954. Once again, the Empire had Swindon all to itself in the matter of professional theatre, but, in the event, proved unable to take advantage of the potential this presented.

The last full year of the Empire Theatre was 1954, a year of mixed fortunes, with seats selling at between two shillings and four shillings. The 'girlie' shows continued. *Honky-Tonk*, 'The Burlesque Leg Show' featured dancer Sheila Atha, and 'The Britvic Lovelies', and marked the beginning of the career of now veteran performers Jimmy and Brian Patton. Amongst others of the genre were *We Couldn't Wear Less*, *Why Cover Girls* (which featured international cover girl Coral 'The Body' Gaye, who went on to star in Paul Raymond productions), *Girl Show*, *Follies of Montmartre*, and *Fluff and Nonsense*, which featured some dancers called 'The Fluffettes'. The patrons of *Shapes and Surprises* were treated to 'the exotic Marlene', who posed naked; and then fan-dance queen Phyllis Dixey returned with her 'genteel stripping' in another *Peek-a-Boo*. Some way above all of this mediocre nudity was Paul Raymond's *Paris After Dark*, the 'French African, Latin Quarter' revue, which toured the country, and which also came to Swindon in 1954. It featured 'The Native Mating Dance', 'Art Studies from the Harlem Night Clubs of Paris' and 'The Reefer Dance'. It must have sounded very exotic to Swindonians in 1954.

This kind of show was not exclusive to Swindon's Empire, of course; a rash of young, naked women spread around the provincial theatres in the 1950s, as managers tried desperately to revive their flagging fortunes by forsaking the family audiences in the hope of appealing mostly to men. Ultimately, it failed, and it has been said that the 'girlie' show concept actually accelerated the demise of so many of the venues that presented it. The sad fact is, the British have never done nude entertainment well, and certainly not with the kind of verve, sparkle, gaiety and lightness of spirit that characterises the way naked bodies are presented elsewhere in the world. They still do not, but in the 1950s, nudity was a sordid, inhibited pastime, wooden in its execution. The draconian censorship laws then pertaining, concerning what naked women could and could not do on stage, did nothing to alleviate this. At best, they were trundled around on moveable podiums, and the different coloured lights that flickered around their flesh, in the hands of experienced lighting assistants, could suggest an element of movement where none in reality occurred. The experiment in on-stage, revue-style nudity really failed because it was necessarily so controlled that it was badly and boringly done. Even the male audiences got fed up with it.

Midgets frequently appeared on the stage at the Empire, usually as one element in an act, invariably presented as a caricature of themselves; they were almost always the subject of comical abuse at the hands of other members of the act who were not vertically challenged. However, the greatest concentration of little people came to the Swindon theatre in 1954 in the shape of Burton Lester's (World Famous) Midgets, which featured Henry Behrens, who was then officially the smallest man alive. There were about forty in the ensemble, including Gloria and her educated dogs; clowns, singers, dancers, a violinist, an accordion player, and Roulette – 'The Human Top'. Hetty Mack, 'the midget granny', sang comedy songs, Ann Day did impersonations, and a miniature Wee Jock McGregor performed as 'Will Fyffe'. The production enabled the Empire to once again show off its ability to mount lighted water spectacles, in Cooper's Festival Fountains.

Several all-male shows were presented at the Empire in 1954, including *Soldiers in Skirts* and *Call us Mister*; there was variety with Stan Stennett, and Sid Millward and the Nitwits, and the Four Ramblers made a return visit. After Phyllis Dixey, the theatre closed for three months, then reopened in October with the play *Affairs of State,* by Louis Verneuil. This was followed by several other plays, including *Dial M for Murder, Someone Waiting* and *The Little Hut*, all recent West End hits. By now, Alan Crooks had become the resident manager at the Empire. He initiated a series of big band concerts, and, over the winter months, Swindon's music lovers were treated to Eric Winstone and his Orchestra, Frank Weir and his Orchestra with singer Denny Dennis, Freddie Randall and his Band, and Teddy Foster and his Band.

The pantomime *Robinson Crusoe*, which featured Joyce Golding, Dorothy Black, Leslie Sarony and Afrique, proved to be the last production ever to play the Empire Theatre, although the first-night audience had no idea of the difficulties into which it was about to run. The pantomime opened on 27 December 1954, but it soon became apparent that the members of the company were not going to be paid their full wages. When the interval curtain came down one night, they threatened to walk out; hurried talks took place, and the audience remained in their seats wondering why the curtain had not risen on the second half. They became restless and began to sing 'Why Are We Waiting'. After a long delay, the pantomime was resumed, but further negotiations took place afterwards and the artistes were persuaded to stay and continue the run only after representatives of Equity and the Variety Artists Federation intervened, coming to Swindon to broker a special contract with Alan Crooks guaranteeing that Ralph Birch would pay his full share of the expenses and wages. Crooks also gave the cast free rail tickets back to London. The contract specified that wages and other pantomime expenses would be shared between Ralph Birch and John D Robertson Ltd, the management presenting the show, and the free rail tickets fulfilled Robertson's part of the guarantee. Birch also agreed to waive certain dues, and agreed deductions such as those for the hire of scenery and performing right fees. *Robinson Crusoe* ran until January 22nd 1955. Reg Swinson, the General Secretary of the VAF was in Swindon when the company left, to ensure that all conditions were met.

The outgoing pantomime was to be followed two days later for a short season by *Aladdin*, which had been playing at Folkestone, with Empire favourites Albert Grant and Renee Beck. The Swindon production of *Robinson Crusoe* was scheduled to replace *Aladdin* at Folkestone, where there had also been some financial irregularities. It was also revealed that, as a result of rate claims in 1954, Swindon Corporation had successfully petitioned an order for the compulsory winding-up of Ralph Birch Entertainments Ltd, made in the Chancery Division by Mr Justice Vaisey.

*Aladdin* was the show that never opened at the Empire. The disputes and problems behind the scenes at each theatre, both of which were controlled by associate companies, of which Ralph Birch was the managing director. In Swindon, Alan Crooks was told by letter that the *Aladdin* company and scenery would arrive by road on the Sunday before the show was due to open. He, and the theatre staff, waited at the theatre all Sunday afternoon while Mollie Tanner, whose pupils were the dancers in the show, rehearsed her girls for the show that would never open.

Suddenly the bomb dropped. Mollie was told by Dorothy Rice, former secretary and now the assistant manager, to get her costumes out by 5.30 or they could be seized. Crooks announced that *Aladdin* would not be playing, and that around £500 of advance bookings would have to be returned. He also gave a provisional week's notice to the thirty-seven people who made up the theatre's staff and the pit orchestra, dependent on whether another production could be found. Mollie Tanner was the last performer to leave the stage of the Empire Theatre; no other production ever took place there. The premises were locked up, and soon began to look bleak and forlorn.

Over the previous three decades, several different companies had been involved in running the business side of the theatre, and the day-to-day management had passed through a number of hands. But who actually owned the bricks and mortar? The answer was Jack Gladwin, now retired and living in Brighton. In 1955, he placed the sale of the building into the hands of Swindon estate agent and property entrepreneur Peter Long. The *Evening Advertiser* reported that the leasehold of the building was up for sale for £10,000. Peter Long held discussions with various London theatre managements, who were of the opinion that the Empire had a very remote chance of succeeding in the future as a live theatre. That being the case, he set about trying to find a sponsor who would be willing to convert the building into a ballroom and general entertainment venue. Long wanted to form a company to take it on, and thought that an additional £10,000 would be needed to carry out the extent of the conversion needed to make it a going concern. He also calculated that as a dance and music hall it would have running costs of about £300 per week, and an income of about £500 per week. The total outlay of £20,000 would put the building on its feet, would be the basis for a solid business venture, and could prove to be an asset to the town. The solution would be an individual or company backer willing to either buy the building outright or take on the funding for his idea. Peter Long also thought it might be possible to form a company and sell 20,000 shares at £1 each. Suddenly, he abandoned the idea as being too expensive. Matters were back at square one.

Towards the end of October 1955, Viciris, who had been the under-lessees of the Arcadia Picture Palace in Swindon since 1933, expressed an interest in buying the Empire. The previous month, the company had applied to renew its lease of the Arcadia, but this had met with opposition from Morses Limited, the Swindon department store, who were the landlords of the property. If Viciris was going to have problems with its Regent Street premises, and even if that matter were to be satisfactorily resolved, the Empire would be a good venue to have under its wing. Peter Long announced that Viciris, if successful, would return the Empire to a cinema; work on altering and renovating the place could begin almost at once, and he expected the cinema to open early in 1956. Mr Long said that his idea had been to sell the freehold of the Empire to Swindon Town Council. He disclosed that the cinema group The Odeon Circuit had expressed an interest in buying the former town hall in Regent Circus, the property of the local authority, which he felt the council could have sold to them for £100,000, using around £30,000 of the money to buy the Empire. In council hands, it could have become part of the cultural life of Swindon, incorporated into the whole area of libraries and arts centres, and thereby run under the auspices of the Swindon Libraries, Museums & Arts Committee. The council was not interested; the Viciris deal fell through.

In April 1956, Jack Gladwin successfully applied to Swindon Council to use the site for a variety of purposes other than that of a theatre, and instructed Harold Loveday of the Swindon firm of auctioneers, Loveday and Loveday, to inform prospective buyers that the site could be used for showrooms with offices, with or without flats above; for a block of flats; as a restaurant and/or ballroom; or as a block of offices or shops with offices and/or flats above. Mr Gladwin was prepared to sell the freehold 'at a suitable price' and revealed he could have sold the premises on many occasions, but they were still leased to Elcock of Park Productions. He added that he was hoping to make a move soon and would still like to see the Empire re-open as a theatre. A notice appeared outside the building stating that it was to be auctioned by Loveday and Loveday on 21 November 1956, at the Goddard Arms Hotel, High Street, Old Town.

Jack Gladwin attended the sale. He wanted to be rid of the place, but no-one was prepared to pay even the low reserve of £7,000 that had been set to reflect this. Fortunately, Harold Loveday's notes, made on the day, reveal that immediately after the failed auction, he was approached privately, and the building changed hands for the reserve price. Exactly who the buyer was remains a mystery, but, in August 1957, Haverstock Investments Limited, property developers and London finance company, registered the freehold of 'The Empire Theatre, Swindon, Wilts.' with H.M. Land Registry. Then, for a while, they did nothing with it.

In February 1959, the *Wiltshire Gazette & Herald* reported that H. Harris, a director of Haverstock Investments Limited, had bought the building and the site, revealed that the theatre would be pulled down in the 'very near future', and that shops and offices were to be built on the land. There would be ground-floor shops, including a loading bay, and two or three floors of offices above. Harris believed the new building would be completed and ready for occupation within a year. Demolition of the Empire by Clarke Brothers of Swindon began on 16 March 1959, when workmen started to remove slates and rafters from the roof. The whole demolition process took about three months. People bought the timber, and used it to make garden sheds. For many years afterwards, a house near to the site of the Empire had a lean-to, made entirely from the floorboards of the former stage. Bits of the masonry were appropriated and set up as garden ornaments. The red velvet front curtains were sold in sections. Heath's School of Dancing, in Bath Road, bought twenty seats from the back of the stalls, which were removed in blocks of six and transported by the demolition firm, F.R. Gould.

As soon as the site was flattened, a new block was built there by the Swindon firm R.J. Leighfield & Sons; it was named Empire House, and opened in 1960. (This was also the year in which, on 13 May, Ralph Birch Entertainments Limited was dissolved.) The site occupied 10,000 square feet; the ground floor of the new building covered 8,500 square feet, and each of the first and second floors was 6,000 square feet. The frontages to Groundwell Road and Clarence Street were 120 feet and 90 feet respectively. Lettings were made by Loveday & Loveday, and occupiers initially consisted of a doctor's surgery, a chemist's shop, a launderette, and other commercial premises, with the valuation offices above. An Italian restaurant has been a long-time occupier of part of the block. The launderette was said to have been haunted by spirits that once inhabited the Empire Theatre, and one summer's afternoon it inexplicably exploded, injuring the proprietor and her son and causing mayhem to the flow of traffic.

Immediately, there were calls for Swindon to provide another custom-built theatre. In 1956, Peggy Miles, a twenty-six-year-old typist working at the Vickers-Armstrong aircraft factory, and who had been involved with the Swindon Repertory Company Limited, called for live theatre to be revived in Swindon. At a meeting held in the Mechanics' Institute, attended by only thirty people, it was agreed that 'most people in Swindon had no interest in repertory'. An elected committee working through neighbourhood workers would canvass the opinions of residents living in new peripheral housing estates.

In May 1959, when parts of the old Empire were still in situ, filling passers-by with mixed emotions, a pressure group called Swindon Live Theatre Campaign, led by Peggy Miles, fired its first real salvo in the fight to reserve a central site on which a new theatre might be built. This group estimated that it would cost around £50,000 to build a theatre that would seat some 800 people. At the time, this financial estimate was reasonable for such a modest theatre, but the suggested capacity showed that it was based on the perceived immediate requirement rather than any future potential. The shots were aimed at Swindon Borough Council, which still thought too parochially to achieve anything of note; so perhaps things were kept within what were considered to be the kind of parameters they might accept. Peggy was confident that the money could be raised, but was less enthusiastic about the local authority's commitment. It would be heart-breaking, she told a public meeting at the town hall on 6 May, if they were able to raise the money and then found they did not have a site on which to build the theatre.

The dichotomy for the successor was every bit as complex as that which had exercised Ernest Carpenter, nearly three-quarters of a century earlier. Was the potential audience in Swindon's catchment area of the late 1960s large enough to support the size of theatre that many people were demanding? What they wanted was a theatre that was sufficiently large to gain recognition as a national entertainment venue: one that would attract the huge acts of the day; and one that would really underline Swindon's investment in culture. They saw it as the town's opportunity to break away from its poor image in that respect, and from its reputation for not thinking big enough, or far enough ahead. Eventually, Swindon did get a new theatre. At its peak, the old Empire could accommodate an audience of 1,600; just over 600 patrons were needed to fill the Wyvern, which opened in 1971.

*The Dancing Years by Ivor Novello is an example of the kind of big musical that occasionally came to the Empire in its last few years. Other Novello works performed at Swindon during this period were Careless Rapture, Crest of a Wave, and Glamorous Nights.*

*A change of programme cover in the late 1940s depicted theatrical masques and the Park Theatrical Productions logo. But by now the company was in financial trouble and the theatre was about to enter its final phase.*

Frankie Howerd topped the bill in this 1949 vehicle hung onto one of his catch-phrases, namely Ladies and Gentle-men, but it was Norman Wisdom who apparently stole the show. At that time, both men were about three years into a professional stage career as professional entertainers; for Howerd it would be one of troughs and come-backs, whilst Wisdom expanded gradually into different areas of the industry and achieved continuous acclaim in each.

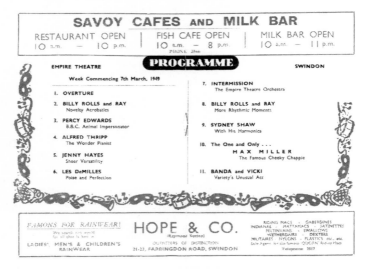

The 'one and only' Max Miller, arguably the greatest comedian ever to tread the board of the Empire, came in 1949 and again in 1952. On the first occasion, one of the supporting acts was Percy Edwards, the voice artist who impersonated animals and birds in a professional career that lasted for six decades.

*Graham Nelson's Juveniles were a group of young Swindon dancers put together in 1949 to perform in Mother Goose at the end of the year. They rehearsed in Swindon, but are here seen in Trafalgar Square, London on a day out. Left to right from they are: (back row) Carol Allen, Judith Chappell, Shirley Whitehead, Myra Burrows, Shirley Randall, Jean Browning, Janet Hawkins (front row) Valerie Whitfield, Marlene Jones, Joan Browning, Janet Pullen, Iris Titchener, Pat O'Neil.*

*The Mother Goose dancers of 1949 rehearsing in a room at the White House public house, Corporation Street, Swindon, where one of them lived. The troop consisted of Joan Browning, Jean Browning, Judith Chappell, Janet Hawkins, Janet Pullen, Pat O'Neil, Shirley Whitehead, Marlene Jones, Carol Allen, Iris Titchener, Valerie Whitfield, Shirley Randall, Myra Burrows, June Cockbill, Mavis Harvey, Rosemary Goddard, Maureen Cockram, Barbara Matin, Pat Casey, Shirley Whittingham, Irene Holton.*

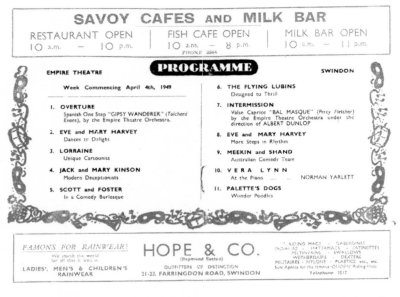

## SAVOY CAFES AND MILK BAR

| RESTAURANT OPEN | FISH CAFE OPEN | MILK BAR OPEN |
|---|---|---|
| 10 a.m. — 10 p.m. | 10 a.m. — 8 p.m. | 10 a.m. — 11 p.m. |

PHONE 2566

### PROGRAMME

EMPIRE THEATRE                                                           SWINDON

Week Commencing April 4th, 1949

**1. OVERTURE**
Spanish One Step "GIPSY WANDERER" (Tolchard Evans), by the Empire Theatre Orchestra.

**2. EVE and MARY HARVEY**
Dances to Delight

**3. LORRAINE**
Unique Cartoonist

**4. JACK and MARY KINSON**
Modern Deceptionists

**5. SCOTT and FOSTER**
In a Comedy Burlesque

**6. THE FLYING LUBINS**
Designed to Thrill

**7. INTERMISSION**
Valse Caprice "BAL MASQUE" (Percy Fletcher) by the Empire Theatre Orchestra under the direction of ALBERT DUNLOP

**8. EVE and MARY HARVEY**
More Steps in Rhythm

**9. MEEKIN and SHAND**
Australian Comedy Team

**10. VERA LYNN**
At the Piano .... .... NORMAN YARLETT

**11. PALETTE'S DOGS**
Wonder Poodles

---

**FAMOUS FOR RAINWEAR!**
We search the world for all that is best in

LADIES', MEN'S & CHILDREN'S
RAINWEAR

## HOPE & CO.
(Raymond Sutton)

OUTFITTERS OF DISTINCTION
21-23, FARRINGDON ROAD, SWINDON

RIDING MACS · GABERDINES
INDIARAGS · MATTAMACS · JATENETTES
MELTONIANS · SWALLOWS
WETHERGAIRS · DEXTERS
MILITAIRES · NYLONS · PLASTICS etc., etc.
Sole Agents for the famous 'QUOFIX' Riding Macs

Telephone 3517

*Vera Lynn, the forces sweetheart, came to Swindon on a variety bill in the spring of 1949.*

*The Empire's house staff of usherettes and commissionaires pose in the stalls of the theatre for this 1946 picture. Sixth from the left is house manager Cedric Green.*

(above) The Swindon Musical Society's production of Carmen in 1950 was part of the Borough of Swindon's 50th anniversary celebrations. It included a number of local artists, such as Ray Nash, Raymond Hatherall, Lorna Cantor, Jack Winter and Lionel Rayner, who were stalwarts of the amateur theatre in the town.

(right) When in 1950 the Empire advertised that it was to give away a tricycle to a three-year old at each performance of Cinderella, Shirley Lafford of Clifton Street was one who successfully 'blew out' Rudolph the Red-nosed Reindeer's nose, encouraged by Buttons (played by Terry O'Neill) to secured the prize. Here she is riding it at home.

EMPIRE THEATRE
SWINDON
Licensee and Manager : W. S. BOBBY

SUNDAY, DECEMBER 10th

ARTHUR HOWES
Presents—

THE SQUADRONAIRES
DANCE ORCHESTRA

Featuring

ROY EDWARDS ★ THE QUADS
and FIRTH ARCHER

Programme - - 3d.

THE PUPILS OF TANWOOD STUDIO

Present a

DANCING
MATINEE

in aid of the

H.M.S. AFFRAY RELIEF FUND

at

THE EMPIRE THEATRE, SWINDON

on

SATURDAY, JUNE 23rd, 1951

Commencing 2.30 p.m.

*

PROGRAMME 6d.

Printed by The Swindon Press Ltd., Newspaper House, Swindon, Wilts.

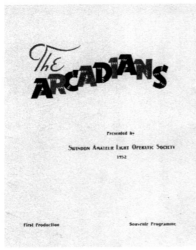

(top left) The Squadronaires Dance Orchestra came to the Empire as part of a series of Sunday concerts that were put on in the 1950s. The band was formed during the Second World War as the morale-boosting Royal Air Force Dance Orchestra, and the name it took post-war as a civilian band was simply the one by which it had been popularly known when a military outfit. It was phenomenally successful in its broadcasts, residencies and when on tour.

(top right) In June 1951, Mollie Tanner hired the Empire Theatre and put on a matinee in aid of the HMS Affray relief fund. This was a Royal Navy submarine that had been launched in 1944 but was lost at sea with seventy five people on board, in mysterious circumstances during a simulated war exercise on 16 April 1951. The pupils from Mollie's Tanwood Studio danced their way through a programme of thirty-two songs and disciplines.

(above) The Swindon Amateur Light Operatic Society was formed in 1951, and its first public performance was The Arcadians, presented at the Empire in 1952. It mounted two more productions, The Desert Song in 1953 and The Vagabond King in 1954, before the theatre closed.

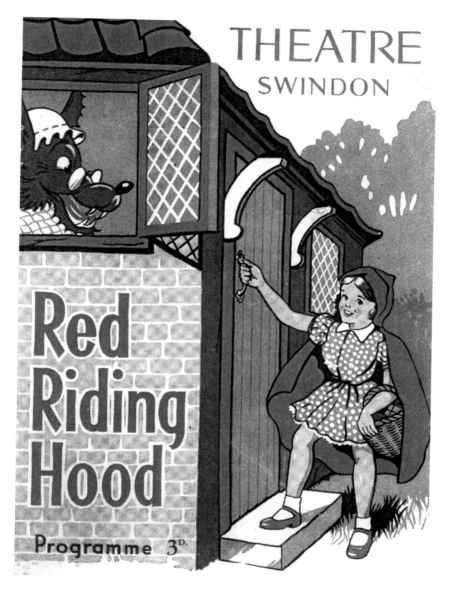

The pantomime Red Riding Hood, staged at the Empire in 1951, was the first to include girls from Mollie Tanner's Tanwood School of Dance, run by the eponymous 'Miss Mollie', accompanied by her husband John who had previously played piano with the Modernaires Show Band. Red Riding Hood was billed as 'a Harry Lester's Hayseeds pantomime' and the girls were named 'Mollie Tanner's Little Sweethearts' for the occasion. They became a pantomime fixture at the Empire until it closed.

(left) Design was definitely not the strong point of the Empire's publicity: one downward stroke with the baton held like that and it would probably spring right across the footlights; and the fringing to the curtains look like Christmas decorations. It all had the appearance of being tired and downbeat, a 'feel' that was by now pervading all areas of the theatre.

(below) Mollie Tanner's girls perform in the 'waterfalls of Scotland' scene in Babes in the Wood, the Empire's 1952 pantomime. This production somehow managed to combine a rocky landscape north of the border (giving the theatre the opportunity to feature its ability to produce cascades of water on the stage) with scenes in Sherwood Forest, Nottingham.

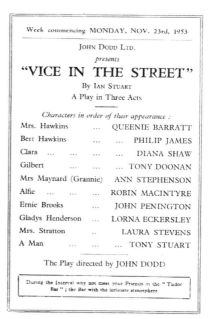

Week commencing MONDAY, NOV. 23rd, 1953

JOHN DODD LTD.

*presents*

## "VICE IN THE STREET"

By IAN STUART

A Play in Three Acts

*Characters in order of their appearance :*

| | |
|---|---|
| Mrs. Hawkins | QUEENIE BARRATT |
| Bert Hawkins | PHILIP JAMES |
| Clara | DIANA SHAW |
| Gilbert | TONY DOONAN |
| Mrs Maynard (Grannie) | ANN STEPHENSON |
| Alfie | ROBIN MACINTYRE |
| Ernie Brooks | JOHN PENINGTON |
| Gladys Henderson | LORNA ECKERSLEY |
| Mrs. Stratton | LAURA STEVENS |
| A Man | TONY STUART |

The Play directed by JOHN DODD

During the Interval why not meet your Friends in the " Tudor
Bar " ; the Bar with the intimate atmosphere

*(above)  Vice in the Streets was the kind of drama that was touring in 1953, when theatre managements hoped it would sound gritty enough to attract adult audiences. The Evening Advertiser's reviewer, pompously wrote that 'it cannot be described as a serious study of juvenile delinquency for it makes no attempt to get to the root of the problem'. He continued 'razor blades are much in evidence, and the audience is even treated to a coshing'. On the stage, one hopes.*

*(right)  In 1954, the theatre's cover design went for sophistication. It was an odd choice; theatregoers had not dressed like this since the 1930s, and probably never in Swindon. Also, the style was quite out of tune with the general tenor of the productions then being mounted at the Empire. It was a brave face being put on a deteriorating situation.*

(above) *Reefer Girl, like* Vice in the Street, *had all the promise of a hard-hitting drama with a sufficiently high sleaze content to be typical of the genre. It was 'the true story of events in the life of a drug addict' which the management respectfully suggested should not be seen by children under eighteen. The Evening Advertiser reported that it was a lurid record of a ruthless young spiv's activities as drug-peddler, murderer and seducer, which takes place in a squalid dockside apartment that 'includes a prostitute who smokes marijuana cigarettes and plies her trade behind a flimsy curtain, and an idiot cripple who takes cocaine injections'.*

(opposite, above) *The 1954 production of* Why Cover Girls *was one in the run of 'girlie' shows that really took off with* Strike a Nude Note *(a variety show with elements of striptease) in 1951 and thereafter came regularly to the Empire. In 1954, patrons were also offered* We Couldn't Wear Less, Paris After Dark, Follies Montmartre, Shapes and Surprises, Fluff and Nonsense, *and* Peek-a-Boo.

(opposite, below) *Phyllis Dixey, the accomplished fan dancer who had previously played the Empire in 1949, was a star in her own right, providing a variety bill with high-end nudity. Following her five-year incumbency at the Whitehall Theatre, London, where, from 1942, she had introduced striptease (in contrast to nude tableaux) into the West End, she was now into a decade of touring the provinces where audiences were more appreciative of what she always considered to be an art form. The 'Queen of Striptease' returned to the Empire in 1954.*

Week commencing MONDAY, APRIL 26th, 1954
Twice Nightly 6.30 and 8.40

Don Nichols says "THIS'LL MAKE YOU WHISTLE" as he asks

## "WHY COVER GIRLS?"

1  Overture

2  Let's start on the front page and meet CORAL GAYE and the Teenage Pin-Ups

3  "Lively Laughs"
   with JIMMY FRENCH, Don Nichols, Ella Nore, Shelagh Duffy and Frankie Parker

4  Ella Nore and the Teenagers

5  MR. FRENCH gets "AN EARFUL!"

6  "Show Piece"

7  Musical Director Ray Long earns his money!

8  MR. FRENCH offers "A Helping Hand"

9  Britain's Youngest Equilibrists—
                        The Three Brooklyns

10  "HIT PARADE"—bringing the Melodies of the Moment

11  Intermission

During the Interval why not meet your Friends in the "Tudor Bar"; the Bar with the intimate atmosphere.

## PEEK-A-BOO

1  SNUFFY introduces ... ... The Girls

2  SNUFFY AND AUDREY

3  THE VAGA MODELS in "The Can-Can"

4  BILLY REVEL & PAT FIELDS
                    Those Friendly Enemies

5  DOROTHY REID & MACK introduce :-
   "A Wee Drop of Scotch"
   with The Vaga Models, Jack Tracy
   and introducing

6  The One and Only
   PHYLLIS DIXEY

   INTERVAL

During the Interval why not meet your Friends in the "Tudor Bar"; the Bar with the intimate atmosphere

Silver Jubilee **25th** year of production

# SWINDON MUSICAL SOCIETY

PRESENTS

Massenet's Opera

# CINDERELLA

Musical Director : H. S. FAIRCLOUGH, Mus. Bac.

## EMPIRE THEATRE : SWINDON

Monday, 5th April, 1954, and week

Commencing at 7.30 p.m.

★

THIS OPERA IS PRESENTED WITH THE SUPPORT
OF THE ARTS COUNCIL OF GREAT BRITAIN

★

Hon. Treasurer : B. L. MONAHAN
Hon. Secretary : A. B. SIDDONS
Hon. Patrons' Secretary : EDITH A. WARD

DESIGNED AND PRINTED BY GEO. T. SIMPSON AND SON AT THE SIGNCRAFT PRESS IN SWINDON

*The Swindon Musical Society had been in existence for a quarter of a century when it performed Massenet's opera Cinderella at the Empire in 1954.*

(right) When the theatre opened in 1898 a seat in the grand circle, as it was then called, cost one shilling. The weekly wage for the kind of non-professional occupations being carried out in Swindon at the end of the 19th century would have been a little over £1 per week; half a century later, it was just in excess of £8 per week. This dress circle ticket was sold for a 1954 performance of Caroll Levis Discoveries, a spin-off from the television show of a similar name, that at Swindon starred Barry Took, and Violet Pretty who later became famous as actress Ann Heywood

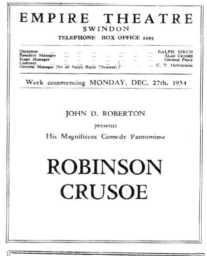

(above, and overleaf) The last production at the Empire Theatre for which a printed programme was issued proved to be the 1954 pantomime Robinson Crusoe. It starred the great comic songwriter Leslie Sarony, the impressionist Afrique who was enjoying something of a revival at the time, and the actress Penelope Gray. Joyce Golding played Mrs Crusoe, and the Evening Advertiser remarked that its only fault was to have a female playing the part of a pantomime dame.

*The pantomime Aladdin was scheduled to follow Robinson Crusoe at the Empire in late January 1955. As staff waited for the scenery to arrive, and Mollie Tanner's juveniles rehearsed on stage, word came that Aladdin was not on its way. Mollie was the last person to leave the stage as the Empire Theatre closed for what would prove to be the last time.*

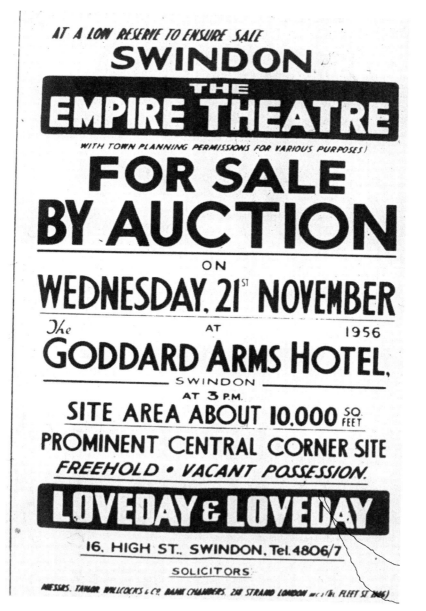

When the Empire closed, Jack Gladwin still owned the bricks and mortar. He negotiated with the local authority for a change of use for the site, and eventually put the sale of the building into the hands of Harold Loveday of the Swindon firm Loveday & Loveday, estate agents and auctioneers.

*Clarke Brothers of Swindon were contracted to take down the Empire Theatre, which they achieved over three months in the spring of 1959. This is a picture of the forlorn building, four years after the theatre closed, and just before demolition work started.*

*The proud coronet, wrapped around the entrance from the 1920s, is showing signs of neglect, and the fascia board, for so long the proclaimer of whatever was on offer within, is now disintegrating.*

*The great ogee-arched, open scrolled pediment with its decorative cresting and moulded strings and pinnacles, was the crowning glory of the south façade. The designers had concentrated a whole range of architectural decorative techniques into what was the central bay above the original front doors, and the ultimate destruction of this whole section, including the area immediately beneath the pediment, was a great loss to the town.*

*The first ladder goes up against the front elevation, as work begins to tear down the fabric.*

(above) Demolition begins at the top in March 1959 as workmen start to take down the roof, stacking such slates that can be salvaged. In this picture, one man is using a sledgehammer to remove the ridge tiles.

(left) The great pediment, wrapped in scaffolding, is about to come down.

*The auditorium has gone, exposing the stage area. The last safety curtain, no longer packed with advertisements, clings to its position, and a piece of curtain hangs mournfully from above. A small boy has managed to climb the ladder onto the rubble-strewn stage, standing now in the sunlight where so often the spotlight played.*

*The last stage of demolition, in May 1959. Only the stage, the fly tower and the cramped backstage areas with their mean dressing rooms, corridors, and staircases have yet to be pulled down.*

As soon as the theatre was demolished, the Swindon building firm of R.J. Leighfield & Sons constructed this office block on the site. This picture shows it nearing completion, just before being opened as Empire House in 1960. The letting agents were Loveday & Loveday, who had sold the Empire Theatre three and a half years previously.

More than half a century after it was built, and no longer labelled Empire House, the ground floor of the building in 2012 is packed with restaurants and fast food outlets.

# 8

# *A view from the stalls*

AS A YOUNG boy, Mark Child was often taken to the Empire Theatre, and has very strong memories of the place and of some of the acts he saw there. This chapter is his first-hand account of what the theatre meant to him, how it affected him then, and how it nurtured a life-long love of live performance.

Between 1947 and 1955, my maternal grandparents regularly patronised the Empire Theatre. On arriving for a performance, they usually bought tickets for the following week's show, before entering the auditorium and taking their places for the current production, always in the same two seats in the centre of the front row of the stalls. Very often, from 1949 when I was six years old, they bought three tickets, and took me with them.

At this point, I must declare something of an interest. The maternal grandmother in the above-mentioned duo was the daughter of James G. Jarman, who trod the boards from the late 1880s as music hall artiste 'Ted Jarman, Humorist'. He took the character of a country yokel, dressed in an authentic Somerset smock, gaiters and boots; sang ballads and recited monologues, and could apparently 'get a tune out of anything'. Among the objects out of which he was allegedly able to coax music were, conventionally, a cornet and a banjo; others items included a musical saw, bones and spoons. During my childhood, these were all crammed inside a large trunk in my grandmother's box room, together with his stage clothes, and numerous theatre posters and programmes that attested to the presence on many bills of Ted Jarman, Humorist. By the time I, as an adult, wished to lay claim to this treasure trove, my grandmother had disposed of everything except for two photographs, which I still have to this day. These show Ted in full costume, said to be singing 'She's Proud and She's Beautiful' in one, and in the other reciting 'The Turmut Hower'.

I do not know whether Ted Jarman ever had the Swindon theatre's stage beneath his feet; the sad fact is that although I remember leafing through the stash of posters and playbills as a small boy, I now have no documentary evidence of anywhere that he performed. Nor have I inherited his musical gene; but if he had a gene labelled 'love of theatre', then he handed that on to me at birth. I used to sit in the Empire with my grandparents and imagine on the stage a portly man in smock and gaiters, leaning on a tree trunk against a pastoral 'flat', or piece of scenery, and singing with orchestral accompaniment. How I applauded with my heart.

A large building may seem extraordinarily so to a very young boy, and there is no doubt that, externally and internally, the Empire Theatre presented imposing aspects of scale. By the same yardstick, a confined space will seem larger than it actually is to one who is vertically challenged. Yet the booking hall of the Empire always appeared to be a cramped corridor, wedged in between – on one side – a row of glazed doors that opened onto the pavement, and, on the other, the stalls in the auditorium. Perhaps this space was narrow because it was designed only to accommodate people as they advanced towards the booking office, but in reality had to deal with loiterers and such pressing throngs as required ingress and egress at each performance. It seemed always to be a claustrophobic glasshouse, solid with people. Its doors were made of metal and were glazed; they were ill-fitting, rattled in windy weather, and made a loud noise when they crashed shut.

The box office was also glazed, and money and tickets changed hands through a hole in the glass barrier. On each side of the box office there were doors that led directly into the stalls, and at the eastern end of the booking corridor was a staircase that eventually admitted firstly into the dress circle, and later into the upper circle and 'the gods'. There was also a side entrance to the theatre from Clarence Street. This admitted, via a mean stairway that had all the hallmarks of being the equivalent of a tradesman's entrance, to the upper reaches of the interior. On the opposite side of the building, down an alleyway off Groundwell Road, was the stage door.

The gods, being the haunt of the seriously impoverished, sat precipitously at the rear of the upper circle. It was a damp place of inaudibility, and smelled more strongly of disinfectant than did the rest of the theatre, and was at turns either unbelievably foetid and hot, or more frequently uncomfortably chilled, depending on whether or not a small door to one side had been left open. It was here that I sat with my parents, who were not habitual theatregoers and who felt that anything other than the cheapest seats were a waste of money, especially when they insisted on taking me to pantomimes. In this latter argument I heartily concurred; I have never liked pantomimes, neither then nor since. They are tinged with the memory of coming in off the cold street and spending the next couple of hours on a hard seat, with the smell of disinfectant blowing on a chill wind about the ears. Their dramatis personae seemed inexplicable to me, even as a small boy. The antics of ugly sisters, washerwomen, broker's men, inept robbers and the like seemed downright silly. I never understood why young women had to pretend to be young men; why elderly males contrived to be asexual females of a certain age; and I did not appreciate audience participation that only prolonged the agony of what were already over-long productions. I did not want to be selected to go on the stage, where I might receive sweets or a balloon for making a fool of myself, and could not understand any other child wishing to do so. Quite possibly they did not wish it for themselves either, for it occurred to me that whenever one of the more ridiculous members of the cast called for children to be passed onto the stage, it was always the mothers who leapt to their feet, and feverishly thrust forward their charges.

One of the least pleasant experiences of a visit to the Empire Theatre at Swindon was the degree to which its cleaners were over-zealous in their use of disinfectant. The smell of this gave the impression that one was seated in a public toilet. Nothing that took place on the stage ever ameliorated this unpleasant aroma. It assailed the nostrils of the audience, and to such a degree that most of them left the building during the intervals, preferring to cleanse their lungs with replenishing cold, and frequently foggy, night air rather than cleansing their palates with tubs of antiseptic-tasting ice cream. The other distressing feature of the theatre was the Arctic temperature that often prevailed within. The building had twelve exits, three of which led from the stage area. It was the considered opinion of theatregoers that, whatever the outside weather conditions, the exits were all left open by a management anxious to assuage (and if so, always in vain) the noisome properties of the disinfectant. Regular patrons, whose seats were at the rear of the dress circle, arrived for the performance, on all but the most balmy of evenings, with blankets with which to envelop themselves. They knew that when the wind was in the right direction, there was a permanent draught from the doorways on each side of the crescent of seats, and that this invariably came accompanied by a piercing whistle. It could easily drown out quieter passages of dialogue.

Life in the front of the stalls was altogether better, and I absolutely loved the variety shows. They all began in the same way. One took one's seat facing the safety curtain; there had been several of these during the theatre's history, and they were packed with advertisements. A few minutes before the production was due to begin, the safety curtain was raised, revealing a red plush curtain with gold trimmings, and the chatter in the audience was reduced to a low hum. The gentlemen of the pit orchestra began to emerge one by one from beneath the stage, and were applauded as they made their way to their seats and began to tune up. There were nine or ten of them, and the double bass player always stood on the left-hand side with his instrument. The percussionist was to the right, next came the strings, and then the woodwind and brass sections. The pianist sat next to the conductor.

When the orchestra was settled, the conductor appeared from a side entrance in the stalls, and was greeted with sustained applause as he made his way towards the orchestra. He let himself into the orchestra pit, closing the door behind him, then bowed to the audience, turned, and raised his baton. At this point, much shuffling of feet and banging of seats occurred as the audience stood up for the National Anthem; having got it out of the way, they sat down again. The conductor fiddled with his sheet music, and checked that the assembled orchestra on each side of him was ready. Satisfied, his baton jerked briefly upwards, descended with a fast, long stroke, and the band burst into a satisfying musical canter. The lights in the auditorium were lowered and a spotlight was directed on to the red curtain.

As each member of the band attempted to outrace his companions to the finishing note, the red curtain was raised to reveal whatever was the first turn to take the stage. On each side of the opening, a light-box sprang into life, revealing the figure 1. The figures thus displayed during the course of the performance accorded with those printed in the programme. It was quite irrelevant, since only those people seated within the light from the stage could read their programmes, anyway. Most people did not know the interval had arrived until the red curtain, which could also sweep down from each side of the stage, stayed down; the safety curtain was lowered, and the ice-cream sellers came into the auditorium, carrying trays of small, dumpy pots of Lyons ice-cream and wooden spatulas to use as spoons.

The penultimate conductor of the Empire Theatre pit orchestra was (Thomas) 'Tim' Coxon (who afterwards occasionally stood in for his successor, Charlie Comley, who had previously – as a member of the orchestra – sometimes stood in for him). Coxon was a spare man, when I knew him, with grey, wavy hair, and an invalid wife; he also had the reputation of being short-tempered and careful with money. The son of a musical family, he played piano and violin, and had come from Hartlepool in 1924 to join the Empire Theatre orchestra, and he initially lived in a flat in Victoria Road, later moving to Westmorland Road. When the Empire was a cinema, Coxon obtained employment as a mechanic at the Victoria Garage in nearby Durham Street, and was still there whilst conducting the Empire's orchestra in his spare time.

He succeeded Albert Dunlop to the position of musical director in 1949, and occupied it until 1952. Whereas Dunlop maintained a suave air and an upright posture when in musical motion, Coxon's style of conducting was rather more frenetic. His arms flayed like broken windmill sails, his torso moved jerkily forwards and backwards from the waist, and as the evening progressed, his hair flew ever more wildly about his head. It was said that Tim Coxon's animation and increasingly dishevelled appearance was, for the observant connoisseur, an extra act on the bill.

Another employee of the Victoria Garage, (John) 'Jock' Walker, who wore round-framed National Health spectacles, kept tropical fish, and regularly played saxophone and clarinet in the Empire's orchestra. He was an old hand on the Swindon music scene, who played with most of the local dance bands from the 1930s. Bert Fluck, Diana Dors's father, was sometimes the pianist in the Empire band. This gathering of amateur Swindon musicians lurched a loud but indifferently musical path through variety bills at the Empire. Touring musical productions often brought their own musicians.

Today, I have brief, mental snapshots of only some of the acts I saw on the Empire's stage in my childhood. Most of the rest, largely forgettable even in their time, have long been irretrievably banished from memory. There were unremarkable magicians galore, emaciated acrobats on equipment made of tubular steel, various fey young ladies and their performing creatures, jugglers plentiful, miscellaneous speciality acts, and insipid vocalists who rallied in support and appeared time and again on the bill provided by the Bernard Delfont Agency. Memories of them coalesce into a monotonous sum of disengaged and disparate parts, mercifully lost to the mind.

It was Al Read's appearance at the Empire that introduced me to the concept of a comedian's catchphrase, and the seemingly inexplicable affect that it has on audiences. He had not long been an entertainer when he came to Swindon in the 1950s, and I remember nothing about his general performance, but suppose that he was joking along to the polite laughter that usually greeted comedians in Swindon, when suddenly he said something that I did not quite catch, and the entire audience roared with laughter. The whole atmosphere in the room changed, and thereafter the assembly chortled heartily and good humouredly at everything he said. People who hitherto had just been staring at the performer on the stage, now turned to those in the seats next to them and nodded with broad smiles on their faces.

My grandparents explained that Al Read had said 'Right Monkey', and that it was his catchphrase, but they were quite unable to put any meaning to it. Why then, had they laughed like everyone else? Why should someone suddenly say something quite meaningless, apropos of absolutely nothing, yet engender such a seemingly absurd response? And how often could a comedian repeat the same phrase before the circumstances became a cliché, and the repetition became boring? Apparently, for ever. In the years that followed, I learnt to listen out for catchphrases, and soon realised that the earlier they were said (Tommy Trinder, for example, actually came on stage saying 'Ho! Ho! You Lucky People', before he uttered another word) the better received was the comedian's act. Perhaps that is the purpose of the catchphrase: to give the audience something familiar that warms them to the entertainer. Personally, I think catchphrases are just boring, repetitive nonsense; but I have Al Read at the Empire to thank for first drawing my attention to them.

The point of the mostly forgettable support acts was to enhance the reputation of the top of the bill. I have information that suggests I once saw Potter and Carole, whoever they were, having 'Fun on Mother's Settee', but recall nothing of it. Perhaps it was a speciality act that performed with furniture. One act that fascinated me as a child was Shek Ben Ali, real name Mohan Ali, a magician from Calcutta who rushed about the stage in turban and eastern costume muttering 'nothing in; nothing out', which appeared to be his catchphrase. Another was Karina, who, when I was about twelve years old, appeared on a variety bill at the Empire in a number of 'exotic poses' and performed a tassel dance. She was known as 'the sauciest tassel dancer of them all', and soon after her appearance at Swindon she went on to top the bill in her own show, *Pardon My Tassel*.

Hugely popular, if always inexplicably so to me, was Morton Fraser's Harmonica Gang, whom I saw at the Empire on several occasions; I would have preferred that I hadn't. Fraser and his eight-piece ensemble played accordions, and harmonicas of various widths. They literally piled themselves in a heap around a single microphone and breathlessly pounded away at their instruments at breakneck speed. The Gang had been formed during the late war when Fraser, previously a solo harmonica player, teamed up with some like-minded musicians and found that their combined reedy screeching found favour with audiences. I thought it was a dreadful row, only relieved when their sound was swamped by that of the accompanying pit orchestra, which, mercifully, was often. Every time they turned up at the Empire, they wore different clothes; sometimes they looked like hillbillies from backwoods America, sometimes London spivs of the forties, complete with trilby hats. Why should they cluster around a microphone with massed trilby hats bobbing up and down? Nor did I enjoy their humour, which seemed to devolve on such a degree of physical contact with the diminutive Tiny Ross, the dwarf comedian of the outfit, that he in consequence spent much of his time on the floor. The Gang were always well received by the Swindon audience, with the notable exception of one seat in the stalls.

When the hilarious Morris and Cowley came to the Empire, the only prop they needed was a bench. Harry and Frank Birkenhead began playing these two old soldiers in the 1920s; they named the act after the Morris motor vehicle works and the location of the factory at Cowley, Oxford, in a career lasting nearly half a century. Most audiences thought of them as portraying Chelsea Pensioners, and although their quasi-military greatcoats were really quite amorphous, it suited their act to be ambivalent in the matter. By the time they came to Swindon, in the 1950s, Morris and Cowley had long been a comfortable vertebra in the backbone of variety.

Their bench was usually set up against any suitable scenery – at Swindon it was a parkland setting – revealed by the opening curtains. Then the orchestra struck up 'Boys of the Old Brigade', and the pair of doddery old soldiers appeared, from stage left, one several paces behind the other, and both hobbling along, with some difficulty, on walking sticks. Be-whiskered, medals festooning their greatcoats, they sat down with apparent discomfort, and then began a series of comical reminiscences of things they were once able to do but which were now denied them by the frailties of advancing years. At one point in their act, an attractive female passed before them, engendering much wobbling of legs and an attempt by one of them to follow her, whilst the other restrained him with a walking stick. It was that kind of obvious, sexist and stereotypical approach that delighted audiences in those days, and made Morris and Cowley an act that was very popular with the paying public.

A regular at the Empire was a young woman – whose name escapes me – dressed in a Miss Havisham-style wedding dress, from the recesses of which, feathers occasionally fluttered, thereby telegraphing the imminent appearance of her performing doves. Whether by training or accident, one of the birds usually escaped the confines of the proscenium and launched an apparent bid for freedom in the upper circle. Eventually, it would be persuaded to return, and the genial audience always sighed collectively when the bird flew back, and then they loudly applauded its return to a cage on stage. I remember Bob Bennard and his pigeons, equally as boring, and some of the seemingly interminable canine acts: Louise and her dogs, Gloria and her *educated* dogs, Palette's Wonder Poodles, and Betty Kayes and her performing Pekineses spring unhappily to mind.

Then there was the comedy magician 'The Great Claude'. Both he and the female with the moulting doves, indifferent acts both, appeared so regularly at the Swindon Empire that one could only assume they were permanently 'resting' (probably no further away than the wings) and were therefore available at a moment's notice. Upon reflection, it is perhaps unkind to refer disparagingly to Claude, for he was the only performer I recall to have a visual catchphrase to finish the act, and for which the entire audience waited. As his pedantic act unfolded to desultory applause, so would Claude change the legend on a flip chart, at the side of the stage, which initially bore the words 'The Great Claude'. At the denouement of his ultimate trick, he would rush across and, with a great flourish, turn the final page to reveal 'The Great Clod'. As the curtains swept down from each side, the whole audience always erupted in agreement with the sentiment, leaping from their seats, stamping their feet, and wildly applauding as the pit orchestra roared into a cacophony of musical ecstasy.

Occasionally, staggering out of the mental mist, I recall real stars: the likes of the voluminous comedian Max Bacon, with a little ukulele; George Formby, with a larger one and an even bigger grin;

Frankie Howerd (who was received with less enthusiasm than was a young Norman Wisdom on the same bill); and Wilson, Keppell, and (one of their various) Betty. Jack Wilson and Joe Keppell were no strangers to the Empire, and I saw them on more than one occasion. So much of their work is still available on film that their act requires no description here, except to say that they were a huge hit with Empire Theatre audiences. Unlike many acts of the period whose words and actions were sterile over several decades, comedians in particular, Wilson, Keppell and Betty manipulated their formula within the basic concept, danced to different tunes, and thereby kept their act fresh. I used to think they must be unique, that no-one would dare copy them. But there was, in London, a wonderful group of buskers called The Roadstars, whom I frequently saw entertaining theatre queues, and who were often to be found performing in Leicester Square. They could be every bit as good. It is a tribute to Wilson, Keppell and Betty that, many years later, when the BBC ran a television series on music hall and variety, theirs were the most asked-for clips by the general public.

The actor Leon Cortez had his car de-coked (we call it a service now) at the Victoria Garage whilst he was at the Empire, and gave signed photographs of himself to the clerk who booked it in and the mechanic who did the job. Someone else who was free with his signed publicity photographs was Arthur English, who came to the Empire as a very new comedian (his career only began in 1949), but who had enjoyed a meteoric rise in popularity through his work on radio. He was well liked by my whole family. English worked in the theatre without any kind of backdrop that might detract from the visual joke he presented on stage. His persona was the wartime 'spiv', dressed in a jacket with wide shoulder pads, a huge floral kipper tie, and a wide-brimmed trilby hat. I see him now, seemingly an infusion of nervous tension, moving jerkily about the stage and delivering a series of shaggy dog-type jokes at incredible (and ever-increasing) speed, in a contrived Cockney accent. His patter grew to a crescendo of momentum, ending with the most famous of his catchphrases, 'Play the music, open the cage'; whereupon Charlie Comley and the pit orchestra obliged, and the audience showed its appreciation.

Memorable musical comedy acts I well remember seeing at the Empire included Sid Millward and his Nitwits, which featured a dwarf in a dress suit, an 'ancient' bearded individual, a character with a heavily bandaged foot, several very hairy musicians, and an energetic black drummer in a little pork-pie hat, who rolled his eyes and played the buffoon. A similar ensemble was Dr Crock and the Crackpots. The names of these top-of- the-bill acts would now be considered politically incorrect, but they were of their time. These hilarious musical comedy turns were well-loved performers, who spent as much time messing about on the stage as they did actually playing tunes. Dr Crock's real name was Harry Hines, and the bands shared the same drummer, Charlie Rossi. Both Millward and Hines were clarinet and saxophone players who had previously played with well-known British dance bands.

In the 1950s, there were occasions when the number of acts on the bill fell short of the clientele's expectations, failed to turn up, or were insufficient in quantity. At such times, the Empire Theatre's pit orchestra was removed from its dungeon, and pressed into service on the stage. In fact, it was probably a misnomer to refer to the Empire's musicians as the 'pit orchestra'. Certainly, the stalls were raked, but only with a modest gradient, and the orchestra was installed at the lowest level; but even when the musicians were seated, the heads of some of them were above the sight line of the stage, when viewed from the stalls. One always knew when the comedian or other non-musical act had given the trigger phrase that signified the imminent close of their act: the double bass player got to his feet fractionally before the conductor, because he needed a second or two longer to manoeuvre the instrument into the correct position.

Two acts absolutely stand out, and I can recreate both of them in my mind, with a great degree of clarity. The first was Phyllis Dixey, the 'Queen of Striptease', the fan dancer who came to the Empire with her naked tableaux show. In those days, nudes could appear on stage only if they did not move. The Windmill Theatre in London got round this by standing their naked girls on revolving plinths; no such furniture existed in Swindon's neck of the provinces.

No artiste had greater reason to despair of the climate at the Empire Theatre than Phyllis, who first played there in 1949. Later, demonstrating considerable pluck, poor memory, or a skin hardened by years in draughty theatres, she gave it another go in 1954. Many readers will recall, even better than I, the rather naturally stern, but athletically bodied Miss Dixey. She was the *éminence grise* of the *tableau vivant* and, in her time, the unassailable exponent of the fan dance. I saw her by accident on her earlier appearance at the Swindon Empire, when I was six years old, and just after her tableaux had proved sufficiently mobile to attract the attention of the Watch Committee (or whatever they were then called), where her *Peek-a-Boo* show had played the previous week. There, the eagle-eyed, puritanical curmudgeons had detected movements where movements should not have been. They had observed parts that should not have been observed. Miss Dixey, called to account under the laws of censorship then pertaining, had been reprimanded and was chastened. But she was also doubtless heartened by the publicity this generated in the local press. It guaranteed full houses at Swindon, her next point of display. She determined to give the patrons a good time when she and her company arrived at the Empire Theatre.

The 'accident', previously mentioned, by which I was introduced to the 'Queen of Striptease', was an apparent failure on the part of my grandparents to read the newspapers. They went to the Empire every week, and booked their customary seats in the front row of the stalls as a matter of course. Believing *Peek-a-Boo* would prove to be just another variety show, they had bought three tickets, and took me along. When interrogated later by my outraged parents, my grandparents maintained that they had not previously heard of Phyllis Dixey and might have supposed that she was a singer. In the event, neither Miss Dixey nor any of the females in her splendid company were inclined to sing.

In those days, Phyllis Dixey's trademark fan dance (two fans) was presented immediately before the interval. Prior to that, one had to suffer endless and tiresome interruptions by her husband, Jack Tracy, in the guise of Snuffy the comedian. There were also a couple of mediocre speciality acts to suffer (in 1949 these were Kenyots Acrobats and Avangers continental specialists), and some ensemble work by the company.

The main ensemble piece in Phyllis Dixey's *Peek-a-Boo* of 1949 was described as a 'Scottish Ballet'. In this, much use was made of the theatre's water supply, a convenience that had been a feature of Swindon's Empire since the day it opened, when it advertised 'a curtain of water that could be utilised at a moment's notice between the proscenium and the audience in the case of fire'. (A pity, one feels, it was not utilised more readily to dilute the disinfectant.)

It was certainly utilised for the Scottish Ballet. The stage of the Empire Theatre was awash with water. There were tableaux amidst fountains, tableaux with waterfalls, and tableaux whose participants seemed to be paddling about for no discernible reason. Naked girls posed in stationary groups, in accordance with the Lord Chamberlain's requirements. Others, wearing pseudo-bearskin hats, sporrans hung loosely about the waist, long plaid socks and nothing else, marched about in time with the music. Any value in the sporrans by way of concealment was negated by the degree of elasticity in their restraining straps, and the vigorous way in which the company applied itself to the Scottish Ballet. The Lord Chamberlain's intentions in proscribing such energetic movements, no doubt accorded with what my parents would have deemed to be proper. Seated in the middle of the front row of the stalls, however, I learnt rather more about the female anatomy than any of them would have wished.

Much the same could be said for the 'Eastern Ballet' after the interval, during which the curtain of water was not required. This ballet was, I recall, a gauzy, diaphanous and more leisurely undertaking in which the by-now increasingly familiar female components were displayed in a harem setting. And then came Miss Dixey's *pièce de résistance*, her 'Bride's Dream'.

When *Peek-a-Boo* returned to the Swindon Empire in 1954, it had hardly changed in essence; it was the same mix of musical tableaux and speciality acts, and contained more leaden humour from Snuffy. By that time, Jack Tracy was described in the programme as 'Mr Phyllis Dixey'. Had she waited another five years and then returned to Swindon in 1959, Phyllis Dixey would doubtless have found me, at sixteen years of age, more attentive of her blandishments and more appreciative of their educational value. Sad to say, however, she would also have found a large, and then newly made, gap in the streetscape of Swindon, where until very recently its Empire Theatre had stood.

The other act that had a huge effect on me – the circumstances of which I have never forgotten – was the comedian Max Miller. He came twice to the Empire, and those were the only times I ever actually *saw* his act. (We did not have television until after he had retired; I otherwise only heard him on the wireless, and on his gramophone recordings.) On each occasion, there was a gradual build-up of suppressed energy and anticipation as the support acts progressed according to the numbers in the light-boxes. The act immediately preceding Max Miller need not have bothered; by the time the curtains closed upon the forlorn performer, the auditorium was palpably electric. Had the audience held hands, they might have lit up Swindon.

A spotlight played on the right-hand side of the stage, from where the artiste was expected to emerge, and the band struck up his signature tune, 'Mary from the Dairy'. The curtains parted to reveal a painted backdrop – possibly the Embankment, but I am not certain – and the orchestra laid into Mary with ever-increasing speed. Miller timed his entrance to perfection, just a few seconds later than one might expect, and the audience exploded. There is no other word for the euphoria and adulation that must have threatened the roof, if not the very foundations of the Empire Theatre.

Dressed in a cross between a suit of pyjamas and plus fours, of mainly red flowers on a yellow background, and topped by a trilby hat, Miller advanced towards the audience with his arms held out on each side. He placed a foot on the footlights, leaned forward, and beckoned, conspiratorially. He leaned backwards, looking right and left into the wings. Then he was off, like a verbal greyhound, pacing up and down, holding the audience in helpless laughter to the point of immobility, engaging them and at the same time carrying out a one-sided dialogue with the unseen management off-stage (this was also a style adopted by Frankie Howerd in his stage act). Max Miller may have drained his Empire Theatre audiences and sent them home weak with laughter, but nobody else ever had such an uplifting effect on Swindon's theatregoers of the post-war era of austerity. He had a catchphrase: 'Miller's the name, lady; there'll never be another'. The fact is, there never was before him, and there has certainly never been since. No entertainer whom I have seen in the flesh since the 1950s has ever generated an atmosphere of such intensity in an audience; if I had known the Empire Theatre only for this, it would have been worth it.

# Productions 1898 - 1955

| Date | Title/Event | Playwright/Author<br>l= lyrics; m= music | Category | Performers |
|---|---|---|---|---|
| 07/02/1898 | Dick Wittington | | Panto | Jennie Armstrong, Albert James, Beatie Kent, Geo Danvers Jun, G Montrose, A Richards |
| 14/02/1898 | As above | | | |
| 21/02/1898 | Charley's Aunt | Brandon Thomas | Play | Henry Crisp |
| 22/02/1898 | Charley's Aunt | Brandon Thomas | Play | Henry Crisp |
| 23/02/1898 | Charley's Aunt | Brandon Thomas | Play | Henry Crisp |
| 24/02/1898 | One of the Bravest | | Play | |
| 25/02/1898 | One of the Bravest | | Play | |
| 26/02/1898 | One of the Bravest | | Play | |
| 28/02/1898 | Aladdin | | Panto | |
| 07/03/1898 | The Gay Parisienne | l George Dance, m Ivan Caryll | Musical | Sinetta Marsden, George Ascot, May Laurie |
| 14/03/1898 | Oriental America | | Revue | Sidney Woodward, Inez Clough |
| 21/03/1898 | The World's Verdict | | Play | |
| 28/03/1898 | Faust | Gounod | Opera | Rouseby's Grand Opera  Co inc Arthur Rouseby, Maude Crombie |
| 29/03/1898 | Il Trovatore | Verdi | Opera | Rouseby's Grand Opera  Co inc Arthur Rouseby, Maude Crombie |
| 30/03/1898 | Bohemian Girl | Balfe | Opera | Rouseby's Grand Opera  Co inc Arthur Rouseby, Maude Crombie |
| 31/03/1898 | Tannhauser | Tannhauser | Opera | Rouseby's Grand Opera  Co inc Arthur Rouseby, Maude Crombie |
| 01/04/1898 | Cavalleria Rusticana/ I Pagliacci | Mascagni/ Leoncavallo | Opera | Rouseby's Grand Opera  Co inc Arthur Rouseby, Maude Crombie |
| 02/04/1898 | Maritana | Vincent Wallace | Opera | Rouseby's Grand Opera  Co inc Arthur Rouseby, Maude Crombie |
| 04/04/1898 | The New Boy | | Play | A B Tapping, Edith Blande |
| 11/04/1898 | On the Frontier | | Play | John Soden, Anna de Grey |
| 18/04/1898 | The Skirt Dancer | l E Mansell, m H Trotere | Musical | Sinetta Marsden, Thomas C Wray, Charles Sequin |
| 25/04/1898 | | | Variety | Marvellous Steens, Lena Snaith |
| 02/05/1898 | The Death or Glory Boys | E Hill Mitchelson | Play | E Hill Mitchelson, Henry George |
| 09/05/1898 | Tom, Dick and Harry | | Play | Edward Bonfield, W S Stevenson |
| 16/05/1898 | Two Little Vagabonds | Arthur Shirley, George Sims | Play | Wilfred Beaumont, Miss J Holford- Berringer |
| 23/05/1898 | The Still Alarm | Joseph Arthur | Play | Bellindon Clark, Nina Vincent |
| 30/05/1898 | The Lady Slavey | l George Dance, m John Crook | Musical | Eva Graham, Frank Sherlock |
| 06/06/1898 | The Greed of Gold | | Play | Chas A Carlile, Morton Powell |
| 13/06/1898 | Our Sailor Lad | | Musical | Fred J Kirke, Nell Ascott |
| 20/06/1898 | Sons of the Sea | | Play | Horace Dawson, Emily Stevens |

| Date | Title/Event | Playwright/Author l= lyrics; m= music | Category | Performers |
|---|---|---|---|---|
| 01/08/1898 | The Colonial Premier | W T McClellan | Play | William Allonby, Harvey White, Bertha Grahame |
| 08/08/1898 | In the Ranks | George Sims and H Pettit | Play | Lynn Harding, James Hare |
| 15/08/1898 | Mr Carpenter's Variety Company | | Variety | Les Tells, Le Barr, D J Pedley |
| 22/08/1898 | Proof | | Play | Malcolm Cherry, Charles Draycott |
| 29/08/1898 | The Sign of the Cross | Wilson Barrett | Play | Gwendoline Floyd, Gertrude Bernette |
| 05/09/1898 | Jane Shore | | Play | |
| 12/09/1898 | The French Maid | l Basil Hood, m Walter Slaughter | Musical | Maude Marriott, Emily Beauchamp, Hettie Edwards |
| 19/09/1898 | A Night Out | | Play | E W Garden, George Mallett |
| 26/09/1898 | Soldiers of the Queen | | Play | Horace Butler, Nelson Ramsey |
| 03/10/1898 | Charley's Aunt | Brandon Thomas | Play | E Lovets Fraser, F Wilkinson, Gertrude Stevens |
| 10/10/1898 | Yeoman of the Guard | l WS Gilbert, m Arthur Sullivan | Opera | D'Oyly Carte No 1 Opera Co inc Adeline Vaudrey, H M Russell, Charles R Wallen |
| 11/10/1898 | Yeoman of the Guard | l WS Gilbert, m Arthur Sullivan | Opera | D'Oyly Carte No 1 Opera Co inc Adeline Vaudrey, H M Russell, Charles R Wallen |
| 12/10/1898 | The Mikado | l WS Gilbert, m Arthur Sullivan | Opera | D'Oyly Carte No 1 Opera Co inc Adeline Vaudrey, H M Russell, Charles R Wallen |
| 13/10/1898 | The Mikado | l WS Gilbert, m Arthur Sullivan | Opera | D'Oyly Carte No 1 Opera Co inc Adeline Vaudrey, H M Russell, Charles R Wallen |
| 14/10/1898 | HMS Pinafore | l WS Gilbert, m Arthur Sullivan | Opera | D'Oyly Carte No 1 Opera Co inc Adeline Vaudrey, H M Russell, Charles R Wallen |
| 15/10/1898 | The Grand Duchess | Offenbach | Opera | D'Oyly Carte No 1 Opera Co inc Adeline Vaudrey, H M Russell, Charles R Wallen |
| 17/10/1898 | Black Eyed Susan | | Play | Roy Redgrave, Ethel Griffies, Alfred Rouseby |
| 24/10/1898 | Uncle Tom's Cabin | Harriet Beecher Stowe | Play | J H Renny, John Henry Roberts |
| 31/10/1898 | The Circus Girl | l Adrian Ross, Harry Greenbank, m Ivan Caryll | Musical | Ada Claire, Dalton Somers, Ethel Netherton |
| 07/11/1898 | The Secrets of the Harem | | Play | Ada Oakley, Henry Rutland |
| 14/11/1898 | Mary Queen of Scots | | Play | Mrs Bandmann- Palmer Co, Kate Walburn, Trant Fagan |
| 15/11/1898 | Hamlet | William Shakespeare | Play | Mrs Bandmann- Palmer Co, Kate Walburn, Trant Fagan |
| 16/11/1898 | East Lynne | from Mrs Henry wood | Play | Mrs Bandmann- Palmer Co, Kate Walburn, Trant Fagan |
| 17/11/1898 | Mary Queen of Scots | | Play | Mrs Bandmann- Palmer Co, Kate Walburn, Trant Fagan |
| 18/11/1898 | The School for Scandal | Richard Brinsley Sheridan | Play | Mrs Bandmann- Palmer Co, Kate Walburn, Trant Fagan |

| Date | Title/Event | Playwright/Author l= lyrics; m= music | Category | Performers |
|---|---|---|---|---|
| 19/11/1898 | East Lynne | from Mrs Henry wood | Play | Mrs Bandmann- Palmer Co, Kate Walburn, Trant Fagan |
| 21/11/1898 | The Geisha | l Harry Greenbank, m Sidney Jones | Musical | Lillian Hubbard, Edward Carlton |
| 28/11/1898 | Our Volunteers | F Maxwell | Play | Sydney Arnold, W S Hartford, Constance Medwyn |
| 05/12/1898 | The Skirt Dancer | l E Mansell, m H Trotere | Musical | Fanny Wright, Thomas C Wray, Fred A Ellis |
| 12/12/1898 | Mr Carpenter's Second Grand Variety Co | | Variety | Daisy Martell, W H Perret, Maude Mortimer |
| 19/12/1898 | The Three Musketeers | | Play | |
| 20/12/1898 | First Grand Benefit for Mr Carpenter | | | |
| 26/12/1898 | Rogues and Vagabonds | E Hill-Mitchelson, F Benton | Play | |
| 02/01/1899 | The Swiss Express | | Play | The Two Renads, Horatio Sinclair, E G Merrie |
| 09/01/1899 | My Friend the Prince | Justin Huntley McCarthy | Play | Frank Beresford, J H Beaumont, Olive Loftus Leyton, Frederick Mouillot |
| 16/01/1899 | The Two Little Vagabonds | Arthur Shirley, George Sims | Play | Ethel Bracewell, Gracie Jones |
| 23/01/1899 | The Bohemian Girl | Balfe | Opera | Rouseby Grand Opera Co, Mr and Mrs Rouseby, Fred Clendon, Therese Gilbert |
| 24/01/1899 | Daughter of the Regiment | Donizetti | Opera | Rouseby Grand Opera Co, Mr and Mrs Rouseby, Fred Clendon, Therese Gilbert |
| 25/01/1899 | Maritana | Vincent Wallace | Opera | Rouseby Grand Opera Co, Mr and Mrs Rouseby, Fred Clendon, Therese Gilbert |
| 26/01/1899 | The Bohemian Girl | Balfe | Opera | Rouseby Grand Opera Co, Mr and Mrs Rouseby, Fred Clendon, Therese Gilbert |
| 27/01/1899 | Faust | Gounod | Opera | Rouseby Grand Opera Co, Mr and Mrs Rouseby, Fred Clendon, Therese Gilbert |
| 28/01/1899 | Maritana | Vincent Wallace | Opera | Rouseby Grand Opera Co, Mr and Mrs Rouseby, Fred Clendon, Therese Gilbert |
| 30/01/1899 | Green Bushes | | Play | Morley Carroll, Matt Wilkinson, Lottie Pearce |
| 06/02/1899 | Aladdin | | Panto | Flo Conlan, Estha Stella, John G Brett |
| 13/02/1899 | A London Mystery | William Bourne | Play | M Thorpe, Walter Kellson, Charlotte Bellinger |
| 20/02/1899 | A Trip to Chinatown | l Charles H Hoyt, m Percy Gaunt | Musical | Wilfred Shine, J W Hooper, Freda Spry |
| 27/02/1899 | Cinderella | | Panto | |
| 06/03/1899 | The Silver King | Wilson Barrett | Play | Claude King, Frances Wetherell, Tom Poulton |
| 13/03/1899 | Mr Carpenter's Great Variety Company | | Variety | Connie Williams, R W Bentley Professor Vallence |
| 20/03/1899 | The Death or Glory Boys | E Hill Mitchelson | Play | Theo Balfour, E Hill- Mitchelson, Alice Balfour |

| Date | Title/Event | Playwright/Author<br>l= lyrics; m= music | Category | Performers |
|------|-------------|----------------------------------------|----------|------------|
| 27/03/1899 | The Scales of Justice | | Play | Douglas Bruce, Fred Cherry |
| 03/04/1899 | A Pair of Spectacles | Sydney Grundy | Play | George Elton. George Gold, Emeline Holt |
| 10/04/1899 | Mr Joseph Poole's Myriorama | | | |
| 17/04/1899 | As above | | | |
| 24/04/1899 | Tommy Atkins | Arthur Shirley, Ben Landeck | Play | F Eustace, Arthur E Godfrey |
| 01/05/1899 | The Girl of my Heart | | Play | George Mitchell, C L Dering, Cora Deane |
| 08/05/1899 | La Poupee | l G Byng, m E Audran | Musical | Gus Danby, Arthur Burdett, Gertrude Griffith, |
| 11/05/1899 | The Middleman | Henry Arthur Jones | Play | F Ronald Bayne, Edgar H Flood, Cecil Massey |
| 15/05/1899 | A Life's Revenge | Walter Howard | Play | Marie Dagmar, Walter Roberts, Kathleen Eckhart |
| 22/05/1899 | Between the Lights | | Play | Leslie Carter, William Craston |
| 29/05/1899 | The Lucky Star | | Opera | D'Oyly Carte Opera Co, inc Charles R Wallen, Helier Le Maistre, H M Russell |
| 30/05/1899 | The Lucky Star | | Opera | D'Oyly Carte Opera Co, inc Charles R Wallen, Helier Le Maistre, H M Russell |
| 31/05/1899 | The Mikado | l WS Gilbert, m Arthur Sullivan | Opera | D'Oyly Carte Opera Co, inc Charles R Wallen, Helier Le Maistre, H M Russell |
| 01/06/1899 | The Golden Chance | St Auban Miller | Play | Taliesyn G Davies, Nesta Sandford |
| 05/06/1899 | Mr Ernest Carpenter's Great Variety Co | | Variety | Elsie May, Bob Hutt, Musical Minim, Maud Mortimer |
| 12/06/1899 | One of the Family | l Frank Dix, Frank Ayrton, m Henry W May, Arnold Cooke | Musical | George Handel, Henry Egington, Harry Brayne |
| 19/06/1899 | Dishonoured | Arthur St John | Play | ArthurSt John, C B Fountaine, Ida St John |
| 26/06/1899 | The Principal Boy | l Guy d'Lanor, m Arnold Cooke | Musical | James Grant, Percy Knight, J E Nightingale, Maud Prenton |
| 03/07/1899 | The Terrors of Paris | E Hill Michelson | Play | Lewis Gilbert, C W Spencer, Trissie Humpheries |
| 07/08/1899 | Sins of the Fathers | W J McKay, W Davidson | Play | Wallace Davidson, John Wilkinson |
| 14/08/1899 | In Old Kentucky | Charles T Dazey | Play | J George Steel, Lillieth Leyton |
| 21/08/1899 | At Duty's Call | | Play | |
| 28/08/1899 | East Lynne | Mrs Henry Wood | Play | Leonard Yorke, Ernest Montefiore, Belle Valpe |
| 04/09/1899 | Black or White | l Mark Melford m J Crook | Musical | Arthur Ring, Wallace Widdicombe, Minna Louis |
| 11/09/1899 | Lady Godiva | Max Goldberg | Play | Jean De Burgoyne, Lillian O'Dell, Clifford Rean |
| 18/09/1899 | Our Boys | H J Byron | Play | Ernest Carpenter, Mrs Carpenter, A M Seaton |

| Date | Title/Event | Playwright/Author<br>l= lyrics; m= music | Category | Performers |
|---|---|---|---|---|
| 25/09/1899 | How London Lives | Arthur Shirley, M Field | Play | Kate Tyndall, Graham Price |
| 02/10/1899 | A Trip to Chicago | Fred Lyster, Charles F Sheridan | Musical | Dolly Lovell, Walter Sealby |
| 09/10/1899 | Saucy Sally | | Play | E J Lonnen, Lawrence Brough, Amy Singleton |
| 16/10/1899 | Les Cloches de Corneville | | Musical | J W Handley, George A Fox, William Everard |
| 23/10/1899 | Streets of London | Dion Boucicault | Play | Charles Grant, Clifford Spencer |
| 30/10/1899 | Maritana | Vincent Wallace | Opera | Neilson Grand Opera Co inc Austin Boyd, T H Wood, Constance St Bride |
| 31/10/1899 | Bohemian Girl | Balfe | Opera | Neilson Grand Opera Co inc Austin Boyd, T H Wood, Constance St Bride |
| 01/10/1899 | Lily of Killarney | Julius Benedict | Opera | Neilson Grand Opera Co inc Austin Boyd, T H Wood, Constance St Bride |
| 02/10/1899 | Maritana | Vincent Wallace | Opera | Neilson Grand Opera Co inc Austin Boyd, T H Wood, Constance St Bride |
| 03/10/1899 | Faust | Gounod | Opera | Neilson Grand Opera Co inc Austin Boyd, T H Wood, Constance St Bride |
| 04/10/1899 | Bohemian Girl | Vincent Wallace | Opera | Neilson Grand Opera Co inc Austin Boyd, T H Wood, Constance St Bride |
| 06/11/1899 | Master and Man | | Play | J W Baxter, Robert Lislemore, Charles Dudley |
| 13/11/1899 | The Belle of New York | L C S McLellan m G Kerker | Musical | Charles J Cunningham, Sam T Pearce, Maud Darling |
| 20/11/1899 | Harbour Lights | G R Simms, H Pettitt | Play | W S Hartford, Kate Brand, J S Crawley, H Aylmer |
| 27/11/1899 | The Little Minister | J M Barrie | Play | Bangley Imeson, Molly Pearson |
| 04/12/1899 | Uncle Tom's Cabin | Harriet Beecher Stowe | Play | Bentic Rowe, J H Rennie, Charles Harrington |
| 11/12/1899 | What happened to Jones | George Broadhurst | Play | |
| 12/12/1899 | What happened to Jones | George Broadhurst | Play | |
| 13/12/1899 | What happened to Jones | George Broadhurst | Play | |
| 14/12/1899 | The Liars | Henry Arthur Jones | Play | C E Bedells, Frank Goldsmith |
| 15/12/1899 | The Liars | Henry Arthur Jones | Play | C E Bedells, Frank Goldsmith |
| 16/12/1899 | The Liars | Henry Arthur Jones | Play | C E Bedells, Frank Goldsmith |
| 26/12/1899 | The Two Hussars | | Play | Harry Bruce, Marguerite Trevosper |
| 01/01/1900 | The French Spy | E Hill-Michelson | Play | Amy Sangster, Fred Benton, Berkeley Perkins |
| 08/01/1900 | Frivolity | | Musical | Harry Leopold, Herbert Lewis |

| Date | Title/Event | Playwright/Author<br>l= lyrics; m= music | Category | Performers |
|------|-------------|------------------------|----------|------------|
| 15/01/1900 | Professor Crocker's 30 educated horses | | Variety | |
| 22/01/1900 | Rogues and Vagabonds | E Hill-Michelson, F Benton | Play | H J Fowler, H Kirby |
| 29/01/1900 | Swiss Express | | Musical | Charles Renad, Fred Renad, W Bailey |
| 05/02/1900 | Cinderella | | Panto | Edith Lyddon, Lydia Cosman |
| 12/02/1900 | Cinderella | | Panto | |
| 19/02/1900 | Two Little Drummer Boys | Walter Howard | Play | Walter Howard, Agnes Howard, Courtenay Robinson |
| 26/02/1900 | Dick Whittington | | Panto | Mabel Wynne, George Campbell |
| 05/03/1900 | Honour Thy Father | | Play | Clavering Craig, John Barton, Helen Clavering Craig, Russell Spiers |
| 12/03/1900 | Two Orphans | | Play | Harry Dornton, Mrs H Hampton, J W Henson |
| 19/03/1900 | | | Dance | Mdlle Jenny Mills (Transformation Dancer), Rouletta, Royal Corries |
| 26/03/1900 | The Mercilless World | | Play | Ernest Keand, Leslie Carter, Cora Deane |
| 02/04/1900 | Dandy Fifth | l George Sims, m C Corrie | Musical | Frank Barclay, Trueman Towers, Zoe Gilfillan |
| 09/04/1900 | Soldiers of the Queen | | Play | Herbert Hollister, Lewis Leslie, Jeannie Burgoyne |
| 16/04/1900 | Denounced | | Play | Cyril Harrison, Clifton Boyne, Katie Froude |
| 23/04/1900 | Held by the Enemy | William Gillette | Play | Douglas Vigors, Charles Leicester, Evelyn Maule |
| 30/04/1900 | Jack o' hearts | | Play | Sydney Vereker, Marie De Burgh |
| 03/05/1900 | Rose of Persia | l Basil Hood, m Arthur Sullivan | Opera | D'Oyly Carte Opera Co |
| 04/05/1900 | Rose of Persia | l Basil Hood, m Arthur Sullivan | Opera | D'Oyly Carte Opera Co |
| 05/05/1900 | Rose of Persia | l Basil Hood, m Arthur Sullivan | Opera | D'Oyly Carte Opera Co |
| 07/05/1900 | The Golden Ladder | Wilson Barrett | Play | Harry Percival, Mary Austin |
| 14/05/1900 | La Poupee | l George Byng, m Edward Audran | Musical | Gus Danby, Gertrude Griffith |
| 21/05/1900 | A Trip to Chicago | Fred Lyster, Charles F Sheridan | Musical | Walter Sealby, Clifford Campbell |
| 28/05/1900 | Ticket of Leave Man | Tom Taylor | Play | Ernest Carpenter, Amy Sangster |
| 04/06/1900 | A Foot at the Altar | | Play | W E Langley, Beryl Montague |
| 11/06/1900 | My Sweetheart | | Musical | John F Lambe, Florence Carlile |
| 18/06/1900 | Lost in London | | Play | Beresford Whitcomb, Maude Walsh |
| 25/06/1900 | The Skirt Dancer | L E Mansell, m H Trotere | Musical | Julia Kent, Charles Sequin |
| 02/07/1900 | When a Man's Married | | Musical | Charles Adeson, Joe E Nightingale |

| Date | Title/Event | Playwright/Author<br>l= lyrics; m= music | Category | Performers |
|---|---|---|---|---|
| 06/08/1900 | In Old Kentucky | | Play | Laura Burt, George Steel |
| 13/08/1900 | Great Temptations | | Musical | Doris Brookes, Charles Carter, Archie Selwyn |
| 20/08/1900 | Florodora | l Ernest Boyd-Jones, m Leslie Stuart | Musical | Lilian Stanley, Gus Danby |
| 27/08/1900 | A Dark Secret | | Play | Byron Douglass, Hugh Marston, Lily Pearl |
| 03/09/1900 | Fun on the Bristol | | Musical | Maurice Love, Chas Fisher |
| 10/09/1900 | The Sign of the Cross | Wilson Barrett | Play | Richard Hoodless, D Lewin Mannington |
| 17/09/1900 | Hearts are Trumps | Cecil Raleigh | Play | Italia Conti, Edwin Palmer, Margaret Saville |
| 24/09/1900 | Frivolity | | Musical | The Leopolds |
| 01/10/1900 | The Worst Woman in London | Walter Melville | Play | Nellie Lauraine, Fred Dobell |
| 08/10/1900 | Somebody's Sweetheart | Edward Marris | Musical | Ethel M Ward, Melville Bickford, Philip Sefton |
| 15/10/1900 | The Span of Life | Sutton Vane Snr | Play | Arthur Bawtree, Gracie Murielle |
| 22/10/1900 | Rose of Persia | l Basil Hood, m Arthur Sullivan | Opera | D'Oyly Carte Opera Co, Manfred Russell, Adeline Vaudrey |
| 23/10/1900 | Rose of Persia | l Basil Hood, m Arthur Sullivan | Opera | D'Oyly Carte Opera Co, Manfred Russell, Adeline Vaudrey |
| 24/10/1900 | Rose of Persia | l Basil Hood, m Arthur Sullivan | Opera | D'Oyly Carte Opera Co, Manfred Russell, Adeline Vaudrey |
| 25/10/1900 | Stars of the Night | | Variety | Hugh Dempsey, Roscoe's performing pig, dog and roosters, Leglare Troupe |
| 26/10/1900 | Stars of the Night | | Variety | Hugh Dempsey, Roscoe's performing pig, dog and roosters, Leglare Troupe |
| 27/10/1900 | Stars of the Night | | Variety | Hugh Dempsey, Roscoe's performing pig, dog and roosters, Leglare Troupe |
| 29/10/1900 | The Little Drummer Boys | Walter Howard | Play | Edward Bikker, Fred Emery, Agnes Howard |
| 05/11/1900 | The Belle of New York | l C M S McLellan, m Gustave Kerker | Musical | Tom J Morton, Norman Page, Maud Darling, Enspie Bowman |
| 12/11/1900 | The Power of Gold | | Play | Charles Aldridge, Ethel Tinsley, Mary Ford |
| 19/11/1900 | White Heather | Henry Hamilton, Cecil Raleigh | Play | Batho Griffiths, Reginal Ian Penny |
| 26/11/1900 | Cissy | l W H Dearlove, m J Franklin | Musical | Adeline Yohle, Charles J Barber, Pick-me-up Acrobatic Troupe |
| 03/12/1900 | The King of Crime | Arthur Shirley, Ben Landeck | Play | Samuel Livesey, Maud Hildyard |
| 10/12/1900 | The Silver Cross | | Musical | Fred A Marston, Maud Western |
| 17/12/1900 | Nell Gwynn | | Play | Beatrice Wilson, Norman V Norman |
| 18/12/1900 | Nell Gwynn | | Play | Beatrice Wilson, Norman V Norman |
| 19/12/1900 | Nell Gwynn | | Play | Beatrice Wilson, Norman V Norman |

| Date | Title/Event | Playwright/Author<br>l= lyrics; m= music | Category | Performers |
|------|-------------|-------------------------------------------|----------|------------|
| 20/12/1900 | David Garrick | Thomas William Robertson | Play | Norman V Norman, Beatrice Wilson |
| 21/12/1900 | David Garrick | Thomas William Robertson | Play | Norman V Norman, Beatrice Wilson |
| 22/12/1900 | Nell Gwynn | | Play | Norman V Norman, Beatrice Wilson |
| 26/12/1900 | Showman's Sweetheart | Arthur Law | Play | Katie Berry, Welton Dale |
| 31/12/1900 | Rip Van Winkle | l H B Farnie, m Planquette | Opera | John Ridding, Jessie Melville |
| 07/01/1901 | Joan of Arc | | Panto | Will Sherlock, Alice Ramsdale, Bros Risto contortionists |
| 14/01/1901 | The Lady of Ostend | F C Burnand | Play | Stanley cooke, Lawrence Brough |
| 21/01/1901 | Two Little Vagabonds | Arthur Shirley, George Sims | Play | Lizzie Hall, Miss Grenville, F Booth Conway |
| 28/01/1901 | Puss in Boots | J Hickory Wood | Panto | Peter Fannon, J Foreman, Gus Wheatman |
| 04/02/1901 | On Her Majesty's Service | Walter Melville, Milton Jones | Play | Harry Marlowe, Henry St Leger |
| 11/02/1901 | Cinderella | | Panto | Lillie Pearl, Edward Grey, Dan Idle |
| 18/02/1901 | The Second Mrs Tanqueray | Arthur Wing Pinero | Play | Muriel Wylford, Guy Carew, George Riddell |
| 19/02/1901 | Magda | Hermann Sudermann | Play | Muriel Wylford, Guy Carew, George Riddell |
| 25/02/1901 | Merry Madcap | Victor Stevens | Musical | Victor Stevens, Ada Willoughby, Nora Millington |
| 04/03/1901 | The Executioner's Daughter | E Hill-Michelson | Play | W H Sharpe, Charles Coleman, Kenneth Black |
| 11/03/1901 | The Dandy Fifth | l George Sims, m Clive Corrie | Musical | Frank Barclay, Zoe Gilfillan, Geo Delaforce |
| 18/03/1901 | In the Shadow of Night | | Play | George Harvard, Kate Hullan |
| 25/03/1901 | The Swiss Express | | Play | Two Renads ( Charles and Frederick), Aimee Rowe |
| 01/04/1901 | Grand Novelties | | Variety | Leoni Clarke with Boxing Kangaroo, Professor Carson, Cinematographic show |
| 08/04/1901 | The French Spy | E Hill-Michelson | Play | Kathleen Eckart, Fred Benton |
| 15/04/1901 | In Old Madrid | | Musical | Fred J Kirke, Nell Ascott, Walter T Hybert |
| 22/04/1901 | The Dandy Doctor | l Edward Marris, m Dudley Powell | Musical | Witty Watty Walton, Florence Smithers, Ethel M Ward |
| 29/04/1901 | Florodora | l Ernest Boyd-Jones, m Leslie Stuart | Musical | Florence Burdett, Gus Daney |
| 06/05/1901 | Woman and Wine | Arthur Shirley | Play | Edith Blande, Vernon Sansbury |
| 13/05/1901 | David Garrick | Thomas William Robertson | Play | Norman V Norman, Beatrice Wilson |
| 14/05/1901 | Nell Gwynn | | Play | Norman V Norman, Beatrice Wilson |
| 15/05/1901 | David Garrick | Thomas William Robertson | | Norman V Norman, Beatrice Wilson |

| Date | Title/Event | Playwright/Author l= lyrics; m= music | Category | Performers |
|------|-------------|------------------|----------|------------|
| 16/05/1901 | Lady of Lyons | Edward Bulwer-Lytton | Play | Norman V Norman, Beatrice Wilson |
| 17/05/1901 | Still Waters Run Deep | Tom Taylor | Play | Norman V Norman, Beatrice Wilson |
| 18/05/1901 | Nell Gwynn | | Play | Norman V Norman, Beatrice Wilson |
| 20/05/1901 | Olivette | Edmond Audran | Musical | Chrissie Saumarez, Irene Marriott, Leslie Holland, Robert Eadie |
| 27/05/1901 | The Bohemian Girl | Balfe | Opera | F S Gilbert's Celebrated English Opera Co, Constance St Bride, T H Wood |
| 27/05/1901 | Maritana | Vincent Wallace | Opera | F S Gilbert's Celebrated English Opera Co, Constance St Bride, T H Wood |
| 28/05/1901 | Il Trovatore | Verdi | Opera | F S Gilbert's Celebrated English Opera Co, Constance St Bride, T H Wood |
| 29/05/1901 | Faust | Gounod | Opera | F S Gilbert's Celebrated English Opera Co, Constance St Bride, T H Wood |
| 03/06/1901 | The Slave Girl | | Play | Jerrold Heather, Nina Vaughton, Stanley Gordon |
| 10/06/1901 | East Lynne | Mrs Henry Wood | Play | Frances Wolvington, E V Campbell, Cecil M Yorke |
| 17/06/1901 | Carl the Clockmaker | Harry Starr | Musical | Harry Starr, Ethel Danbury, Fred W Graham |
| 24/06/1901 | Delivered from Evil | Frank Dix | Play | Frank Dix, Sidney Sarl, Elsie Evelyn Hill |
| 01/07/1901 | Shadows of a Great City | Joseph Jefferson | Play | Harry Foxwell, Eleanor Reardon, E Carter Livesey |
| 05/08/1901 | Somebody's Sweetheart | Edward Marris | Musical | Winifred Preece, Austin Lenton |
| 12/08/1901 | The Silver King | Wilson Barrett | Play | Herbert Ford, Ethel Gordon, Edward J George |
| 19/08/1901 | Alone in London | Robert Buchanan, Harriet Jay | Play | F Joynson Powell, W H Brougham |
| 26/08/1901 | Secrets, or the Cross and the Crescent | | Play | George Rydon, Nellie Merton, John F Preston |
| 02/09/1901 | Gentleman Joe, the Hansom Cabbie | l Basil Hood, m Walter Slaughter | Musical | Chal T Chaloner, May Mars, Lottie Leonora |
| 09/09/1901 | While London Sleeps | Charles Darrell | Play | Lester Collingwood, Frederick Ross |
| 16/09/1901 | Programme of Novelties | | Variety | Salambo and Ollivette, Eire Salambo, Cyril Dare |
| 23/09/1901 | A Chinese Honeymoon | l George Dance, m Harry Talbot | Musical | Picton Roxborough, Frank Sutton, Harry Kilburn, Lily Soutter |
| 30/09/1901 | Dare Devil Dorothy | l Wilfred Carr, m K Ernest Irving | Musical | Helene India, Percy Yorke |
| 07/10/1901 | The 10.30 Down Express | | Play | Edward L Garside, John Hignett, Ella Vane |
| 14/10/1901 | San Toy | L Harry Greenbank, Adrian Ross, m Sidney Jones | Musical | J Edward Fraser, Gertrude Gillian |
| 21/10/1901 | Jacko | | Musical | Harry Rogerson, John Fuller, Lauri Wylie |

| Date | Title/Event | Playwright/Author l= lyrics; m= music | Category | Performers |
|------|-------------|--------------------------------------|----------|------------|
| 28/10/1901 | A Woman Adrift | W T McCLellan | Play | Marie Polini, Ernest Keand, Artie Keand, Violet Keand |
| 04/11/1901 | A Fool's Paradise | Sydney Grundy, | Play | Lillian Herries, Charles Doran, Fred Sergeant |
| 05/11/1901 | The Profligate | Arthur Pinero | Play | Lillian Herries, Charles Doran, Fred Sergeant |
| 06/11/1901 | The Notorious Mrs Ebsmith | Arthur Pinero | Play | Lillian Herries, Charles Doran, Fred Sergeant |
| 07/11/1901 | The Casino Girl | H B Smith, L Englander | Musical | Max Copeland, Charles R Walenn, Mrs Arthur Rouseby |
| 08/11/1901 | The Casino Girl | H B Smith, L Englander | Musical | Max Copeland, Charles R Walenn, Mrs Arthur Rouseby |
| 09/11/1901 | The Casino Girl | H B Smith, L Englander | Musical | Max Copeland, Charles R Walenn, Mrs Arthur Rouseby |
| 11/11/1901 | Passion of Life | | Play | Augustine Alexander, Samuel James |
| 12/11/1901 | Passion of Life | | Play | Augustine Alexander, Samuel James |
| 13/11/1901 | Passion of Life | | Play | Augustine Alexander, Samuel James |
| 14/11/1901 | The Emerald Isle | l Basil Hood, m Arthur Sullivan, Edward German | Opera | Manfred Russell, Charles R Walenn, Mrs Arthur Rouseby |
| 15/11/1901 | The Emerald Isle | l Basil Hood, m Arthur Sullivan, Edward German | Opera | Manfred Russell, Charles R Walenn, Mrs Arthur Rouseby |
| 16/11/1901 | The Emerald Isle | l Basil Hood, m Arthur Sullivan, Edward German | Opera | Manfred Russell, Charles R Walenn, Mrs Arthur Rouseby |
| 18/11/1901 | The Sign of the Cross | Wilson Barrett | Play | Richard Hoodless, Dorothy Thomas |
| 25/11/1901 | The Music Hall Girl | W T McCLellan | Musical | Julia Kent, Alex Keith |
| 02/12/1901 | Two Little Sailor Boys | Walter Howard | Play | W H Hallatt, Blanche Steele |
| 09/12/1901 | The Christian | | Play | Laura Walker, Hilliard Vox |
| 16/12/1901 | The Worst Woman in London | Walter Melville | Play | Hugh Metcalfe, Phil Harper, Fred Dobell |
| 26/12/1901 | The Major | | Musical | John Clegg, Ada Wallis, Lizzie M'Quire |
| 30/12/1901 | A Royal Divorce | | Play | |
| 06/01/1902 | Rich and Poor of London | Max Goldberg | Play | Fred Clifton, Georgia Walton, Ada Oakley |
| 13/01/1902 | The Ladies' Maid | l C A Lord, m Ernest Hastings | Musical | Chal T Chaloner, Frank Hemming, Lilian Besant, The Two Graces |
| 20/01/1902 | Babes in the Wood | J Hickory Wood | Panto | Frank Crouch, Leonard Theil, Tom Wallace |
| 27/01/1902 | As above | | | |
| 03/02/1902 | The Stolen Birthright | Sydney Spencer | Musical | Charles Draycott, Rosalind Scott Watson |
| 10/02/1902 | Robinson Crusoe | | Panto | Constance St Bride, Harry Buss, Polly Prim |
| 17/02/1902 | The Shadows of a Great City | Joseph Jefferson | Play | Harry Foxwell, Howell Travis, Eleanor Reardon |
| 24/02/1902 | A Trip to Blackpool | Russell Bogue | Musical | Russell Bogue, Nellie V Warden |
| 04/03/1902 | A Message from Mars | Richard Ganthony | Play | F Vernon Travers, William Lockhart, Margaret Savill |

| Date | Title/Event | Playwright/Author<br>l= lyrics; m= music | Category | Performers |
|------|-------------|------------------------------------------|----------|------------|
| 10/03/1902 | On the Frontier | | Play | Alice Rees, Arthur T Lennard, Geo Carrington |
| 17/03/1902 | Blue Beard | | Panto | Cissie Moxon, Frank Lorenzi, W Lorenzi |
| 24/03/1902 | Variety Combination | | Variety | De Lille (illusionist), The Great Hulbert (ventriloquist) |
| 31/03/1902 | A Noble Brother | | Play | Charles Carte, Doris Brookes |
| 07/04/1902 | What Became of Totman | l Augustus Hammond, m Arnold Cooke | Musical | Billy Harman, Marguerite Roath |
| 14/04/1902 | An Eye for an Eye | | Play | Gerald Kaye-Souper, Isabel Egremont, Julian Hartleigh |
| 21/04/1902 | San Toy | l Harry Greenbank, Adrian Ross, m Sidney Jones | Musical | E Stratton Staples, Daisy Wallace, Gertrude Gilliam, J Edward Fraser |
| 28/04/1902 | A Little Outcast | | Play | Nina Vaughton, Jerrold Heather |
| 05/05/1902 | The Money Market | | Musical | W Mowbray Harle, C J Barber |
| 12/05/1902 | Voices of London | William Bourne | Play | E Penn Lewer, Tom Taylor, Mary Dawson |
| 19/05/1902 | The Lady Slavey | l George Dance, m John Crook | Musical | Eva Graham, Frank Sherlock, J C Graves |
| 26/05/1902 | The French Spy | E Hill-Michelson | Play | Kathleen Eckhart, George Mitchell, Berkeley Perkins |
| 02/06/1902 | Faust | Gounod | Opera | Neilson Grand Opera Co inc Marshall Vincent, Hilton St Just, Vera Visard |
| 03/06/1902 | Maritana | Vincent Wallace | Opera | Neilson Grand Opera Co inc Marshall Vincent, Hilton St Just, Vera Visard |
| 04/06/1902 | Daughter of the Regiment | Donizetti | Opera | Neilson Grand Opera Co inc Marshall Vincent, Hilton St Just, Vera Visard |
| 05/06/1902 | Bride of Lammermore | Donizetti | Opera | Neilson Grand Opera Co inc Marshall Vincent, Hilton St Just, Vera Visard |
| 06/06/1902 | Faust | Gounod | Opera | Neilson Grand Opera Co inc Marshall Vincent, Hilton St Just, Vera Visard |
| 07/06/1902 | Bohemian Girl | Balfe | Opera | Neilson Grand Opera Co inc Marshall Vincent, Hilton St Just, Vera Visard |
| 09/06/1902 | Man's Enemy, or the Downward Path | | Play | Effie Bartlett, Evelyn Clare, Edward E Louis |
| 16/06/1902 | Queen of Hearts | | Musical | Walter Blake, Fred Zeitz, Julie Temple |
| 23/06/1902 | Under Remand | Eric Hudson, Reginald Stockton | Play | Marguerite Thorne, J Wilton Richards |
| 30/06/1902 | My Sweetheart | | Musical | W H Montgomery, Maudie Vincent, J E Manning |
| 04/08/1902 | The New Mephisto | l George Dance, m Ernest Vousden | Musical | Albert Weston, WH Kirby, Daisy Sylverton, Marian Armitage |
| 11/08/1902 | The Grip of Iron | Arthur Shirley | Play | Fred Powell, Andrew Liston |

| Date | Title/Event | Playwright/Author<br>l= lyrics; m= music | Category | Performers |
|---|---|---|---|---|
| 18/08/1902 | Two Little Vagabonds | Arthur Shirley, George Sims | Play | F Stuart Innes, J O Monkhouse |
| 25/08/1902 | Gay Grisette | l George Dance, Carl Kiefert | Musical | Charles Adeson, Max Copland, Nellie Hodson |
| 01/09/1902 | Othello | William Shakespeare | Play | Osmond Tearle Co, Carrie Baillie, Norman Partlege, Leonard Shepherd, Godfrey Tearle |
| 02/09/1902 | Merchant of Venice | William Shakespeare | Play | Osmond Tearle Co, Carrie Baillie, Norman Partlege, Leonard Shepherd, Godfrey Tearle |
| 03/09/1902 | Hamlet | William Shakespeare | Play | Osmond Tearle Co, Carrie Baillie, Norman Partlege, Leonard Shepherd, Godfrey Tearle |
| 04/09/1902 | Romeo and Juliet | William Shakespeare | Play | Osmond Tearle Co, Carrie Baillie, Norman Partlege, Leonard Shepherd, Godfrey Tearle |
| 05/09/1902 | Julius Caesar | William Shakespeare | Play | Osmond Tearle Co, Carrie Baillie, Norman Partlege, Leonard Shepherd, Godfrey Tearle |
| 06/09/1902 | Richard the Third | William Shakespeare | Play | Osmond Tearle Co, Carrie Baillie, Norman Partlege, Leonard Shepherd, Godfrey Tearle |
| 08/09/1902 | The Belle of New York | l C S McLellan, m Gustav Kerker | Musical | Arthur Poole, J Carlyle, Edmund Sherras |
| 15/09/1902 | Honour thy Father | C A Clarke, H R Silva | Play | Arthur Knight, Mary Vere, Charles Fancourt |
| 22/09/1902 | The Dandy Fifth | l George Sims, m Clarence C Corrie | Musical | Alan Turner, Pauline Hague, Marjorie Cecil |
| 29/09/1902 | Sherlock Holmes | A Conan Doyle, W Gillette | Play | J B Crawley, Allan Wilkie, Beatrice Whitney |
| 06/10/1902 | Otto the Outcast | Harry Starr | Musical | Harry Starr, Ethel Danbury, Fred W Graham |
| 13/10/1902 | A Chinese Honeymoon | l George Dance, m Harry Talbot | Musical | Tom Redmond, Gwennie Harcourt |
| 20/10/1902 | The Lights o' London | G R Sims | Play | James C Aubrey, Jeannie Burgoyne |
| 27/10/1902 | Kitty Grey | l J Smyth Piggot, m Lionel Monckton, Howard Talbot etc | Musical | Madeline Rees, Bert Byrne, Percy Carr, Tom Graves |
| 03/11/1902 | Two Little Heroes | Eric Hudson, C Longden | Play | Eric Hudson, W Fraser-Brunner, Marie Robson |
| 10/11/1902 | Sporting Life | C Raleigh, Seymour Hicks | Play | Hilliard Vox, V St Lawrence |
| 17/11/1902 | The Messenger Boy | l Adrian Ross m Lionel Monckton | Musical | Alfred Donohue, R White Jr, Eva Sandford |
| 24/11/1902 | A Royal Divorce | | Play | J H Clyndes, Margaret Watson |
| 01/12/1902 | On Active Service | Herbert Leonard | Play | Hartwell J Kirby, Grace Lester |
| 08/12/1902 | Uncle Tom's Cabin | | Play | Ben Rowe, Fred J Kaye, Kitty Wood |
| 15/12/1902 | | | Variety | Lady Wrestlers, Henderson and Stanley ( instrumentalists) |
| 26/12/1902 | A Mother's Love | | Play | Fred Connynghame, John Dunbar, Ethel Gordon |

| Date | Title/Event | Playwright/Author l= lyrics; m= music | Category | Performers |
|------|-------------|------------------------------------|----------|------------|
| 27/12/1902 | A Mother's Love | | Play | Fred Connynghame, John Dunbar, Ethel Gordon |
| 29/12/1902 | Judy; a Child of the streets | | Play | Florrie Groves, George Kirk, F Joynson Powell |
| 05/01/1903 | Somebody's Sweetheart | Edward Marris | Musical | Bertram Damer,Lennox Chandler, Mena Eckerman |
| 12/01/1903 | The Ladies' Maid | l C A Lord, m Ernest Hastings | Musical | Flo Gordon, Larry Clements, HarryHerbert |
| 19/01/1903 | Little Bo-Peep | Martin Byam | Panto | Lily Rouletta, Frances Manners, Mark Tyme, Ted Squires |
| 26/01/1903 | Little Bo-Peep | | | |
| 02/02/1903 | Driven from Home | | Play | Percy Wright, F Lyndon, Albert Clark |
| 09/02/1903 | The Assasin | E Hill-Michelson | Play | E Hill-Michelson, F W Freeman, Amy Ellam |
| 16/02/1903 | Message from Mars | Richard Ganthony | Play | William H Sams, Percy Tyler, William Lockhart |
| 23/02/1903 | The Gay Parisienne | l George Dance, m Ivan Carryl | Musical | Nellie Hodson, Tom May, Madge Soutter |
| 02/03/1903 | Little Lord Fauntleroy | | Play | Master Vivian Thomas, Walter Russell |
| 09/03/1903 | His Majesty's Guests | | Play | Walter Purvis, George Hudson, Cora Duncan |
| 16/03/1903 | Aladdin | | Panto | Daisy Silcott, Irene Rose, Julian Mack |
| 23/03/1903 | Why Men Love Women | Walter Howard | Play | Alfred Panmuir, Annie Saker, Clinton Baddeley |
| 30/03/1903 | Three Little Maids | Paul Rubens | Musical | Lily Elsie ( later the original Merry Widow), Gus Danby |
| 06/04/1903 | The Dandy Doctor | l Edward Marris, m Dudley Powell | Musical | Edward Marris, Ethel M Ward, James Danvers, Florence Smithers |
| 13/04/1903 | For the Woman he Loves | M Wallerton, F Gilbert | Play | Nina Vaughton, Marie McAulay, William J Miller |
| 20/04/1903 | A Trip to Chicago | Fred Lyster, Charles F Sheridan | Musical | Walter Sealby, Chrissie Ralland, Mabel Sealby |
| 27/04/1903 | A Country Girl | l Adrian Ross m Lionel Monckton | Musical | Francis Ludlow, C F Cooke, John Osborne |
| 04/05/1903 | A Grip of Iron or the Stranglers of Paris | J A Atkins, Arthur Shirley | Play | Fred Powell, Florence Nelson, Andrew Liston, Allan Wilkie |
| 11/05/1903 | The Fatal Wedding | Theo Kremer | Play | Rosie Campbell, Randolfo Reade, Burton Cooke |
| 18/05/1903 | The Swiss Express | | Musical | Charles Renad, Frederick Renad, Wilford Bailey |
| 25/05/1903 | Jack's Sweetheart | l J Fletcher Sansome, m A Leopold, A Sheldrake | Musical | Fletcher Sansome, Will Percy |
| 01/06/1903 | Man to Man | William Bourney | Play | H E Chattell, Hettie Chattell, Horace Dawson |
| 08/06/1903 | Grand Variety | | Variety | Apollo ( Scottish athlete), Tani (Japanese wrestler), Curtis Leo (Juggler) |
| 15/06/1903 | Otto the Outcast | Harry Starr | Musical | Harry Starr, Ethel Danbury, Fred W Graham |

| Date | Title/Event | Playwright/Author<br>l= lyrics; m= music | Category | Performers |
|---|---|---|---|---|
| 22/06/1903 | The Heart of a Hero | Lingford Carson | Play | Fred Goddard, Jerrold Ord, Owen Remonde |
| 29/06/1903 | The Scales of Justice | | Play | Jackson Hayes, Florrie Kelsey |
| 03/08/1903 | The Hero of the Flag | Sydney Spenser | Play | Lizzie Hall, Sydney Spenser, A W Munroe |
| 10/08/1903 | Admiral Jack | | Musical | Barry Lupino, Arthur Ricketts, Fred May |
| 17/08/1903 | Her Second Time on Earth | Walter Melville | Play | Edith Blande, Eric Hudson |
| 24/08/1903 | The Black Bishop | Barry Williams | Play | Guinevere Shilton, Albert Guyon |
| 31/08/1903 | Dangerous Women | F A Scudamore | Play | Lillie Monckton, Gladys Newcombe |
| 07/09/1903 | Florodora | l Ernest Boyd-Jones, Leslie Stuart | Musical | Anne Braddon, Edward Thirlbury, Hilda Dugdale, George Wilson |
| 14/09/1903 | When London Sleeps | Charles Darrell | Play | Violet Langley, Jack Haddon, Frank Strickland |
| 21/09/1903 | Merchant of Venice | William Shakespeare | Play | Osmond Tearle Co, Alexander Marsh, Carrie Baillie, Baliol Holloway, |
| 22/09/1903 | As You Like It | William Shakespeare | Play | Osmond Tearle Co, Alexander Marsh, Carrie Baillie, Baliol Holloway, |
| 23/09/1903 | David Garrick | Thomas William Robertson | Play | Osmond Tearle Co, Alexander Marsh, Carrie Baillie, Baliol Holloway, |
| 24/09/1903 | Hamlet | William Shakespeare | Play | Osmond Tearle Co, Alexander Marsh, Carrie Baillie, Baliol Holloway, |
| 25/09/1903 | Macbeth | William Shakespeare | Play | Osmond Tearle Co, Alexander Marsh, Carrie Baillie, Baliol Holloway, |
| 26/09/1903 | Othello | William Shakespeare | Play | Osmond Tearle Co, Alexander Marsh, Carrie Baillie, Baliol Holloway, |
| 28/09/1903 | The Gay Grisette | l George Dance, m Carl Kiefert | Musical | Lilian Stanley, Will Hindson, Chas Adeson |
| 05/10/1903 | A Chinese Honeymoon | l George Dance m Harry Talbot | Musical | Gwennie Harcourt, Maud Terry, Tom W Conway |
| 12/10/1903 | The Private Secretary | Charles Hawtrey | Play | George Helm, Geo Nelson Wallace |
| 19/10/1903 | Bound to Win | Mrs Kimberley | Play | F G Kimberley, Lottie Addison (Mrs Kimberley) |
| 26/10/1903 | The Eternal City | Hall Caine | Play | D Lewin Mannering, Beatrice Bevan |
| 02/11/1903 | All at Sea | l E Paulton, m W Arthur | Musical | Harry Phydora, Julia Kent, Edward Lowe |
| 09/11/1903 | A Bid for Fortune | Barry Williams | Play | Mary Fuleton, Kenneth Smith, Marie Robson |
| 16/11/1903 | The Traitor | E Hill-Michelson | Play | Benaley Evans, Stephen E Scanlon Edwin Jenner |
| 23/11/1903 | A Trip to Chinatown | l Charles Hoyte, m Edward Solomon | Musical | Robert Perris, Eva Purcell |
| 30/11/1903 | The Geisha | l Harry Greenbank, m Sidney Jones | Musical | Dorothy Steele, Edward Ramsdale |

| Date | Title/Event | Playwright/Author l= lyrics; m= music | Category | Performers |
|---|---|---|---|---|
| 07/12/1903 | The Mariners of England | Robert Buchanan, Harriet Jay | Play | E R Abbott Co, Clifford Clifford , Ada Abbott |
| 08/12/1903 | The Mariners of England | Robert Buchanan, Harriet Jay | Play | E R Abbott Co, Clifford Clifford , Ada Abbott |
| 09/12/1903 | The Mariners of England | Robert Buchanan, Harriet Jay | Play | E R Abbott Co, Clifford Clifford , Ada Abbott |
| 10/12/1903 | East Lynne | Mrs Henry Wood | Play | E R Abbott Co, Clifford Clifford , Ada Abbott |
| 11/12/190 | East Lynne | Mrs Henry Wood | Play | E R Abbott Co, Clifford Clifford , Ada Abbott |
| 12/12/1903 | The Mariners of England | Mrs Henry Wood | Play | E R Abbott Co, Clifford Clifford , Ada Abbott |
| 14/12/1903 | Man and Wife | Walter Howard | Play | T E Ward Co,John F Traynor, Wilson Coleman, Miss Ward |
| 15/12/1903 | Man and Wife | Walter Howard | Play | T E Ward Co,John F Traynor, Wilson Coleman, Miss Ward |
| 16/12/1903 | Man and Wife | Walter Howard | Play | T E Ward Co,John F Traynor, Wilson Coleman, Miss Ward |
| 17/12/1903 | Her Wedding Day | | Play | T E Ward Co,John F Traynor, Wilson Coleman, Miss Ward |
| 18/12/1903 | Her Wedding Day | | Play | T E Ward Co,John F Traynor, Wilson Coleman, Miss Ward |
| 19/12/1903 | Her Wedding Day | | Play | T E Ward Co,John F Traynor, Wilson Coleman, Miss Ward |
| 26/12/1903 | Our Sailor Lad | l F J Kirke, m G Dixon | Musical | Fred J Kirk, Nell Ascott |
| 28/12/1903 | Our Sailor Lad | l F J Kirke, m G Dixon | Musical | Fred J Kirk, Nell Ascott |
| 29/12/1903 | Our Sailor Lad | l F J Kirke, m G Dixon | Musical | Fred J Kirk, Nell Ascott |
| 30/12/1903 | Our Sailor Lad | l F J Kirke, m G Dixon | Musical | Fred J Kirk, Nell Ascott |
| 31/12/1903 | In Old Madrid | | Musical | Fred J Kirk, Nell Ascott |
| 01/01/1904 | In Old Madrid | | Musical | Fred J Kirk, Nell Ascott |
| | In Old Madrid | | Musical | Fred J Kirk, Nell Ascott |
| 04/01/1904 | My Lady Molly | l G H Jessop, Percy Greenbank, Sidney Jones | Musical | Gertrude Melville, Muriel Chester, Reginald Kenneth |
| 11/01/1904 | Sentenced for Life | | Musical | G Rutherford, Charles Grant |
| 18/01/1904 | Runaways | l "Jacob Sugarman", m F Knight Pearce | Musical | John Geraint |
| 25/01/1904 | Babes in the Wood | J Hickory Wood | Panto | Nellie Cozens, Arthur Godfrey, Veronica Brady |

| Date | Title/Event | Playwright/Author<br>l= lyrics; m= music | Category | Performers |
|---|---|---|---|---|
| 01/02/1904 | Her One Great Sin | Frank M Thorne | Play | Blanche St Albans, Sam Arthur, J Lester Jackson |
| 08/02/1904 | Judy, or the Fatal Hand | | Play | Florrie Groves, George Kirke |
| 15/02/1904 | The Crimson Club | W Hall, W James | Play | Gus C Livesey, Miss N A Livesey |
| 22/02/1904 | Between Two Women | Frederick Melville | Play | Frank Robertson, Marie Robson, Marie McAuley, Tubby Edlin |
| 29/02/1904 | What Became of Mrs Rackett | l Charles Townsend, m Charles Dixon | Musical | Edith Madelle, Emily Kelsey, Jack Hames |
| 07/03/1904 | Little Red Riding Hood | | Panto | Lily Iris, Nellie Burdett, Dave O'Toole |
| 14/03/1904 | Bigamy | Fred Moule | Play | Grace Lester, Graham Wood, Edward Fryer |
| 21/03/1904 | His Majesty's Guests | Herbert Danley` | Musical | Harry Roxbury, Jasmine Newcombe |
| 28/03/1904 | A Sailor's Sweetheart | | Play | Adam Barton, Alfred Goddard |
| 04/04/1904 | A Showman's Sweetheart | l Arthur Law, Guy Eden, m George Byng | Musical | Chal T Chaloner, Campbell Goldsmith, Julie Alexander |
| 11/04/1904 | Dare Devil Dorothy | l Wilfred Carr, m K Ernest Irving | Musical | Marjorrie Cecil, Wm Francis Green, Henry C Ward, Nellie Harcourt |
| 20/04/1904 | The Idol of Kano | l W F Hewer, m T P Arkell | Opera | Pollie Finn, Frank G Bayly, Chris Fielder |
| 25/04/1904 | The Temptress | Wm P Sheen | Play | Grace E Leslie, George Daner |
| 02/05/1904 | Sinbad the Sailor | | Panto | Daisy De Roy, Tom Griffin, Will Letters, Henry Revell |
| 09/05/1904 | A King Amongst Men | Charles Aldin | Play | Frank Eden, Tom Taylor, Marie Robertson |
| 16/05/1904 | Variety | | Variety | Dr Walford Bodie, World's greatest hypnotist, electrician and scientist |
| 23/05/1904 | Her Second Time on Earth | Walter Melville | Play | Grace Heywood, Bernard Mervyn |
| 30/05/1904 | Somebody's Sweetheart | Edward Marris | Musical | Melville Bickford, Josie Bickford, Nell Ascott |
| 06/06/1904 | Maritana | Vincent Wallace | Opera | Elster-Grime Grand Opera Co inc Marie Elster, F Hargrave, Michael Kemble |
| 07/06/1904 | Daughter of the Regiment | Donizetti | Opera | Elster-Grime Grand Opera Co inc Marie Elster, F Hargrave, Michael Kemble |
| 08/06/1904 | Maritana | Vincent Wallace | Opera | Elster-Grime Grand Opera Co inc Marie Elster, F Hargrave, Michael Kemble |
| 09/06/1904 | Bohemian Girl | Balfe | Opera | Elster-Grime Grand Opera Co inc Marie Elster, F Hargrave, Michael Kemble |
| 10/06/1904 | Faust | Gounod | Opera | Elster-Grime Grand Opera Co inc Marie Elster, F Hargrave, Michael Kemble |
| 11/06/1904 | Bohemian Girl | Balfe | Opera | Elster-Grime Grand Opera Co inc Marie Elster, F Hargrave, Michael Kemble |
| 13/06/1904 | The Woman He Loved | | Play | Nina Vaughton, E Avinal |
| 20/06/1904 | Lady Godiva | Max Goldberg | Play | Hilda Shirley, F B Wolfe |
| 27/06/1904 | David Garrick | Thomas William Robertson | Play | E Hoggan-Armadale, Henry Moxon, Fred Cherry, Marie Florence |

| Date | Title/Event | Playwright/Author<br>l= lyrics; m= music | Category | Performers |
|---|---|---|---|---|
| 28/06/1904 | Sleigh Bells | | Play | E Hoggan-Armadale, Henry Moxon, Fred Cherry, Marie Florence |
| 29/06/1904 | David Garrick | Thomas William Robertson | Play | E Hoggan-Armadale, Henry Moxon, Fred Cherry, Marie Florence |
| 30/06/1904 | Vicar of Wakefield | | Play | E Hoggan-Armadale, Henry Moxon, Fred Cherry, Marie Florence |
| 01/07/1904 | The Lady of Lyons | Edward Bulwer-Lytton | Play | E Hoggan-Armadale, Henry Moxon, Fred Cherry, Marie Florence |
| 02/07/1904 | The Robbery of the Lyons Mail | | Play | E Hoggan-Armadale, Henry Moxon, Fred Cherry, Marie Florence |
| 01/08/1904 | The Lady of Ostend | Sir Francis Burnand | Play | Lawrence Brough, Percy Marshall, Kate Milford |
| 08/08/1904 | A Trip to China Town | l Charles Hoyte, m Edward Solomon | Musical | Lesie Newman, Jerrold Manville, Harriet Fawn |
| 15/08/1904 | Zaza | | Play | Ethel Warwick, Eric Maine |
| 22/08/1904 | A Trip to Rum Fum | | Musical | Cissie Moxon, W Garvey |
| 29/08/1904 | Shadows of a Great City | Joseph Jefferson | Play | Harry Foxwell, Sheila Foxwell, Howell Travis |
| 05/09/1904 | Frivolity | | Musical | Willie Leopold, John Leopold Jr, Bert Lloyd |
| 12/09/1904 | David Garrick | Thomas William Robertson | Play | Alexander Marsh Co, Carrie Baillie |
| 13/09/1904 | Hamlet | William Shakespeare | Play | Alexander Marsh Co, Carrie Baillie |
| 14/09/1904 | Merchant of Venice/ Hamlet | William Shakespeare | Play | Alexander Marsh Co, Carrie Baillie |
| 15/09/1904 | What a Woman Did | | Play | Alexander Marsh Co, Carrie Baillie |
| 16/09/1904 | School for Scandal | Richard Brinsley Sheridan | Play | Alexander Marsh Co, Carrie Baillie |
| 17/09/1904 | Lady of Lyons | Edward Bulwer-Lytton | Play | Alexander Marsh Co, Carrie Baillie |
| 19/09/1904 | The Mockery of Marriage | | Play | Florence Zillwood, Arthur Wimpenny, Frank Dalton |
| 26/09/1904 | The New Commander | | Musical | Grace Warne, George Gordon |
| 03/10/1904 | The Manxman | Wilson Barrett | Play | Alfred B Cross, Minnie Watersford |
| 10/10/1904 | The Girl from Japan | l Wilfred Carr, m Colet Dare | Musical | Nellie Valentine, S Lockeridge, Madie Scott |
| 17/10/1904 | The Midnight Mail | Arthur Shirley | Play | George Harvard, Ada Oakley, Fred G Evison |
| 24/10/1904 | The Cherry Girl | l Aubrey Hopwood, m Ivan Caryll | Musical | Elsie Molloy, Katie May, Dorothy Frostick |
| 31/10/1904 | The Bells of Haslemere | Sydney Grundy, H Pettit | Play | |
| 07/11/1904 | The Ladies Maid | l C A Lord, m Ernest Hastings | Musical | Isa Bowman, Chal T Chaloner |

| Date | Title/Event | Playwright/Author<br>l= lyrics; m= music | Category | Performers |
|------|-------------|-------------------------------|----------|------------|
| 14/11/1904 | My Lady Molly | l G H Jessop, m Sidney Jones | Musical | Arthur Powell, Mabel Lait |
| 21/11/1904 | Her Forbidden Marriage | Frederick Melville | Play | Horace Hunter, Isla Garner Vane |
| 28/11/1904 | Two Little Sailor Boys | Walter Howard | Play | Marie Daventry, Blanche Steele |
| 05/12/1904 | The Lady Slavey | l George Dance, m John Crook | Musical | Addie Lennard, Frank Sherlock |
| 12/12/1904 | The Anarchist Terror | | Play | Edward Neville, Lois Esmond |
| 13/12/1904 | The Anarchist Terror | | Play | Edward Neville, Lois Esmond |
| 14/12/1904 | The Sorrows of Satan | from Marie Corelli | Play | Edward Neville, Lois Esmond |
| 15/12/1904 | The Sorrows of Satan | from Marie Corelli | Play | Edward Neville, Lois Esmond |
| 16/12/1904 | The Sorrows of Satan | from Marie Corelli | Play | Edward Neville, Lois Esmond |
| 17/12/1904 | The Sorrows of Satan | from Marie Corelli | Play | Edward Neville, Lois Esmond |
| 19/12/1904 | The Christian | | Play | Grace Chalmers, Hillard Vox |
| 26/12/1904 | The Revenge | E Hill-Michelson | Play | E Hill- Michelson, Violet Carlyle |
| 02/01/1905 | Florodora | l Ernest Boyd-Jones, m Leslie Stuart | Musical | Gus Danby, Daisy Lake, Miss F M Newman |
| 09/01/1905 | La Poupee | l George Byng, m Edward Audran | Musical | Edward Thirlby, Cissie Wade |
| 16/01/1905 | The Female Swindler | Walter Melville | Play | |
| 23/01/1905 | Dick Whittington | J Hickory Wood | Panto | Bob Hutt, Madeline Rees, Fred Dart, Arthur Godfrey |
| 30/01/1905 | A Woman's Devotion | | Play | Mrs Morton Powell, Alwynne Ermon |
| 06/02/1905 | Miss Mischief | l Reginald Bacchus, m Osmond Carr | Musical | Evelyn Hughes, Cecil Curtis |
| 13/02/1905 | A Victim of Villainy | Walter Howe | Play | Walter Howe, Rosa Lehman |
| 20/02/1905 | Three Little Maids | l Paul Rubens, Percy Greenbank, m Paul Rubens | Musical | |
| 27/02/1905 | Are you a Mason | Leo Dietricht-stein | Play | Harry ashford, Arthur Claremont |
| 06/03/1905 | Robinson Crusoe | | Panto | Bob King, Walter Kooney, Ethel Campbell |
| 13/03/1905 | The Sleigh Bells | | Play | E Hoggan-Armadale, Marie Florence |
| 14/03/1905 | The Vicar of Wakefield | | Play | E Hoggan-Armadale, Marie Florence |
| 15/03/1905 | David Garrick | Thomas William Robertson | Play | E Hoggan-Armadale, Marie Florence |
| 16/03/1905 | Lady of Lyons | Edward Bulwer-Lytton | Play | E Hoggan-Armadale, Marie Florence |

| Date | Title/Event | Playwright/Author<br>l= lyrics; m= music | Category | Performers |
|---|---|---|---|---|
| 17/03/1905 | David Garrick | Thomas William Robertson | Play | E Hoggan-Armadale, Marie Florence |
| 18/03/1905 | The Sleigh Bells | | Play | E Hoggan-Armadale, Marie Florence |
| 20/03/1905 | The Traitor | E Hill-Michelson | Play | John E Carlyle, Stephen E Scanlon |
| 27/03/1905 | Aladdin | | Panto | Beatrice Varley, Albert Williams |
| 03/04/1905 | Hearts Adrift | | Play | Julian Cross, Celestine Bertram |
| 10/04/1905 | My Sweetheart | | Musical | Minnie Palmer, Robert H Howard |
| 17/04/1905 | The London Fireman | Arthur Shirley, G Conquest | Play | J Forbes Knowles, Ed L Garside |
| 24/04/0905 | The Officers' Mess | l Cyril Hurst, m Mark Strong | Musical | T E Conover, Gladys Huxley, Grace Heywood |
| 01/05/1905 | A Hot Night | Milton Ray | Musical | Alf Bishop, Madeline L'Estrange |
| 08/05/1905 | The Dandy Doctor | l Edward Marris, m Dudley Powell | Musical | Edward Marris, Florence Smithers |
| 15/05/1905 | Carlton and his Star Vaudeville Co | | Variety | |
| 22/05/1905 | A Mother's Love | F l Connynghame | Play | Fred Connynghame, Violet Macaree |
| 29/05/1905 | What a Woman Did | | Play | Dora Price, William A Armour |
| 05/06/1905 | A Gay Girl | l Edward Devreve, m Guieppe Leone | Musical | |
| 07/06/1905 | Grand Variety Programme | | Variety | Sister Edenes, Mrs Richens, Belle Thomas, H E Phillips |
| 12/06/1905 | Fred Harcourt's Vaudeville Co | | Variety | The Ettenas, Lilian Warren, Happy Attwood, Fred Harcourt |
| 19/06/1905 | J A Huxley's Grand Vaudeville Co | | Variety | Tom Cannon (Wrestler), Blanche Newman |
| 26/06/1905 | A Woman's Revenge | Henry Pettit | Play | Winifred Chalmers, Henry L Osmond |
| 03/07/1905 | | | Variety | Mark Anthony, Dennis Drew, Belle Thomas |
| 07/08/1905 | Frank Harcourt's New London Vaudeville | | Variety | Harry Grey, Babs Lloyd, Casino Girls |
| 14/08/1905 | The Convicts Daughter | | Play | Frank Bertram, J K Walton, Edith Savery |
| 21/08/1905 | Swiss Express | | Musical | Frank Renad, Frederick Renad, Fowler Thatcher, Lily Beverley |
| 28/08/1905 | Sunday | Thomas Raceward | Play | May Congden, William Lockhart |
| 04/09/1905 | Tommy Atkins | Arthur Shirley, Ben Lander | Play | Horace Denton, J M Troughton, Elizabeth Watkins |
| 11/09/1905 | Bid for Fortune | Barry Williams | Play | Edith Blair-Staples, Henry Watchman |
| 18/09/1905 | For the King | Walter Howard, S T Pease | Play | Sidney T Pease, Walter Bentley, Phyllis Orme |

| Date | Title/Event | Playwright/Author l= lyrics; m= music | Category | Performers |
|------|-------------|------------------------|----------|-----------|
| 25/09/1905 | Treasure Island | l Peter Eland, m Vincent Exley | Musical | J C Bland, Joe Monkhouse |
| 02/10/1905 | Beauty and the Barge | W W Jacobs, L N Parker | Play | Maitland Marler, Lillian Hallows |
| 09/10/1905 | The Silver King | Henry Arthur Jones | Play | Stephen T Ewart, Daisy Scudamore, Edward J George |
| 16/10/1905 | The Girl from Japan | l Wilfred Carr, m Colet Dare | Musical | Percy Baverstock, Edward Kipling, Dorothy Glenton |
| 23/10/1905 | The Love that Women Desire | G Carlton Wallace | Play | Lydia Donovan, G Carlton Wallace, David G Noble, Alice N Livesey |
| 30/10/1905 | In Old Kentucky | C T Dazey, Arthur Shirley | Play | Miss A F Hermann, Charles A Leicester |
| 06/11/1905 | As Midnight Chimes | Edward Marris | Play | Kenneth Smith, Nina Vaughton, Dtanley S Gordon, James Salter |
| 13/11/1905 | Faust | Gounod | Opera | Moody-Manners Grand Opera Co inc Enriqueta Chrichton, Albert Bower, Ethel Cadman |
| 14/11/1905 | Tannhauser | Wagner | Opera | Moody-Manners Grand Opera Co inc Enriqueta Chrichton, Albert Bower, Ethel Cadman |
| 15/111905 | Maritana | Vincent Wallace | Opera | Moody-Manners Grand Opera Co inc Enriqueta Chrichton, Albert Bower, Ethel Cadman |
| 16/11/1905 | Lohengrin | Wagner | Opera | Moody-Manners Grand Opera Co inc Enriqueta Chrichton, Albert Bower, Ethel Cadman |
| 17/11/1905 | Cavalleria Rusticanna/ I Pagliacci | Mascagni/ Leoncavallo | Opera | Moody-Manners Grand Opera Co inc Enriqueta Chrichton, Albert Bower, Ethel Cadman |
| 18/11/1905 | Carmen  mat | Bizet | Opera | Moody-Manners Grand Opera Co inc Enriqueta Chrichton, Albert Bower, Ethel Cadman |
| 18/11/0905 | Bohemian Girl | Balfe | Opera | Moody-Manners Grand Opera Co inc Enriqueta Chrichton, Albert Bower, Ethel Cadman |
| 20/11/1905 | Les Cloches de Corneville | l Henry Brougham Farnie, m Robert Planquette | Opera | Marian Ayling, E St Alban, George E Fox |
| 27/11/1905 | Hamlet | William Shakespeare | Play | Osmond Tearle Co, Alexander Marsh, Carrie Baillie, Cyril Grier, Fanny Chamberlain |
| 28/11/1905 | Merchant of Venice | William Shakespeare | Play | Osmond Tearle Co, Alexander Marsh, Carrie Baillie, Cyril Grier, Fanny Chamberlain |
| 29/11/1905 | Romeo and Juliet | William Shakespeare | Play | Osmond Tearle Co, Alexander Marsh, Carrie Baillie, Cyril Grier, Fanny Chamberlain |
| 30/11/1905 | Julius Caesar | William Shakespeare | Play | Osmond Tearle Co, Alexander Marsh, Carrie Baillie, Cyril Grier, Fanny Chamberlain |
| 01/12/1905 | David Garrick | Thomas William Robertson | Play | Osmond Tearle Co, Alexander Marsh, Carrie Baillie, Cyril Grier, Fanny Chamberlain |

| Date | Title/Event | Playwright/Author l= lyrics; m= music | Category | Performers |
|---|---|---|---|---|
| 02/12/1905 | Othello | William Shakespeare | Play | Osmond Tearle Co, Alexander Marsh, Carrie Baillie, Cyril Grier, Fanny Chamberlain |
| 04/12/1905 | The New Mephisto | l George Dance, m Ernest Vousden | Musical | Sam Walsh, David James |
| 08/12/1905 | The Duke of Kilkrankie | | Opera | |
| 11/12/1905 | The Village Blacksmith | G Carlton Wallace | Play | Sam Livesey, Joseph Carter, Miss E Kay |
| 18/11/1905 | Leah Kleschna | C M S McLellan | Play | H Cooper Cliffe, Maud Hoffman |
| 26/12/1905 | The Golden Ladder | Wilson Barrett, G R Sims | Play | H Cullenford, Alice Capel, J Milne Taylor |
| 01/01/1906 | The Price of her Soul | William Herbert | Play | John B Shinton, Ada M Ryder |
| 08/01/1906 | The Walls of Jericho | Alfred Sutro | Play | Florence Jackson, Herbert Bunston |
| 15/01/1906 | The Orchid | l Adrian Ross, m Ivan Carryl | Musical | |
| 22/01/1906 | Robinson Crusoe | J Hickory Wood | Panto | Maisie Ellinger, Veronica Brady. Tom Owen |
| 29/01/1906 | Sapho | Birkett Winning | Play | Annie Bell, Pringle Roberts |
| 05/02/1906 | Babes in the Wood | J Hickory Wood | Panto | Ernestine Desborough, Florence Arnold |
| 12/02/1906 | Dare Devil Dorothy | l Wilfred Carr, m K Ernest Irving | Musical | Nellie Harcourt, Arthur Verne |
| 19/02/1906 | The Breed of the Treshams | John Rutherford | Play | Henry Belding, Florence Tressilian, Hamilton Deane |
| 26/02/1906 | Rip Van Winkle | Fred Storey | Play | Fred Storey, Lilian Holmes |
| 05-Mar | Goody Two Shoes | Ernest and Mrs Carpenter | Panto | Harriet Fawn, May Fallowfield, Dave O'Toole |
| 12/03/1906 | Sergeant Brue | l J Hickory Wood, m Liza Lehman | Musical | J Harold Carson, Miss Reydon-Dallas |
| 19/03/1906 | None but the Brave Deserve the Fair | Arthur Shirley, Sutton Vane | Play | Amy Hermann, Stanley Bedwell, Herbert Evelyn |
| 26/03/1906 | After the Ball | l B Clair, m G Leone | Musical | Florence Smithers, Gibson Girls, V Widdicombe |
| 02/04/1906 | The Wearin' o' the Green | Walter Howard | Musical | Chalmers Mackey, Nana Flensberg, Mrs Chalmers Mackey |
| 09/04/1906 | Kitty Grey | l J Smyth Piggot, m Lionel Monkton, Howard Talbot etc | Musical | |
| 16/04/1906 | Cingalee | l Adrian Ross, Percy Greenbank, m Lionel Monckton | Musical | Edith Harmer, Tom Payne, Minnie Muir |
| 23/04/1906 | The Duffer | Weedon Grossmith | Play | E H Wynne, Nellie Griffin |
| 30/04/1906 | The Christian | Hall Caine | Play | Grace Chalmers, Frank Tennant |

| Date | Title/Event | Playwright/Author l= lyrics; m= music | Category | Performers |
|------|-------------|------------|----------|-----------|
| 07/05/1906 | Claudian | Wilson Barrett | Play | William Maclaren, Lily Bandmann, Chal T Chaloner, Carlotta Anson |
| 14/05/1906 | Uncle Tom's Cabin | from Harriet Beecher Stowe | Play | J Carr, J H Rennie |
| 21/05/1906 | Sailors of the King | Frank Bateman | Play | Charles Harrington, Sylvia Stella |
| 28/05/1906 | Cousin Kate | Herbert Henry Davies | Play | Lilias Earle, Percy Hutchison |
| 04/06/1906 | The Country Mouse | | Play | Lilias Earle, Percy Hutchison |
| 05/06/1906 | The Country Mouse | | Play | Lilias Earle, Percy Hutchison |
| 06/06/1906 | The Country Mouse | | Play | Lilias Earle, Percy Hutchison |
| 07/06/1906 | The Country Mouse | | Play | Lilias Earle, Percy Hutchison |
| 08/16/1906 | The Country Mouse | | Play | Lilias Earle, Percy Hutchison |
| 09/06/1906 | On the Love Path | C M S McLellan | Play | Lilias Earle, Percy Hutchison |
| 11/06/1906 | Empire Theatrescope and Vaudeville Co | | Variety | Zelda (musician), T C Jacques (actor vocalist), Boden & Bell (cyclists) plus pictures |
| 18/06/1906 | Alfred Manners Vaudeville Co | | Variety | Leo Fallowfield (Comedian), Doris Randall (sand dancer), Harriet Fawn (Chanteuse) |
| 25/06/1906 | The Still Alarm | Joseph Arthur | Play | Cecil Du Gue, Matthew H Glenville, Fred Osmond |
| 06/08/1906 | Under Two Flags | Edward Elaner | Play | Mary Thorne, Mark Blow |
| 13/08/1906 | Beauty and the Beast | l H B Levy, m C Sherrington | Panto | Wee Georgie Wood, Dolly Dodds, May Gibson |
| 20/08/1906 | The Spider and the Fly | Arthur Shirley, Sutton Vane | Play | Nina Vaughton, Stanley Gordon, Fred Terris |
| 27/08/1906 | Driven from Home | | Play | Felix Pitt, Frances Ruttledge, Clement Wakefield, Percy Dawsone |
| 03/09/1906 | The Prodigal Parson | F l Connyng-hame | Play | W V Garrod, Bertha Kingston |
| 10/09/1906 | Bluebell in Fairyland | l Aubrey Hopwood, Charles H Taylor, m Walter Slaughter | Musical | Lily Eyton, Laurence Emery |
| 17/09/1906 | When London Sleeps | Charles Darrell | Play | M Scuddamore, Sam Arthur |
| 24/09/1906 | Vaudeville Co | | | |
| 01/10/1906 | A Destroyer of Men | Sidney Spencer, Clarence Burnette | Play | Gladys Lloyd, Charles Bickell |
| 08/10/1906 | East Lynne | From Mrs Henry Wood | Play | Julie Kennard, Harry Nunn |
| 09/10/1906 | East Lynne | From Mrs Henry Wood | Play | Julie Kennard, Harry Nunn |
| 10/10/1906 | East Lynne | From Mrs Henry Wood | Play | Julie Kennard, Harry Nunn |

| Date | Title/Event | Playwright/Author<br>l= lyrics; m= music | Category | Performers |
|------|-------------|-------------------------------------|----------|------------|
| 11/10/1906 | Blue Moon | l Percy Greenbank, m Howard Talbot, Paul Rubens | Musical | Mdlle E Naudin, V Wallace, A Burton |
| 12/10/1906 | Blue Moon | l Percy Greenbank, m Howard Talbot, Paul Rubens | Musical | Mdlle E Naudin, V Wallace, A Burton |
| 13/10/1906 | Blue Moon | l Percy Greenbank, m Howard Talbot, Paul Rubens | Musical | Mdlle E Naudin, V Wallace, A Burton |
| 15/10/1906 | Saturday to Monday | l F Karno, m D Powell | Musical | Rolando Martin, Amy Rogerson |
| 22/10/1906 | Carmen | Bizet | Opera | Moody-Manners Opera Co inc Zellie De Lussan, Marshall Vincent, Maurice Paul |
| 23/10/1906 | Faust | Gounod | Opera | Moody-Manners Opera Co inc Zellie De Lussan, Marshall Vincent, Maurice Paul |
| 24/10/1906 | Bohemian Girl | Balfe | Opera | Moody-Manners Opera Co inc Zellie De Lussan, Marshall Vincent, Maurice Paul |
| 25/10/1906 | Il Trovatore | Verdi | Opera | Moody-Manners Opera Co inc Zellie De Lussan, Marshall Vincent, Maurice Paul |
| 26/10/1906 | Tannhauser | Wagner | Opera | Moody-Manners Opera Co inc Zellie De Lussan, Marshall Vincent, Maurice Paul |
| 27/10/1906 | Lohengrin  mat | Wagner | Opera | Moody-Manners Opera Co inc Zellie De Lussan, Marshall Vincent, Maurice Paul |
| 27/10/1906 | Maritana  eve | Vincent Wallace | Opera | Moody-Manners Opera Co inc Zellie De Lussan, Marshall Vincent, Maurice Paul |
| 29/10/1906 | San Toy | l Harry Greenbank, m Sidney Jones | Musical | Mora Hersee, Mabel Carr |
| 05/11/1906 | The Trumpet Call | George Sims, R Buchanan | Play | Doris Gilham, Leonard Yorke |
| 12/11/1906 | Florodora | l Ernest Boyd-Jones, Leslie Stuart | Musical | Josephine Sullivan, A E Passmore |
| 19/11/1906 | The Streets of London | Dion Boucicault | Play | William Rokeby, Riddell Robinson. Dorothy Casey |
| 26/11/1906 | The Earl and the Girl | l Percy Greenbank, m Ivan Carryl | Musical | Alfred Donohoe, Thomas Kennard |
| 03/12/1906 | The French Spy | E Hill-Michelson | Play | Madge Devereux, Beresford Lovet |
| 10/12/1906 | Star Vaudeville Artistes | | | |
| 17/12/1906 | The Conscript | Wybert Clive | Play | E Bellenden Clarke, Lilian Ross |
| 26/12/1906 | Sinbad the Sailor | N Maurice, A Manners | Panto | Fanny Robbins, Nora Haywood, Will Crackles |
| 14/01/1907 | At Cripple Creek | Hall Reid | Play | Stanley Bedwell, Agnes Verity |
| 21/01/1907 | Dick Whittington | | Panto | Emily Taylor, Chas Wood, Rosalie Jacobi |

| Date | Title/Event | Playwright/Author l= lyrics; m= music | Category | Performers |
|------|-------------|---------------------------------------|----------|------------|
| 28/01/1907 | Sentenced for Life | Frank Bateman | Play | E Vaughan, Edwin B Jones |
| 04/02/1907 | The Breed of the Treshams | John Rutherford | Play | H Tripp Edgar, Celestine Bertram |
| 11/02/1907 | Little Red Riding Hood | | Panto | Josie Tuden, Mabel Kessler |
| 18/02/1907 | Sunday | | Play | Thomas Racewards, Emilie Polini |
| 25/02/1907 | The Shulamite | C Askew, Edward Knoblauch | Play | Algernon J Hicks, Miss Shepherd |
| 04/02/1907 | The Lights of London | George Sims | Play | C F Colling, Jeann Burgoyne |
| 26/08/1907 | The White Chrysanthemum | l Arthur Anderson, m Howard Talbot | Musical | Lillian Hubbard, Victor Kahn, Harriet Fawn |
| 02/09/1907 | The Cingalee | l Adrian Ross, m Lionel Monckton | Musical | Tom Payne, Lydia Flop, Marjorie Grey |
| 09/09/1907 | The Still Alarm | Joseph Arthur | Play | Mathew H Glenville, Elinor Fordham, Fred Osmond |
| 16/09/1907 | The Pet of the Embassy | Albert E Wilson, Sidney F Bailey | Musical | Ethel Dunford, Florence Watson |
| 23/090/907 | The Knave of Hearts | Gladys Ungar | Play | H A Sainsbury, Leon M Lion, Nina Sevening, Haidee Wright |
| 30/09/1907 | Finest Variety Company | | Variety | Hilda Mascott ( comedienne and dancer), Leo King, (actor and vocalist) |
| 07/10/1907 | Two Little Vagabonds | George Sims, Arthur Shirley | Play | Violet Ellicott, Wilson Coleman |
| 14/10/1907 | Woman and Wine | Arthur Shirley, Ben Landeck | Play | E Vivian Edmonds, Cissie St Elmo |
| 21/10/1907 | The Torreador | l Adrian Ross, m Ivan Caryll | Musical | W Strong, Ivy Moore |
| 28/10/1907 | Sleeping Beauty | | Panto | Wee Georgie Wood, Dolly Dodds, May Gibson, Stanley Jefferson (Stan Laurel) |
| 04/11/1907 | The Girl from Japan | l Wilfred Carr, m Colet Dare | Musical | Florence Wilton, Percy Baverstock |
| 11/11/1907 | Sherlock Holmes | | Play | Hamilton Stewart, Ryland Leigh |
| 18/11/1907 | The Gayest of the Gay | Arthur Shirley, Eric Hudson | Play | Ernest Owtrimm, Laura Walker |
| 25/11/1907 | The Ugliest Woman on Earth | Frederick Melville | Play | Beatrice Homer, Philip Darien, Tubby Edlin, Nellie Jackson |
| 26/12/1907 | | | Variety | M'lle Ampere, Peggy Pride, Bicknelle, Empire Pictures, Zaro and Arno |
| 30/12/1907 | | | Variety | Fred Poplar, Kitty Wager, Lillian Rigby, Russell Carr, Empire Pictures |
| 06/01/1908 | Christine | Augusta Tulloch | Play | Mack Ollive, Walter Wade |
| 13/01/1908 | | | Variety | Three Romas Ruby Emmerson, Empire Bioscope |

| Date | Title/Event | Playwright/Author<br>l= lyrics; m= music | Category | Performers |
|------|-------------|------------------------------------------|----------|------------|
| 20/01/1908 | | | Variety | Tom Davies Trio ( motoring in mid air), Marl, Sisters Gladwin |
| 27/01/1908 | Puss In Boots | | Panto | Daisy Silcott, Madge Field, Charles Ashdowne |
| 03/02/1908 | | | Variety | Hackenschmidt v Rogers (Wrestling), Ryder Sloane, Carl Howarsd |
| 10/02/1908 | | | Variety | Two Rubies, Royal Dreadnoughts (Rifle act), Empire Pictures |
| 17/02/1908 | | | Variety | Four Juggling Breens, Beatrice Willey, Fitzboys |
| 24/02/1908 | | | Variety | Unthan (armless sharp shooter), Molly Augarde (Comedienne), Harry Nation |
| 02/03/1908 | | | Variety | Bonnie Godwin's Apollo Piccanninnies, Bert Williams (Vent), Empire Pictures |
| 09/03/1908 | | | Variety | Tarro Myaki (Ju Jitsu, wrestler), Medley Barrett (comedian), Empire Pictures |
| 16/03/1908 | | | Variety | Elliott Savannas(in Palace of Orpheus), Baby Sisters Herbert, Empire Pictures |
| 23/03/1908 | | | Variety | Harry Tate's No 1 Co in "Motoring", Ida Brophy (comedienne), Frank Gee |
| 30/03/1908 | | | Variety | Datas(Memory man), Mark Leslie (coon comedian), Leonie de Lausanne (Rifle) |
| 06/04/1908 | | | Variety | Mysterious Mahatmas (Psychic), Maggie Rimmer (comedienne) Maggie Rimmer |
| 13/04/1908 | | | Variety | Whisper (juggler), Beattie Bloom (Comedienne) Fred Ginnett's Hunting Morn |
| 20/04/1908 | | | Variety | Dusty Rhodes (comedian), Madame Collard (Animal act), Miss Florence (mimic) |
| 27/04/1908 | The Dairy Maids | l Paul Rubens, Arthur Wimpweris, m Paul Rubens | Musical | Dan Agar, Maud Lucy |
| 04/05/1908 | | | Variety | Hall and Earle (eccentrics), Cambo (musical monkey), Jimmy James (comedian) |
| 11/05/1908 | | | Variety | Chung Ling Soo (Chinese Illusionist),Millie Denham (comedian), |
| 18/05/1908 | | | Variety | Lyons Trio (pantomimists), Dora Martin (trapeze), Harry Cotton (comedian) |
| 25/05/1908 | | | Variety | Mechanical, Minstrels, Judge' s marvellously trained cockatoos, Percy Honri |
| 01/06/1908 | | | Variety | Caupitt (conjurer), Harry Bedford (comedian), Garland & Douglas |
| 08/06/1908 | | | Variety | Randolph King, (Quick change), Robbie Roy (Scottish comedian), |
| 15/06/1908 | | | Variety | Joe Peterman's Co in "Singing servant", Ford and Barras (dancers) |
| 22/06/1908 | | | Variety | Les Berthos (acrobats), De Bierce (illusionist), Clothilde (Cockatoos) |

| Date | Title/Event | Playwright/Author<br>l= lyrics; m= music | Category | Performers |
|------|-------------|------------------------------------------|----------|------------|
| 29/06/1908 | | | Variety | R G Knowles (comedian), Helen Stuart (singer), Jock McKay (Scotttish comedian |
| 03/08/1908 | | | Variety | Five Vernons,(xylophonistso, Edith Garrick (contortionist),Harry Taft (with horse) |
| 10/08/1908 | | | Variety | Hinton and Wootton (football match on bicyles), Sears (Illusionist) |
| 17/08/1908 | | | Variety | Three demons (cyclists), Rosslyn (wizard), Wallace (boy juggler) |
| 24/08/1908 | | | Variety | Mlle de Rose, (baritone), Carrie Laurie's Juveniles, Wild, Willie& West (navvies& acrobats) |
| 31/08/1908 | | | Variety | Werds (grotesque acrobat), Davis and Gledhill(roller cyclists), Thoba (juggler) |
| 07/09/1908 | | | Variety | |
| 14/09/1908 | | | Variety | Billy (educated horse), Maude and Gill (acrobatic dogs) |
| 21/09/1908 | | | Variety | Brinn (strongman, "Pastimes on a battleship", Effie White (kaleidescope dancer) |
| 28/09/1908 | | | Variety | La Freya (electrical novelty), Columbia Comedy Trio (opera and humour) |
| 05/10/1908 | | | Variety | John Grun Marx (strongman) The Great Zerbinis (musical speciality) |
| 12/10/1908 | | | Variety | Les Barrois, (acrobats), Frank Hartley (boy juggler) |
| 19/10/1908 | The Merry Maid | | Musical | Vivian Wakeman, May Gibson, Wee Georgie Wood* |
| 26/10/1908 | A Mountain Bell | | Musical | Lena Maitland, Edward O'Brian |
| 02/11/1908 | | | Variety | Maitland Marler, (comedian), Johnnie and Charlie, (eccentric tumblers) |
| 09/11/1908 | | | Variety | Arthur Frine's Mascots (refined entertainers), George Ripley,(comedian) |
| 16/11/1908 | Florodora | l Ernest Boyd-Jones, m Leslie Stuart | Musical | Gus Danby, Daisy Lake, Lillie Blyth |
| 23/11/1908 | A Lancashire Lad | G Carlton Wallace | Play | Alec Alexander, T G Vane |
| 30/11/1909 | Amasis | l Frederick Fenn, m Philip Michael Faraday | Musical | W H Denny, Mabel Burnage |
| 07/12/1908 | The Prince and the Beggar Maid | Walter Howard | Play | Walter Howard, Ethel Bracewell, Alfred Brandon |
| 14/12/1908 | Beggar Girl's Wedding | Walter Melville | Play | Otto Minster, Vashti Wynne |
| 26/12/1908 | Raffles | from E W Hornung | Play | Reginald Dance, Edward Irwin, Francis, Tetheradge |
| 29/12/1908 | Raffles | | | |

| Date | Title/Event | Playwright/Author<br>l= lyrics; m= music | Category | Performers |
|------|-------------|------------------------------------------|----------|------------|
| 04/01/1909 | Leah Kleschna | C W S McLellan | Play | William Clayton, Arthur Leigh, Charles Barrett |
| 11/01/1909 | The House that Jack Built | | Panto | Evelyn Major, Florrie Taylor, Stanley Jefferson (Stan Laurel) |
| 18/01/1909 | The Fatal Wedding | Theo Kremer | Play | Cecil A Melton, Ethel Kay, Elaine Vanburgh |
| 25/01/1909 | Cinderella | | Panto | Maude Mortimer, Corinne Leon, Edith Banwell, Annie Cohen |
| 01/02/1909 | East Lynne | from Mrs Henry Wood | Play | Edmund Kennedy, Julie Kennard, Frank G Bayley |
| 02/02/1909 | East Lynne | from Mrs Henry Wood | Play | Edmund Kennedy, Julie Kennard, Frank G Bayley |
| 03/02/1909 | East Lynne | from Mrs Henry Wood | Play | Edmund Kennedy, Julie Kennard, Frank G Bayley |
| 04/02/1909 | Gay Gordons | l Arthur Wimperis, m Guy Jones | Musical | Gladys Archbutt, Mabel Dent, Frank Lincoln |
| 05/02/1909 | Gay Gordons | l Arthur Wimperis, m Guy Jones | Musical | Gladys Archbutt, Mabel Dent, Frank Lincoln |
| 06/02/1909 | Gay Gordons | l Arthur Wimperis, m Guy Jones | Musical | Gladys Archbutt, Mabel Dent, Frank Lincoln |
| 08/02/1909 | London Variety Co | | Variety | Arthur Kenny (cyclist), Odeyne Spark (comedienne), Rosina (instrumentalist) |
| 15/02/1909 | Two Little Vagabonds | George Sims, Arthur Shirley | Play | Leonora Castelle, George Denham |
| 22/02/1909 | The Cingalee | l Adrian Ross, m Lionel Monckton | Musical | Mollie Wolstenholme, Arthur Carwright |
| 01/03/1909 | White Edged Tools | H Armitage | Play | William Grant, Marie Leonhard |
| 08/03/1909 | The Catch of the Season | l Charles H Taylor, m Herbert E Haines, Evelyn Baker | Musical | Dorothea Clarke, William Greene |
| 15/03/1909 | The Sailor's Wedding | | Play | R A Greene, Miss M Sadie |
| 22/03/1909 | Her Love Against the World | Walter Howard | Play | F Emery, Lewis Gilbert, Rosie St John |
| 29/03/1909 | The Flower Girl | William T Gliddon | Musical | Eva Nelson, R Cranny |
| 05/04/1909 | Monster Vaudeville Entertainment | | Variety | Bert Wickham (strong man), Mlle De Rose (female baritone), Kavados (juggler) |
| 12/04/1909 | Second to None | Walter Howard | Play | C W Spencer, Leonard Williams, Miss Ward |
| 19/04/1909 | Two Lancashire Lads in London | Arthur Shirley, Sutton Vane | Play | George Rammell, Chris Mason |
| 26/04/1909 | | | Variety | Vonetta (illusionist), Carl Bennie (ventiloquist), Zasma (gymnast) |
| 03/05/1909 | Dare Devil Dorothy | l Wilfred Carr, m K Ernest Irving | Musical | Nellie Valentine, Nellie Harcourt, George Handel |

| Date | Title/Event | Playwright/Author<br>l= lyrics; m= music | Category | Performers |
|------|-------------|------------------------------|----------|-----------|
| 10/05/1909 | | | Variety | Mlle Bartonelli (contortionist), Four Eugenes (gymnasts), |
| 17/05/1909 | For Wife and Kingdom | Ward Baily | Play | Mathew H Glenville, Hettie Zillwood, Fred Osmond |
| 24/05/1909 | The Great White Chief | Lingford Carson | Play | Charles Homer, Pollie Denville, Hugh Brady |
| 31/05/1909 | Her Secret Lover | Mrs G F Kimberley | Play | Fred W Goddard, Arthur Preston, Amy Ellam, Cissie St Elmo |
| 07/06/1909 | Bluebeard | | Play | Daisy Lake, H L Davies, Walter B Freer |
| 14/06/1909 | Was she to Blame | Mrs G F Kimberley | Play | Mrs F G Kimberley, Mr F G Kimberley |
| 21/06/1909 | | | Variety | Marie Dreams (girl baritone), The Paolias (athletes), Maude Mortimer (singer) |
| 19/07/1909 | Midget Minstrels | | Variety | Harold Pyott (23ins), Gladys Wyse |
| 26/07/1909 | | | Variety | Elliott Savanas (Palace of Orpheus), Primavesi ( Juggling Milkman) |
| 02/08/1909 | Two Little Drummer Boys | Walter Howard | Play | Edward Bikker, Eva Rogers |
| 09/08/1909 | | | Variety | Albert Troupe (lady equilibrists), Alice Lingard (comedienne), Kinnard (juggler) |
| 10/08/1909 | | | Variety | Albert Troupe (lady equilibrists), Alice Lingard (comedienne), Kinnard (juggler) |
| 11/08/1909 | | | Variety | Albert Troupe (lady equilibrists), Alice Lingard (comedienne), Kinnard (juggler) |
| 12/08/1909 | The Flag Lieutenant | W P Brury, L Trevor | Play | Edgar Kent |
| 13/08/1909 | The Flag Lieutenant | W P Brury, L Trevor | Play | Edgar Kent |
| 14/08/1909 | The Flag Lieutenant | W P Brury, L Trevor | Play | Edgar Kent |
| 16/08/1909 | The Prince and the Beggar Maid | Walter Howard | Play | Walter Howard, Annie Saker |
| 23/08/1909 | | | Variety | Mlle Sidi Minerva (poseur), Argo ( farm yard mimic), James Willard (Ace of Hearts) |
| 30/08/1909 | Sexton Blake | | Play | Murray Yorke, Will Glaze, Betty Seymour, Fred Terriss |
| 06/09/1909 | A Chinese Honeymoon | l George Dance, m Howard Talbot | Musical | Gwennie Harcourt, Will Harman, Gladys Ivery |
| 13/09/1909 | Lucky Durham | Wilson Barrett | Play | Edmund Kennedy, Arthur Leigh, Nellie Bonner, Florence Tressilion |
| 20/09/1909 | The Explorer | W Somerset Maugham | Play | Herbert Ford, Zerlina Harrington |
| 27/09/1909 | The Village Blacksmith | G Carlton Wallace | Play | Sam Livesey, Maggie Edwards |

| Date | Title/Event | Playwright/Author l= lyrics; m= music | Category | Performers |
|------|-------------|------------------------------------|----------|------------|
| 04/10/1909 | The King of Cadonia | l Adrian Ross, m Sidney Jones | Musical | Conway Dixon, Netta Lynde |
| 11/10/1909 | Our Miss Gibbs | l Adrian Ross, m Lionel Monckton | Musical | Jessie Lonnen, Eustice Burnaby, Theodore Leonard |
| 18/10/1909 | The Devil | Franz Molnar | Play | Murray Carson, Marie Rignold |
| 25/10/1909 | A Country Girl | l Adrian Ross, Lionel Monckton | Musical | Coningsby Brierley, St John Hamund, Daphne Hope |
| 01/11/1909 | The Earl and the Girl | Percy Greenbank, m Ivan Carryl | Musical | Bert Beswick, George McCloskie, Beatrice Hayden |
| 08/11/1909 | The Walls of Jericho | Alfred Sutro | Play | Rutland Barrington, Ethelbert Edwardes, Ethel Trevor Lloyd |
| 15/11/1909 | An Englishman's Home | Guy du Maurier | Play | Frank Bradley, Marguerite Unett |
| 22/11/1909 | The New Barmaid | l Frederick Bowyer, W Edward Sprange, m John Crook | Musical | E H Bertram, Florrie Millington, Charles Adeson |
| 29/11/1909 | A Thief in the Night | G Carlton Wallace | Play | Stanley Bedwell, Herbert Carr, Yvonne Q Orchardson |
| 06/12/1909 | A Royal Divorce | | Play | Violet Ellicott, Keith Fraser |
| 13/12/1909 | Captain Jack | | Play | Dora Pass, E H De Quincy |
| 20/12/1909 | | | Variety | Louie Freear, Charles Douglas, Eva Dickson |
| 27/12/1909 | The Cotton Spinner | Frank Harvey | Play | Mary Austin, E Vivian Edmonds |
| 03/01/1910 | Raffles | | Play | Reginald Dance, Frances Titheradge, Oswald Griffiths |
| 10/01/1910 | A Broken Heart | | Play | Sheila Walsh, Harry Cullenford |
| 17/01/1910 | The Forty Thieves | | Panto | Marie Reeve, Mary Otto, Johnny Johnston |
| 24/01/1910 | The Flag Lieutenant | W PG Drury, Leo Trevor | Play | Hastings Lynn, Frederick Lester |
| 31/01/1910 | Dick Whittington | | Panto | Murray King, Gertrude Gilliam, Tom Wallis |
| 07/02/1910 | Sherlock Holmes | | Play | H Hamilton Stewart. Charles Brandon, Mary Beatrice |
| 14/02/1910 | The Dairymaids | l Paul Rubens, Arthur Wimperis, m Paul Rubens | Musical | Edwin Doods, Edie Martin, Dorothy Grasdorff |
| 21/02/1910 | Swiss Express | | Musical | Charles Renad, Frederick Renad |
| 28/02/1910 | Her Forbidden Marriage | Frederick Melville | Play | Louis Hector, Alice Bowes |
| 07/03/1910 | A White Man | Edward Milton Royle | Play | Guy Hastings, Kathleen Maude, Hilda Barita |
| 14/03/1910 | Alone in London | R Buchanan, H Jay | Play | Nellie Clyde, Russell Norrie, Charles Gibbon |

| Date | Title/Event | Playwright/Author l= lyrics; m= music | Category | Performers |
|------|-------------|----------------------------------------|----------|------------|
| 21/03/1910 | The Sins of the Fathers | Wallace Davidson | Play | Max Coutts, Edith Blande |
| 28/03/1910 | The Arcadians | l Arthur Wimperis, m Lionel Monckton, Howard Talbot | Musical | Charles A Stephenson, Alfred Beers |
| 04/03/1910 | A Message from Mars | Richard Ganthony | Play | F Vernon Travers, William H Brougham |
| 11/04/1910 | Way Out West | James Booth | Play | James Booth, Millar Anderson |
| 18/04/1910 | The Gay Gordons | l Arthur Wimperis, m Guy Jones | Musical | Frank Lincoln, May Yates, Edwin Dodds |
| 25/04/1910 | Hush Money | | Play | Horace Denton, Ernest Imeson |
| 02/05/1910 | The Bondman | Hall Caine | Play | Philip Darien, Stanley Harrison, Violet Macaree, W H Rotheram |
| 09/05/1910 | The Merry Widow | l Adrian Ross, Franz Lehar | Musical | Mary Ridley, Robert Needham |
| 16/05/1910 | Almost his Bride | | Play | Stephen Pritt, George R J Justin, R F Stacey |
| 17/05/1910 | A Woman's Passion | | Play | Stephen Pritt, George R J Justin, R F Stacey |
| 18/05/1910 | Almost his Bride | | Play | Stephen Pritt, George R J Justin, R F Stacey |
| 19/05/1910 | A Woman's Passion | | Play | Stephen Pritt, George R J Justin, R F Stacey |
| 21/05/1910 | A Woman's Passion | | Play | Stephen Pritt, George R J Justin, R F Stacey |
| 23/05/1910 | | | Variety | Rapolie (Juggler), Maudie Laurel (comedienne, acrobatic dancer) |
| 30/05/1910 | | | Variety | Albert Tofts (living statuary), The Arnolds (Cabinet mystery) |
| 06/06/1910 | The Love of the Princess | | Play | Frank Harvey, John Burton, May Beatrice |
| 13/06/1910 | | | Variety | Harry Raymond & Little Ivy (coon singer & child dancer), Maggie Rimmer |
| 20/06/1910 | | | Variety | 3 Spanish Armadas (tight rope dancers), Dott & Williams (Sand dancers) |
| 11/07/1910 | | | Variety | Sarnthaler Group ( Int songs & dances), Stanley Bros, (cycle& motor cycle act) |
| 18/07/1910 | | | Variety | Millie Doris (eccentric comedienne), Zaida (high wire), Maningos (equilibrists) |
| 25/07/1910 | Our Flat | Mrs Musgrave | Play | Murray King, Louis West |
| 01/08/1910 | Her Fatal Marriage | | Play | Jerrold Heather, Hilda Shirley |
| 08/08/1910 | Hamlet | William Shakespeare | Play | Alexander Marsh Co, Carrie Baillie, May Grimshaw |
| 09/08/1910 | Romeo and Juliet | William Shakespeare | Play | Alexander Marsh Co, Carrie Baillie, May Grimshaw |
| 10/08/1910 | David Garrick/Sleigh Bells | Thomas William Robertson | Play | Alexander Marsh Co, Carrie Baillie, May Grimshaw |

| Date | Title/Event | Playwright/Author<br>l= lyrics; m= music | Category | Performers |
|------|-------------|-------------------------------------------|----------|------------|
| 11/08/1910 | The Taming of the Shrew | William Shakespeare | Play | Alexander Marsh Co, Carrie Baillie, May Grimshaw |
| 12/08/1910 | Merry Wives of Windsor | William Shakespeare | Play | Alexander Marsh Co, Carrie Baillie, May Grimshaw |
| 13/08/1910 | Othello | William Shakespeare | Play | Alexander Marsh Co, Carrie Baillie, May Grimshaw |
| 15/08/1910 | The Bad Girl of the Family | Frederick Melville | Play | Alice Esther Belmore, Sydney Lynn, Edith Evans |
| 22/08/1910 | The Midnight Wedding | Walter Howard | Play | A E Winnington Barnes, Stuart Black, Lilian Hallows |
| 29/08/1910 | Niobe | Harry & Edward Paulton | Play | Charles Macdona, Miss K Connaught |
| 05/09/1910 | The Queen of the Fair | l R C Thorp, m B Horsfall | Musical | Basil Horsfall, Albert Chapman, Senora Dalmada |
| 12/09/1910 | His Real Wife | Charles C Clarke | Play | T Edward Ward, Clifford Rean, Miss Ward |
| 19/09/1910 | Miss Hook of Holland | Paul Rubens | Musical | Dorothy Southgate, Alfred Wellesley, Harry Brayne |
| 26/09/1910 | The Apple of Eden | G Carlton Wallace | Play | Janet Alexander, Lauderdale Maitland, Stephen E Scanlon |
| 03/10/1910 | Was She to Blame | Mrs Kimberley | Play | Fred Conyngham, Georgie Delara |
| 10/10/1910 | Havana | l Adrian Ross, m Leslie Stuart | Musical | Miss Bliss, John Sanderbrook |
| 17/10/1910 | Jane Shore | | Play | F B Wolfe Co, Edith Lorraine |
| 18/10/1910 | Merchant of Venice | William Shakespeare | Play | F B Wolfe Co, Edith Lorraine |
| 19/10/1910 | Three Musketeers | | Play | F B Wolfe Co, Edith Lorraine |
| 20/10/1910 | Lady Godiva | Max Goldberg | Play | F B Wolfe Co, Edith Lorraine |
| 21/10/1910 | Two Orphans of Paris | | Play | F B Wolfe Co, Edith Lorraine |
| 22/10/1910 | The King of Crime | Arthur Shirley, Ben Landeck | Play | |
| 24/10/1910 | The Arcadians | l Arthur Wimperis, m Lionel Monckton, Howard Talbot | Musical | Alfred Beers, Molly McIntyre, Charles Stephenson |
| 31/10/1910 | The King's Romance | E Vivian Edmonds | Musical | E Vivian Edmonds, Mary Austin, Arthur Estcourt |
| 07/11/1910 | Lucky Durham | Wilson Barrett | Play | Edmund Kennedy, Arthur Leigh, Nellie Bonser |
| 08/11/1910 | Lucky Durham | Wilson Barrett | Play | Edmund Kennedy, Arthur Leigh, Nellie Bonser |
| 09/11/1910 | Lucky Durham | Wilson Barrett | Play | Edmund Kennedy, Arthur Leigh, Nellie Bonser |
| 10/11/1910 | Our Miss Gibbs | l Adrian Ross, m Leslie Stuart | Musical | Daisy Wallace, Vincent Erin |
| 11/11/1910 | Our Miss Gibbs | l Adrian Ross, m Leslie Stuart | Musical | Daisy Wallace, Vincent Erin |

| Date | Title/Event | Playwright/Author  l= lyrics; m= music | Category | Performers |
|------|-------------|------------------------------|----------|------------|
| 12/11/1910 | Our Miss Gibbs | l Adrian Ross, m Leslie Stuart | Musical | Daisy Wallace, Vincent Erin |
| 14/11/1910 | Paying Their Price | James Willard | Play | James Willard, Fred Wilson, Margaret Tueski, Lily Lloyd |
| 21/11/1910 | Beauty and the Barge | W W Jacobs, L N Parker | Play | Maitland Marler, Hilda Vaughan |
| 28/11/1910 | When Knights Were Bold | Charles Marlow | Play | H Langdon Bruce, Violet Noel, Lena Flowerdew |
| 05/12/1910 | The Boy King | Walter Howard | Play | Walter Howard, Annie Saker |
| 12/12/1910 | Hop o' my Thumb | | Panto | Georgie Harris, Harold Pyott, Daisy Wood |
| 19/12/1910 | Dare Devil Dorothy | l Wilfred Carr, m K Ernest Irving | Musical | D Desmonde, W Ashley |
| 26/12/1910 | The Missing Maid | l George de Lara, m William T Gliddon, Jacques Henri | Musical | Nellie Lang, Will Smith, Reggie Gray |
| 02/01/1911 | Two Lancashire Lasses in London | Arthur Shirley | Play | Robert Gilbert, Walter H Wilson, Florence Zillwood, Mabel Coleman |
| 09/01/1911 | Cinderella | | Panto | Kitty Upton, Elsie Lisle, Stafford Hilliard, Harry Hilliard |
| 16/01/1911 | The Girl Who lost Her Character | Walter Melville | Play | Lorraine Stevens, W Kellson |
| 23/01/1911 | Jack and the Beanstalk | | Panto | Madge O'Neill, Harry Howe |
| 30/01/1911 | The Ruin of her Life | Mrs Morton Powell | Play | Mrs Charles Sugden, A B McKay, Maud Randford |
| 06/02/1911 | Charley's Aunt | Brandon Thomas | Play | Hugh Wakefield, Cecil Kerr, Robert Burnett |
| 13/02/1911 | Aladdin | | Panto | Ethel Ward, Jack McKenzie |
| 20/02/1911 | A Criminal's Bride | | Play | |
| 27/02/1911 | Chasing Cynthia | Frank Stanmore | Musical | Kitty Hyde, Frank Stanmore, Jerrold Manville |
| 06/03/1911 | The Love Waltz | | Musical | George Fox, Rosa Mai, Senora Delmada, George Carroll |
| 13/03/1911 | The Sins of London | Walter Melville | Play | Austen Milroy, Ethel Bracewell |
| 20/03/1911 | The Girl from Nowhere | | Musical | Henry Hare, Dan Ugar |
| 27/03/1911 | The Dandy Doctors | l Edward Maris, m Dudley Powell | Musical | Marie Ault, Tom E Sinclair, Jessica Brooke |
| 03/04/1911 | Queen of the Wicked | Ronald Grahame | Play | Edith Blande, Henry W Haschman |
| 10/04/1911 | The Village Blacksmith | G Carlton Wallace | Play | Sam Livesey, Maggie Edwards |
| 17/04/1911 | The Scarlet Sin | George Sims, Arthur Shirley | Play | William Clayton, Edward Lowrie, Patey Trounsell |
| 24/04/1911 | The Arcadians | l A Wimperis, m L Monckton | Musical | Charles A Stephenson, Alfred Beers, Vivien Carter |
| 01/05/1911 | A Chinese Honeymoon | l George Dance, m Harry Talbot | Musical | Gwennie Harcourt, Edward Thirlby |
| 08/05/1911 | The Christian | Hall Cane | Play | Marcus Draper, Gladys Purnell |

| Date | Title/Event | Playwright/Author<br>l= lyrics; m= music | Category | Performers |
|------|-------------|--------------------------------------------|----------|------------|
| 15/05/1911 | The Face at the Window | F Brooke Warren | Play | Constance Glenabyn, T W Dunscombe |
| 21/05/1911 | | | Variety | Carl Hertz & Co (illusionists), Polo & Florence (equilibrists) |
| 28/05/1911 | The Merry Widow | l Adrian Ross, m Franz Lehar | Musical | Gladys Lancaster, Robert Needham |
| 05/06/1911 | The Wages of Sin | Frank Harvey | Play | Grace Warner, George Gordon |
| 06/06/1911 | The Wages of Sin | Frank Harvey | Play | Grace Warner, George Gordon |
| 07/06/1911 | Lady Audley's Secret | from Mary Elizabeth Braddon | Play | Grace Warner, George Gordon |
| 08/06/1911 | Lady Audley's Secret | from Mary Elizabeth Braddon | Play | Grace Warner, George Gordon |
| 09/06/1911 | Lady Audley's Secret | from Mary Elizabeth Braddon | Play | Grace Warner, George Gordon |
| 10/06/1911 | The Wages of Sin | Frank Harvey | Play | Grace Warner, George Gordon |
| 12/06/1911 | | | Variety | "My Star" ( child comedienne), Henry Tate & Co |
| 19/06/1911 | | | Variety | Alec Hurley (coster comedian), Four Chums (hoops), Ben Lewin (impersonator) |
| 26/06/1911 | | | Variety | Daisy Meads (comedienne), L B Athol (monologues), Flying Julians (gymnasts) |
| 03/07/1911 | | | Variety | G H Elliott and Company of Chocolate Coloured Coons, Merry& Bright |
| 24/07/1911 | | | Variety | Elliott Savanas (musical act) Tom Taylor& Co (Comedy sketches) |
| 31/07/1911 | The Silver King | Henry Arthur Jones | Play | Arthur Rooke, Madge Trenchard, Ernest E Imeson |
| 07/08/1911 | The Outcast of the Family | | Play | Wybert Clive, David Blair, Freda Beckett |
| 14/08/1911 | David Garrick/ The Corsican Brothers | Thomas William Robertson/ Dion Bouccicault | Play | Alexander Marsh Co, Carrie Baillie, Wilson Gunning, May Grimshaw |
| 15/08/1911 | Taming of the Shrew | William Shakespeare | Play | Alexander Marsh Co, Carrie Baillie, Wilson Gunning, May Grimshaw |
| 16/08/1911 | Merry Wives of Windsor | William Shakespeare | Play | Alexander Marsh Co, Carrie Baillie, Wilson Gunning, May Grimshaw |
| 17/08/1911 | Trilby/Married by Accident | Clifford Rean/ | Play | Alexander Marsh Co, Carrie Baillie, Wilson Gunning, May Grimshaw |
| 18/08/1911 | Twelfth Night | William Shakespeare | Play | Alexander Marsh Co, Carrie Baillie, Wilson Gunning, May Grimshaw |
| 19/08/1911 | Hamlet | William Shakespeare | Play | Alexander Marsh Co, Carrie Baillie, Wilson Gunning, May Grimshaw |
| 21/08/1911 | Second to None | Walter Howard | Play | Edward E Ashby, Miss Ward |

| Date | Title/Event | Playwright/Author<br>l= lyrics; m= music | Category | Performers |
|---|---|---|---|---|
| 28/08/1911 | The Breed of the Treshams | John Rutherford | Play | Sydney Bland, Frank Danby |
| 04/09/1911 | With Edged Tools | Henry Seton Merriman | Play | Richard Hicks, Campbell Goldsmid, Hamilton Deane, Stanley Bedwell |
| 11/09/1911 | The Bad Girl of the Family | Frederick Melville | Play | Florrie Kelsey, Charles Yorke |
| 18/09/1911 | The Wild Girl of the Family | Mrs F G Kimberley | Play | Mrs F G Kimberley, Algernon Hicks |
| 25/09/1911 | The Prince and the Beggar Maid | Walter Howard | Play | Gladys Leslie, Henry Hallatt |
| 02/10/1911 | | | Variety | The Seddons (jugglers), Nell Cotter (comedienne), Harry Brookes (comedienne) |
| 03/10/1911 | | | Variety | The Seddons (jugglers), Nell Cotter (comedienne), Harry Brookes (comedienne) |
| 04/10/1911 | | | Variety | The Seddons (jugglers), Nell Cotter (comedienne), Harry Brookes (comedienne) |
| 05/10/1911 | Our Miss Gibbs | l Adrian Ross, m Leslie Stuart | Musical | Florence Ray, Chris Wren |
| 06/10/1911 | Our Miss Gibbs | l Adrian Ross, m Leslie Stuart | Musical | Florence Ray, Chris Wren |
| 07/10/1911 | Our Miss Gibbs | l Adrian Ross, m Leslie Stuart | Musical | Florence Ray, Chris Wren |
| 09/10/1911 | Passers- By | C Haddon Chambers | Play | Lewis Edgarde, Amy Ravenscroft |
| 16/10/1911 | Faust | Gounod | Opera | Moody-Manners Opera Co inc William Anderson, Florence Morden, Olive Westwood |
| 17/10/1911 | Carmen | Bizet | Opera | Moody-Manners Opera Co inc William Anderson, Florence Morden, Olive Westwood |
| 18/10/1911 | Maritana | Vincent Wallace | Opera | Moody-Manners Opera Co inc William Anderson, Florence Morden, Olive Westwood |
| 19/10/1911 | Daughter of the Regiment | Donizetti | Opera | Moody-Manners Opera Co inc William Anderson, Florence Morden, Olive Westwood |
| 20/10/1911 | Lohengrin | Wagner | Opera | Moody-Manners Opera Co inc William Anderson, Florence Morden, Olive Westwood |
| 21/10/1911 | Il Trovatore   mat | Wagner | Opera | Moody-Manners Opera Co inc William Anderson, Florence Morden, Olive Westwood |
| 21/10/1911 | Bohemian Girl  eve | Balfe | Opera | Moody-Manners Opera Co inc William Anderson, Florence Morden, Olive Westwood |
| 23/10/1911 | The Still Alarm | Joseph Arthur | Play | Matthew H Glenville, George Arthur, Rene Belle Douglas |
| 30/10/1911 | What the Butler Saw | | Play | Lionel Rignold |
| 31/10/1911 | What the Butler Saw | | Play | Lionel Rignold |
| 01/11/1911 | What the Butler Saw | | Play | Lionel Rignold |
| 02/11/1911 | The Dollar Princess | Leo Fall | Musical | Fred Leslie, Fred Maguire, Norah Barry |
| 03/11/1911 | The Dollar Princess | Leo Fall | Musical | Fred Leslie, Fred Maguire, Norah Barry |

| Date | Title/Event | Playwright/Author<br>l= lyrics; m= music | Category | Performers |
|---|---|---|---|---|
| 04/11/1911 | The Dollar Princess | Leo Fall | Musical | Fred Leslie, Fred Maguire, Norah Barry |
| 06/11/1911 | The Eternal City | Hall Caine | Play | Marcus Draper Co, Gladys Purnell, Norman Purnell |
| 07/11/1911 | The Christian | Hall Caine | Play | Marcus Draper Co, Gladys Purnell, Norman Purnell |
| 08/11/1911 | The Eternal City | Hall Caine | Play | Marcus Draper Co, Gladys Purnell, Norman Purnell |
| 09/11/1911 | The Eternal City | Hall Caine | Play | Marcus Draper Co, Gladys Purnell, Norman Purnell |
| 10/11/1911 | The Christian | Hall Caine | Play | Marcus Draper Co, Gladys Purnell, Norman Purnell |
| 11/11/1911 | The Eternal City | Hall Caine | Play | Marcus Draper Co, Gladys Purnell, Norman Purnell |
| 13/11/1911 | The Belle of New York | l CSM McLellan, m Gustav Kerker | Musical | Empsie Bowman, Frank Lawton |
| 20/11/1911 | The Sky Skipper | l Arthur E Ellis, E W Rogers, m Arthur Rigby | Musical | Arthur Rigby, Jack McKenzie, Gwen Clifford |
| 21/11/1911 | The Sky Skipper | l Arthur E Ellis, E W Rogers, m Arthur Rigby | Musical | Arthur Rigby, Jack McKenzie, Gwen Clifford |
| 22/11/1911 | The Sky Skipper | l Arthur E Ellis, E W Rogers, m Arthur Rigby | Musical | Arthur Rigby, Jack McKenzie, Gwen Clifford |
| 23/11/1911 | The Girl in the Train | | Musical | Stella Gastelle, Bay Russell |
| 24/11/1911 | The Girl in the Train | | Musical | Stella Gastelle, Bay Russell |
| 25/11/1911 | The Girl in the Train | | Musical | Stella Gastelle, Bay Russell |
| 27/11/1911 | The Girl Who Knew a Bit | Charles Darrell | Play | Harold Weston, Vashti Wynne |
| 04/12/1911 | The Speckled Band | Arthur Conan Doyle | Play | Grendon Bentley, Harold S Standing, E Vassel Vaughan |
| 11/12/1911 | | | Variety | Netta & Jetta (comedy duo), Madame Holt's Juvenile Follies |
| 18/12/1911 | Two Little Vagabonds | Arthur Shirley, George Sims | Play | Ethel Kay, Ernest Owtram |
| 26/12/1911 | His Indian Wife | Travis Green & A Hinton | Play | Leila Zellwood, Leonard Williams |
| 01/01/1912 | The Mousme | l Arthur Wimperis, m Howard Talbot, Lionel Monckton | Musical | Victor Gouriet, Sybil Coulthurst |
| 08/01/1912 | The Coastguard's Daughter | J A Campbell | Play | T Lionel Ellis, Alice Bowes |
| 15/01/1912 | The Cingalee | l Adrian Ross, m Lionel Monckton | Musical | Lional Yeoman, Florrie Greensmith |
| 22/01/1912 | Babes in the Wood | | Panto | Jack Cromo, Will Terry, Agnes Tandy |
| 29/01/1912 | The World, the Flesh and the Devil | Lesser Columbus | Play | Maud Hildyard |

| Date | Title/Event | Playwright/Author l= lyrics; m= music | Category | Performers |
|------|-------------|----------------------------------------|----------|------------|
| 05/02/1912 | Little Red Riding Hood | | Panto | George Campbell, The Bernhardts, Bessie Esmond, Florrie Arthur |
| 12/02/1912 | Miss Hook of Holland | Paul Rubens | Musical | Arthur Wellesley, Percy Cahill |
| 19/02/1912 | A Girl's Cross Roads | Walter Melville | Play | Marion Fawcett, Edward Valentine, Dorrie Roberts |
| 26/02/1912 | Claudian | Wilson Barrett | Play | William MacLaren, Lily C Bandman |
| 05/03/1912 | The Fatal Wedding | Theodore Kremer | Play | Cecil A Melton, Elaine Vanburgh, Rosie Trenchard |
| 12/03/1912 | Babes in the Wood | | Panto | Naughton & Gold, George Grogie, George Brooks |
| 19/03/1912 | The Dairy Maids | l Paul Rubens, Arthur Wimperis, m Paul Rubens, F Tours | Musical | Edwin Dodds, Katie Yates, Edie Martin |
| 25/03/1912 | The Quaker Girl | l Adrian Ross, Percy Greenbank, m Lionel Monckton | Musical | Effie Vincent, Leslie Henson |
| 01/04/1912 | Little Red Riding Hood | | Panto | Lena Stanton, Rex Kempton, Hilda Trelawney |
| 08/04/1912 | The Cattle Thief | | Play | George A Street |
| 15/04/1912 | The Beggar Princess | Mrs Cassidy | Play | J Rice Cassidy, Mrs Cassidy |
| 22/04/1912 | | | Variety | Yamamoto Kyoshi Troupe (equilibrists), Mlle Roseau's Nine Toy Dogs |
| 29/04/1912 | | | Variety | De Biere (illusionist), Harry Harvey (pattering postman),Dora MacKay (chorus comedienne) |
| 06/05/1912 | Alias Jimmy Valentine | Paul Armstrong | Play | J Hamilton Stewart, John Richter |
| 13/05/1912 | | | Variety | Herbert Lloyd &Co, (comedy burlesque), Gracie Lawn (comedienne), Three Romas (cyclists) |
| 20/05/1912 | | | Variety | Arthur Roberts & Co ("The Girl Who Lost her Honeymoon), Olive West (comedienne) |
| 27/05/1912 | | | Variety | Imperial Russian Dancers, Carta & Martziana (equilibrists with "The Dog Actor") |
| 03/06/1912 | | | Variety | Elsie Arnold & Lil Dunlop (Gipsey vocalists), George Belling (humourist with 4-legged comedians) |
| 10/05/1912 | | | Variety | James Hendon (whistling cowboy), Cecil Gray & Dora Eastlake in "Tomorrow's dawn") |
| 17/06/1912 | Temptress of Paris | Herbert Fuller | Play | Agnes Collier, Herbert Fuller, Paul Beckett |
| 24/06/1911 | The Sledge Hammer | Wilson Barrett | Play | Bertha Kingston, W V Garrod |
| 01/07/1912 | Queen of the Redskins | Emma Litchfield | Play | Hilda Shirley, Jerrold Heather |
| 29/07/1912 | | | Variety | Bros Lloyd & co (Tight- Rope), Elsie Ridgeley & Co (in "Affinities" melodrama) |

| Date | Title/Event | Playwright/Author<br>l= lyrics; m= music | Category | Performers |
|---|---|---|---|---|
| 05/08/1912 | | | Variety | Sears (American illiusionist), Daisy Bright (Rag-time), Dolly Harmer, (Comedienne) |
| 12/08/1912 | | | Variety | Tinka Troupe (Japanese equilibrists), La Belle Nello (contortionist), Connie Mascot, (comedienne |
| 19/08/1912 | The Colombo Girl | l Wilfred Carr, m Harry Richardson | Musical | Wilfred Carr, May Warden, Nellie Harcourt |
| 26/08/1912 | | | Variety | Jungle Children (Patsy & Sally, chimpanzees), Bert Williams, (vent.), Lily Esplin (comedienne) |
| 02/09/1912 | Merchant of Venice | William Shakespeare | Play | Alexander Marsh Co, Carrie Baillie, May Grimshaw, Wilson Gunning |
| 03/09/1912 | Julius Caesar | William Shakespeare | Play | Alexander Marsh Co, Carrie Baillie, May Grimshaw, Wilson Gunning |
| 04/09/1912 | Romeo and Juliet | William Shakespeare | Play | Alexander Marsh Co, Carrie Baillie, May Grimshaw, Wilson Gunning |
| 05/09/1912 | Tale of Two Cities | | Play | Alexander Marsh Co, Carrie Baillie, May Grimshaw, Wilson Gunning |
| 06/09/1912 | Midsummers Night Dream | William Shakespeare | Play | Alexander Marsh Co, Carrie Baillie, May Grimshaw, Wilson Gunning |
| 07/09/1912 | Three Musketeers | Clifford Rean | Play | Alexander Marsh Co, Carrie Baillie, May Grimshaw, Wilson Gunning |
| 09/09/1912 | Faust | Gounod | Opera | Joseph O'Mara Grand Opera Co inc,Edith Eavns, Maria Le Fre, Kingsley Lark, Joseph O'Mara |
| 10/09/1912 | Il Trovatore | Verdi | Opera | Joseph O'Mara Grand Opera Co inc,Edith Eavns, Maria Le Fre, Kingsley Lark, Joseph O'Mara |
| 11/09/1912 | Maritana | Vincent Wallace | Opera | Joseph O'Mara Grand Opera Co inc,Edith Eavns, Maria Le Fre, Kingsley Lark, Joseph O'Mara |
| 12/09/1912 | Carmen | Bizet | Opera | Joseph O'Mara Grand Opera Co inc,Edith Eavns, Maria Le Fre, Kingsley Lark, Joseph O'Mara |
| 13/09/1912 | Tannhauser | Wagner | Opera | Joseph O'Mara Grand Opera Co inc,Edith Eavns, Maria Le Fre, Kingsley Lark, Joseph O'Mara |
| 14/09/1912 | Faust   mat | Gounod | Opera | Joseph O'Mara Grand Opera Co inc,Edith Eavns, Maria Le Fre, Kingsley Lark, Joseph O'Mara |
| 14/09/1912 | Bohemian Girl | Balfe | Opera | Joseph O'Mara Grand Opera Co inc,Edith Eavns, Maria Le Fre, Kingsley Lark, Joseph O'Mara |
| 16/09/1912 | The Lifeguardsman | Walter Howard | Play | Ernest H G Cox, Miriam Pritchett, Alfred Goddard |
| 23/09/1912 | The Waltz Dream | l Adrian Ross, m Oscar Strauss | Musical | |

| Date | Title/Event | Playwright/Author l= lyrics; m= music | Category | Performers |
|---|---|---|---|---|
| 30/09/1912 | The Slave Girl | | Play | Miss Ward, Amy Height, S Elwyn- Leslie, Fred Rivers |
| 07/10/1912 | The Glad Eye | Jose G Levy | Play | F Clive Ross, Sam Wilkinson |
| 14/10/1912 | A Country Girl | l Adrian Ross, m Lionel Monckton | Musical | Arthur Staples, Ellaline Thorne, Douglas Philips |
| 21/10/1912 | From Convent to Throne | J A Campbell | Play | Dorrie Roberts, Roland Daniel, William Calvert, Wilton Read |
| 28/10/1912 | Allah's Orchard | Emma Litchfield | Play | Floence Zillwood, Arthur Hinton, Eric Leighton, Olive Purcess |
| 04/11/1912 | Peggy | | Musical | Harry Phydora, Lulu Evans |
| 11/11/1912 | After Midnight | | Play | Arthur Hawtree, Ida Heron, Benson North |
| 18/11/1912 | The Chocolate Soldier | l Stanislaus Strange, m Oscar Straus | Musical | Villiers Arnold, Alice Coverick |
| 25/11/1912 | Master of the Mill | | Play | George Littleton Holydale, Ellis Dight |
| 02/12/1912 | The Girl in the Picture | l Isa Bowman, m Harry Richardson | Musical | Isa Bowman, Frank Barclay, Hylton Warde |
| 09/12/1912 | The Sleeping Beauty | | Panto | Kitty Rafferty, Evelyn Major, Wee Georgie Harris |
| 16/12/1912 | | | Variety | Chung Sing Loo (illusionist), Mlle Marjutti (Lissom lady), George Maston (Yorkshire comedian) |
| 23/12/1912 | Nick Carter, Detective | Arthur Shirley, Ben Landreck | Play | Chas Bardon, Violet Somerville, Walter Clarke |
| 30/12/1912 | The Count of Luxembourg | Franz Lehar | Musical | |
| 06/01/1913 | The Monk and the Woman | Frederick Melville | Play | Ronald Adair, Lewis Mannering, Vernon Sansbury |
| 13/01/1913 | The Woman in the Case | Clyde Fitch | Play | Martin Henry, Olive Warne, Rita Jonson |
| 20/01/1913 | The Merry Widow | l Adrian Ross, m Franz Lehar | Musical | Gladys Lancaster, Robert needham, Alfred Beers |
| 27/01/1913 | Jack and Jill | | Panto | Lily Leonhard, Indiana Lindsay, Arthur Anarto |
| 03/02/1913 | Jack and Jill | | | |
| 10/02/1913 | Milestones | Arnold Bennett, Edward Knoblauch | Play | Gerald Mirriellees, Hilda Gregory |
| 17/02/1913 | King of the Wild West | | Play | Young Buffalo, Lilian Maude, Arthur C Goff |
| 24/02/1913 | Robinson Crusoe | | Panto | Tom Hume, Dorothy Veitch |
| 03/03/1913 | The Barrier | Rex Beach | Play | Arthur Leigh, Louis Hector, Florence Tressilion |
| 10/03/1913 | Carmen | Bizet | Opera | Moody-Manners Opera Co inc Florence Morden, Zellie de Lussan |
| 11/03/1913 | Elijah | Mendelssohn | Opera | Moody-Manners Opera Co inc Florence Morden, Zellie de Lussan |

| Date | Title/Event | Playwright/Author<br>l= lyrics; m= music | Category | Performers |
|---|---|---|---|---|
| 12/03/1911 | Lohengrin | Wagner | Opera | Moody-Manners Opera Co inc Florence Morden, Zellie de Lussan |
| 13/03/1913 | Samson and Delilah | Saint-Saens | Opera | Moody-Manners Opera Co inc Florence Morden, Zellie de Lussan |
| 14/03/1913 | Romeo and Juliet | Gounod | Opera | Moody-Manners Opera Co inc Florence Morden, Zellie de Lussan |
| 15/03/1913 | Rigoletto  mat | Verdi | Opera | Moody-Manners Opera Co inc Florence Morden, Zellie de Lussan |
| 15/03/1913 | Faust    eve | Gounod | Opera | Moody-Manners Opera Co inc Florence Morden, Zellie de Lussan |
| 17/03/1913 | The Gambler | Sheila Walsh | Play | Scott Leighton, Sheila Walsh, Dane Clarke |
| 24/03/1913 | A Thief in the Night | G Carlton Wallace | Play | Naylor Grimson, Elizabeth Watkins |
| 31/03/1913 | The Prisoner of Zenda | Anthony Hope, Edward Rose | Play | Claud A Lister, Dorothy Overend |
| 07/04/1913 | The Cingalee | l Adrian Ross, m Lionel Monckton | Musical | Daisy Lake, Sam Locridge, Walter Uridge |
| 14/04/1913 | His Indian Wife | Travis Green, Arthur Hinton | Play | Leonard Williams, Irene Aitcheson, Tod Squires |
| 21/04/1913 | The Arcadians | l Arthur Wimperis, Lionel Monckton | Musical | Alfred Selby, Edward Jefferson, Walter Elabert, Minnie Rayner |
| 28/04/1913 | Miss Hook of Holland | Paul Rubens | Musical | Fred J Little, George F Ide, Helene Moore, Gladys Ashton |
| 05/05/1913 | | | Variety | John Lawson (in "Humanity"), Susie Potter Brown (Ragtime comedienne), Cook (juggler) |
| 12/05/1913 | King of the Gipseys | Emma Litchfield | Play | Sidney Bland, Josephine Ricchards, F Leighton Courteney |
| 19/05/1913 | | | Variety | Gicardo ( backward juggler), Fred Karno |
| 26/05/1913 | | | Variety | Maude May Murray (electrical aerial dance), Fred Karno presents "Flats" |
| 02/06/1913 | | | Variety | |
| 09/06/1913 | | | Variety | Babie Beattie (child marvel in song and dance), Juggling Geraldos, 5 Vernons (xylophonists) |
| 16/06/1913 | | | Variety | |
| 23/06/1913 | | | Variety | Baroness Von Lutzel (Horses & Dogs) ,La Vie (Artistic panel poses),The Slaters (comedians |
| 30/06/1913 | | | Variety | Vasco (mad musician), Maurin's Marvellous Fountains, |
| 21/07/1913 | | | Variety | Three Royal Matsuis (Japanese water jugglers), Wee Dot & Doris(Juvenile entertainers) |
| 28/07/1913 | | | Variety | Astley's American Circus, Delroys (negro musical comedy specialists), Millwards (equilibrists) |

| Date | Title/Event | Playwright/Author<br>l= lyrics; m= music | Category | Performers |
|---|---|---|---|---|
| 04/08/1913 | | | Variety | Mizuno Troupe, (Japanese entertainers),Beatrice Bonny & Sister (Refined singing and dancing) |
| 11/08/1913 | | | Variety | Capt Taylors Wonderful Baboons & Dog Actors, Judges Cockatoos, Parrots & Macaws |
| 18/08/1913 | Jane | Harry Nichols, William Lestocq | Play | Sebastion Smith, Jenny Lynn |
| 25/08/1913 | An Oath of Vengeance | Ward Bailey | Play | T Arthur Ellis, Elsie Marriott Watson, George Gaisford |
| 01/09/1913 | Tale of Two Cities | | Play | Alexander Marsh Co, Carrie Baillie, Wilson Gunning, May Grimshaw |
| 02/09/1913 | Bishop's Candlesticks/ Trilby | Norman McKinnel/ Clifford Rean | Play | Alexander Marsh Co, Carrie Baillie, Wilson Gunning, May Grimshaw |
| 03/09/1913 | Three Musketeers | Clifford Rean | Play | Alexander Marsh Co, Carrie Baillie, Wilson Gunning, May Grimshaw |
| 04/09/1913 | Oliver Twist | | Play | Alexander Marsh Co, Carrie Baillie, Wilson Gunning, May Grimshaw |
| 05/09/1913 | Nell Gwynn | Clifford Rean | Play | Alexander Marsh Co, Carrie Baillie, Wilson Gunning, May Grimshaw |
| 06/09/1913 | Taming of the Shrew | William Shakespeare | Play | Alexander Marsh Co, Carrie Baillie, Wilson Gunning, May Grimshaw |
| 06/09/1913 | David Garrick/ The Sleigh Bells | Thomas William Robertson | Play | Alexander Marsh Co, Carrie Baillie, Wilson Gunning, May Grimshaw |
| 08/09/1913 | The Flag Lieutenant | W G Drury, Leo Trevor | Play | Frederick Meads, Aiden Lovett, Elizabeth Dundas |
| 11/09/1913 | Hindle Wakes | Stanley Houghton | Play | Lilian Deane, Doris Ward, Claremont Gaskell, Charles W Dockwray |
| 15/09/1913 | The Girl from Nowhere | | Musical | Edwin Dodds, Lilian Laurent, Nellie James |
| 22/09/1913 | The Catch of the Season | l Charles H Taylor, m Herbert E Haines, Evelyn Baker | Musical | Morant Weber, Phyllis Hughes |
| 29/09/1913 | Oh! I Say! | Sidney Blow, Douglas Hoare | Play | Freddy Bentley, Stafford Dicken |
| 06/10/1913 | The Miracle | John Maclaren, Alfred Denville | Play | Kate Saville, Elsie Shelton |
| 13/10/1913 | A Butterfly on the Wall | Edward C Hemmerde, Francis Nielson | Play | Cecil Brooking, Douglas Greet, Mary Douglas |
| 20/10/1913 | La Poupee | l George Byng, m Edward Audran | Musical | Arthur Lenville, Bertram Whit, Winifred Dunkley |
| 27/10/1913 | Woman and Wine | Arthur Shirley, Ben Landeck | Play | Dalton H Keand, Edward Valentine, Nannie Mead |
| 03/11/1913 | The Chocolate Soldier | l Stanislau Stange, Oscar Straus | Musical | Aubrey Millward, Edith St George. W P Morgan |

| Date | Title/Event | Playwright/Author l= lyrics; m= music | Category | Performers |
|---|---|---|---|---|
| 10/11/1913 | Inconstant George | Gladys Ungar | Play | N Carter Slaughter, Hilda Glynne, A V Bramb |
| 17/11/1913 | The Speckled Band | | Play | Julian Cross, A Corney-Grain, Agnes Marey, Dorothy Cross |
| 24/11/1913 | The Girl on the Train | l Adrian Ross, m Leo Fall | Musical | Bay Russell, Frank Harrison, Ethel Oliver |
| 01/12/1913 | Its Never Too Late to Mend | Charles Reade | Play | Geoffrey Pattrick, Emmie Barton |
| 08/12/1913 | The Revue Girl | W S Ivory, Kenneth Morrison | Musical | Lily Wallbrook, Eight Varsity Girls, Cathleen Cavanagh |
| 15/12/1913 | Queen of the Air | Edward Thane | Play | Joseph Millane, Joseph Magrath, Mabel Rose |
| 24/12/1913 | Cinderella | | Panto | Hazel Deane, Harry Rouseby, Dan Belmore, Randolph Sutton |
| 05/01/1914 | For her Children's Sake | Theodore Kremer | Play | Aylmer J Williams, Hugh Clayton, Dora Pass |
| 12/01/1914 | Robinson Crusoe | | Panto | Iris Belshaus, Nellie Turner, Phil Lester, Edie Martin |
| 19/01/1914 | Indian Girl's Devotion | F N Brownmann | Play | Mathew H Glenville, Edmund Blake, Genna Lyndon |
| 26/01/1914 | The Pride of the Mill | Sheila Walsh | Play | Sheila Walsh, Fred H Constable, Harrison For John Prescott |
| 02/02/1914 | The Quaker Girl | l, Adrian Ross, m Lionel Monckton | Musical | Christine Owens, Nellie Cozens, Harry W Bentham |
| 09/02/1914 | The Headmaster | Wilfred T Coleby, Edgar Knobloch | Play | Charles Windermere, Mollie Maitland, Rene Mowbray |
| 16/02/1914 | Little Red Riding Hood | | Panto | Gracie Rosslyn, Carlotta Sylvana, Edith Beverley, Fred Walker |
| 23/02/1914 | The Ever Open Door | G R Sims, H H Herbert | Play | Mabel Mannering, Terence Byron |
| 02/03/1914 | The Sunshine Girl | l Paul Rubens, A Wimperis, m Paul Rubens | Musical | Grace Wray, Nellie Cozens, Joseph Magrath |
| 09/02/1914 | Who's the Lady | Jose S Levy | Play | Percy Marmont, Frank Bradley, Barbara Gott, Marga La Rubia, Irene Hentschel |
| 16/03/1914 | Little Miss Ragtime | l Isa Bowman, m William Neale | Musical | Josephine Ellis, Isa Bowman, May Warden, A Passmore |
| 23/03/1914 | The Whip | Cyril Raleigh, Henry Hamilton | Play | Arthur Keane, Ernest James |
| 30/03/1914 | The Sledge Hammer | Wilson Barrett | Play | W V Garrod Co, David Maxwell, W V Garrod |
| 31/03/1914 | A Wife for a Day | W V Garrod | Play | W V Garrod Co, David Maxwell, W V Garrod |
| 01/04/1914 | A Wife for a Day | W V Garrod | Play | W V Garrod Co, David Maxwell, W V Garrod |
| 02/04/1914 | A Country Girl in London | W V Garrod | Play | W V Garrod Co, David Maxwell, W V Garrod |

| Date | Title/Event | Playwright/Author l= lyrics; m= music | Category | Performers |
|------|-------------|------------|----------|------------|
| 03/04/1914 | A Country Girl in London | W V Garrod | Play | W V Garrod Co, David Maxwell, W V Garrod, |
| 04/04/1914 | The Sledge Hammer | W V Garrod | Play | W V Garrod Co, David Maxwell, W V Garrod, |
| 06/04/1914 | Miss Lamb of Canterbury | l Sylvester Stuart, | Musical | Henry L Osmond, Ethel Glyde |
| 13/04/1914 | Dare-Devil Dorothy | l Wilfred Carr, m K Ernest Irving | Musical | Dorothy Desmonde, Nellie Harcourt |
| 20/04/1914 | Hullo, What's On | | Revue | Lena stanton, Lena Joseph, Ted Cartright |
| 27/04/1914 | A Blind Girl's Love | H F Housden | Musical | George Steele, Frank Hartie |
| 04/05/1914 | Gipsey Love | l Adrian Ross, m Franz Lehar | Musical | Sybil Coulthurst, Goedon Yates, Alfred Beers |
| 11/05/1914 | Tom, Dick and Harry | | Play | George Abel, Stella Campbell, Ormonde Wynne |
| 18/05/1914 | Ragtime Girl | | Revue | Trixie and Trix, Ted Freeling, Will Parkin |
| 25/05/1914 | The Glad Eye | Jose G Levy | Play | Stanley Laithbury, Beatrice West, Gwen Ffrangon-Davies |
| 01/06/1914 | The Woman Who Atoned | | Play | Kathleen Montagu, R S Ravenscroft, Valerie Russell |
| 08/06/1914 | Lucky Liza | Fred Locke | Musical | Dickie Clare, Minnie Millward |
| 09/06/1914 | Lucky Liza | Fred Locke | Musical | Dickie Clare, Minnie Millward |
| 10/06/1914 | Lucky Liza | Fred Locke | Musical | Dickie Clare, Minnie Millward |
| 11/06/1914 | Dolly Dye | | Musical | Dickie Clare, Minnie Millward |
| 12/06/1914 | Dolly Dye | | Musical | Dickie Clare, Minnie Millward |
| 13/06/1914 | Dolly Dye | | Musical | Dickie Clare, Minnie Millward |
| 15/06/1914 | Find the Lady | | Revue | Harry Ray, Harry Calden, Lily Calden |
| 22/06/1914 | Violet and Pink | | Musical | Gus Oxley, Rene Ash, Lauri Aster, Molly Buckley |
| 29/06/1914 | All Aboard | | Revue | Harry Melody, Josie Lawrence, Venton Swift |
| 20/07/1914 | Now We Know | | Revue | Billie Moran, Billy Fry |
| 27/07/1914 | A Place in the Sun | Cyril Harcourt | Play | Alfred Goddard, H F Maltby |
| 03/08/1914 | Wait and See | | Revue | Harry Monkhouse, Emmie King |
| 10/08/1914 | Baby Mine | Margaret Mayo | Play | Betty Fairfax, Keith Kenneth |
| 17/08/1914 | All the Nice Girls | | Revue | Jack McKenzie, Viola Rene |
| 24/08/1914 | What ho, Tango | | Revue | Tom Tutty, Chic Biarritz Dancers, Six Pretty Amsterdamsters, Dancing Mclloyds |
| 31/08/1914 | Taming of the Shrew | William Shakespeare | Play | Alexander Marsh Co, Carrie Baillie, Oswald Dobson |
| 01/09/1914 | Sorrows of Satan | | Play | Alexander Marsh Co, Carrie Baillie, Oswald Dobson |
| 02/09/1914 | The Corsican Brothers | Dion Bouccicault | Play | Alexander Marsh Co, Carrie Baillie, Oswald Dobson |

| Date | Title/Event | Playwright/Author<br>l= lyrics; m= music | Category | Performers |
|---|---|---|---|---|
| 03/09/1914 | Napoleon and his Washer Woman | | Play | Alexander Marsh Co, Carrie Baillie, Oswald Dobson |
| 04/09/1914 | Moths | | Play | Alexander Marsh Co, Carrie Baillie, Oswald Dobson |
| 05/09/1914 | Merchant of Venice mat | William Shakespeare | Play | Alexander Marsh Co, Carrie Baillie, Oswald Dobson |
| 05/09/1914 | The Corsican Brothers eve | Dion Bouccicault | Play | Alexander Marsh Co, Carrie Baillie, Oswald Dobson |
| 07/09/1914 | The Midnight Mail | Arthur Shirley | Play | Albert Sinclair, Charles Carte |
| 14/09/1914 | Oh!, Oh!, Delphine | l C M S McLellan ,m Ivan Carryl | Musical | Walter Thomas, Edwin Dodds, Ruby Vivian, Kathleen Gordon |
| 21/09/1914 | Carmen | Bizet | Opera | Joseph O'Mara Opera Co inc Joseph O'Mara, Teify Davies |
| 22/09/1914 | Faust | Gounod | Opera | Joseph O'Mara Opera Co inc Joseph O'Mara, Teify Davies |
| 23/09/1914 | Bohemian Girl | Balfe | Opera | Joseph O'Mara Opera Co inc Joseph O'Mara, Teify Davies |
| 24/09/1914 | Tannhauser | Wagner | Opera | Joseph O'Mara Opera Co inc Joseph O'Mara, Teify Davies |
| 25/09/1914 | Cavalleria Rusticanna/ I Pagliacci | Mascagni/ Leoncavallo | Opera | Joseph O'Mara Opera Co inc Joseph O'Mara, Teify Davies |
| 26/09/1914 | Il Trovatore mat | Verdi | Opera | Joseph O'Mara Opera Co inc Joseph O'Mara, Teify Davies |
| 26/09/1914 | Maritana eve | Vincent Wallace | Opera | Joseph O'Mara Opera Co inc Joseph O'Mara, Teify Davies |
| 28/09/1914 | The New Boy | | Play | Violet Engefield, Sam Lysons, Howard Gridland, Wyn Weaver, Helen Sainsbury |
| 05/10/1914 | Brewster's Millions | Winchell Smith, Bryan Ongley | Play | Henry Hampson, Winifred Wing |
| 12/10/1914 | All Moonshine | | Revue | Tom Talbot, Maud Clothier |
| 19/10/1914 | Oh, I Say | | Revue | Freddy Bentley, Stafford Dickens, Diana Cortis |
| 26/10/1914 | Potash and Perlmutter | Montague Glass | Play | Sam Lewis, Douglas Lloyd |
| 02/11/1914 | The Pearl Girl | l Basil Hood, m Howard Talbot, Hugo Felix | Musical | Margot Joyce, Ellis Carlile, Kenneth Ware |
| 09/11/1914 | The Girl on the Film | l James T Tanner, m Walter Kollo, Albert Szirmai | Musical | Edith Drayson, Leslie Hawkins |
| 16/11/1914 | Princess Caprice | M Leo Fall | Musical | Aubrey Millward, Coningsby Brierley, Nan Rose, May Stevenson |
| 23/11/1914 | The Lady Slavey | l George Dance, m A Crook | Musical | Frank H Crimp, Daisy Bray, Jean Lester |
| 30/11/1914 | Maskelyn and Devant's Mysteries | | Revue | W Littlejohn, E Morehen, Nellie Norway, Charles Morritt |
| 07/12/1914 | Cut it Out | | Revue | Ian Dermont, Muriel Kelly, Tom Dean |
| 14/12/1914 | Well, I Never | | Revue | Marie Lumberg, Tiny Hettie |

| Date | Title/Event | Playwright/Author<br>l= lyrics; m= music | Category | Performers |
|---|---|---|---|---|
| 23/12/1914 | Jack and the Beanstalk | | Panto | Betty Beryl, Queenie Roy, Billy Taylor |
| 28/12/1914 | Jack and the Beanstalk | | | |
| 04/01/1915 | The Quaker Girl | l Adrian Ross, m Lionel Monckton | Musical | Georgie Corlass, Nellie Vancourt |
| 11/01/1915 | Mary Latimer-Nun | Eva Elwes | Play | Laura Walker |
| 18/01/1915 | The Cingalee | l Adrian Ross, m Lionel Monckton | Musical | Stella Gastelle, Queenie Lang |
| 25/01/1915 | A Heritage of Hate | Arthur Shirley | Play | Sam Livesey |
| 01/02/1915 | Dick Whittington | | Panto | Freda Waring, Josey Leyton |
| 08/02/1915 | Margaret of the Red Cross | | Play | Florence Tresillion |
| 15/02/1915 | The Girl from Utah | l Adrian Ross, m Sidney Jones | Musical | Gladys Trevor. |
| 22/02/1915 | Grumpy | | Play | Chas Windermere |
| 01/03/1915 | The Story of the Rosary | Walter Howard | Play | R Scrope-Quentin, Millicent Hallett, G H Mulcaster |
| 08/03/1915 | Lucky Durham | Wilson Barrett | Play | Armitage and Leigh Co, Arthur Leigh, Louis Hector, Marguerite Cellier, Stanley Bedwell |
| 09/03/1915 | Leah Kleschna | C W S McLellan | Play | Armitage and Leigh Co, Arthur Leigh, Louis Hector, Marguerite Cellier, Stanley Bedwell |
| 10/03/1915 | Lucky Durham | Wilson Barrett | Play | Armitage and Leigh Co, Arthur Leigh, Louis Hector, Marguerite Cellier, Stanley Bedwell |
| 11/03/1915 | Leah Kleschna | C W S McLellan | Play | Armitage and Leigh Co, Arthur Leigh, Louis Hector, Marguerite Cellier, Stanley Bedwell |
| 12/03/1915 | Leah Kleschna | C W S McLellan | Play | Armitage and Leigh Co, Arthur Leigh, Louis Hector, Marguerite Cellier, Stanley Bedwell |
| 13/03/1915 | The Barrier | Rex Beach | Play | Armitage and Leigh Co, Arthur Leigh, Louis Hector, Marguerite Cellier, Stanley Bedwell |
| 15/03/1915 | The Dollar Princess | l Adrian Ross, m Leo Fall | Musical | Martin Iredale, Nancy Gibbs |
| 22/03/1915 | A Soldier's Honour | Mrs F G Kimberley | Play | Victor Ray |
| 29/03/1915 | Paying the Price | James Willard | Play | Austin Leigh, James Williams |
| 05/04/1915 | A Place in the Sun | Cyril Harcourt | Play | Alexander Marsh, Carrie Baillie, J Edward Witty, Manning Sproston, Stella Campbell |
| 12/04/1915 | Mischeivous Molly | | Musical | Hilda Playfair, Leonard Wallis |
| 19/04/1915 | The Still Alarm | Joseph Arthur | Play | Mathew H Glanville |
| 26/04/1915 | Little Miss Ragtime | l Isa Bowman, m W Neale | Musical | Alec Godfrey, Isa Bowman, Alec Green, Alec Godfrey |
| 03/05/1915 | | | Variety | Horace Goldin (The royal Illusionist) and Co |
| 10/05/1915 | All the Nice Girls | | Revue | Viola Rene, Kenneth Seymour |
| 17/05/1915 | It's a Long Way to Tipperary | Henrietta Schrier, Lodge-Percy | Play | Henrietta Schrier |

| Date | Title/Event | Playwright/Author<br>l= lyrics; m= music | Category | Performers |
|------|-------------|------------------------------------------|----------|------------|
| 24/05/1915 | Merry Miss Madcap | l Isa Bowman, m William Neale | Musical | George Young, Tina Frank |
| 31/05/1915 | Come in Miss | | Revue | |
| 07/06/1915 | The Girl from Nowhere | | Musical | Harry Ugar, Lily Elsie |
| 14/06/1915 | The Girl in the Train | | Musical | Bert Murray, Kathleen Severn |
| 21/06/1915 | All Change Here | | Musical | Havana Girls, Donna Rita |
| 28/06/1915 | The Dutch Hussars | | Musical | Jake Friedman, Florence Hunton & Specialities |
| 05/07/1915 | S'Nice | | Revue | Espinosa, Eva Kelland, Harry Ray, Stratton Mills |
| 12/07/1915 | Think it Over | | Revue | Lotte Stoned, Rosa Ray |
| 19/07/1915 | Not a Word | | Revue | Bert Danson, Carton, Ormono |
| 26/07/1915 | A Devonshire Girl | | Revue | Lomax & Cissie, Dinkie Dunn, Esse Gipsey |
| 02/08/1915 | Sheba | | Revue | Katarina Renoff |
| 09/08/1915 | Lovely Woman | | Revue | Finlay Dunn, Ruby Vivian |
| 16/08/1915 | Pleased to Meet you | | Revue | Vivien Carter, Stanley Kirk, Edwin Sykes |
| 23/08/1915 | The Belle of New York | l C M S McLellan, m Gustav Kerker | Musical | Edith Drayton, Hilda Harris, Philip Leslie |
| 30/08/1915 | All Square | | Revue | Fred Bluett, Jack Warman, Mabel and Cilff Diamond |
| 06/09/1915 | Tales Of Hoffman | Offenbach | Opera | Carl Rosa Opera Co, William Wegener, Muriel Terry, Dorothy Robson |
| 07/09/1915 | Carmen | Bizet | Opera | Carl Rosa Opera Co, William Wegener, Muriel Terry, Dorothy Robson |
| 08/09/1915 | Magic Flute | Mozart | Opera | Carl Rosa Opera Co, William Wegener, Muriel Terry, Dorothy Robson |
| 09/09/1915 | Faust | Gounod | Opera | Carl Rosa Opera Co, William Wegener, Muriel Terry, Dorothy Robson |
| 10/09/1915 | Aida | Verdi | Opera | Carl Rosa Opera Co, William Wegener, Muriel Terry, Dorothy Robson |
| 11/09/1915 | Tales Of Hoffman  mat | Offenbach | Opera | Carl Rosa Opera Co, William Wegener, Muriel Terry, Dorothy Robson |
| 11/09/1915 | Bohemian Girl  eve | Balfe | Opera | Carl Rosa Opera Co, William Wegener, Muriel Terry, Dorothy Robson |
| 13/09/1915 | Florodora | l Ernest Boyd-Jones, m Leslie Stuart | Musical | |
| 20/09/1915 | The Arcadians | l Arthur Wimperis, m Lionel Monckton | Musical | Minnie Rayner |
| 27/09/1915 | The Balkan Princess | l Paul Rubens, Arthur Wimperis, m Paul Rubens | Musical | May Stevenson |

| Date | Title/Event | Playwright/Author<br>l= lyrics; m= music | Category | Performers |
|---|---|---|---|---|
| 04/10/1915 | The Girl in the Taxi | l Arthur Wimperis, Frederick Fenn, m Jean Gilbert | Musical | Cathie Ferguson, Fred Rolph, Fred Randall |
| 11/10/1915 | The Little Michus | l Percy Greenbank, m Andre Messager | Musical | Herbert Williams, Gertrude Lawrence, Etta Belle |
| 18/10/1915 | The Merry Widow | l Adrian Ross, m Franz Lehar | Musical | George Edwarde's Co, Alfred Beers, Harold Bradley, Pat Cannon |
| 19/10/1915 | The Merry Widow | l Adrian Ross, m Franz Lehar | Musical | George Edwarde's Co, Alfred Beers, Harold Bradley, Pat Cannon |
| 20/10/1915 | The Merry Widow | l Adrian Ross, m Franz Lehar | Musical | George Edwarde's Co, Alfred Beers, Harold Bradley, Pat Cannon |
| 21/10/1915 | Gipsy Love | l Adrian Ross, m Franz Lehar | Musical | George Edwarde's Co, Alfred Beers, Harold Bradley, Pat Cannon |
| 22/10/1915 | Gipsy Love | l Adrian Ross, m Franz Lehar | Musical | George Edwarde's Co, Alfred Beers, Harold Bradley, Pat Cannon |
| 23/10/1915 | Gipsy Love | lAdrian Ross, m Franz Lehar | Musical | George Edwarde's Co, Alfred Beers, Harold Bradley, Pat Cannon |
| 25/10/1915 | A Pair of Silk Stockings | Cyril Harcourt | Play | Hilda Sims, Jane Comfort, Charles Steuart |
| 01/11/1915 | The Cinema Star | l Harry Graham, Percy Greenbank, m Jean Gilbert | Musical | Walter Brodie, Guy Buckland, Ethel Moore, Beryl Jackson |
| 08/11/1915 | The Pearl Girl | l Basil Hood, m Howard Talbot, Hugo Felix | Musical | Eileen Molteno. Audrey Leslie, Eric J Stone |
| 15/11/1915 | The Geisha | l Harry Greenbank, m Sidney Jones | Musical | Florence Jenkins, W Williams, Edna Earl, Edward Carlton |
| 22/11/1915 | The Dancing Mistress | l J T Tanner, Adrian Ross, m Lionel Monckton | Musical | Laura Wright, Percy Cahill, Cissie Sephton |
| 29/11/1915 | Faust | Gounod | Opera | Harrison Frewin Opera co, John Harrison, Kingsley Lark, Raymonde Amy |
| 30/11/1915 | Tannhauser | Wagner | Opera | Harrison Frewin Opera co, John Harrison, Kingsley Lark, Raymonde Amy |
| 01/12/1915 | Rigoletto | Verdi | Opera | Harrison Frewin Opera co, John Harrison, Kingsley Lark, Raymonde Amy |
| 02/12/1915 | Maritana | Vincent Wallace | Opera | Harrison Frewin Opera co, John Harrison, Kingsley Lark, Raymonde Amy |
| 03/12/1915 | Carmen | Bizet | Opera | Harrison Frewin Opera co, John Harrison, Kingsley Lark, Raymonde Amy |
| 04/12/1915 | Il Trovatore  mat | Verdi | Opera | Harrison Frewin Opera co, John Harrison, Kingsley Lark, Raymonde Amy |
| 04/12/1915 | Bohemian Girl  eve | Balfe | Opera | Harrison Frewin Opera co, John Harrison, Kingsley Lark, Raymonde Amy |
| 06/12/1915 | When Knights Were Bold | Charles Marlowe | Play | Bromley Challenor |

| Date | Title/Event | Playwright/Author l= lyrics; m= music | Category | Performers |
|---|---|---|---|---|
| 13/12/1915 | Kitty Grey | l Adrian Ross, m Lionel Monckton | Musical | Madge Brown |
| 20/12/1915 | The Red Heads | | Revue | |
| 27/12/1915 | Brides | | Revue | |
| 03/01/1916 | The Marriage Market | l Frederick Jarman, m Chevalier Legrand | Musical | H Dobell Lyle, Winifred Browne |
| 10/01/1916 | Aladdin | | Panto | Willie Lassam, Will Judge |
| 17/01/1916 | Aladdin | | Panto | |
| 24/01/1916 | The Story of the Rosary | Walter Howard | Play | Millicent Hallatt, Herbert Mansfield, Gertrude Harrison |
| 31/01/1916 | Pygmalion | George Bernard Shaw | Play | Florence Jackson, Gordon Bailey. Harry Parker |
| 07/02/1916 | Cinderella | | Panto | Lillie Ennis, Ruth Shannon |
| 14/02/1916 | Diplomacy | Victorien Sardou | Play | Aubrey Mallaieu, Ethel Bracewell |
| 21/02/1916 | Peaches | l Sydny Blow, Douglas Hare, m Philip Braham | Musical | Frank Butt, Madge Haines |
| 28/02/1916 | The Lady's Maid | l C A Lord, Ernest Hastings | Musical | Herbert Williams, Hilda Playfair |
| 06/03/1916 | I'm Sorry | | Revue | Willie Cave, Jimmy Cozens, Evelyn Grace |
| 13/03/1916 | Oh! You Must | | Revue | Flora Cromer, Arthur Dixon |
| 20/03/1916 | Ever Been Had | | Revue | Nat Lewis, Violette McCauley, Marie Sobonoff (The Human Bird) |
| 27/03/1916 | S' Whats the Matter | | Revue | Lena Stanton, Lena Joseph, Harry Joseph |
| 03/04/1916 | Sugar and Spice | | Revue | Gaby Davis, Bert Beswick |
| 10/04/1916 | Smile, Please | | Revue | Billy Brown, Barney O'Reilley |
| 17/04/1916 | The Dream Girl | | Revue | Lillie Soutter, Will B Wilby |
| 24/04/1916 | Good Evening | | Revue | Mona Vivian, Tom Drew |
| 01/05/1916 | What Happened to Jones | George Broadhurst | Play | C Vernon Proctor, Edward Mervyn |
| 08/05/1916 | Spots | | Revue | Freda Spry, W Townsend, |
| 15/05/1916 | Pretty Darlings | | Revue | Myra Hamilton, Dorothea Trowell, George West, Will Fennings |
| 22/05/1916 | All of a Sudden Peggy | Ernest Denny | Play | Rita Sponti |
| 29/05/1916 | Show Me the Way to Your Heart | | Revue | Olive Williams, Hilda Vivian, Bert Lennard |
| 05/06/1916 | Our Miss Cinders | l W T Ivory, Frederick Baugh, m Kenneth Morrison | Musical | J T McMillan, Frank Barclay |
| 12/06/1916 | The Dream Girl | | Revue | Daisy Squelch, Lillie Soutter, Will B Wilby |
| 19/06/1916 | Somebody's Looking | | Revue | Frank Crouch, Honor Bright |

| Date | Title/Event | Playwright/Author l= lyrics; m= music | Category | Performers |
|------|-------------|----------------------------------------|----------|------------|
| 26/06/1916 | All Change Here | | Revue | Donna Rita, Fred Roma, Kitty Temple |
| 03/07/1916 | Think of me | | Revue | Mabel Millar, Harry Clayton, Bert Melville |
| 10/07/1916 | Behind the Scenes | | Revue | Meg Hamilton, Jack Cromo |
| 17/07/1916 | The Girl in the Taxi | l Arthur Wimperis, m Jean Gilbert | Musical | Douglas Vine, Gwladys Gaynor, Douglas Byng |
| 24/07/1916 | Find the Lady | | Musical | Blanche Merryweather, Harry Ray |
| 31/07/1916 | Oh, So Dainty | | Revue | Donald Brown, E Leslie Coupe |
| 07/08/1916 | Knick-Knacks | | Revue | Sid Cotterell, Lily St John |
| 14/08/1916 | Oh, I Say | | Revue | Frederick Bentley, Marjorie Battis |
| 15/08/1916 | My Aunt | | Revue | Frederick Bentley, Marjorie Battis |
| 16/08/1916 | Oh, I Say | | Revue | Frederick Bentley, Marjorie Battis |
| 17/08/1916 | Oh, I Say | | Revue | Frederick Bentley, Marjorie Battis |
| 18/08/1916 | My Aunt | | Revue | Frederick Bentley, Marjorie Battis |
| 19/08/1916 | Oh, I Say | | Revue | Frederick Bentley, Marjorie Battis |
| 21/08/1916 | The Devonhire Girl | | Revue | Emilie Sheppard, Will martinette |
| 28/08/1916 | My Lady Frayle | l Arthur Wimperis, m Howard Talbot, Herman Finck | Musical | Hilda Charteris, Ursula Felton, Edgar Stanmore |
| 04/09/1916 | The Cinema Star | | Musical | V Thomas, Lilian Davis |
| 11/09/1916 | We're Getting Busy | | Revue | Laura Dyson, Edward Curtis, Randal Cardigan, Bert Lennard |
| 18/09/1916 | The Dutch Hussars | | Musical | Florence Hunton, Jake Friedman |
| 25/09/1916 | Ye Gods | | Play | Ivor Bernard, Estelle Van Gene |
| 02/10/1916 | A Little Bit of Fluff | Walter W Ellis | Play | Keith Shepherd, Norah Burke |
| 09/10/1916 | Some Girls | | Revue | Jackson Owen, Millie Hall |
| 16/10/1916 | Pearl of the Orient | | Revue | Marie Santoy, Happy Attwood |
| 23/10/1916 | Fads and Fancies | | Revue | Joe Hayman, Mildred Franklin |
| 30/10/1916 | Find the Woman | | Play | Arthur Leigh & Armitage Co, Arthur Leigh, Jessie Belmore, George Belmore, Louis Hector |
| 31/10/1916 | Find the Woman | | Play | Arthur Leigh & Armitage Co, Arthur Leigh, Jessie Belmore, George Belmore, Louis Hector |
| 01/10/1916 | Find the Woman | | Play | Arthur Leigh & Armitage Co, Arthur Leigh, Jessie Belmore, George Belmore, Louis Hector |
| 02/11/1916 | The Lion and the Mouse | Charles Klein | Play | Arthur Leigh & Armitage Co, Arthur Leigh, Jessie Belmore, George Belmore, Louis Hector |
| 03/11/1916 | The Lion and the Mouse | Charles Klein | Play | Arthur Leigh & Armitage Co, Arthur Leigh, Jessie Belmore, George Belmore, Louis Hector |
| 04/11/1916 | Lucky Durham | Wilson Barrett | Play | Arthur Leigh & Armitage Co, Arthur Leigh, Jessie Belmore, George Belmore, Louis Hector |
| 06/11/1916 | Going Strong | | Bur-lesque | Percy Johnson, Violet Gower |

| Date | Title/Event | Playwright/Author l= lyrics; m= music | Category | Performers |
|------|-------------|----------------------------------------|----------|------------|
| 13/11/1916 | Eliza Comes to Stay | H V Esmond | Play | Nellie Bowman, Ernest Jeffrey |
| 20/11/1916 | Pardon Me | | Revue | Clarice Farrey, James Jewel, Herbert Jewel |
| 27/11/1916 | It's a Bargain | | Revue | Archie Pitt, Gracie Fields, Pat Aza |
| 04/12/1916 | Rosebuds | | Revue | Chas E Brandelle, Bertha Brandelle |
| 11/12/1916 | A Pair of Silk Stockings | Cyril Harcourt | Play | Charles Stewart, Elsa Hall, Esme Wynne |
| 18/12/1916 | Au Revoir Paris | | Revue | Marie Terry, Marie Cliff |
| 26/12/1916 | Frills and Fancies | | Revue | Rosalie Jacobi |
| 01/01/1917 | Tiger's cub | George Potter | Play | Sam Livesey |
| 08/01/1917 | | | Variety | The Great Rameses (Royal Magician in Egyptian Temple of Mystery) |
| 15/01/1917 | The Story of the Rosary | Walter Howard | Play | Herbert Mansfield, W J Miller |
| 22/01/1917 | Red Riding Hood | | Panto | Marjorie Cecil, Charlie Hennessey |
| 29/01/1917 | Shell Out | | Revue | Ambrose Thorne, Florence Williams |
| 05/02/1917 | Some Girls | | Revue | Mabel Hirst, Vena Vilmar |
| 12/02/1917 | The Lion and the Mouse | Charles Klein | Play | Jessie Belmore, Louis Hector |
| 13/02/1917 | The Lion and the Mouse | Charles Klein | Play | Jessie Belmore, Louis Hector |
| 14/02/1917 | The Barrier | Rex Beach | Play | Jessie Belmore, Louis Hector |
| 15/02/1917 | The Hypocrites | Henry Arthur Jones | Play | Jessie Belmore, Louis Hector |
| 16/02/1917 | Lucky Durham | Wilson Barrett | Play | Jessie Belmore, Louis Hector |
| 17/02/1917 | Lucky Durham | Wilson Barrett | Play | Jessie Belmore, Louis Hector |
| 19/02/1917 | Dick Whittington | | Panto | Madoline Rees |
| 26/02/1917 | Paris to Maidenhead | | Revue | Ivy Proudfoot, Heather Evans |
| 05/03/1917 | The Man who Stayed at Home | Lechmere Worrall, J Harold Terry | Play | Owen Cassidy, Howard Brennan |
| 12/03/1917 | Jack and the Beanstalk | | Panto | Lena Stanton, Harry Joseph |
| 19/03/1917 | Outcast | | Play | Muriel Johnston, Nevil Brook, Ranee Brook |
| 26/03/1917 | Eliza Comes to Stay | H V Esmond | Play | Nellie Bowman, Gerard A Neville |
| 02/04/1917 | My Lady Frayle | l Arthur Wimperis, m Howard Talbot, Herman Finck | Musical | Hilda Charteris, Queenie Gwynne |
| 09/04/1917 | Frolics | | Revue | |
| 16/04/1917 | Tonight's the Night | l Paul Rubens, Percy Greenslade, m Paul Rubens | Musical | |
| 23/04/1917 | Keep the Home Fires Burning | | Play | Roy Sefridge, Edgar Milton, |
| 24/04/1917 | Keep the Home Fires Burning | | Play | Roy Sefridge, Edgar Milton, |

| Date | Title/Event | Playwright/Author l= lyrics; m= music | Category | Performers |
|---|---|---|---|---|
| 25/04/1917 | Keep the Home Fires Burning | | Play | Roy Sefridge, Edgar Milton, |
| 26/04/1917 | Shadows of A Great City | Herbert Blache, Aaron Hoffmann | Play | Roy Sefridge, Edgar Milton, |
| 27/04/1917 | Shadows of A Great City | Herbert Blache, Aaron Hoffmann | Play | Roy Sefridge, Edgar Milton, |
| 28/04/1917 | Keep the Home Fires Burning | | Play | Roy Sefridge, Edgar Milton, |
| 30/04/1917 | Betty | l Adrian Ross, m Paul Rubens | Musical | Doris Williams, Stephen Langton |
| 07/05/1917 | Peg O' My Heart | J Hartley Manners | Play | Ethel O'Shea, William Kershaw |
| 14/05/1917 | Heave Ho! | | Revue | Rene Ash, Walter Ash |
| 21/05/1917 | Hip, Hip, Hooray | | Revue | Dsid Le Fre, Nora Dwyer |
| 28/05/1917 | Fall In! | | Musical | Horace Jones, Queenie Essex |
| 04/06/1917 | I'm Sorry | | Revue | Mabel Hind, Victor Tyler |
| 11/06/1917 | Rosebuds | | Revue | Nat Lewis, Bertha Brandelle |
| 18/06/1917 | The Belle of New York | l C M S McLellan, m Gustav Kerker | Musical | Walter Uridge, Joe Tate, May Ronane |
| 25/06/1917 | All Aboard | | Revue | Jackson Moore, Chris Baker, Gladys Mavius |
| 02/07/1917 | S'Hush | | Revue | Nora Kebble, Harry Shaw |
| 09/07/1917 | Pass On Please | | Revue | Chas Gladwell, Leslie Rome, Gracie Rivers |
| 16/07/1917 | Some Treasure | | Musical | Sis brothers Luck, Billy Lytton, Anna Hornby |
| 23/07/1917 | Dream Girl | | Revue | Daisy Squelch, Lillie Souttar |
| 30/07/1917 | Gold and Syrup | | Revue | Edward Denham, Maisie Terris, Vivien Carter |
| 06/08/1917 | A Bunch of Beauty | | Revue | Jack Mackenzie, Viola Rene |
| 13/08/1917 | In Cupid's Garden | | Musical | A G Spry, May Warden |
| 20/08/1917 | Forty Winks | | Revue | Tom Gibbs, Ella Addison |
| 27/08/1917 | Don't Crush | | Revue | Sid Dee, Dorothy Vere |
| 03/09/1917 | The Glad Eye | Jose Levy | Play | Martin Henry, Violet Blyth-Pratt |
| 04/09/1917 | The Glad Eye | Jose Levy | Play | Martin Henry, Violet Blyth-Pratt |
| 05/09/1917 | The Glad Eye | Jose Levy | Play | Martin Henry, Violet Blyth-Pratt |
| 06/09/1917 | Who's the Lady | | Play | Martin Henry, Violet Blyth-Pratt |
| 07/09/1917 | Who's the Lady | | Play | Martin Henry, Violet Blyth-Pratt |
| 08/19/1917 | Who's the Lady | | Play | Martin Henry, Violet Blyth-Pratt |
| 10/09/1917 | The Hypocrites | Henry Arthur Jones | Play | H Armitage & Arthur Leigh Co, Jessie Belmore, Louis Hector, Harold French |
| 11/09/1917 | The Hypocrites | Henry Arthur Jones | Play | H Armitage & Arthur Leigh Co, Jessie Belmore, Louis Hector, Harold French |
| 12/09/1917 | The Hypocrites | Henry Arthur Jones | Play | H Armitage & Arthur Leigh Co, Jessie Belmore, Louis Hector, Harold French |

| Date | Title/Event | Playwright/Author l= lyrics; m= music | Category | Performers |
|------|-------------|----------------------------------------|----------|------------|
| 13/09/1917 | Find the Woman | | Play | H Armitage & Arthur Leigh Co, Jessie Belmore, Louis Hector, Harold French |
| 14/09/1917 | Find the Woman | | Play | H Armitage & Arthur Leigh Co, Jessie Belmore, Louis Hector, Harold French |
| 15/09/1917 | The Lion and the Mouse | Charles Klein | Play | H Armitage & Arthur Leigh Co, Jessie Belmore, Louis Hector, Harold French |
| 17/09/1917 | Dr Wake's Patient | W Gayer Mackay, Robert Ord | Play | H Armitage & Arthur Leigh Co, Jessie Belmore, Louis Hector, Harold French |
| 18/09/1917 | Dr Wake's Patient | W Gayer Mackay, Robert Ord | Play | H Armitage & Arthur Leigh Co, Jessie Belmore, Louis Hector, Harold French |
| 19/09/1917 | Dr Wake's Patient | W Gayer Mackay, Robert Ord | Play | H Armitage & Arthur Leigh Co, Jessie Belmore, Louis Hector, Harold French |
| 20/09/1917 | Lucky Durham | Wilson Barrett | Play | H Armitage & Arthur Leigh Co, Jessie Belmore, Louis Hector, Harold French |
| 21/09/1917 | Lucky Durham | Wilson Barrett | Play | H Armitage & Arthur Leigh Co, Jessie Belmore, Louis Hector, Harold French |
| 22/09/1917 | The Barrier | Rex Beach | Play | H Armitage & Arthur Leigh Co, Jessie Belmore, Louis Hector, Harold French |
| 24/09/1917 | Sherlock Holmes | | Play | H Hamilton Stewart, Ethel Trevor Lloyd |
| 01/10/1917 | Tina | l Paul Rubens, Percy Greenbank, m Paul Rubens | Musical | Frederick Lloyd, Peggy Shannon |
| 08/10/1917 | The Silver King | Henry Arthur Jones | Play | C W Somerset, Wilfred Denyer |
| 15/10/1917 | Razzle Dazzle | | Revue | Harry Cole, Edna Morgan |
| 22/10/1917 | Leah Kleschna | C W S McLellan | Play | H Armitage & Arthur Leigh's Company, William Clayton, Harold French, Arthur Leigh |
| 23/10/1917 | Leah Kleschna | C W S McLellan | Play | H Armitage & Arthur Leigh's Company, William Clayton, Harold French, Arthur Leigh |
| 24/10/1917 | Leah Kleschna | C W S McLellan | Play | H Armitage & Arthur Leigh's Company, William Clayton, Harold French, Arthur Leigh |
| 25/10/1917 | The Lion and the Mouse | Charles Klein | Play | H Armitage & Arthur Leigh's Company, William Clayton, Harold French, Arthur Leigh |
| 26/10/1917 | Deep Purple | Paul Armstrong | Play | H Armitage & Arthur Leigh's Company, William Clayton, Harold French, Arthur Leigh |
| 27/10/1917 | The Hypocrites mat | Henry Arthur Jones | Play | H Armitage & Arthur Leigh's Company, William Clayton, Harold French, Arthur Leigh |
| 27/10/1917 | Deep Purple | Paul Armstrong | Play | H Armitage & Arthur Leigh's Company, William Clayton, Harold French, Arthur Leigh |
| 29/10/1917 | Half Past Eight | | Revue | Ambrose Thorn, Edwin Dodds |
| 05/11/1910 | All Women | | Musical | Lily Long, Florence Smithers |
| 12/11/1917 | Mr Wu | Harry M Vernon | Play | George Butler, Evelyn Laye, Barbara Everest, Renee Brook |

| Date | Title/Event | Playwright/Author<br>l= lyrics; m= music | Category | Performers |
|---|---|---|---|---|
| 19/11/1917 | Broadway Jones | George M Cohan | Play | Wilbur Langton, Arthur Selwyn, Lorn MacNaughton |
| 26/11/1917 | The Bing Boys Are Here | | Revue | Bert Beswick, Walter Westwood |
| 03/12/1917 | A Bunch of Beauty | | Revue | Jack Mackenzie, Viola Rene |
| 10/12/1917 | Search Lights | Horace Annesley Vachell | Play | Arthur Bawtree, Leo Casselli |
| 17/12/1917 | Beauchamp and Beecham | Sara Jeanette Duncan | Play | Jack Crichton, Douglas Cecil |
| 24/12/1917 | Aladdin | | Panto | Lill Carr, Jack Withare |
| 31/12/1917 | The Girl from Ciros | Pierre Veby, tr by Jose G Levy | Play | Paul Hansall, Albert Kavanagh |
| 07/01/1918 | Beauty and the Beast | | Panto | Madge Lester, Dave Clarke, Barry Gilmour |
| 14/01/1918 | Beauty and the Beast | | Panto | |
| 21/01/1918 | The Happy Day | l Adrian Ross, Paul Rubens m,Sidney Jones, P Rubens | Musical | Enid Sass, Drew McIntosh, Frances Mc Leish |
| 28/01/1918 | Monty's Flapper | Walter W Ellis | Play | Sam Lysons, Zoe Davis |
| 04/02/1918 | For Sweethearts and Wives | Arthur Roseberry | Play | W J Blunt, Renand Lockwood |
| 11/02/1918 | All British | | Revue | George Carroll, Jack Watt, May Hill |
| 18/02/1918 | Some Treasure | | Revue | Six Brothers Luck, Ernie Bee, E Lynd |
| 25/02/1918 | Eliza Comes to Stay | H V Esmond | Play | Juanita Charlton, Cyril Austin-Lee |
| 04/03/1918 | My Lady Frayle | l Arthur Wimperis m, Howard Talbot, Herman Finck | Musical | Hilda Charteris, Harry Norton, Kathleen Millar, Erhel Callaman |
| 11/03/1918 | The Cinema Star | | Musical | Frank H Dale, Reg Sackville-West, Doris Passmore |
| 18/03/1918 | The Carnival Girl | | Musical | Cyril Dunn, Jill Joy |
| 25/03/1918 | Frills and Fancies | | Musical | Lorna Della, George Gregory |
| 01/04/1918 | The Marriage Market | l Frederick Jarman, m Chevalier Legrand | Musical | Victor Kerr, Alfred Passmore |
| 08/04/1918 | Oh! I Say | Sidney Blow, Douglas Hoare | Play | Yourke Challenor, Harry Cartwright, Gladys Archbutt |
| 15/04/1918 | The Arcadians | l Arthur Wimperis, m Lionel Monckton | Musical | William Kokeby, Mabelle George |
| 22/04/1918 | Inside the Lines | Earl Derr Biggers | Play | Frederick Victor, C Worldley, Husle, May Edward Saker |
| 29/04/1918 | Look Pleasant | | Musical | Ernest Ball, Katherine Kay |
| 06/05/1918 | John Raymond's Daughter | Eva Elwes | Play | Wilson Benge, Sadie Smith |

| Date | Title/Event | Playwright/Author<br>l= lyrics; m= music | Category | Performers |
|------|-------------|-------------------------------------------|----------|------------|
| 13/05/1918 | Mirth and Melody | | Musical | Billy Howard, George Gee |
| 20/05/1918 | Maid of the Midnight Sun | l Louis Casson, m Geoffrey Blackmore | Musical | Fred J Little, Fred Lyne, May Shilli |
| 27/05/1918 | Maid of the Mountains | l Harry Graham, m Harold Fraser-Simpson | Musical | Vera McDonald, Teddy Brogden |
| 03/06/1918 | The Dream Girl | | Revue | Daisy Squelch, Edwin Sykes, Gus Ern |
| 10/06/1918 | Gay Paree | | Musical | Ted Larkum, Billy Larkum, Allan Napier |
| 17/06/1918 | Air Birds | | Revue | Billy Lytton, Oscar Luck |
| 24/06/1918 | Go As You Please | | Revue | Jack Cromo, Peggy Hamilton |
| 01/07/1918 | Over the Top | | Revue | Fred Hastings, Billy Amstell |
| 08/07/1918 | The Lifeguardsman | Walter Howard | Play | Nina Oldfield, Norman Howard |
| 15/07/1918 | Bluff Boys | | Revue | Harry Ray, Lillie Calden |
| 22/07/1918 | Entre Nous | | Revue | W L Rowland, Cora Lingard |
| 29/07/1918 | My Son Sammy | | Revue | Arthur White, Lily Lonsdale, Walter Lawley |
| 05/08/1918 | Fiddle-de- dee | | Revue | Stan Paskin, Kitty Emson |
| 12/08/1918 | The Prince and the Beggar Maid | Walter Howard | Play | Ethel Wensley, Ledward Harris, Grace Stafford |
| 19/08/1918 | The Girl from Ciro's | Pierre Veby, tr by Jose G Levy | Play | Mabel Hirst, Sam Lysons |
| 26/08/1918 | Il Trovatore | Verdi | Opera | Allington Charsley Opera Co, Gwynne Davis, Gladys Parr, Walter Barrett, Ethel Austin |
| 27/08/1918 | Faust | Gounod | Opera | Allington Charsley Opera Co, Gwynne Davis, Gladys Parr, Walter Barrett, Ethel Austin |
| 28/08/1918 | Bohemian Girl | Balfe | Opera | Allington Charsley Opera Co, Gwynne Davis, Gladys Parr, Walter Barrett, Ethel Austin |
| 29/08/1918 | Rigoletto | Verdi | Opera | Allington Charsley Opera Co, Gwynne Davis, Gladys Parr, Walter Barrett, Ethel Austin |
| 30/08/1918 | Rose of Castille | Balfe | Opera | Allington Charsley Opera Co, Gwynne Davis, Gladys Parr, Walter Barrett, Ethel Austin |
| 31/08/1918 | Daughter of the Regiment  mat | Donizetti | Opera | Allington Charsley Opera Co, Gwynne Davis, Gladys Parr, Walter Barrett, Ethel Austin |
| 31/08/1918 | Maritana  eve | Vincent Wallace | Opera | Allington Charsley Opera Co, Gwynne Davis, Gladys Parr, Walter Barrett, Ethel Austin |
| 02/09/1918 | The Story of the Rosary | Walter Howard | Play | Evelyn Carlton, Violet Bray-Weaver |
| 09/09/1918 | High Jinks | l Otto Harbach, m Rudolf Friml | Musical | Harry Merrylees, Hamilton Edwards |
| 16/09/1918 | The Belle of New York | l, C M S McLellan, m Gustave Kerker | Musical | Walter Urige, Winnie Goodwin |
| 23/09/1918 | The Carnival Girl | | Musical | Cyril Dunn, Billy Rutherford, Vicky Gerard |
| 30/09/1918 | Carminetta | l Andre Barde, m Emile Lassaily | Musical | |

| Date | Title/Event | Playwright/Author l= lyrics; m= music | Category | Performers |
|---|---|---|---|---|
| 07/10/1918 | The Amazing Marriage | G Carlton Wallace | Play | Theo Balfour, G Carlton Wallace |
| 14/10/1918 | Real Sports | | Revue | Hettie Gale, Dave O'Toole |
| 21/10/1918 | Peg O' My Heart | J Hartley Manners | Play | Nancy Mortimer, Richard Custance |
| 28/10/1918 | San Toy | l Harry Greenbank, Adrian Ross, m Sidney Jones | Musical | Marguerite Moreton, Conway Dixon, Edward Carlton, Netta Lynde |
| 29/10/1918 | San Toy | l Harry Greenbank, Adrian Ross, m Sidney Jones | Musical | Marguerite Moreton, Conway Dixon, Edward Carlton, Netta Lynde |
| 30/10/1918 | San Toy | l Harry Greenbank, Adrian Ross, m Sidney Jones | Musical | Marguerite Moreton, Conway Dixon, Edward Carlton, Netta Lynde |
| 31/10/1918 | The Geisha | l Harry Greenbank, m Sidney Jones | Musical | Marguerite Moreton, Conway Dixon, Edward Carlton, Netta Lynde |
| 01/10/1918 | A Greek Slave | l Harry Greenbank, Adrian Ross, m Sidney Jones | Musical | Marguerite Moreton, Conway Dixon, Edward Carlton, Netta Lynde |
| 02/10/1918 | The Geisha | l Harry Greenbank, m Sidney Jones | Musical | Marguerite Moreton, Conway Dixon, Edward Carlton, Netta Lynde |
| 04/11/1918 | The Love Charm | | Musical | Gertie Orchard, Maisie Lynn |
| 11/11/1918 | Betty | l Adrian Ross, m Paul Rubens | Musical | Dorothy Hersie, Leonard Edwards |
| 18/11/1918 | Fragments | | Revue | Bijou Dreno, Sylvia Petina |
| 25/11/1918 | The Man from Toronto | Douglas Murray | Play | Florrie Bond, Robert Carey Fairfax, Ronald Ward |
| 02/12/1918 | Searchlights | Horace Annesley Vachell | Play | Louis Hector, Marion Fawcett, Jessie Belmore |
| 03/12/1918 | Searchlights | Horace Annesley Vachell | Play | Louis Hector, Marion Fawcett, Jessie Belmore |
| 04/12/1918 | Searchlights | Horace Annesley Vachell | Play | Louis Hector, Marion Fawcett, Jessie Belmore |
| 05/12/1918 | Miss Elizabeth's Prisoner | E Lyall Swete, R N Stephens | Play | Louis Hector, Marion Fawcett, Jessie Belmore |
| 06/12/1918 | Miss Elizabeth's Prisoner | E Lyall Swete, R N Stephens | Play | Louis Hector, Marion Fawcett, Jessie Belmore |
| 0712/1918 | Miss Elizabeth's Prisoner | E Lyall Swete, R N Stephens | Play | Louis Hector, Marion Fawcett, Jessie Belmore |
| 09/12/1918 | What happened to Jones | George Broadhurst | Play | Louis Hector, Marion Fawcett, Jessie Belmore |
| 10/12/1918 | What happened to Jones | George Broadhurst | Play | Louis Hector, Marion Fawcett, Jessie Belmore |

| Date | Title/Event | Playwright/Author<br>l= lyrics; m= music | Category | Performers |
|---|---|---|---|---|
| 11/12/1918 | What happened to Jones | George Broadhurst | Play | Louis Hector, Marion Fawcett, Jessie Belmore |
| 12/12/1918 | The Woman in the Case | Lyle Fitch | Play | Louis Hector, Marion Fawcett, Jessie Belmore |
| 13/12/1918 | The Woman in the Case | Lyle Fitch | Play | Louis Hector, Marion Fawcett, Jessie Belmore |
| 14/12/1918 | The Woman in the Case | Lyle Fitch | Play | Louis Hector, Marion Fawcett, Jessie Belmore |
| 15/12/1918 | The Woman in the Case | Lyle Fitch | Play | Louis Hector, Marion Fawcett, Jessie Belmore |
| 16/12/1918 | Closed | | | |
| 24/12/1918 | Dick Whittington | | Panto | Alva Young, Ted Young, Syd Franks |
| 30/12/1918 | The Luck of the Navy | Clifford Mills | Play | Kenneth Kent, Patricia Selbourne |
| 06/01/1919 | Seven Days Leave | Walter Howard | Play | Hilliard Vox, Lilian Christine |
| 13/01/1919 | Aladdin | | Panto | Hetty Gale, Freddie Regent |
| 20/01/1919 | Jack Horner | | Panto | Rose Hamilton, Nella Della, Walter Dale |
| 27/01/1919 | The Bing Boys | | Revue | Gus Oxley, Sydney T Pease |
| 03/02/1919 | Sweethearts and Wives | | Play | Renand Lockwood, Roy Cuthbertson |
| 10/02/1919 | Mother Hubbard | | Panto | Harry Attwood, Harriet Fawn |
| 17/02/1919 | Odds On | | Revue | W H Kirby, Hilda Cross |
| 24/02/1919 | Mr Mayfair | | Revue | Herbert Darnley, Claude Lester |
| 03/03/1919 | Hullo Baby | | Revue | Bernard Mervyn, Guy Fields, Dorothea Lester |
| 10/03/1919 | Bubbly | m Philip Braham | Musical | Ivy Tresmand, Ernest, Seebold |
| 17/03/1919 | Violette | l Norman Slee, m John Ansell | Musical | Reginald Sheridan, Edna Coombs |
| 24/03/1919 | Yes, Uncle | l Clifford Grey, m Nat D Ayer | Musical | Leonard Neville, Katie Vesey |
| 31/03/1919 | You Never Know | from Feydeau, La Puce d'Oreille | Play | Bertram Fryer, Olive Eltone, Grace Illingworth |
| 07/04/1919 | Merchant of Venice | William Shakespeare | Play | Henry Baynton, Alice De Grey |
| 08/04/1919 | Hamlet | William Shakespeare | Play | Henry Baynton, Alice De Grey |
| 09/04/1919 | Romeo and Juliet | William Shakespeare | Play | Henry Baynton, Alice De Grey |
| 10/04/1919 | Merry Wives of Windsor | William Shakespeare | Play | Henry Baynton, Alice De Grey |
| 11/04/1919 | Twelfth Night | William Shakespeare | Play | Henry Baynton, Alice De Grey |
| 12/04/1919 | Henry V | William Shakespeare | Play | Henry Baynton, Alice De Grey |
| 14/04/1919 | A Country Girl | l Adrian Ross, m Lionel Monckton | Musical | E Floyd Gwynne, Mabel Medrow |
| 21/04/1919 | Tina | l Paul Rubens, Percy Greenbank, m Paul Rubens | Musical | Harry Norton, Marjorie Ellanby |

| Date | Title/Event | Playwright/Author<br>l= lyrics; m= music | Category | Performers |
|---|---|---|---|---|
| 28/04/1919 | Arlette | l Clifford Grey,<br>m Guy L Feuvre,<br>Ivor Novello | Musical | Prue Temple, Gerard Neville |
| 05/05/1919 | The Knife | Eugene Walter | Play | Arthur Ellis, Frank Strickland, Renee Bevan |
| 12/05/1919 | The Better 'Ole | Bruce<br>Barnsfather,<br>Arthur Eliot | Play | Martin Adeson, Wilfred Norman, Jack Gordon |
| 19/05/1919 | The Maid of the<br>Mountains | l Harry Graham,<br>m Harold Fraser-<br>Simson | Musical | Mabell Hurst, Leonard Tremaynem Fred Payne |
| 26/05/1919 | All Over the Shop | | Revue | Billy Bernhardt, Amy Stewart, Arthur Leslie*? |
| 02/06/1919 | What Next | | Revue | Mabelle Thorne, Anna Hornby, George Cooper |
| 09/06/1919 | The Misleading Lady | Charles<br>Goddard, Paul<br>Dickie | Play | Rollo Balmain, S Brooke Warren |
| 16/06/1919 | The Silver Crucifix | Robert Hughes,<br>Walter Howard | Play | Lillian Hallowes, Terrence Maxwell, Norman<br>Leyland |
| 23/06/1919 | Upside Down | | Revue | Ruby Kimberley, Robert Armstrong |
| 21/07/1919 | Strawberries and Cream | | Revue | Ernie Bee, Harriet Fawn |
| 28/07/1919 | Na Poo | | Revue | Jackson Owen, Jenny Lamonte |
| 04/08/1919 | The Secret Service Girl | Royce Carlton | Play | Jessie Belmore, Richard Minster, Pete Leslie |
| 11/08/1919 | The Bluff Boys | | Revue | Harry Ray, Lillie Calden, Harry Valden |
| 18/08/1919 | The Man from Toronto | Douglas Murray | Play | Nell Carter, Clive Currie, Ronald T Ward |
| 25/08/1919 | A Pair of Spectacles | Sydney Grundy | Play | Alexander Marsh, Carrie Baillie, Wilfred<br>Lawson |
| 26/08/1919 | The Vicar of Wakefield | | Play | Alexander Marsh, Carrie Baillie, Wilfred<br>Lawson |
| 27/08/1919 | A Place in the Sun | Cyril Harcourt | Play | Alexander Marsh, Carrie Baillie, Wilfred<br>Lawson |
| 28/08/1919 | Dr Wake's Patient | W Gayer McKay,<br>Robert Ord | Play | Alexander Marsh, Carrie Baillie, Wilfred<br>Lawson |
| 29/08/1919 | A Snug Little Kingdom | Mark Ambient | Play | Alexander Marsh, Carrie Baillie, Wilfred<br>Lawson |
| 30/08/1919 | David Garrick    mat | Thomas William<br>Robertson | Play | Alexander Marsh, Carrie Baillie, Wilfred<br>Lawson |
| 01/09/1919 | Pygmalian | George Bernard<br>Shaw | Play | Lionel Leonard, Tom Mowbray, Muriel Kidner |
| 08/09/1919 | Rigoletto | Verdi | Opera | Allington Charsley Grand Opera Co inc<br>Michael Kemble, Jeanne Jeune |
| 09/09/1919 | Satanella | Balfe | Opera | Allington Charsley Grand Opera Co inc<br>Michael Kemble, Jeanne Jeune |
| 10/09/1919 | Maritana | Vincent Wallace | Opera | Allington Charsley Grand Opera Co inc<br>Michael Kemble, Jeanne Jeune |

| Date | Title/Event | Playwright/Author l= lyrics; m= music | Category | Performers |
|------|-------------|----------------------------------------|----------|------------|
| 11/09/1919 | The Hugenots | Mayerbeer | Opera | Allington Charsley Grand Opera Co inc Michael Kemble, Jeanne Jeune |
| 12/09/1919 | Lohengrin | Wagner | Opera | Allington Charsley Grand Opera Co inc Michael Kemble, Jeanne Jeune |
| 12/09/1919 | Il Trovatore | Verdi | Opera | Allington Charsley Grand Opera Co inc Michael Kemble, Jeanne Jeune |
| 13/09/1919 | Bohemian Girl   eve | Balfe | Opera | Allington Charsley Grand Opera Co inc Michael Kemble, Jeanne Jeune |
| 15/09/1919 | Three weeks | Roy Horniman adapted from Elinor Glyn | Play | Gladys Purnell, Herbert Mansfield |
| 22/09/1919 | Nothing but the Truth | James Montgomery | Play | Reginald Andrews, Alexander Bradley |
| 29/09/1919 | Cash on Delivery | Seymour Hicks | Play | Stanley Brett, Nora O'Malley |
| 06/10/1919 | The Rotters | H P Maltby | Play | Fred Glover, Edith Finlay |
| 13/10/1919 | Bubbly | | Revue | Edmund Russell, Edith Payne |
| 20/10/1919 | The Quaker Girl | l Adrian Ross, Percy Greenbank m, Lionel Monckton | Musical | Louis Wigley, Ivy Luck, Maude Denny |
| 27/10/1919 | Broadway Jones | George M Cohan | Play | Geoffrey Saville, Eva Lytton-Gray |
| 03/11/1919 | The Sign of the Cross | Wilson Barrett | Play | William McLaren, Gladys Morris, Edwin Beverley |
| 10/11/1919 | High Jinks | | Musical | Chas E Paton, Keith Sydney |
| 17/11/1919 | The Prince and the Beggar Maid | Walter Howard | Play | Jessie Belmore, Henry Hallett, Charity Wynne |
| 24/11/1919 | Oh! Joy! | l Anne Caldwell m Jerome Kern | Musical | Dorothy Meade, Peggy Shannon, Nelson Hancock |
| 01/12/1919 | Toto | l Arthur Henderson m Archibold Joyce, Merlin Morgan | Musical | Elsie Steadman, Eric Masters, Louie Rene |
| 08/12/1919 | My Son Sammy | Ernest Dottridge, Arthur White | Musical | Arthur White, Lily Lonsdale, Walter Lawley |
| 15/12/1919 | Tommy French's Wife | Charles Darrell | Play | Effie Bartlett, Tom C Leybourne |
| 24/12/1919 | Jack and Jill | | Panto | Billy Martin, Trixie Kay |
| 29/12/1919 | Jack and Jill | | Panto | |
| 05/01/1920 | The Luck of the Navy | Clifford Mills | Play | Norman C Cannon, Daphne Riggs |
| 12/01/1920 | The Forty Thieves | Herbert Lloyd | Panto | Billy Douglas, Bert McNulty, Ruby Blick |
| 19/01/1920 | Seven Days Leave | Walter Howard | Play | Henry Lonsdale, Millicent Hallett |
| 26/01/1920 | Cinderella | | Panto | Gay Silvani, Gwladys Hay-Dillon |
| 02/02/1920 | A Week-End | Walter W Ellis | Play | Josephine Richards, Christopher Steele |
| 09/02/1920 | A Chinese Honeymoon | l George Dance, m Howard Talbot | Musical | Victor Crawford, Grace Henderson |

| Date | Title/Event | Playwright/Author l= lyrics; m= music | Category | Performers |
|---|---|---|---|---|
| 16/02/1920 | Her Love Against the World | Walter Howard | Play | Ivy Shepperd, Henry Hallatt |
| 23/02/1920 | The Rose of Araby | l Harold Simpson, m Merlin Morgan | Musical | Phyllis Dupree, Connie Hilliard, Leslie Ward |
| 01/03/1920 | The Belle of New York | l C S M McLellan, m Gustav Kerker | Musical | Walter Uridge, Evelyn Ray |
| 08/03/1920 | La Poupee | l George Byng, m Edward Audran | Musical | Stella Gastelle, Harry C Parker |
| 15/03/1920 | The Better 'Ole | Bruce Barnsfather, Arthur Eliot | Play | Martin Adeson, Wilfred Norman, Cyril Weldon |
| 22/03/1920 | The Taming of the Shrew | William Shakespeare | Play | Henry Baynton Co, Gertrude Gilbert |
| 23/03/1920 | Hamlet | William Shakespeare | Play | Henry Baynton Co, Gertrude Gilbert |
| 24/03/1920 | The Merry Wives of Windsor | William Shakespeare | Play | Henry Baynton Co, Gertrude Gilbert |
| 25/03/1920 | Much Ado About Nothing | William Shakespeare | Play | Henry Baynton Co, Gertrude Gilbert |
| 26/03/1920 | The Tempest | William Shakespeare | Play | Henry Baynton Co, Gertrude Gilbert |
| 27/03/1920 | As You Like It  Mat | William Shakespeare | Play | Henry Baynton Co, Gertrude Gilbert |
| 27/03/1920 | The Bells, preceded by David Garrick | / Thomas William Robertson | Play | Henry Baynton Co, Gertrude Gilbert |
| 29/03/1920 | Les Cloches de Cornveille | Robert Planquette | Opera | Fredk G Lloyd Opera Co inc Gwladys Newth, Ian McRobert, Alan Johnstone |
| 05/04/1920 | Dorothy | Alfred Cellier | Opera | Fredk G Lloyd Opera Co inc Gwladys Newth, Ian McRobert, Alan Johnstone |
| 06/04/1920 | Dorothy | Alfred Cellier | Opera | Fredk G Lloyd Opera Co inc Gwladys Newth, Ian McRobert, Alan Johnstone |
| 07/04/1920 | Dorothy | Alfred Cellier | Opera | Fredk G Lloyd Opera Co inc Gwladys Newth, Ian McRobert, Alan Johnstone |
| 08/04/1919 | La Cigale | Edmond Audran | Opera | Fredk G Lloyd Opera Co inc Gwladys Newth, Ian McRobert, Alan Johnstone |
| 09/04/1919 | La Cigale | Edmond Audran | Opera | Fredk G Lloyd Opera Co inc Gwladys Newth, Ian McRobert, Alan Johnstone |
| 10/04/1919 | La Cigale | Edmond Audran | Opera | Fredk G Lloyd Opera Co inc Gwladys Newth, Ian McRobert, Alan Johnstone |
| 12/04/1920 | The Bing Boys on Broadway | | Revue | Frank Weir, Fay Govan |
| 19/04/1920 | The Tiger's Cub | George Potter | Play | Nellie Morris, C Cranleigh-Andrews |
| 26/04/1920 | Baby Bunting | l Clifford Grey, m Nat D Ayer | Musical | Teddy Brogden, Aileen Firminger |

| Date | Title/Event | Playwright/Author<br>l= lyrics; m= music | Category | Performers |
|------|-------------|------------------------------------------|----------|------------|
| 03/05/1920 | The Maid of the Mountains | l Harry Graham, m Harold Fraser-Simpson | Musical | Nora Bird, Beatrice Boater, H M White |
| 10/05/1920 | The Girl for the Boy | l Percy Greenbank, m Howard Carr, Bernard Rolt | Musical | |
| 17/05/1920 | Carminetta | l Andre Barde m Emile Lassaily | Musical | Kenneth Ware, Vivien Carter |
| 24/05/1920 | The Gondoliers | l W S Gilbert, m Arthur Sullivan | Opera | D'oyly Carte Opera Co inc Frank Steward, Maura Canning, Elsie Coram |
| 25/05/1920 | Iolanthe | l W S Gilbert, m Arthur Sullivan | Opera | D'oyly Carte Opera Co inc Frank Steward, Maura Canning, Elsie Coram |
| 26/05/1920 | Mikado | l W S Gilbert, m Arthur Sullivan | Opera | D'oyly Carte Opera Co inc Frank Steward, Maura Canning, Elsie Coram |
| 27/05/1920 | The Gondoliers | l W S Gilbert, m Arthur Sullivan | Opera | D'oyly Carte Opera Co inc Frank Steward, Maura Canning, Elsie Coram |
| 28/05/1920 | Iolanthe | l W S Gilbert, m Arthur Sullivan | Opera | D'oyly Carte Opera Co inc Frank Steward, Maura Canning, Elsie Coram |
| 29/05/1920 | Mikado  mat | l W S Gilbert, m Arthur Sullivan | Opera | D'oyly Carte Opera Co inc Frank Steward, Maura Canning, Elsie Coram |
| 29/05/1920 | Mikado  eve | l W S Gilbert, m Arthur Sullivan | Opera | D'oyly Carte Opera Co inc Frank Steward, Maura Canning, Elsie Coram |
| 31/05/1920 | Why Men Love Women | Walter Howard | Play | Ivy Shepperd, Harry Bristow |
| 07/06/1920 | All Over the Ship | | Revue | Ida Taylor, Freddie Foss |
| 14/06/1920 | The Blindness of Virtue | Cosmo Hamilton | Play | Louis Hector, Marguerite Cellier |
| 21/06/1920 | Five Nights | Victoria Cross | Play | Frank G Cariella, Helen Hardy |
| 28/06/1920 | Tatters | | Musical | Arthur E Pringle, Leah Marlborough |
| 05/07/1920 | Clementina | l E T Bennett, Fred Adlington, m Frederick T Bennett | Musical | Bert Murray, Albert Whitmore, May Barry |
| 12/07/1920 | Who's Wife | | Play | Percy Francis, Graham Pockett |
| 19/07/1920 | Some Kiss | | Revue | Jack Marks, Josie Rene |
| 26/07/1920 | Three Weeks | Roy Horniman adapted from Elinor Glyn | Play | Gladys Purnell, Herbert Mansfield |
| 02/08/1920 | Eastern Nights | | Revue | Ruby Kimberley, Bobbie Graham |
| 09/08/1920 | The Dream Girl | l Norman Lee, m Joe Morrison | Musical | Randolph Sutton, Maisie Terriss |
| 16/08/1920 | As You Were | Arthur Wimperis | Revue | Nan Stuart, Jack Tully |
| 23/08/1920 | K'Night of the Garter | | Revue | Jackson Owen, Alf Shaw, Ivy Bevans |
| 30/08/1920 | Jack O'Jingles | Leon M Lion, Malcolm Cherry | Play | Violet Farebrother, Henry Hallett |
| 06/09/1920 | Tales of Hoffman | Offenbach | Opera | Royal Carl Rosa Opera Co inc Parry Jones, Gladys Seager |

| Date | Title/Event | Playwright/Author<br>l= lyrics; m= music | Category | Performers |
|------|-------------|------------------------------------------|----------|------------|
| 07/09/1920 | Faust | Gounod | Opera | Royal Carl Rosa Opera Co inc Parry Jones, Gladys Seager |
| 08/09/1920 | Maritana | Vincent Wallace | Opera | Royal Carl Rosa Opera Co inc Parry Jones, Gladys Seager |
| 09/09/1920 | Carmen | Bizet | Opera | Royal Carl Rosa Opera Co inc Parry Jones, Gladys Seager |
| 10/09/1920 | Tannhauser | Wagner | Opera | Royal Carl Rosa Opera Co inc Parry Jones, Gladys Seager |
| 11/09/1920 | Tales of Hoffman   mat | Offenbach | Opera | Royal Carl Rosa Opera Co inc Parry Jones, Gladys Seager |
| 11/09/1920 | Bohemian Girl   eve | Balfe | Opera | Royal Carl Rosa Opera Co inc Parry Jones, Gladys Seager |
| 13/09/1920 | Lucky Durham | Wilson Barrett | Play | H Armitage & A Leigh Co inc Hamilton Deane, Winifred Willard, Helena Pickard, Arthur Leigh |
| 14/09/1920 | With Edged Tools | Henry Seton Merrriman | Play | H Armitage & A Leigh Co inc Hamilton Deane, Winifred Willard, Helena Pickard, Arthur Leigh |
| 15/09/1920 | The Hypocrites | Henry Arthur Jones | Play | H Armitage & A Leigh Co inc Hamilton Deane, Winifred Willard, Helena Pickard, Arthur Leigh |
| 16/09/1920 | Passers By | C Haddon Chambers | Play | H Armitage & A Leigh Co inc Hamilton Deane, Winifred Willard, Helena Pickard, Arthur Leigh |
| 17/09/1920 | Masters of the House | | Play | H Armitage & A Leigh Co inc Hamilton Deane, Winifred Willard, Helena Pickard, Arthur Leigh |
| 18/09/1920 | The Barrier | Rex Beach | Play | H Armitage & A Leigh Co inc Hamilton Deane, Winifred Willard, Helena Pickard, Arthur Leigh |
| 20/09/1920 | Pretty Peggy | l Douglas Furber, m A Emmett Adams | Musical | Gerald Neville, Jane Ayr, Elaine Rosslyn |
| 27/09/1920 | The Quaker Girl | l Adrian Ross, Percy Greenbank m, Lionel Monckton | Musical | Ivy Luck, Charles Wingrove |
| 04/10/1920 | The Girl in the Taxi | l Arthur Wimperis, m Jean Gilbert | Musical | |
| 11/10/1920 | The Silver King | Henry Arthur Jones | Play | Effie Bartlett, S Herbert Humber |
| 18/10/1920 | The Catch of the Season | l Charles H Taylor, m Herbert E Haines, Evelyn Baker | Musical | Joan Clarkson, Stanley Brett |
| 25/10/1920 | Toto | l Arthur Anderson, m Archibold Joyce, Merlin Morgan | Musical | |

| Date | Title/Event | Playwright/Author<br>l= lyrics; m= music | Category | Performers |
|------|-------------|------------------------------------------|----------|------------|
| 01/11/1920 | Yes, Uncle | l Clifford Grey, m Nat D Ayer | Musical | Sybil Woodruffe, Dan Brooker, Alec Young |
| 08/11/1920 | Irene | l Joseph McCarthy, m Harry Tierney | Musical | Dorothy O'Shann, Gladys Tudor, Claude Baily |
| 15/11/1920 | The Naughty Wife | Fred Jackson | Play | Frederick Burtwell, Billie Sinclair |
| 22/11/1920 | Rose of Araby | l Harold Simpson, m Merlin Morgan | Musical | Ethel Erskine, Adrian Burgon |
| 29/11/1920 | Romance | Edward Sheldon | Play | Frances Dillon, Vincent Clive |
| 06/12/1920 | The Country Girl | l Adrian Ross, Percy Greenbank m, Lionel Monckton | Musical | Frederick Ives, Ellaline Thorne, Elsie Bennett |
| 13/12/1920 | Kiss Call | l Adrian Ross, Percy Greenbank, m Ivan Caryll | Musical | Herbert T Mundin, Ivan Leslie |
| 20/12/1920 | Aladdin | | Panto | Ethel Leslie, Dick Ray |
| 27/12/1920 | Aladdin | | | |
| 03/01/1921 | Humpty Dumpty | | Panto | Leo Bliss, Ted Lacy, Ena Cairns |
| 10/01/1921 | Humpty Dumpty | | | |
| 17/01/1921 | The Face at the Kitchen | F Brooke Warren | Play | Alec Alexander, Charles H Lester |
| 21/01/1921 | Special matinee | | | Forbes Robertson |
| 24/01/1921 | Dick Whittington | | Panto | Billy Kirton, Gerald Meade |
| 31/01/1921 | The Home of the Fairies | Mrs Kimberley | Play | Robert Faulkner, Nancy Roberts, Arthur E Pringle |
| 07/02/1921 | The Merchant of Venice | William Shakespeare | Play | Charles Doran Co, Eric Adney, Muriel Hutchinson, Donald Wolfit, Edith Sharpe |
| 08/02/1921 | Julius Caesar | William Shakespeare | Play | Charles Doran Co, Eric Adney, Muriel Hutchinson, Donald Wolfit, Edith Sharpe |
| 09/02/1921 | The Taming of the Shrew | William Shakespeare | Play | Charles Doran Co, Eric Adney, Muriel Hutchinson, Donald Wolfit, Edith Sharpe |
| 10/02/1921 | Hamlet | William Shakespeare | Play | Charles Doran Co, Eric Adney, Muriel Hutchinson, Donald Wolfit, Edith Sharpe |
| 11/02/1921 | The Tempest | William Shakespeare | Play | Charles Doran Co, Eric Adney, Muriel Hutchinson, Donald Wolfit, Edith Sharpe |
| 12/02/1921 | The Merchant of Venice mat | William Shakespeare | Play | Charles Doran Co, Eric Adney, Muriel Hutchinson, Donald Wolfit, Edith Sharpe |
| 12/02/1921 | Macbeth eve | William Shakespeare | Play | Charles Doran Co, Eric Adney, Muriel Hutchinson, Donald Wolfit, Edith Sharpe |
| 14/02/1921 | The Sleeping Beauty | | Panto | Victor Wakeman, Ernie Leno, Kitty Falkons, Marie Lumberg |
| 21/12/1921 | Afgar | l Douglas Furber, m Charles Cuvillier | Musical | Doris Thomas, Bert Harland, Hilda Cross |

| Date | Title/Event | Playwright/Author<br>l= lyrics; m= music | Category | Performers |
|---|---|---|---|---|
| 28/02/1921 | Paddy, the Next Best Thing | W Gayer McKay, Robert Ord | Play | Muriel Munro, Maisie Bell, Daisy Norman |
| 07/03/1921 | Hello, America | | Revue | Doody Hurl, Peggy O'Dare |
| 14/03/1921 | His Little Widows | l Rita Johnson Young, m William Schroeder | Musical | Leslie Hyde, Elsie Lisle |
| 21/03/1921 | The Boy | l Adrian Ross, Percy Greenbank, m Lionel Monckton | Musical | Edward Lewis, Beatrice Raymond |
| 28/03/1921 | Tilly of Bloomsbury | Ian Hay | Play | Cynthia Murtagle, Walter Hudd |
| 04/04/1921 | Dream Girl | l Norman Lee, m Joe Morrison | Revue | Randolph Sutton, Maisie Terriss, Edwin Sykes |
| 11/04/1921 | The Right to Strike | Ernest Hutchinson | Play | Mr and Mrs F Marriott Watson |
| 18/04/1921 | Jack in the Box | l Joseph Hayman, m Kenneth Morrison | Revue | Jack Warman, Dorothy Venton, Harry Hartley |
| 25/04/1921 | Joy Bells | | Revue | Stan Paskin, Daisy Hurdle |
| 02/05/1921 | Justice for the Wife | | Play | Dollie Douglas, Jack Sommers |
| 09/05/1921 | The Man from Toronto | Douglas Murray | Play | Iris Hoey, Victor Bogetti |
| 16/05/1921 | Eastern Nights | Mrs Kimberley | Musical | Ruby Kimberley, Will Harris |
| 23/05/1921 | Morocco Bound | l Adrian Ross, m F Osmond Carr | Musical | Fred Woglast, Jack Tregale, Georgina Fisher, Paddy Dupres |
| 30/05/1921 | Lucky Durham | Wilson Barrett | Play | Hamilton Deane, Winifred Willard, Helena Pickard, Arthur Leigh |
| 31/05/1921 | Lucky Durham | Wilson Barrett | Play | Hamilton Deane, Winifred Willard, Helena Pickard, Arthur Leigh |
| 01/06/1921 | The Lion and the Mouse | Charles Klein | Play | Hamilton Deane, Winifred Willard, Helena Pickard, Arthur Leigh |
| 02/06/1921 | The Lion and the Mouse | Charles Klein | Play | Hamilton Deane, Winifred Willard, Helena Pickard, Arthur Leigh |
| 03/06/1921 | The Hypocrites | Henry Arthur Jones | Play | Hamilton Deane, Winifred Willard, Helena Pickard, Arthur Leigh |
| 04/06/1921 | The Hypocrites | Henry Arthur Jones | Play | Hamilton Deane, Winifred Willard, Helena Pickard, Arthur Leigh |
| 06/06/1921 | The Blindness of Virtue | Cosmo Hamilton | Play | Hamilton Deane, Winifred Willard, Helena Pickard, Arthur Leigh |
| 07/06/1921 | The Blindness of Virtue | Cosmo Hamilton | Play | Hamilton Deane, Winifred Willard, Helena Pickard, Arthur Leigh |
| 08/06/1921 | The Blindness of Virtue | Cosmo Hamilton | Play | Hamilton Deane, Winifred Willard, Helena Pickard, Arthur Leigh |
| 09/06/1921 | Leah Kleschna | C W S McLellan | Play | Hamilton Deane, Winifred Willard, Helena Pickard, Arthur Leigh |

| Date | Title/Event | Playwright/Author l= lyrics; m= music | Category | Performers |
|------|-------------|----------------------|----------|------------|
| 10/06/1921 | Leah Kleschna | C W S McLellan | Play | Hamilton Deane, Winifred Willard, Helena Pickard, Arthur Leigh |
| 11/06/1921 | Leah Kleschna | C W S McLellan | Play | Hamilton Deane, Winifred Willard, Helena Pickard, Arthur Leigh |
| 13/06/1921 | What Next | | Revue | Tommy Nellsdon, Mabelle Thorne, Phil Luck, James Luck, George Luck |
| 20/06/1921 | Carmello | l John Bond, Frederick Ramsdale, m H Lyton Norman | Musical | Haydon Scott, Bob Selvidge, Hilda Paul |
| 27/06/1921 | Tatters | Mrs Kimberley | Musical | Gladys Warland, Marion Ryder |
| 04/07/1921 | A Broken Heart | | Play | Harry Foxwell, Sheila Walsh, Roty Selfridge, Arthur Leslie, Lillian Maitland |
| 05/07/1921 | A Broken Heart | | Play | Harry Foxwell, Sheila Walsh, Roty Selfridge, Arthur Leslie, Lillian Maitland |
| 06/07/1921 | The Young Minister | Sheila Walsh | Play | Harry Foxwell, Sheila Walsh, Roty Selfridge, Arthur Leslie, Lillian Maitland |
| 07/07/1921 | The Young Minister | Sheila Walsh | Play | Harry Foxwell, Sheila Walsh, Roty Selfridge, Arthur Leslie, Lillian Maitland |
| 08/07/1921 | The Wife and the Other Woman | Sheila Walsh | Play | Harry Foxwell, Sheila Walsh, Roty Selfridge, Arthur Leslie, Lillian Maitland |
| 09/07/1921 | The Wife and the Other Woman | Sheila Walsh | Play | Harry Foxwell, Sheila Walsh, Roty Selfridge, Arthur Leslie, Lillian Maitland |
| 11/07/1921 | Only a Mill Girl | Sheila Walsh | Play | Harry Foxwell, Sheila Walsh, Roty Selfridge, Arthur Leslie, Lillian Maitland |
| 12/07/1921 | Only a Mill Girl | Sheila Walsh | Play | Harry Foxwell, Sheila Walsh, Roty Selfridge, Arthur Leslie, Lillian Maitland |
| 13/07/1921 | East Lynne | From Mrs Henry Wood | Play | Harry Foxwell, Sheila Walsh, Roty Selfridge, Arthur Leslie, Lillian Maitland |
| 14/07/1921 | East Lynne | From Mrs Henry Wood | Play | Harry Foxwell, Sheila Walsh, Roty Selfridge, Arthur Leslie, Lillian Maitland |
| 15/07/1921 | The Old Times Are back Again | | Play | Harry Foxwell, Sheila Walsh, Roty Selfridge, Arthur Leslie, Lillian Maitland |
| 16/07/1921 | The Old Times Are back Again | | Play | Harry Foxwell, Sheila Walsh, Roty Selfridge, Arthur Leslie, Lillian Maitland |
| 18/07/1921 | The Lady Slavey | l George Dance, m John Crook | Musical | |
| 25/07/1921 | Find the Lady | | Revue | Harry Ray, Lillie Calden |
| 01/08/1921 | Kiddie O' Mine | Mrs Kimberley | Musical | Gladys Warland, Madge Trevelyan, Harry Cullenford |
| 08/08/1921 | Zig Zag | | Revue | Stan Paskin, Maisie Terriss |
| 15/08/1921 | Knights of the Garter | | Revue | Jackson Owen, Edna Payne, Lily Tando |
| 22/08/1921 | Kick Off | | Revue | Dick Ray, Florence Thurston, May Shill |
| 29/08/1921 | Romance of the Rosary | Herbert Shelley | Play | Frank Henry, Gilbert Lonsdale, M dana |
| 05/09/1921 | My Old Dutch | Arthur Shirley, Albert Chevalier | Play | Albert Chevalier, Dorothy Turner, Charles Fawcett |

| Date | Title/Event | Playwright/Author<br>l= lyrics; m= music | Category | Performers |
|---|---|---|---|---|
| 12/09/1921 | Lord Richard in the Pantry | Sidney Blow, Douglas Hoare | Play | Lillie Soutter, Richard Cooper |
| 19/09/1921 | Missy Jo | l Harry Graham, m Harold Fraser-Simpson | Musical | Ethel Erskine, Gordon Sherry, Lauderdale Maitland |
| 26/09/1921 | Kissing Time | l Guy Bolton, P G Wodehouse, m Ivan Caryll | Musical | Leo Franklin, Helen Rose Innes |
| 03/10/1921 | Macbeth | William Shakespeare | Play | Charles Doran, Edith Sharpe, Neil Porter Arthur Young |
| 04/10/1921 | The Tempest | William Shakespeare | Play | Charles Doran, Edith Sharpe, Neil Porter Arthur Young |
| 05/10/1921 | Twelth Night | William Shakespeare | Play | Charles Doran, Edith Sharpe, Neil Porter Arthur Young |
| 06/10/1921 | Henry V | William Shakespeare | Play | Charles Doran, Edith Sharpe, Neil Porter Arthur Young |
| 07/10/1921 | As You Like It   Mat | William Shakespeare | Play | Charles Doran, Edith Sharpe, Neil Porter Arthur Young |
| 08/10/1921 | Midsummer- mat, Taming Shrew- Eve | William Shakespeare | Play | Charles Doran, Edith Sharpe, Neil Porter Arthur Young |
| 10/10/1921 | Who's Hooper | l Clifford Grey, m Ivor Novello, Howard Thompson | Musical | Rowland Hill, Lola Raine |
| 17/10/1921 | Don Q's Love Story | H Hesketh Prichard | Play | Ernest E Morris, Ethel Wensley |
| 24/10/1921 | A Night Out | l Clifford Grey, m Willie Redstone | Musical | Nellie Cozens, Frank W Dale |
| 31/10/1921 | Fair and Warmer | Avery Hopwood | Play | Wyn Weaver, Dorothy Neave |
| 07/11/1921 | The Gipsey Princess | Erik Kalman | Musical | Ethel Cadman, Dewey Gibson, Renee Sutton, R Barrett Lennard |
| 14/11/1921 | French Leave | Reginald Berkeley | Play | Alexander Bradley, Reginald Dane, Marie Royter |
| 21/11/1921 | Tonight's the Night | l Paul Rubens, Percy Greenbank, m Paul Rubens | Musical | R Hughes, Betty Green, D Liddington |
| 28/11/1921 | The Sign of the Cross | Wilson Barrett | Play | William Mclaren, Lily C Bandman, Nellie Masterson |
| 05/12/1921 | Joy Bells | | Revue | Tom Heathfield, Daisy Hurdle, Edna Myra |
| 12/12/1921 | Three Wise Fools | Austin Strong | Play | Angela McKay, Frank Moore |
| 19/12/1921 | Mother Goose | | Panto | Teddy Brogden, Dan Lawley, Jose Barclsy Gammon |
| 26/12/1921 | Cinderella | | Panto | Ruby Kertheen, Marie Folloy, Newham & Latimer |
| 02/01/1922 | Cinderella | | | |

| Date | Title/Event | Playwright/Author l= lyrics; m= music | Category | Performers |
|------|-------------|------------------|----------|------------|
| 09/01/1922 | The Blue Lagoon | Norman Macowan, Charlton Mann | Play | Stella Florence, Dennis Trent |
| 16/01/1922 | The Garden of Allah | Robert Hichens | Play | Stephen T Ewart, Lilian Hallows, Hamilton Stewart |
| 23/01/1922 | Little Red Riding Hood | Mrs Kimberley | Panto | Evelyn Rogers, Josie Leyton, Allan Hanbury |
| 30/01/1922 | Romance | Edward Sheldon | Play | Isobel Carma, Frank Lacy, Arnold Rayner |
| 06/02/1922 | Jack and the Beanstalk | | Panto | Bert King, Monte Christo, Hilda Paul |
| 13/02/1922 | The Sleeping Beauty | | Panto | Kitty Falkons, Victor Wakeman, Ernie Leno |
| 20/02/1922 | The Rose of Araby | l Harold Simpson, m Merlin Morgan | Musical | Kennneth Ware, Muriel Bentham, Lily Moore, Dick Evans |
| 27/02/1922 | A Southern Maid | l Harry Graham, m Harold Fraser-Simpson | Musical | Mae Blundell, Cecil Dereham |
| 06/03/1922 | The Arcadians | Arthur Wimperis, m Lionel Monckton, Howard Talbot | Musical | Dan Rolyat, George Welford, Winifred Doran |
| 13/03/1922 | Chu Chin Chow | l Oscar Asche, m Frederick Norton | Musical | Victor Fairley, Doris Gordon |
| 20/03/1922 | The Knave of Diamonds | Ethel M Dell | Play | Josset Ellis, Frank Pettingell |
| 27/03/1922 | One Night of Folly | Mrs Kimberley | Musical | Pauline Naunton, Ernest Massingham, Eric Wingfield |
| 03/04/1922 | Wedding Bel(le)s | | Revue | Gilbert Payne, Harry Matto, James Daly, Melville Birley |
| 10/04/1922 | Hello, Venus | | Revue | Tom Frewer, Harold Sydney, Clifford Hayden |
| 17/04/1922 | Sunbeams | | Revue | Fred Fields, Rob Elton |
| 24/04/1922 | The Romany Maid | | Revue | Mamie Worth, Maggie McKenzie, Lewis Grey |
| 01/05/1922 | Seven Days Leave | Walter Howard | Play | Josset Ellis, Lydia Mannington |
| 08/05/1922 | Heads and Tails | | Revue | Lynn Wright, George Norton, Sadie Boston |
| 15/05/1922 | Zig Zag | | Revue | Bryan Herbert, Maisie Terriss |
| 22/05/1922 | The Lads of the Village | Clifford Harris, "Valentine" | Musical | Wilfred Essex, Irene Desmond |
| 24/05/1922 | Burgomaster of Stilemonde - matinee | Maurice Maeterlinck | Play | Sir John Martin-Harvey, Miss N De Silva |
| 29/05/1922 | The Very Idea | William Le Baron | Play | Easten Pickering, Walter Hilliard, Ethel King |
| 05/06/1922 | Kid of Arizona | Mrs Kimberley | Play | Dora Martin, Edie Macklin |
| 12/06/1922 | Kick Off | | Revue | Dick Ray, Florence Thurston, May Shill |
| 19/06/1922 | Broadway Jones | George M Cohan | Play | Harry Piddock, Maisie Crowley, Nellie Sheffield |
| 26/06/1922 | Brown Sugar | Lady Lever | Play | Eileen Beldon, Colin Clive, Winifred Oughton |

| Date | Title/Event | Playwright/Author<br>l= lyrics; m= music | Category | Performers |
|------|-------------|------------------------------------------|----------|------------|
| 03/07/1922 | A Mother Should Tell | Dorothy Mullord, Ivan Patrick | Play | Dorothy Mullord, Chas A Baker, Lillian Drake, Maud Linden |
| 10/07/1922 | Twiddly Bits | Mrs Kimberley | Revue | Fred Lloyd, Etta Ray |
| 17/07/1922 | The Rotters | H F Maltby | Play | Frank Lichfield, Edith Finlay |
| 24/07/1922 | What Next | | Revue | Tommy Neildon, Marjorie Manners, Dorothy Venton |
| 31/07/1922 | The Fun Shop | | Revue | Fred Miller, Millie Deane, Freda Francis |
| 07/08/1922 | Scarlet Runners | W H Briggs | Revue | Bobbie Howes, Grace Wilson |
| 14/08/1922 | Little Biddie O'Farrell | Madge Douglas | Musical | Madge Douglas, Laurie Wright |
| 21/08/1922 | All Put | | Revue | Eva Barnes, Page and Webbb, Ivy Proudfoot |
| 28/08/1922 | The Little Damozel | Monckton Hoffe | Play | Cecile Barclay, Rupert Lister |
| 29/08/1922 | The Little Damozel | Monckton Hoffe | Play | Cecile Barclay, Rupert Lister |
| 30/08/1922 | The Great Adventure | Arnold Bennett | Play | Cecile Barclay, Rupert Lister |
| 31/08/1922 | The Great Adventure | Arnold Bennett | Play | Cecile Barclay, Rupert Lister |
| 01/09/1922 | Captain Drew On Leave | Hubert Henry Davies | Play | Cecile Barclay, Rupert Lister |
| 02/09/1922 | Captain Drew On Leave | Hubert Henry Davies | Play | Cecile Barclay, Rupert Lister |
| 04/09/1922 | Oh! Laugh | | Revue | Ireland Cutter, Tom Maynard, Pat Aza |
| 11/09/1922 | The Circus Queen | | Circus | Charlie Jones*, Evelyn Bebenna, Kenneth Ware |
| 18/09/1922 | Kiddie O' Mine | Mrs Kimberley | Musical | Nellie Corben, Peggy Triggs |
| 25/09/1922 | Sally | l Clifford Grey, m Kerome Kern | Musical | Teddy Brogden, Isabel Dorothy, Hilda Cooper |
| 02/10/1922 | Mr Tower Of London | | Revue | Gracie Fields, Archie Pitt |
| 09/10/1922 | Maid of the Mountains | l Harry Graham, m Harold Fraser-Simpson | Musical | Vera MacDonald, Ernest Shannon |
| 16/10/1922 | Lord Richard in the Pantry | Sidney Blow, Douglas Hoare | Play | Lilliie Soutter, Percy Crawford |
| 23/10/1922 | Betty | l Adrian Ross, Paul Rubens, m Paul Rubens | Musical | Constance Neville, Claude Bailey, Myles Clifton |
| 30/10/1922 | Bulldog Drummond | Sapper | Play | W Austin, Kathleen Kilfoyle, Audrey Dale |
| 06/11/1922 | My Nieces | l Percy Greenbank, m Howard Talbot | Musical | Biba Delabere, Winifred Hare, Sam Wilkinson, Gladys Chapelle |
| 13/11/1922 | Mary | l Otto Harbach, m Louis A Hirsch | Musical | Rita Moir, George Turner, Beatrice Borer |
| 20/11/1922 | O Lady O | | Revue | Eva Kelland, Arthur Rigby, Ada Booth, Alexander Dane |
| 27/11/1922 | Sybil | m Victor Jacobi | Musical | Dolly Varden, Fay Norris, Reg Fanton |

| Date | Title/Event | Playwright/Author<br>l= lyrics; m= music | Category | Performers |
|------|-------------|----------------------|----------|------------|
| 04/12/1922 | The Quaker Girl | l Adrian Ross, Percy Greenbank m, Lionel Monckton | Musical | Peggy Mortimer, Bee O'Connor, Jack O'Shea |
| 11/12/1922 | Splinters of 1922 | | Revue | Archie Glen, Cyril Haydon, Leslie Thurstons |
| 18/12/1922 | Footlight Frolics | | Revue | Billy Blackburn, Frank Farrell, Kitty Austen |
| 26/12/1922 | Dick Whittington | | Panto | Ida Conroy, Pattie St Clair |
| 01/01/1923 | Dick Whittington | | Panto | |
| 08/01/1923 | The Home of the Fairies | Mrs Kimberley | Musical | Nellie Corbin, Edwin Gorse |
| 15/01/1923 | Babes in the Wood | Mrs Kimberley | Panto | Estella Hall, Mabel Evelyn, Eileen Joyce |
| 22/01/1923 | The Sign on the Door | Channing Pollock | Play | Edwin Cooper, T A Shannon, Phyllis Sinclair |
| 29/01/1923 | Cinderella | | Panto | Eva Linacre, Jill Jayes, Jack Hayes, Tom Ashby |
| 05/02/1923 | Tonight's the Night | l Percy Greenbank, Paul Rubens, m Paul Rubens | Musical | Herbert Darnley, Hilda Halfnight |
| 12/02/1923 | John Glaydes | Alfred Sutro | Play | Hamilton Deane, Nancy De Silva, Nan Braunton, Dora Patrick |
| 13/02/1923 | The Ware Case | George Pleydell Bancroft | Play | Hamilton Deane, Nancy De Silva, Nan Braunton, Dora Patrick |
| 14/02/1923 | The Thief | Cosmo Gordon Lennox | Play | Hamilton Deane, Nancy De Silva, Nan Braunton, Dora Patrick |
| 15/02/1923 | Robin's Father | Rudolf Besier | Play | Hamilton Deane, Nancy De Silva, Nan Braunton, Dora Patrick |
| 16/02/1923 | The Missing Volume | Charles Hannon | Play | Hamilton Deane, Nancy De Silva, Nan Braunton, Dora Patrick |
| 17/02/1923 | Jim the Penman | Sir Charles Young | Play | Hamilton Deane, Nancy De Silva, Nan Braunton, Dora Patrick |
| 19/02/1923 | The Builder of Bridges | Alfred Sutro | Play | Hamilton Deane, Nancy De Silva, Nan Braunton, Dora Patrick |
| 20/02/1923 | Captain Drew On Leave | Hubert Henry Davies | Play | Hamilton Deane, Nancy De Silva, Nan Braunton, Dora Patrick |
| 21/02/1923 | The Old Country | Dion Clayton Calthrop | Play | Hamilton Deane, Nancy De Silva, Nan Braunton, Dora Patrick |
| 22/02/1923 | A Message from Mars | Richard Ganthony | Play | Hamilton Deane, Nancy De Silva, Nan Braunton, Dora Patrick |
| 23/02/1923 | When we were Twenty One | H V Esmond | Play | Hamilton Deane, Nancy De Silva, Nan Braunton, Dora Patrick |
| 24/02/1923 | The Wolf | Eugene Walters | Play | Hamilton Deane, Nancy De Silva, Nan Braunton, Dora Patrick |
| 26/02/1923 | Pit-Pat | | Revue | W L Rowlands, Lilian Major, Val Walker |
| 05/03/1923 | The Dollar Princess | m Leo Fall | Musical | Gracie Hartington, George Byrne |
| 12/03/1923 | The Merchant of Venice | William Shakespeare | Play | Alexander Marsh, Carrie Baillie, G Malcolm Russell, Donald Wolfit |

| Date | Title/Event | Playwright/Author | Category | Performers |
|------|-------------|-------------------|----------|------------|
|      |             | l= lyrics; m= music |        |            |
| 13/03/1923 | Twelfth Night | William Shakespeare | Play | Alexander Marsh, Carrie Baillie, G Malcolm Russell, Donald Wolfit |
| 14/03/1923 | Taming of the Shrew | William Shakespeare | Play | Alexander Marsh, Carrie Baillie, G Malcolm Russell, Donald Wolfit |
| 15/03/1923 | Midsummer Night's Dream | William Shakespeare | Play | Alexander Marsh, Carrie Baillie, G Malcolm Russell, Donald Wolfit |
| 16/03/1923 | As You Like It | William Shakespeare | Play | Alexander Marsh, Carrie Baillie, G Malcolm Russell, Donald Wolfit |
| 17/03/1923 | The Tempest Mat | William Shakespeare | Play | Alexander Marsh, Carrie Baillie, G Malcolm Russell, Donald Wolfit |
| 17/03/1923 | David Garrick and The Sleigh Bells | Thomas William Robertson | Play | Alexander Marsh, Carrie Baillie, G Malcolm Russell, Donald Wolfit |
| 19/03/1923 | Julius Caesar | William Shakespeare | Play | Alexander Marsh, Carrie Baillie, G Malcolm Russell, Donald Wolfit |
| 20/03/1923 | Winter's Tale | William Shakespeare | Play | Alexander Marsh, Carrie Baillie, G Malcolm Russell, Donald Wolfit |
| 21/03/1923 | Romeo and Juliet | William Shakespeare | Play | Alexander Marsh, Carrie Baillie, G Malcolm Russell, Donald Wolfit |
| 22/03/1923 | Twelfth Night | William Shakespeare | Play | Alexander Marsh, Carrie Baillie, G Malcolm Russell, Donald Wolfit |
| 23/03/1923 | Midsummer Night's Dream | William Shakespeare | Play | Alexander Marsh, Carrie Baillie, G Malcolm Russell, Donald Wolfit |
| 24/03/1923 | Merchant of Venice Mat | William Shakespeare | Play | Alexander Marsh, Carrie Baillie, G Malcolm Russell, Donald Wolfit |
| 24/03/1923 | Two Orphans of Paris | Adolphe D'Ennery | Play | Alexander Marsh, Carrie Baillie, G Malcolm Russell, Donald Wolfit |
| 26/03/1923 | Spare Parts | | Revue | Randolph Sutton, Frank Leigh |
| 02/04/1923 | A Few Chips | | Revue | Harry Pidduck, Fred Kitchen |
| 09/04/1923 | Iolanthe | l W S Gilbert m Arthur Sullivan | Musical | Swindon Amateur Musical and Dramatic Society |
| 16/04/1923 | Chu Chin Chow | l Oscar Asche, m Frederick Norton | Musical | Victor Fairly, Fred Marshall, Winifred Wellsworth |
| 23/04/1923 | All Put | | Revue | Austin Webb, Dandy Page |
| 30/04/1923 | Brilliants | | Revue | Billy Russell, Jack Walker, Eva Farrar |
| 07/05/1923 | There You Are Then | | Revue | Teddy Morris, Lily Hartley, Doris Crawford |
| 14/05/1923 | Smilin' Through | Allan Langdon Martin (Jane Cowl, Jane Murfin) | Musical | Allen Hanbury, Jack Darby |
| 21/05/1923 | All Pep | | Revue | Len Kilroy, Norman Astridge, Reg Wakefield |
| 28/05/1923 | OK | | Revue | Nor Kiddie, Carl Mysto |
| 04/06/1923 | She's a Daisy | | Revue | Dan Rolyat, Anita Moir |
| 11/06/1923 | The Way of an Eagle | Ethel M Dell | Play | Reginald Nugent, Jane Welsh, Georgina Wynter |
| 18/06/1923 | Down South | | Revue | Eddie Myers, Jasper White |
| 25/06/1923 | The Fun Shop | | Revue | Fred Miller, Freda Francis, Millie Deane |

| Date | Title/Event | Playwright/Author<br>l= lyrics; m= music | Category | Performers |
|------|-------------|------------------------------------------|----------|------------|
| 02/07/1923 | Happy-Go-Lucky | | Revue | May Erne, Erne Chester, Gladys Hay, George Perry |
| 09/07/1923 | Froth | | Revue | Tommy Lorne, John F Traynor, Sylvia Watt |
| 16/07/1923 | Hoch Aye! | | Revue | Jim Jessiman, George West |
| 23/07/1923 | The Musical Romance | | Revue | F Rowland-Tims, Kathleen Maughan, Dorothy Huxtable, Ivy Hargreaves |
| 30/07/1923 | The Speckled Band | from Arthur Conan Doyle | Play | Cecile Barclay, Rupert Lister |
| 31/07/1923 | The Speckled Band | from Arthur Conan Doyle | Play | Cecile Barclay, Rupert Lister |
| 01/08/1923 | The Speckled Band | from Arthur Conan Doyle | Play | Cecile Barclay, Rupert Lister |
| 02/08/1923 | Raffles | E W Hornung, Eugene Presbrey | Play | Cecile Barclay, Rupert Lister |
| 03/08/1923 | Raffles | E W Hornung, Eugene Presbrey | Play | Cecile Barclay, Rupert Lister |
| 04/08/1923 | Raffles | E W Hornung, Eugene Presbrey | Play | Cecile Barclay, Rupert Lister |
| 06/08/1923 | Shuffle Along | | Revue | Stan Paskin, Dorothy Venton |
| 13/08/1923 | Bill Out Of Work | Mrs Kimberley | Revue | Len Martin, Millicent Burton, George Leslie |
| 20/08/1923 | Sunbeams | | Revue | Fred Wolgast, Murray Mills, Arthur Carvey |
| 27/08/1923 | Heads or Tails | | Revue | George Norton, Lynn Wright |
| 03/09/1923 | Bubble and Squeak | | Revue | Charlie Rich, Elsie Roby, Gracie Gallimore |
| 10/09/1923 | Keep Guessing | | Revue | Lester& Wood, Kitty Evelyn, Fred Anderson |
| 17/09/1923 | A Trip to Paris | | Revue | Fred E Taylor, Bobbie Barker, Pat Iza |
| 24/09/1923 | Laughter (Un) Ltd | | Revue | Vine and Russell, Joe Young |
| 01/10/1923 | Sally | l Guy Bolton, P G Wodehouse, m Jerome Kern | Musical | Beryl Leslie, Teddy Brogden, Roy E Ray |
| 08/10/1923 | Tarzan of the Apes | Herbert Woodgate | Play | Philip Valentine, George Conquest Jnr, Alfred Arno |
| 15/10/1923 | All the Best | | Revue | Gilbert Payne, Bella Moody, Val Morgan |
| 22/10/1923 | Jingles | | Revue | Charlie Jones, Hylda Baker, Ida Conroy |
| 29/10/1923 | The Garden of Harmony | | Variety | Elliott Savonas, Dick Rawson, Eileen Lilley, Jimmy Hughes |
| 05/11/1923 | Her Dancing Partner | Muriel Hine | Play | Aileen Firminger, Geoffrey Fulton, Margaret Bull |
| 12/11/1923 | Whirled into Happiness | l Harry Graham, m Robert Stoz | Musical | Scott Harrold, Dorothy Hersee, George Byrne, Edna Bennett |
| 19/11/1923 | Ambrose Applejohn's Adventure | Walter Hackett | Play | David Hawthorne, Phoebe Hodgson |
| 26/11/1923 | Sleeping Partners | Sacha Guitry | Play | Seymour Hicks, Mabel Green, Stanley Turnball, Frederick Wills |

| Date | Title/Event | Playwright/Author<br>l= lyrics; m= music | Category | Performers |
|---|---|---|---|---|
| 03/12/1923 | Oh I! | | Revue | London Welsh Quartet, Bros Hannaway, Esme Willard |
| 10/12/1923 | The Story of the Rosary | Walter Howard | Play | Annie Saker, Alfred Paumier |
| 17/12/1923 | Unemployed | | Revue | Fred E Moore, Leslie Sears, Harvey West |
| 24/12/1923 | Robinson Crusoe | | Panto | Dorothy Langley, Gus Elton, Dick Royal, Jock Cochrane |
| 31/12/1923 | Robinson Crusoe | | Panto | |
| 07/01/1924 | Tons of Money | Will Evans and Valentine | Play | Richard Lawrence, Adela Raine |
| 14/01/1924 | The House that Jack Built | | Panto | Madge Weston, Gert Orchard |
| 21/01/1924 | Aladdin | | Panto | Gwen Highly, Edith Elen, Jay Highly, J C Morris, Jac Smart |
| 28/01/1924 | Partners Again | Jules Eckert Goodman, Montague Glass | Play | Naylor Grimson, Sam Springston |
| 04/02/1924 | A Week in a Night | | Revue | Sam Mayo, Mabel Marks |
| 11/02/1924 | Wangles | | Revue | Con Ingham, Mabelle George |
| 18/02/1924 | Bluebeard's Eighth Wife | Alfred Savoir | Play | Francis Robert, Leonard Walker, Honor Byrne |
| 25/02/1924 | Top Speed | l Guy Bolton, Bert Kalmar, m Joseph Burke | Musical | Fred E Wynne, Evelyn Kirkby |
| 03/03/1924 | Royal Italian Circus | | Circus | |
| 10/03/1924 | The Rose of Persia | l Basil Hood, m Arthur Sullivan | Musical | Swindon Amateur Musical and Dramatic Society |
| 17/03/1924 | Wild Heather | Dorothy Brandon | Play | Hamilton Deane, Dora Patrick, Nan Braunton, Barrie Livesey |
| 18/03/1924 | The Blindness of Virtue | Cosmo Hamilton | Play | Hamilton Deane, Dora Patrick, Nan Braunton, Barrie Livesey |
| 19/03/1924 | Smith | W Somerset Maugham | Play | Hamilton Deane, Dora Patrick, Nan Braunton, Barrie Livesey |
| 20/03/1924 | The Ware Case | George Pleydell Bancroft | Play | Hamilton Deane, Dora Patrick, Nan Braunton, Barrie Livesey |
| 21/03/1924 | The Wolf | Eugene Walters | Play | Hamilton Deane, Dora Patrick, Nan Braunton, Barrie Livesey |
| 22/03/1924 | The Man from Toronto | Douglas Murray | Play | Hamilton Deane, Dora Patrick, Nan Braunton, Barrie Livesey |
| 24/03/1924 | Pit-Pat | | Revue | Fred Shuff, Lilian Major, Bert Arnold |
| 31/03/1924 | The Carnival | H G M Hardinge, Matheson Lang | Play | Cecile Barclay, Rupert Lister |
| 07/04/1924 | Joy Bells | | Revue | Johnson and Ricard, Clark and Jensen, Peggy Andrews |
| 14/04/1924 | Plum Blossom | | Revue | George Butler, Julie Gilmer |
| 21/04/1924 | The Musical Romance | | Revue | F Rowland -Tims, Pauline Day, Betty Gayford |

| Date | Title/Event | Playwright/Author<br>l= lyrics; m= music | Category | Performers |
|---|---|---|---|---|
| 16/08/1924 | Hey Presto | | Revue | Clive Maskelyn, Stephanie Stephens, Frederick Culpitt, Tom Heathfield |
| 25/08/1924 | April Showers | | Revue | Barry Barnes, Len Martin, Rene Dawson |
| 01/09/1924 | Pops | | Revue | Johnson and Bert, Ethel Erskine, Neville Delmar |
| 08/09/1924 | Stop Flirting | | Musical | Gerald Seymour, Mabel Harley, R O'Malley |
| 15/09/1924 | Joan of Arc | | Play | Atholl Douglas, Maureen O'Mara, Harry Hartley |
| 22/09/1924 | Zip | | Revue | Billy Caryll, Hilda Mundy |
| 29/09/1924 | Irish and Proud of it | | Revue | Joe O'Gorman, James Daly, Monica Daly |
| 06/10/1924 | The Talk of the Town | l Chas H Taylor, m Herbert E Haines | Musical | Cora Goffin, Charles Glover, Vyvyan Pedler |
| 13/10/1924 | Outward Bound | Sutton Vane | Play | Herbert Alexander, Harry Morton |
| 20/10/1924 | Irene | l Joseph McCarthy, m Harry Tierney | Musical | Ursula Hughes, Harry Ray |
| 27/10/1924 | Pins and Needles | | Revue | Binnie Lura, Hal Collins, Horace Kenney |
| 03/11/1924 | Katinka | l Otto Harbach m, Rudolf Friml | Musical | Constance Neville, Richard Teasdale, Norman Greene |
| 10/11/1924 | The Nine O'Clock Revue | | Revue | M Klit Gaarde, Hugh Rene, Gola Betti |
| 17/11/1924 | Ginger | | Revue | Hedge Brothers & Jacobson, Monica Magnet, Dick Tubb |
| 24/11/1924 | The Way of an Eagle | from Ethel M Dell | Play | Guy Buckley, Stella Florence, Frances Midgley |
| 01/12/1924 | Pledges | | Revue | Barney Lando, Brian O'Sullivan, |
| 08/12/1924 | Oceans of Joy | | Revue | George Norton, Lynn Wright |
| 15/12/1924 | Over the Hill | | Play | Clara Santley, Harry Tilbury |
| 24/12/1924 | Babes in the Wood | | Panto | Christine Roy, Fred Lloyd, Joe Archer |
| 29/12/1924 | Babes in the Wood | | Panto | |
| 05/01/1925 | Babes in the Wood | | Panto | |
| 12/01/1925 | Going Up | James Montgomery, Otto Harbach, Jouis Hirsch | Musical | Ivy Close, R Barrett Lennard |
| 19/01/1925 | Jack and the Beanstalk | | Panto | Randolph Sutton, Frank Leigh |
| 26/01/1925 | Lillies of the Field | | Play | Beryl Sidney, Julian D'Albie, Lilian Mason |
| 02/02/1925 | Peter Pan | J M Barrie | Play | Maisie Darrell, Marguerite Moreton, Lionel Gadsen |
| 09/02/1925 | Cinderella | | Panto | Eva Renee, Agnes Rayson |
| 16/02/1925 | The First Kiss | m Pablo Luna | Musical | Ethel Cadman, V Barrett Lennard, May Morton, Denier Warren |
| 23/02/1925 | The Gondoliers | l W S Gilbert, m Arthur Sullivan | Musical | Swindon Amateur Musical and Dramatic Society |

| Date | Title/Event | Playwright/Author<br>l= lyrics; m= music | Category | Performers |
|------|-------------|------------------------------------------|----------|------------|
| 02/03/1925 | The Crimson Alibi | George Broadhurst | Play | Hamilton Deane, Dora Patrick, Barrie Livesey, Jack Howarth, Nan Braunton |
| 03/03/1925 | The Crimson Alibi | George Broadhurst | Play | Hamilton Deane, Dora Patrick, Barrie Livesey, Jack Howarth, Nan Braunton |
| 04/03/1925 | Sherlock Holmes | | Play | Hamilton Deane, Dora Patrick, Barrie Livesey, Jack Howarth, Nan Braunton |
| 05/03/1925 | Sherlock Holmes | | Play | Hamilton Deane, Dora Patrick, Barrie Livesey, Jack Howarth, Nan Braunton |
| 06/03/1925 | Dracula | Hamilton Deane, John L Balderston | Play | Hamilton Deane, Dora Patrick, Barrie Livesey, Jack Howarth, Nan Braunton |
| 07/03/1925 | Dracula | Hamilton Deane, John L Balderston | Play | Hamilton Deane, Dora Patrick, Barrie Livesey, Jack Howarth, Nan Braunton |
| 09/03/1925 | Ring In | | Revue | Rebla, Osborne & Perryer, Victoria Bros, Noni |
| 16/03/1925 | Peeps into 1925 | | Revue | Sam Rayne, Freddie Westcott, Lily Bruce |
| 23/03/1925 | The Officer's Mess | l Sydney Blow, Douglas Hoare, m Philip Braham | Musical | Harold Lane?, Constance Neville |
| 30/03/1925 | Our Liz | | Revue | Lilian Low, Bert Murray |
| 06/04/1925 | Spare Parts | | Revue | Randolph Sutton, Frank Leigh, Maggie McLean, Dorothy Brett |
| 13/04/1925 | Scotch and Polly | | Revue | Tommy Lorne, Sydney Bray, Betty Green |
| 20/04/1925 | Short Stories | | Revue | Teddy Williams, Thelma Hamilton |
| 27/04/1925 | The Belle of New York | l C S M McLellan, m Gustav Kerker | Musical | Johnnie Schofield, Lily Lansdown, Irene Wisher |
| 04/05/1925 | Merchant of Venice | William Shakespeare | Play | Charles Doran, Muriel Hutchinson, Dorothy Francis |
| 05/05/1925 | Julius Caesar | William Shakespeare | Play | Charles Doran, Muriel Hutchinson, Dorothy Francis |
| 06/05/1925 | Macbeth | William Shakespeare | Play | Charles Doran, Muriel Hutchinson, Dorothy Francis |
| 07/05/1925 | Hamlet | William Shakespeare | Play | Charles Doran, Muriel Hutchinson, Dorothy Francis |
| 08/05/1925 | Taming of the Shrew | William Shakespeare | Play | Charles Doran, Muriel Hutchinson, Dorothy Francis |
| 09/05/1925 | As You Like It      Mat | William Shakespeare | Play | Charles Doran, Muriel Hutchinson, Dorothy Francis |
| 09/05/1925 | Merry Wives of Windsor Eve | William Shakespeare | Play | Charles Doran, Muriel Hutchinson, Dorothy Francis |
| 11/05/1925 | 10-1 On | | Revue | Jimmy James, Rene Ray |
| 18/05/1925 | The Rat | Ivor Novello | Play | F V Owen, Kathleen Saintsbury, June Meredith, Eunice Mann |
| 25/05/1925 | Up the River | | Revue | Donald Keir, Reg Marcus |
| 01/06/1925 | Puzzles of 1925 | | Revue | Zoe Corner, Douglas Vine, Bert Weston |

| Date | Title/Event | Playwright/Author<br>l= lyrics; m= music | Category | Performers |
|------|-------------|------------------|----------|-----------|
| 08/06/1925 | Derby Day | | Revue | Neville Graham, Belle Richardson |
| 15/06/1925 | The Side Show | | Revue | Fred Morgan, Harry Arthurs |
| 22/06/1925 | The Goods | | Revue | Jack Cromo, Charles Harvey |
| 29/06/1925 | April Showers | | Revue | Bert Rogers, Nan Hillaby, Barry Barnes |
| 06/07/1925 | A Trip to Paris | | Revue | Len Jackson, Jennie Russell |
| 13/07/1925 | Round the Town | | Revue | Peter Fannan, Gladys Steele |
| 20/07/1925 | London Says Winners/<br>Winners of 1925 | | Revue | Gus Stratton, Hugh Ogilvie, Glyn Grafton |
| 27/07/1925 | Star Shells | | Revue | Bert Norman, Edna Payne |
| 03/08/1925 | Sign On | | Revue | Charles King, Florence Benson |
| 10/08/1925 | Sally | l Clifford Grey,<br>m Jerome Kern | Musical | Frank Dale, Maudie Harris, Elizabeth Kempton |
| 17/08/1925 | Royal Italian Circus | | Circus | |
| 24/08/1925 | The Green Goddess | William Archer | Play | Abraham Soafer, Kathleen Pickard |
| 31/08/1925 | Spasms | | Revue | Lowe and Boden, Claughton Holdsworth,<br>Georgie Trevelyan |
| 07/09/1925 | Attaboy | | Revue | Fred Miller, Irene Shamrock, Millie Deane,<br>Marie Fane (baritone) |
| 14/09/1925 | Stop Flirting | l Fred Jackson,<br>m William Daly,<br>Paul Lannin | Musical | Geoffrey Saville, Ida Walton, Margot Bryant |
| 21/09/1925 | The Dairymaids | l Paul Rubens,<br>Arthur<br>Wimperis, m<br>Paul Rubens | Musical | Avis Robb, Dan Clark |
| 28/09/1925 | Mikado | l W S Gilbert, m<br>Arthur Sullivan | Opera | D'oyly Carte Opera Co inc J Ivan Menzies,<br>Hilton Leyland, Kathleen Anderson |
| 29/09/1925 | Ruddigore | l W S Gilbert, m<br>Arthur Sullivan | Opera | D'oyly Carte Opera Co inc J Ivan Menzies,<br>Hilton Leyland, Kathleen Anderson |
| 30/09/1925 | Iolanthe | l W S Gilbert, m<br>Arthur Sullivan | Opera | D'oyly Carte Opera Co inc J Ivan Menzies,<br>Hilton Leyland, Kathleen Anderson |
| 01/10/1925 | Patience | l W S Gilbert, m<br>Arthur Sullivan | Opera | D'oyly Carte Opera Co inc J Ivan Menzies,<br>Hilton Leyland, Kathleen Anderson |
| 02/10/1925 | Ruddigore | l W S Gilbert, m<br>Arthur Sullivan | Opera | D'oyly Carte Opera Co inc J Ivan Menzies,<br>Hilton Leyland, Kathleen Anderson |
| 03/10/1925 | Iolanthe   mat | l W S Gilbert, m<br>Arthur Sullivan | Opera | D'oyly Carte Opera Co inc J Ivan Menzies,<br>Hilton Leyland, Kathleen Anderson |
| 03/10/1925 | Mikado   eve | l W S Gilbert, m<br>Arthur Sullivan | Opera | D'oyly Carte Opera Co inc J Ivan Menzies,<br>Hilton Leyland, Kathleen Anderson |
| 05/10/1925 | The Last Waltz | m Oscar Straus<br>l Reginald<br>Arkell ? | Musical | Sybil Coulthurst, Denys Erlam |
| 12/10/1925 | The Street Singer | l Percy<br>Greenbank, m<br>Harold Fraser-<br>Simpson | Musical | Maisie Bell, John Careodus, Leedham Stanley |

| Date | Title/Event | Playwright/Author l= lyrics; m= music | Category | Performers |
|------|-------------|----------------------|----------|-----------|
| 19/10/1925 | Carmen | Bizet | Opera | Royal Carl Rosa Opera Co inc Hughes Macklin, Horace Vincent, Gladys Parr |
| 20/10/1925 | Il Trovatore | Verdi | Opera | Royal Carl Rosa Opera Co inc Hughes Macklin, Horace Vincent, Gladys Parr |
| 21/10/1925 | Maritana | Vincent Wallace | Opera | Royal Carl Rosa Opera Co inc Hughes Macklin, Horace Vincent, Gladys Parr |
| 22/10/1925 | Cavalleria Rusticanna/ I Pagliacci | Mascagni/ Leoncavallo | Opera | Royal Carl Rosa Opera Co inc Hughes Macklin, Horace Vincent, Gladys Parr |
| 23/10/1925 | Samson and Delilah | Saint-Saens | Opera | Royal Carl Rosa Opera Co inc Hughes Macklin, Horace Vincent, Gladys Parr |
| 24/10/1925 | Madame Butterfly   mat | Puccini | Opera | Royal Carl Rosa Opera Co inc Hughes Macklin, Horace Vincent, Gladys Parr |
| 24/10/1925 | Faust   eve | Gounod | Opera | Royal Carl Rosa Opera Co inc Hughes Macklin, Horace Vincent, Gladys Parr |
| 26/10/1925 | Madame Pompadour | m Leo Fall | Musical | Doreen Langton, Arthur Lucas |
| 02/11/1925 | Lilac Time | l Adrian Ross, m Franz Schubert | Musical | Courtice Pounds, Marion Bower, Lionel Victor |
| 09/11/1925 | Gipsey Love | l Adrian Ross, m Franz Lehar | Musical | Nancy Parr, Bertram Dench, Roy Lockhart |
| 16/11/1925 | White Cargo | Leon Gordon | Play | Kathleen Boutall, Murray Carrington, Fred Wright |
| 23/11/1925 | Little Nellie Kelly | George M Cohan | Musical | Marjorie Wyn, Fred Kichen Jnr, Regis Toomey |
| 30/11/1925 | Patricia | l Denis Mackail, Greatrex Newman, m Geoffrey Gwyther | Musical | Dorothy Laurie, Franklin Ives, J H Wakefield, Vida England |
| 07/12/1925 | Apple Sauce | | Revue | Stanley Kirkby, Harry Hudson, Lawrie Howe, Ena Foy |
| 14/12/1925 | No, No, Nanette | l Irving Caesar, Otto Harbach, m Vincent Youmans | Musical | Hal Gordon, Gladys Cruikshanks, Frank Hector |
| 24/12/1925 | Jack and Jill | | Revue | Freddie Frome, Dora Dare |
| 04/01/1926 | The Cooptimists | | Revue | Jessie Hitter, Hay Plumb, Kevan bernard, Bernard Ansell |
| 11/01/1926 | Little Jack Horner | | Panto | Jack Cromo, Bob Roberts, Meg hamilton, Dorothy Brett |
| 18/01/1926 | Sammy in Corsica | | Revue | Arthur White, Daisy Brindley, Darroll Richards |
| 25/01/1926 | Our Cabaret | | Revue | Bunny Doyle, Ivy Chase |
| 01/02/1926 | What Ho! | | Revue | Mark Richards |
| 08/02/1926 | Zip | | Revue | Billy Caryll, Hilda Mundy |
| 15/02/1926 | Wait for it | | Revue | Peter Hardy, Rita Moya |
| 22/02/1926 | The Mikado | l W S Gilbert, m Arthur Sullivan | Musical | Swindon Amateur Musical and Dramatic Society |
| 29/02/1926 | Volumes | | Revue | Arthur Forbes, May Yorke |

| Date | Title/Event | Playwright/Author<br>l= lyrics; m= music | Category | Performers |
|---|---|---|---|---|
| 08/03/1926 | Katinka | l Otto Harbach,<br>m Rudolf Friml | Musical | Eileen Moody, Richard Teasdale, Anna Cuka |
| 15/03/1926 | Under Cover | Roy Cooper Megrue | Play | Hamilton Deane, Dora Patrick, Diana Wynyard, Jack Howarth, Stuart Lomath |
| 16/03/1926 | The Faithful Heart | Monckton Hoffe | Play | Hamilton Deane, Dora Patrick, Diana Wynyard, Jack Howarth, Stuart Lomath |
| 17/03/1926 | Dracula | Hamilton Deane, John L Balderston | Play | Hamilton Deane, Dora Patrick, Diana Wynyard, Jack Howarth, Stuart Lomath |
| 18/03/1926 | Dr Wake's Patient | W Gayer Mackay, Robert Ord | Play | Hamilton Deane, Dora Patrick, Diana Wynyard, Jack Howarth, Stuart Lomath |
| 19/03/1926 | Tom, Dick and Harry | | Play | Hamilton Deane, Dora Patrick, Diana Wynyard, Jack Howarth, Stuart Lomath |
| 20/03/1926 | The Dancers | | Play | Hamilton Deane, Dora Patrick, Diana Wynyard, Jack Howarth, Stuart Lomath |
| 22/03/1926 | Mr Tower of London | | Revue | Joe Mitchell, Barbara Bartle, Stanley Durward |
| 29/03/1926 | Me and my Gal | | Revue | Russell Brandow, Fred Brand, Evelyn Taylor |
| 05/04/1926 | Crossing the Line | | Revue | Leonard Morris, Teddie Webb |
| 12/04/1926 | Parish Relief | | Revue | Jack Mayo, Jean Collins |
| 19/04/1926 | Served Hot | | Revue | Jim Nolan, Albert Edwards, Rita Dilston |
| 26/04/1926 | Roses | | Revue | Tom Gamble, Lena Lloyd |
| 03/05/1926 | Snacks | | Revue | |
| 10/05/1926 | Nippy | | Revue | Fred Evison, Joan Hestor, Dorothy Greene |
| 17/05/1926 | Good Times Coming | | Revue | Bert Lawrie, Fred Ward |
| 24/05/1926 | How Dare You | | Revue | Harry Ford, S H Wyndham |
| 31/05/1926 | Fellow Workers | | Revue | Tommy Neldon, Mabelle Thorne, Virgina Davies |
| 07/06/1926 | The New Side Show | | Revue | Will Cave, Monty Goulding, Rays Band |
| 14/06/1926 | Wake Up | | Revue | Jack Gallagher, The Two 'Erbs |
| 21/06/1926 | A Week's Pleasure | | Revue | Betty Fields, Walter Amnet |
| 28/06/1926 | House Hunting | | Revue | Freddie Frome, Lila Vesta |
| 05/07/1926 | See the Point | | Revue | Tom Drew, Ruth Dennis |
| 12/07/1926 | Making Money | | Revue | Dan Raynor, Clairette Ruane |
| 19/07/1926 | | | Variety | Josie Collins, Trevor Watkins, Joe Daly |
| 26/07/1926 | Contrasts | | Revue | Tom Moss, Ethel Orrell |
| 02/08/1926 | Mottoes | | Revue | Sam Mayo, Leon & Alys |
| 09/08/1926 | Red Hot | | Revue | Bobby Kent, Teddie Curtis |
| 16/08/1926 | Still Jazzing | | Revue | Joe Morrison's Panoramic Band, Maisie Terriss, Eleanor Smith |
| 23/08/1926 | Mr Tickle MP | | Revue | Fred Morgan, Albert Letine, Wilma Deane |
| 30/08/1926 | Are You Listening? | | Revue | Billy Lowe, Eva Dennis & Charles Alison |

| Date | Title/Event | Playwright/Author l= lyrics; m= music | Category | Performers |
|------|-------------|---------------------------------------|----------|------------|
| 06/09/1926 | | | Variety | Horace Goldin (Royal Illusionist), Les Eldons, Barrett Clarke |
| 13/09/1926 | Red Tape | | Revue | Billy Camp, Toots Holden, Royal Mail Choir |
| 20/09/1926 | Here's to you | | Revue | Florrie Forde, Bud Flanagan, Chesney Allen, Aleta Turner |
| 27/09/1926 | | | Variety | Howard Flynn's Symphonic Band |
| 04/10/1926 | Cranky | | Revue | Peter Fannan, Florence Williams |
| 11/10/1926 | London Nights, | | Revue | Darby Dale, May Royal, Ivy Helder |
| 18/10/1926 | Our Liz | | Revue | Anna Cuka, Bert Murray, Arthur Garside |
| 25/10/1926 | It Pays to Advertise | Walter Hackett, Roi Cooper Megrue | Play | C Vivian Wallace, D Muir Little, Marjorie Sunley |
| 01/11/1926 | What'll I Do | | Revue | Eddie Walker, Bert Snowden, Millie Jillson, Winifred Laurie |
| 08/11/1926 | The Creaking Chair | Allene Tupper Wilkes | Play | C Brough Robertson, Sybille Olivier, Wallace Court |
| 15/11/1926 | The Rat | Ivor Novello, Constance Collier | Play | Guy Preston, Pauline Loring, Eunice Mann` |
| 22/11/1926 | Just Married | | Play | Arthur Mack, Honor Byrne |
| 29/11/1926 | Veteran Stars of Variety | | Variety | Tom Costello, Arthur Roberts |
| 06/12/1926 | No, No, Nanette | l Irving Caesar, Otto Harbach, m Vincent Youmans | Musical | Jean Colin, Hal Gordon, Frank Hector |
| 13/12/1926 | Magical Moments | | Variety | The Great Carmo |
| 20/12/1926 | Dreams | | Revue | Dick Tubb, Kathy Buckle, Claire Baines |
| 27/12/1926 | Dick Whittington | | Panto | Eddie Lotto, Eddie Venn, Jack Crew |
| 03/01/1927 | Alf's Button | W A Darlington | Play | Dan Booker, Jack Morris |
| 10/01/1927 | Scotch Broth | | Revue | Dave Willis, Alex Foster |
| 17/01/1927 | In Clover | | Revue | Jack Martell, Gladys Roberts |
| 24/01/1927 | Humpty Dumpty | | Panto | Jack Cromo, Meg Hamilton, Teddy Curtis, Dorothy Brett |
| 31/01/1927 | The Street Singer | l Percy Greenbank, m Harold Fraser-Simpson | Musical | Ethel Oliver, John Redmond, Alfred Beers |
| 07/02/1927 | Scotch Mist | Patrick Hastings | Play | Lenore Williams, J Edward Whitty |
| 14/02/1927 | The Real Stuff | | Revue | George Hyam, Chic Hyam, Ladd West |
| 21/02/1927 | The Speed Show | | Revue | Clive Maskelyn, Theda Sisters |
| 28/02/1927 | London- Day and Night | | Revue | Charlie Jones, Phyllis Robb |
| 07/03/1927 | Mercenary Mary | l William Friedlander, Isabel Leighton, m Con Conrad | Musical | Katy Kay, Joan Morgan, William Cromwell |

| Date | Title/Event | Playwright/Author<br>l= lyrics; m= music | Category | Performers |
|---|---|---|---|---|
| 14/03/1927 | Delia | l Harry W Boden, m Hamylton Hope | Musical | Swindon Amateur Musical and Dramatic Society |
| 21/03/1927 | The Ghost Train | Arnold Ridley | Play | Clifford Cobbe, Ethel Warwick |
| 28/03/1927 | Go | | Revue | Bill Caryll, Hilda Mundy, Phyllis Pleydell |
| 04/04/1927 | Lido Lady | l Lorenz Hart, m Richard Rodgers | Musical | Fred Kitchen Jnr, Mabelle George |
| 11/04/1927 | Souvenirs | | Revue | Dick Ray, The Kobes |
| 18/04/1927 | Brighter London | | Revue | Rita Bernard, Teddy Williams, Roy Barbour |
| 25/04/1927 | The Last of Mrs Cheney | Frederick Lonsdale | Play | Hilda Esty Marsh, Frederick Keen, F Wyndham Goldie |
| 02/05/1927 | The Cat Burglars | | Revue | Sam Mayo, Harry Barrett |
| 09/05/1927 | Whirl of the World | | Revue | Dave Bruce, Nellie Turner |
| 16/05/1927 | Irish Follies | | Revue | Lucan & McShane, Bert Arnold |
| 23/05/1927 | Julius Caesar | William Shakespeare | Play | Charles Doran, R Eric Lee, Norman Hault, Dorothy Francis, Jane Foster Baird |
| 24/05/1927 | As You Like It | William Shakespeare | Play | Charles Doran, R Eric Lee, Norman Hault, Dorothy Francis, Jane Foster Baird |
| 25/05/1927 | The Cardinal | Louis N Parker | Play | Charles Doran, R Eric Lee, Norman Hault, Dorothy Francis, Jane Foster Baird |
| 26/05/1927 | Hamlet | William Shakespeare | Play | Charles Doran, R Eric Lee, Norman Hault, Dorothy Francis, Jane Foster Baird |
| 27/05/1927 | Midsummers Night's Dream | William Shakespeare | Play | Charles Doran, R Eric Lee, Norman Hault, Dorothy Francis, Jane Foster Baird |
| 28/05/1927 | Macbeth    mat | William Shakespeare | Play | Charles Doran, R Eric Lee, Norman Hault, Dorothy Francis, Jane Foster Baird |
| 28/05/1927 | Merchant of Venice | William Shakespeare | Play | Charles Doran, R Eric Lee, Norman Hault, Dorothy Francis, Jane Foster Baird |
| 30/05/1927 | All Spice | | Revue | Hayes & Austin, Dora Dale, Lena Lind |
| 06/06/1927 | The Farmer's Wife | Eden Philpotts | Play | F Payne Palmer, E W Avery, Phyllis Birkett |
| 13/06/1927 | Top Hole | | Revue | Gus Chevalier, Sisters Reeve |
| 20/06/1927 | Second to None | | Revue | Edgar Cooke, Kitty & Jack Noyes |
| 27/06/1927 | Broadway Jones | George H Cohan | Play | Harry Pidduck, John J Hooker, Ida Mackay |
| 04/07/1927 | Three Weeks | Roy Horniman adapted from Elinor Glyn | Play | W A Payne-Seddon, Cecile Barclay |
| 11/07/1927 | QUP | | Revue | Trixie Maison, Bud Richie, Mike Morice |
| 18/07/1927 | Patsy From Paris | | | Lillie Soutter, Alexander Loftus, Mary Hayward |
| 25/07/1927 | Rainbows | | Revue | Austin Wood, Kitty Spencer, Billy Faubert, Charles Wingrove |
| 01/08/1927 | Just for Fun | | Revue | Doris Ashton, George West, Ivy Grant |
| 08/08/1927 | Hold Tight | | Revue | Jack Stanley, Doris Vi Driscoll |
| 15/08/1927 | Get Busy | | Revue | Jack Henry, Doris Crawford, |

| Date | Title/Event | Playwright/Author<br>l= lyrics; m= music | Category | Performers |
|------|-------------|------------------------------|----------|------------|
| 22/08/1927 | Casey's Circus | | Revue | |
| 29/08/1927 | The Never Works | | Revue | Dave Morris, Ten Moonies, Eileen Audrey |
| 05/09/1927 | Mustard | Mrs Kimberley | Revue | Aston Brothers, Rolando Martin |
| 12/09/1927 | Tell Me More | l Ira Gershwin,<br>m George<br>Gershwin | Musical | Dan Young, Peggy Abbott, Doris Davis, Jack Deering |
| 19/09/1927 | Still Jazzing | | Revue | Maisie Terriss, Harry Arthurs, Eleanor Smith, Joe Morris And his Panoramic Band, Charlie Wood |
| 26/09/1927 | Rookery Nook | Ben Travers | Play | Lenton Murray, Stanford Holme, Thea Johnson, Alex Begbie |
| 03/10/1927 | Married Life | | Revue | Charles O'Neill, Jean Andrews, Nita Desmond |
| 10/10/1927 | Too Many Cooks | | Revue | Douglas Wakefield, Billy Nelson, Rosie May |
| 17/10/1927 | VA | | Variety | Horace Goldin (Royal Illusionist), Bert Madison, Camille Gillard |
| 24/10/1927 | White Cargo | Leon Taylor | Play | Hodgson Taylor, Charles Hodges, Elsie Goulding, Douglas Quayle |
| 31/10/1927 | The Ringer | Edgar Wallace | Play | W Ellythorne Fraser, Vernon Fortescue, Betty Turner |
| 07/11/1927 | Eliza Comes to Stay | H V Esmond | Play | Juanita Charlton, Gerard Rendle |
| 14/11/1927 | The Joker | | Play | Joan Kingdom, Michael Woods |
| 21/11/1927 | In the Night | Cyril Harcourt | Play | Bristol Little Theatre Co, Charles Cornock, Clive Morton, Murray MacDonald, |
| 22/11/1927 | In the Night | Cyril Harcourt | Play | Bristol Little Theatre Co, Charles Cornock, Clive Morton, Murray MacDonald, |
| 23/11/1927 | In the Night | Cyril Harcourt | Play | Bristol Little Theatre Co, Charles Cornock, Clive Morton, Murray MacDonald, |
| 24/11/1927 | Her Temporary Husband | Edward A Paulton | Play | Bristol Little Theatre Co, Charles Cornock, Clive Morton, Murray MacDonald, |
| 25/11/1927 | Her Temporary Husband | Edward A Paulton | Play | Bristol Little Theatre Co, Charles Cornock, Clive Morton, Murray MacDonald, |
| 26/11/1927 | Her Temporary Husband | Edward A Paulton | Play | Bristol Little Theatre Co, Charles Cornock, Clive Morton, Murray MacDonald, |
| 28/11/1927 | What'll I Do | | Revue | Eddie Walker, Millie Jillson |
| 05/12/1927 | Just Married | | Play | Arthur Mack, Betty Nelson |
| 12/12/1927 | | | Variety | Harry Weldon, Hilda Glyder, Nora Delaney |
| 19/12/1927 | Our Lodger | Mrs Kimberley | Revue | Wal Butler, Patti St Clair, Jack Hayes |
| 26/12/1927 | Babes in the Wood | | Revue | Florrie Forde, Bud Flanagan, Chesney Allen, Aleta Turner |
| 02/01/1928 | Sinbad the Sailor | | Panto | Trixie Maison, Nora Roden, Mike Morice, Yvette Yorke |
| 09/01/1928 | Joking Again | | Revue | Harry Korris, George Melt, Hilda Meacham |
| 16/01/1928 | The Blue Saraphan | | Revue | Cecilia Marion, Maxim Turganoff, Frank Tully |
| 23/01/1928 | On the Panel | | Revue | Rhys Thomas, Tubby Turner |

| Date | Title/Event | Playwright/Author<br>l= lyrics; m= music | Category | Performers |
|------|-------------|------------------------------|----------|------------|
| 30/01/1928 | The Whole Town's Talking | Anita Loos | Play | Guy Vivian, Theo Cotterill |
| 06/02/1928 | Tom Jones | l Charles H Taylor, m Edward German | Musical | GWR Mechanics Institute Amateur Theatrical Society |
| 13/02/1928 | Princess Charming | | Musical | Mytle Stewart, Hugh Osmond, Walter Passmore |
| 20/02/1928 | The Best People | David Gray, Avery Hopwood | Play | Mary Byron, Amy Elstob |
| 27/02/1928 | Surprises | | Revue | Herbert Ray & his Band, Arthur Lewis |
| 05/03/1928 | Ask Beccles | Cyril Campion | Play | Richard Williams, Florrie Kelsey |
| 12/03/1928 | Miss Hook of Holland | l, m, Paul Rubens | Musical | Swindon Amateur Musical and Dramatic Society |
| 19/03/1928 | The Laughter Mixture | | Revue | Gladys Watson, George Norton, Fred Knight, Edith McLeod |
| 26/03/1928 | The Fake | Frederick Lonsdale | Play | Hamilton Deane, Dora Patrick, A Edward Sproston |
| 27/03/1928 | Daddy Long Legs | Jean Webster | Play | Hamilton Deane, Dora Patrick, A Edward Sproston |
| 28/03/1928 | Dracula | Hamilton Deane, John L Balderston | Play | Hamilton Deane, Dora Patrick, A Edward Sproston |
| 29/03/1928 | Lucky Durham | Wilson Barrett | Play | Hamilton Deane, Dora Patrick, A Edward Sproston |
| 30/03/1928 | At the Villa Rose | A E W Mason | Play | Hamilton Deane, Dora Patrick, A Edward Sproston |
| 31/03/1928 | Dracula | Hamilton Deane, John L Balderston | Play | Hamilton Deane, Dora Patrick, A |
| 02/04/1928 | Cranky | | Revue | Peter Fannan, Florence Williams, Maudie Edwards |
| 09/04/1928 | The Fanatics | Miles Malleson | Play | Paul Hansell, Helen Kane |
| 16/04/1928 | The Blue Train | m Robert Stolz | Musical | Billy Fry, Marjorie Lancaster, Kathleen Kilfoyle |
| 23/04/1928 | All Smiles | | Revue | May Royal, Marjorie Lawrence, Billy Rowlands |
| 30/04/1928 | Yellow Sands | Eden Philpotts | Play | Julian D'Albie, Elizabeth Chambers, Esmond Knight |
| 07/05/1928 | The Cooptimists | | Revue | Jessie Hitter, Brewster Meadows |
| 14/05/1928 | All Fun | | Revue | Billie Lane, Dan Rayner |
| 21/05/1928 | Alf's Button | W A Darlington | Play | Jack Morris, Sid Claydon, Daphne Grey |
| 28/05/1928 | Rose Marie | l Oscar Hammerstein, Otto Harbach, m Rudolf Friml | Musical | Nita Croft, Stanley Arthur, Manuel Jones |
| 04/06/1928 | Thark | Ben Travers | Play | Fred Glover, Stanford Holme, Thea Johnston |
| 11/06/1928 | Biddy | Lawrence Cowen | Play | Molly Redmond, Michael Renton |

# ✷ Productions 1898-1955 ✷

| Date | Title/Event | Playwright/Author<br>l= lyrics; m= music | Category | Performers |
|---|---|---|---|---|
| 18/06/1928 | The Kellys and the Cohens | | Revue | Fred Moule, Arthur Woodville |
| 25/06/1928 | Cuckoo in the Nest | Ben Travers | Play | Louis Bradfield Jnr, Dorothy Dale |
| 02/07/1928 | Mademoiselle from Armentieres | | Revue | Pimple, Angus Stron, Millie Constance |
| 09/07/1928 | The More We Laugh Together | | Revue | Fred Renon, Syd Wickard |
| 16/07/1928 | Maria Marten | | Play | Grace Sweeting, R Meadow White |
| 23/07/1928 | Charley's Aunt | Brandon Thomas | Play | Landon Littler, James Duncan |
| 30/07/1928 | Compromising Daphne | Edith Fitzgerald | Play | Edna Howard-Innes, Easten Pickering, Louie Tinsley |
| 06/08/1928 | Oh! You Sailors | | Revue | Billy Blackburn, Jack Sheppard |
| 13/08/1928 | The 100th Chance | from Ethel M Dell | Play | Owen Reynolds, Rozelle Bain, Bruce Baron |
| 20/08/1928 | Birthdays | | Revue | Billy Kray, Nita Desmond |
| 27/08/1928 | The Letter | W Somerset Maugham | Play | Margaret Swallow, H Hodgson-Bentley |
| 03/09/1928 | The Silent House | | Play | Henry Fielding, Joan Marion |
| 10/09/1928 | Sweeney Todd | | Play | Will Haggar, Gene Maurel |
| 17/09/1928 | The Wrecker | Arnold Ridley | Play | Hazel Bainbridge, harry Phydora, Rex De Vigne |
| 24/09/1928 | Hullo Cabaret | | Revue | Betty De Jay, Charlie Wood |
| 01/10/1928 | The Crooked Billet | Dion Titheradge | Play | Quinton McPherson, H Lindsell Stuart |
| 08/10/1928 | Hit the Deck | l Herbert Fields, m Vincent Youmans | Musical | Dora Barnes, Henry Raymond, Joan Fred-Emney, Jack Williams |
| 15/10/1928 | Lady Luck | l Desmond Carter, m H B Hedley, Jack Strachey | Musical | Teddy Brogden, Kathleen Burke |
| 22/10/1928 | Interference | Harold Dearden, Roland Pertwee | Play | Victor Bogetti, Douglas Jefferies |
| 29/10/1928 | My Son John | m Oscar Strauss | Musical | Norman Bowyer, Vera Barker, Richard Williams |
| 05/11/1928 | Devonshire Cream | Eden Philpotts | Play | Fred Rivenshall, Marjorie Battis, William Lorrimer |
| 12/11/1928 | The Terror | Edgar Wallace | Play | H Charles Carew, Edmund Kennedy, Margot Grahame |
| 19/11/1928 | Two White Arms | Harold Dearden | Play | Alma Taylor, George Mannering |
| 26/11/1928 | Right Away | | Revue | Jimmie Bryant, Topsy Turvy Five |
| 03/12/1928 | Lord Babs | Keble Howard | Play | Dan Booker, Basil Bowen |
| 10/12/1928 | Going Strong | | Revue | Albert Bruno, Edith Scott, Gladys Hay |
| 17/12/1928 | The Show Case | | Revue | Bobby Bayes, Johnnie Harris |
| 26/12/1928 | Jack and Jill | | Panto | Florrie Forde, Bud Flanagan, Chesney Allen |
| 31/12/1928 | Cinderella | | Panto | Walter Niblo, Lynda Martell |

| Date | Title/Event | Playwright/Author<br>l= lyrics; m= music | Category | Performers |
|------|-------------|------------------------|----------|-----------|
| 07/01/1929 | Insured | | Revue | Fred Renson, Ruth Dennis, Syd Wickard |
| 14/01/1929 | Brown Birds | | Revue | Jim & Jack, Dorothy Verton |
| 21/01/1929 | Sally | l Clifford Grey, m Jerome Kern | Musical | GWR Mechanics Institute Amateur Theatrical Society |
| 28/01/1929 | Potiphar's Wife | Edgar C Middleton | Play | Bertha Gross, Roy Jackson, Walter Roy, Roland Gillett |
| 04/02/1929 | Come to the Shoq | | Revue | Harry Wray & His White Guards, Beth O'Dare |
| 11/02/1929 | Oh, Kay | l Ira Gershwin, m George Gershwin | Musical | Rita McLean, Denier Warren |
| 18/02/1929 | Constant Nymph | Margaret Kennedy | Play | Nellie Giffiths, Terence Duff |
| 25/02/1929 | The Toreador | l Adrian Ross, P Greenbank, m Ivan Caryll, L Monckton | Musical | Swindon Amateur Musical and Dramatic Society |
| 04/03/1929 | Review of Revues | | Revue | Leslie Fuller, Margate Peddlers |
| 11/03/1929 | Bulldrog Drummond | Gerald Du Maurier, Herman Cyril McNeile | Play | Hamilton Deane, Dora Patrick, Edward Sproston, Mary Sproston |
| 12/03/1929 | At the Villa Rose | A E W Mason | Play | Hamilton Deane, Dora Patrick, Edward Sproston, Mary Sproston |
| 13/03/1929 | The Hypocrites | Henry Arthur Jones | Play | Hamilton Deane, Dora Patrick, Edward Sproston, Mary Sproston |
| 14/03/1929 | Dracula | Hamilton Deane, John L Balderston | Play | Hamilton Deane, Dora Patrick, Edward Sproston, Mary Sproston |
| 15/03/1929 | Daddy Long Legs | Jean Webster | Play | Hamilton Deane, Dora Patrick, Edward Sproston, Mary Sproston |
| 16/03/1929 | Frankenstein | | Play | Hamilton Deane, Dora Patrick, Edward Sproston, Mary Sproston |
| 18/03/1929 | The Squeaker | Edgar Wallace | Play | Victor Bogetti |
| 25/03/1929 | Empire State Circus | | Circus | Funny Harry (Stilts), Eddy & Bobby (Clowns), Frederica's Comedy Troupe of Terriers, Fosset Jockey |
| 01/04/1929 | Introduce Her | | Revue | Fred Brand, Bud Bennett |
| 08/04/1929 | The Alibi | Agatha Christie | Play | Francis L Sullivan |
| 15/04/1929 | The Girl Friend | l Lorenz Hart, m Richard Rodgers | Musical | Frances Davies, Sydney Keith, Edwin Styles |
| 22/04/1929 | | | Variety | Murray, the Australian escapologist |
| 29/04/1929 | The House of the Arrow | A E W Mason | Play | Beckett Bould |
| 06/05/1929 | Plunder | Ben Travers | Play | Roy Futvoy, Ethel Arden |
| 13/05/1929 | Barbed Wire | | Musical | George E Beck, Lucy Adair |

| Date | Title/Event | Playwright/Author<br>l= lyrics; m= music | Category | Performers |
|---|---|---|---|---|
| 20/05/1929 | Her Cardboard Lover | Jacques Deval, tr Valerie Wyngate, P G Wodehouse | Play | Athalie Davies, Derek Waterlow, Charle Cornock |
| 27/05/1929 | Seven Days Leave | J M Barrie | Play | Denville Rep Co, Isla Garnett-Vayne, Wilson Claridge, John Blake |
| 03/06/1929 | Yellow Ticket | Michael Morton | Play | Denville Rep Co, Isla Garnett-Vayne, Wilson Claridge, John Blake |
| 10/06/1929 | The Under Dog | Walter Howard | Play | Denville Rep Co, Isla Garnett-Vayne, Wilson Claridge, John Blake |
| 17/06/1929 | A Butterfly on the Wheel | | Play | Denville Rep Co, Isla Garnett-Vayne, Wilson Claridge, John Blake |
| 24/06/1929 | The Story of the Rosary | Walter Howard | Play | Denville Rep Co, Isla Garnett-Vayne, Wilson Claridge, John Blake |
| 01/07/1929 | The Silver King | Henry Arthur Jones | Play | Denville Rep Co, Isla Garnett-Vayne, Wilson Claridge, John Blake |
| 08/07/1929 | Tilly of Bloomsbury | Dion Titheradge | Play | Denville Rep Co, Isla Garnett-Vayne, Wilson Claridge, John Blake |
| 15/07/1929 | Under Two Flags | from Ouida | Play | Denville Rep Co, Isla Garnett-Vayne, Wilson Claridge, John Blake |
| 22/07/1929 | The Man Who Stayed at Home | J E Harold Terry, Lechmere Worral | Play | Denville Rep Co, Isla Garnett-Vayne, Wilson Claridge, John Blake |
| 29/07/1929 | If Four Walls Told | Edward Percy | Play | Denville Rep Co, Isla Garnett-Vayne, Wilson Claridge, John Blake |
| 30/07/1929 | If Four Walls Told | Edward Percy | Play | Denville Rep Co, Isla Garnett-Vayne, Wilson Claridge, John Blake |
| 31/07/1929 | If Four Walls Told | Edward Percy | Play | Denville Rep Co, Isla Garnett-Vayne, Wilson Claridge, John Blake |
| 01/08/1929 | If Four Walls Told | Edward Percy | Play | Denville Rep Co, Isla Garnett-Vayne, Wilson Claridge, John Blake |
| 02/08/1929 | East Lynne | from Mrs Henry Wood | Play | Denville Rep Co, Isla Garnett-Vayne, Wilson Claridge, John Blake |
| 03/08/1929 | East Lynne | from Mrs Henry Wood | Play | Denville Rep Co, Isla Garnett-Vayne, Wilson Claridge, John Blake |
| 05/08/1929 | League of Neighbours | | Revue | Albert Burton, Vie Vivienne |
| 12/08/1929 | The Twister | | Play | Randolph McLeod, Leila Oakley |
| 19/08/1929 | Hold Tight | | Revue | Jack Stanley, Percy Mavis, Stavanys (Gymnasts) |
| 26/08/1929 | Joy Boat | | Revue | Mark Denison |
| 02/09/1929 | Clowns in Clover | l Ronald Jeans, Donovan Parsons, m Noel Gay | Revue | Phyllis Bourke, Tiny Grayling, Laurence Tiller Girls |
| 09/09/1929 | The Police Force | | Revue | Joe Poynton |
| 16/09/1929 | Evening Stars | | Revue | Florence Smithson |
| 23/09/1929 | One Dam Thing After Another | l Lorenz Hart, m Richard Rodgers | Revue | Connie Graham, Hal Scott, Stan Stanford |

| Date | Title/Event | Playwright/Author<br>l= lyrics; m= music | Category | Performers |
|---|---|---|---|---|
| 30/09/1929 | Sunny | l Otto Harbach, Oscar Hammerstein, m Jerome Kern | Musical | Jack Dwyer, Sheila Page, Elsie Arnold |
| 07/10/1929 | Aloma | John B Hymer, Le Roy Clemens | Play | Olga Murgatroyd, Harry Frearson, Hector McGregor |
| 14/10/1929 | Aug-14 | Herbert Sargent, Con West | Revue | Billy Percy, Mercia Lotinga |
| 21/10/1929 | High Spirits | | Revue | Jack Gallagher, Josie Castalla, Lauri Howard |
| 28/10/1929 | By Candlelight | Siegfried Geyer, Karl Farkas | Play | Georgetta Le Grand, Richard Hatteras |
| 04/11/1929 | Chinese Bungalow | James Corbett, Marian Osmond | Play | George Butler, Rex Harrison |
| 11/11/1929 | See for Yourself | | Revue | Hal Duncan, Sybil Elsie |
| 18/11/1929 | To What Red Hell | Leslie S Hiscott, Percy Robinson | Play | Frederick Peisley, Nan Marriott-Watson |
| 25/11/1929 | The Last Hour | Charles Bennett | Play | Alexander Onslow, Alec Johnstone |
| 02/12/1929 | Laugh it Off | | Revue | Fred Morgan |
| 09/12/1929 | The Silent House | | Play | |
| 16/12/1929 | Merry Moments | | Revue | Mark Rivers, Nina Le Main, Jack Jacobs |
| 26/12/1929 | Robinson Crusoe | | Panto | Eileen Lane, Fay Stedman, Harry Summerson |
| 06/01/1930 | Flying Squad | Edgar Wallace | Play | Clive Woods, Harry Kerr, Dorothy Blair |
| 13/01/1930 | So this is Love | | Musical | Reg Fenton, Reg Andrews, Elsie Arnold |
| 20/01/1930 | 77 Park Avenue | Walter Hackett | Play | Doris Rogers, Jack Knight |
| 27/01/1930 | The Arcadians | l Arthur Wimperis, m Lionel Monckton, Howard Talbot | Musical | GWR Mechanics Institute Amateur Theatrical Society |
| 03/02/1930 | All Right on the Western Front | | Revue | Tom Gamble, Ena Stratton |
| 10/02/1930 | Rope | Patrick Hamilton | Play | Ireland Wood, Edwin Gibson, E W Waddy |
| 17/02/1930 | The Breakaway Revue | | Revue | Bobby Burns |
| 24/02/1930 | A Cup of Kindness | Ben Travers | Play | Laurence Cairn, Elspeth Duxbury, Betty Dorian, Rex Harrison |
| 03/03/1930 | Virginia | l Herbert Clayton, Douglas Furber, m Jack Waller, | Musical | Furness Williams, Helen Cooney, Harry Ray |
| 10/03/1930 | Review of Revues | | Revue | Leslie Fuller's Margate Meddlers |
| 17/03/1930 | Katinka | l Otto Harbach, m Rudolf Friml | Musical | Swindon Amateur Musical and Dramatic Society |
| 24/03/1930 | Bostock's Royal Italian Circus | | Circus | |

| Date | Title/Event | Playwright/Author<br>l= lyrics; m= music | Category | Performers |
|------|-------------|-------------------------|----------|------------|
| 31/03/1930 | The Mile-a- Minute Revue | | Revue | Alice Maude |
| 07/04/1930 | Brass Tacks | | Revue | Joey Porter, Lilian Conan |
| 14/04/1930 | Ever So Good | | Revue | Charles Regan, Winnie Draycrott |
| 21/04/1930 | Parisian Pleasures | | Revue | Tommy Mostoe, Ray Zack |
| 28/04/1930 | This Year of Grace | Noel Coward | Revue | Lily Moore, Ernest Lester, Percy Martin |
| 05/05/1930 | One Dam Thing After Another | l Lorenz Hart, m Richard Rodgers | Revue | Connie Graham, Bert Murray, Lilian Finney |
| 12/05/1930 | On the Road | | Revue | Barry Barnes |
| 19/05/1930 | Lido Follies | | Revue | Raymond Bennett, Fai Robina |
| 26/05/1930 | Clowns in Clover | l Ronald Jeans, Donovan Parsons, m Noel Gay | Revue | Leslie Vernon, Joan Hester |
| 02/06/1930 | One of the Best | | Revue | Jimmy Britton, Tom Deere |
| 09/06/1930 | Let's Laugh | | Revue | Neil Nelson |
| 16/06/1930 | Tres Bon | | Revue | Billy Kray, Gus Granville |
| 23/06/1930 | A Show Superlative | | Revue | Robert Ingalese, Angela Gray |
| 30/06/1930 | Insured | | Revue | Fred Renon, Ruth Dennis |
| 07/07/1930 | Hot Rhythm | | Revue | Billy Rowland, Trixie Maison |
| 14/07/1930 | Just Plain Folk | | Revue | Sandy Dawn, Ettie Howerd |
| 21/07/1930 | Playtime | | Revue | Nora Bancroft, Jean Kennedy |
| 28/07/1930 | The Heart Punch | | Revue | Ted (Kid) Lewis, Claude Gardner |
| 04/08/1930 | The Green Melody | | Revue | Leonard Morris |
| 11/08/1930 | The Novelty Box | | Revue | Harry Korris, Jimmy Charters, Betty Clelland* |
| 18/08/1930 | Speed and Sparkle | | Revue | May Royal, Fred Walker |
| 25/08/1930 | Splendour | | Revue | Dave Morris |
| 01/09/1930 | Fine Feathers | | Revue | Harry Day, Marie Ambrose |
| 08/09/1930 | There's no Argument | | Revue | Teddy Morris and his Band |
| 15/09/1930 | Something New | | Revue | Ted E Ross |
| 22/09/1930 | Happy Days | | Revue | Joe Young, Ida Le Roy |
| 29/09/1930 | The Blue Train | m Robert Stolz | Musical | Ernest Donley |
| 06/10/1930 | Silver Wings | l Dion Titheradge, m Jack Waller, Joseph Tunbridge | Musical | Helen Cooney, Philip Marvin, Karl Melene |
| 13/10/1930 | Lucky Girl | l Douglas Furber, m Phil Charig* | Musical | Hal Gordon, Harry Hartley, Mabs Luyes |
| 20/10/1930 | All Smiles | | Revue | Gladdy Sewell |
| 27/10/1930 | Making Good | | Revue | Douglas Wakefield, Billy Nelson, Edith Fields |
| 03/11/1930 | Follies Bergere Revue | | Revue | Bert Murray, Roger Foster |

| Date | Title/Event | Playwright/Author<br>l= lyrics; m= music | Category | Performers |
|---|---|---|---|---|
| 10/11/1930 | Love Lies | l Desmond Carter, m Hal Brody | Musical | Freddie Foss, Sidney Keith, Myrette Morven |
| 17/11/1930 | | | Variety | George Robey |
| 24/11/1930 | The Show's the Thing | | Revue | Doris Hare |
| 01/12/1930 | Why Goes to Paris | | Revue | Queenie May, Jack Gallagher |
| 08/12/1930 | Journey's End | R C Sherriff | Play | Anthony Enstrell, Henry Ludlow |
| 15/12/1930 | This is Value | | Revue | Bert Clifford, Frankland Gray |
| 22/12/1930 | Cheeky Face | | Revue | Robert Bemant |
| 29/12/1930 | Sez You | | Revue | Walter Niblo, Janice Hart |
| 05/01/1931 | Aladdin | | Panto | Fred Morgan |
| 12/01/1931 | Mickey the Mouse | | Revue | Teddy Morris, Ully Hartley |
| 19/01/1931 | Singing Clown | | Revue | Joe Moss |
| 09/02/1931 | Princess Charming | l Arthur Wimperis, m Albert Szirmai | Musical | GWR Mechanics Institution Amateur Theatrical Society |
| 09/03/1931 | The Vagabond King | l W H Post, Brian Hooker, m Rudolf Friml | Musical | Swindon Amateur Musical and Dramatic Society |
| 14/03/1932 | Florodora | l E Boyd Jones, Paul Rubens | Musical | Swindon Amateur Musical and Dramatic Society |
| 04/04/1932 | The New Moon | l Oscar Hammer-stein, m Sigmund Romberg | Musical | GWR Mechanics Institution Amateur Theatrical Society |
| 09/01/1933 | Robinson Crusoe | | Panto | Renee Roy, Florence Lenner, Monty Higgs |
| 27/03/1933 | The Desert Song | l Oscar Hammer-stein, m Sigmund Romberg | Musical | Swindon Amateur Musical and Dramatic Society |
| 24/04/1933 | The Good Companions | J B Priestley, Edward Knoblock | Play | Clifford Spurr, Gladys Ford-Howitt, Newton Blick, Marie Picquart |
| 01/05/1933 | Rose Marie | l Oscar Hammer-stein, Otto Harbach, M Rudolf Friml | Musical | Great Western (Swindon) Amateur Theatrical Society |
| 10/10/1933 | Bitter Sweet | Noel Coward | Musical | Nan Liddle, Marguerite Moreton, Webster Millar |
| 22/12/1933 | Goody Two Shoes | | Panto | George Young, Hilda campbell Russell, Dave Graves |
| 19/03/1934 | The Three Musketeers | l Clifford Grey, M Rudolf Friml | Musical | Swindon Amateur Musical and Dramatic Society |
| 09/04/1934 | Rio Rita | l Joseph McCarthy, m Harry Tierney | Musical | Great Western (Swindon) Amateur Theatrical Society |

| Date | Title/Event | Playwright/Author<br>l= lyrics; m= music | Category | Performers |
|---|---|---|---|---|
| 10/10/1934 | No, No, Nanette | l Irving Caesar, Otto Harbach, m Vincent Yeomans | Musical | Great Western (Swindon) Amateur Theatrical Society |
| 26/12/1934 | Babes in the Wood | | Panto | Edith James, Olwyn Williams, Bruce Green |
| 11/03/1935 | The Girl Friend | l Lorenz Hart, m Richard Rodgers | Musical | Swindon Amateur Musical and Dramatic Society |
| 08/04/1935 | Viktoria and her Hussar | l Harry Graham, m Paul Abraham | Musical | Great Western (Swindon) Amateur Theatrical Society |
| 23/03/1936 | The Maid of the Mountains | l Harry Graham, m Harold Fraser Simpson | Musical | Swindon Amateur Musical and Dramatic Society |
| 00/12/1936 | Mother Goose | | Panto | Olga May, George Bolton, Valerie Roy, Eva Ellis, Irene Leslie |
| 11/01/1937 | | | Variety | Beryl Orde, Hershel Henlere, Coram and Jerry |
| 08/03/1937 | Good-Night Vienna | l Holt Marvell, m George Posford, | Musical | Swindon Amateur Musical and Dramatic Society |
| 05/04/1937 | Virginia | l Herbert Clayton, Douglas Furber, m Jack Waller | Musical | Great Western (Swindon) Amateur Theatrical Society |
| 12/04/1937 | | | Variety | Nat Gonella and his Georgians, Harry Tate and Son |
| 19/04/1937 | | | Variety | Billy Bennett, Phyllis Robins |
| 26/04/1937 | | | Variety | Yogi Caram Dubilla |
| 03/05/1937 | Jill Darling! | l Desmond Carter, m Vivian Ellis | Musical | Fred Kitchen Jnr, Jeffrey Piddock, Joan Edmundson |
| 10/05/1937 | Grand Coronation Carnival and Cabaret | Grand Coronation Carnival and Cabaret | Variety | Nellie Wallace, Dulcie Dunn, Reg Bullock |
| 17/05/1937 | | | Variety | Flotsam and Jetsam, Ella Shields |
| 24/05/1937 | Distinguished Gathering | James Parrish | Play | Swindon Repertory Company |
| 31/05/1937 | Anthony and Anna | St John Erving | Play | Swindon Repertory Company |
| 07/06/1937 | The Late Christopher Bean | Emlyn Williams | Play | Swindon Repertory Company |
| 14/06/1937 | Living Dangerously | St John Erving | Play | Swindon Repertory Company |
| 21/06/1937 | While Parents Sleep | Anthony Kimmins | Play | Swindon Repertory Company |
| 28/06/1937 | The Trial of Mary Dugan | Bayard Veiller | Play | Swindon Repertory Company |
| 05/07/1937 | Tonight at 8.30 | Noel Coward | Play | Swindon Repertory Company |
| 12/07/1937 | Queer Cargo | Noel Langley | Play | Swindon Repertory Company |
| 19/07/1937 | Spring Tide | George Billam, J B Priestley | Play | Swindon Repertory Company |
| 26/07/1937 | The Man from Toronto | Douglas Murray | Play | Swindon Repertory Company |

| Date | Title/Event | Playwright/Author<br>l= lyrics; m= music | Category | Performers |
|------|-------------|------------------------------------------|----------|------------|
| 02/08/1937 | | | Variety | Tommy Handley, Albert Whelan |
| 09/08/1937 | Going Places | | Variety | Fred Kitchen Jnr |
| 16/08/1937 | Splinters of 1937 | | Revue | Hal Jones, George Ellisia |
| 23/08/1937 | | | Variety | Murray (Escapologist), Kitty Masters, Johnnie Riscoe |
| 30/08/1937 | | | Variety | Leslie Fuller |
| 06/09/1937 | | | Variety | Stanley Holloway, Bartlett and Ross |
| 13/09/1937 | The Belle of New York | l C M S McLellan, Gustav Kerker | Musical | Herbert Darnley, Peggy Inglis |
| 20/09/1937 | | | Variety | Anona Winn, Arthur Prince |
| 27/09/1937 | Blackberries | | Variety | Cole Brothers |
| 04/10/1937 | Stanelli's Stag Party | | Variety | Stanelli, Norman Long |
| 11/10/1937 | Kiss Me, Sergeant | | Revue | Tom Gamble |
| 18/10/1937 | Red, Hot and Blue Moments | | Revue | Sid Field |
| 25/10/1937 | | | Variety | Les Allen |
| 01/11/1937 | Penny Soc-Her Pools | | Revue | Ernie Lotinga |
| 08/11/1937 | Hip- Hip! Zoo-Ray | | Revue | Royal Bengal Tigers, Cossack Riding Acts |
| 07/03/1938 | Yeoman of the Guard | l W S Gilbert, m Arthur Sullivan | Musical | Swindon Amateur Musical and Dramatic Society |
| 04/04/1938 | New Moon | l Oscar Hammer-stein, m Sigmund Romberg | Musical | Great Western (Swindon ) Amateur Theatrical Society |
| 06/03/1939 | Miss Hook of Holland | Paul Rubens | Musical | Swindon Amateur Musical and Dramatic Society |
| 26/12/1939 | Cinderella | | Panto | Betty Hamilton, Frances Hughes, Clifton Court |
| 03/01/1944 | Babes in the Wood | | Panto | |
| 26/12/1944 | Cinderella | | Panto | Anona Winn, Gladys Watson, Tubby West & Bert Bury |
| 24/12/1945 | Aladdin | | Panto | Wally Patch, Bill Waddington, Sylvia Kellaway, Tom Payne |
| 24/12/1946 | Mother Goose | | Panto | Leonard Henry, Tommy Godfrey, Billy Shenton, Barbara Newman |
| 17/03/1947 | Mlada | | Opera | Swindon Musical Society |
| 07/04/1947 | | | Variety | Troise and his Mandoliers |
| 14/04/1947 | | | Variety | Bill Waddington, Charlie Kunz, The Permanes in "The Nightingale's Courtship" |
| 21/04/1947 | | | Variety | Sandy Powell, Eva May Wong, Charles Hague |
| 28/04/1947 | | | Variety | Suzette Tarri, Stanelli, Les Allen |
| 05/05/1947 | | | Variety | Harry Lester and his Hayseeds, Marie Lawton |

| Date | Title/Event | Playwright/Author l= lyrics; m= music | Category | Performers |
|------|-------------|---------------------------------------|----------|------------|
| 12/05/1947 | | | Variety | Elsie and Doris Waters (Gert and Daisy), Hughie Diamond ,Renara |
| 19/05/1947 | | | Variety | Primo Scala and his famous BBC Accordian Band |
| 26/05/1947 | Strike a New Note | | Revue | Freddie Frinton |
| 02/06/1947 | | | Variety | Western Brothers |
| 09/06/1947 | Strike it again | | Revue | Johnny Lockwood |
| 16/06/1947 | | | Variety | Koringa, Peter Sinclair |
| 23/06/1947 | Something to shout about | | Revue | Dick Henderson Jnr |
| 30/06/1947 | Till the end of time | | Film | |
| 07/07/1947 | Sister Kenny | | Film | |
| 04/08/1947 | | | Variety | Sid Millward and the Nitwits |
| 11/08/1947 | | | Variety | Adelaide Hall |
| 18/08/1947 | The Great Lyle and his Magical Revue | | Revue | The Great Lyle |
| 25/08/1947 | So Much the Better | | | Freddie Forbes, Jean Cavell |
| 01/09/1947 | | | Variety | Marie Lloyd Jnr, Jack Train, Tommy Godfrey |
| 08/09/1947 | Desert Song | l O Harbach, Oscar Hammer-stein, m Sigmund Romberg | Musical | Frederick Bentley, Peter Grant |
| 15/09/1947 | | | Variety | Laurel and Hardy, Olga Varona, Two Pirates, Peter Raynor |
| 22/09/1947 | Just William | Alick Hayes | Play | |
| 29/09/1947 | | | Variety | Macari and his Serenaders |
| 06/10/1947 | | | Variety | Henry Hall and his Band |
| 13/10/1947 | | | Variety | Big Bill Campbell |
| 20/10/1947 | Come to the Show-1st Prog | | Revue | Albert Grant, Renee Beck |
| 27/10/1947 | Come to the show -2nd Prog | | Revue | Albert Grant, Renee Beck |
| 03/11/1947 | Come to the Show- 3rd Prog | | Revue | Albert Grant, Renee Beck |
| 10/11/1947 | Come to the Show- 4th Prog | | Revue | Albert Grant, Renee Beck |
| 17/11/1947 | Come to the Show- Final Prog | | Revue | Albert Grant, Renee Beck |
| 01/12/1947 | Sing and Laugh | | Variety | Donald Peers, Dorothy Summers |
| 08/12/1947 | Scotch Express | Scotch Express | Revue | George Burton |
| 15/12/1947 | Ballet | | Ballet | Continental Theatre Ballet |
| 24/12/1947 | Jack and the Beanstalk | | Panto | Dick Ray, Harry Angers |

| Date | Title/Event | Playwright/Author l= lyrics; m= music | Category | Performers |
|------|-------------|---------------------------------------|----------|------------|
| 26/01/1948 | Cinderella | | Panto | Renee Beck, Pat Siddons, Fred Wynne |
| 09/02/1948 | Don Ross's Royal Imperial Circus | | Circus | |
| 16/02/1948 | | | Variety | Dr Crock and his Crackpots |
| 23/02/1948 | | | Variety | Jasper Maskelyn, The Two Leslies (Leslie Sarony, Leslie Michael Cole) |
| 01/03/1948 | | | Revue | Jane ( the famous Cartoon Girl from the Daily Mirror), Ravel |
| 08/03/1948 | Ignorance is Bliss | | Variety | Michael Moore, Gladys Hay, Harold Berens |
| 15/03/1948 | Holiday Mood | | Variety | Billy Carlyle,  Hilda Mundy |
| 22/03/1948 | No Orchids for Miss Blandish | James Hadley Chase | Play | Bryan Spielman |
| 29/03/1948 | | | Variety | Afrique, Billy Matchett |
| 05/04/1948 | Variety | | Variety | Hutch (Leslie Hutchinson) |
| 12/04/1948 | Stars of Command Performance | | Variety | Georgie Wood |
| 19/04/1948 | Hugh the Drover | Vaughan Williams | Opera | Swindon Musical Society |
| 26/04/1948 | Me and my Girl | l L Arthur Rose, Douglas Furber, m Noel Gay | Musical | Laurie Lupino Lane |
| 03/05/1948 | | | Variety | Cavan O'Connor |
| 10/05/1948 | Worms Eye View | R F Delderfield | Play | Molly Hare, O'Donovan Shiell |
| 17/05/1948 | Peace comes to Peckham | R F Delderfield | Play | Wally Patch,  Mona Vivian |
| 24/05/1948 | Snow White and the Seven Dwarfs | | Panto | Olga Fleming, Victor Standing |
| 31/05/1948 | Old Mother Riley and her daughter Kitty | | Revue | Arthur Lucan , Kitty McShane |
| 07/06/1948 | Waltz Dream | l Adrian Ross, m Oscar Straus | Musical | Leo Franklyn, Peter Grant, Leslie Hatton, Olga Gwynne |
| 14/06/1948 | Radio on Parade | | Variety | Peter Brough and Archie Andrews, Peter Cavanagh |
| 21/06/1948 | | | Variety | Clark Brothers, Maurice Rocco, Albert Whelan |
| 28/06/1948 | Radio Forfeits | | Revue | Michael Miles, Joan Winters and Guy Fielding, Senor Wences |
| 05/07/1948 | Show Business | | Revue | Joey Porter,  Peggy Cochrane |
| 12/07/1948 | Hit Parade of 1948 | | Variety | Betty Driver |
| 19/07/1948 | Soldiers in Skirts | | Revue | Joe Stein, Max Carole |
| 26/07/1948 | | | Variety | Richard Murdoch |
| 02/08/1948 | Hollywood Doubles | | Revue | Eddie Lee, Billy Barr, Patricia Sands |
| 09/08/1948 | | | Variety | Allan Jones, Winifred Atwell |
| 16/08/1948 | | | Variety | Leon Cortez, Phyllis Robins, Peter Sinclair |
| 23/08/1948 | Rocky Mountain Rhythm | | Variety | Big  Bill Campbell |

| Date | Title/Event | Playwright/Author<br>l= lyrics;  m= music | Category | Performers |
|------|-------------|-------------------------------------------|----------|-----------|
| 30/08/1948 | | | Variety | Wilson, Keppel and Betty, Jack Simpson and his Radio Sextet |
| 06/09/1948 | The Trinder Show | | Variety | Tommy Trinder, The Tiller Girls |
| 13/09/1948 | | | Variety | Martha Raye |
| 20/09/1948 | | | Variety | George Formby, Arthur Worsley |
| 27/09/1948 | Stars We'll Remember | | Variety | Frank Formby,  Marie Lloyd Junior, Lil O'Gorman |
| 04/10/1948 | | | Variety | Troise and his Mandoliers, Max Bacon |
| 11/10/1948 | | | Variety | Sid Millward and his Nitwits, Leslie Strange, The Karloffs |
| 18/10/1948 | Hellzapoppin | | Revue | Dave and Joe O'Gorman |
| 25/10/1948 | | | Variety | Sandy Lane, Turner Leyton, Rosemary Andree, Pop White and Stagger |
| 01/11/1948 | Your Country Cousins | | Revue | Harry Lester and his Hayseeds |
| 08/11/1948 | BBC Discoveries | | Variety | Carroll Levis, Johnny Lockwood |
| 15/11/1948 | | | Variety | Ivy Benson and her Band |
| 22/11/1948 | Variety | | Variety | Derek Roy, George Meaton, The Permanes, The Jerry Builders |
| 29/11/1948 | Would You Believe it | | Variety | Lofty -   9 ft 3i/2 ins, The Armless Artist, Elroy, Fredel, Crochet |
| 06/12/1948 | Forces Showboat | | Revue | Terry Bartlett,  Colin Ross, Harry Secombe |
| 13/12/1948 | | | Variety | Elsie and Doris Waters (Gert and Daisy), Hal Miller, Chas Carlton |
| 20/12/1948 | Closed | | | |
| 27/12/1948 | Goldilocks and the Three Bears | | Panto | Sally Barnes |
| 24/01/1949 | Babes in the Wood | | Panto | Billy "Uke" Scott |
| 21/02/1949 | Peek A Boo | | Revue | Phyllis Dixey, Jack Tracey, Howard de Courcey |
| 28/02/1949 | | | Variety | Monte Rey, Ronald Frankeau, Terry Hall with Micky Flinn |
| 07/03/1949 | | | Variety | Max Miller, Percy Edwards |
| 14/03/1949 | Don Ross's Royal Imperial Circus | | Circus | |
| 21/03/1949 | Ladies and Gentlemen | | Variety | Frankie Howerd, Norman Wisdom, Janet Brown |
| 28/03/1949 | Sadko | | Opera | Swindon Musical Society |
| 04/04/1949 | | | Variety | Vera Lynn, Scott and Foster, Meekin and Shand |
| 11/04/1949 | Ta- Ra-Rah-Boom-De-Ay | | Revue | Billy Whittaker, Mimi Law |
| 18/04/1949 | Palace of Varieties | | Variety | Ernest Longstaffe, Sunny Rogers |

| Date | Title/Event | Playwright/Author<br>l= lyrics; m= music | Category | Performers |
|------|-------------|------------------------------------------|----------|------------|
| 24/04/1949 | Me and my Girl | l L Arthur Rose, Douglas Furber, m Noel Gay | Musical | Lauri Lupino Lane, Helen Lauder, Nell Emerald |
| 02/05/1949 | Star Wagon | | Variety | Sandy Powell, Kay White, Brian Kent, Madge Kent |
| 09/05/1949 | Star Wagon | | Variety | Sandy Powell, Kay White, Brian Kent, Madge Kent |
| 16/05/1949 | Star Wagon | | Variety | Sandy Powell, Kay White, Brian Kent, Madge Kent |
| 23/05/1949 | Star Wagon | | Variety | Sandy Powell, Kay White, Brian Kent, Madge Kent |
| 30/05/1949 | | | Variety | Primo Scala and his Accordian Band, Molly Ostran, Edward Victor |
| 06/06/1949 | The Belle of New York | l Hugh Morton, m Gustav Kerker | Musical | Wally Patch, Bernard Hunter |
| 13/06/1949 | | | Variety | George Wood, Ronald Chesney, Dennis Noble and Margaret Eaves |
| 20/06/1949 | The Dancing Years | l Christopher Hassall, m Ivor Novello | Musical | Victoria Campbell, Max Oldakre |
| 27/06/1949 | No Room at the Inn | Joan Temple | Play | Diana Chesney, Sheila Eaves, Gladys Dyer, Dorothy Truman Taylor |
| 04/07/1949 | No, No, Nanette | l Otto Harbach, Irving Caesar, m Vincent Youmans | Musical | Reg Palmer, Kim Taylor |
| 11/07/1949 | The Melody Lingers on | | Variety | Issy Bonn |
| 18/07/1949 | Ice Carnival | | Ice Show | |
| 25/07/1949 | | | Variety | Robb Wilton, Walter Jackson |
| 01/08/1949 | Opportunity Knocks | | Talent | Hughie Green, Joe Hale and his Halestones |
| 08/08/1949 | The Geisha | l Harry Greenbank, m Sidney Jones | Musical | Leonard Henry, Mary Allen, Geoffrey Denton |
| 15/08/1949 | | | Variety | Jack Doyle(boxer), Jack (Record Roundup) Jackson, Peter Sinclair |
| 22/08/1949 | The Chocolate Soldier | l Stanislaus Strange, m Oscar Straus | Musical | Jessica James, Roy Royston, Fred Emney |
| 29/08/1949 | | | Variety | Steve Conway, Harold Berens, Winifred Atwell |
| 05/09/1949 | Hellzapoppin | | Revue | Hall, Norman and Ladd, Three Monarchs, Dave and Joe O'Gorman |
| 12/09/1949 | | | Revue | Maskelyn and Femynyne, Jasper Maskelyne and Co, Jane with Little Fritzi |
| 19/09/1949 | | | Variety | Felix Mendelssohn and his Hawaiian Serenadors, Dick Bentley |
| 26/09/1949 | | | Variety | Peter Cavanagh, Bill Kerr, Joan Hinde |

| Date | Title/Event | Playwright/Author l= lyrics; m= music | Category | Performers |
|---|---|---|---|---|
| 03/10/1949 | Madame Butterfly | Puccini | Opera | Imperial Opera Company, John Torney, Victoria Elliott, Charles Danson |
| 04/10/1949 | Faust | Gounod | Opera | |
| 05/10/1949 | Faust | Gounod | Opera | Special appearance of Walter Midgeley |
| 06/10/1949 | Cavalleria Rusticana, I Pagliacci | Mascagni, Cavallo | Opera | |
| 07/10/1949 | Madame Butterfly | Puccini | Opera | |
| 08/10/1949 | Cavalleria Rusticana, I Pagliacci | Mascagni, Cavallo | Opera | |
| 10/10/1949 | Tess and Bill | | Variety | Billy Cotton and His Band, Tessie O'Shea |
| 17/10/1949 | | | Variety | Suzette Tarri, Kay Cavendish |
| 24/10/1949 | Glamorous Night | l Christopher Hassall m Ivor Novello | Musical | Sylvia Cecil, Barry McKay, John McHugh |
| 31/10/1949 | How do Swindon | | Variety | Hetty King, Roy Lester, Billy Scott Kimber, Balliol & Merton |
| 07/11/1949 | | | Variety | Elsie and Doris Waters |
| 14/11/1949 | Hip-Hip-Zoo-Ray | | Circus | Roberts Bros |
| 21/11/1949 | | | Variety | Vic Oliver, Donald B Stewart, Stevils Sisters (m) |
| 28/11/1949 | | | Variety | Robb Wilton, Payne and Hilliard |
| 05/12/1949 | This was the Army | | Revue | Sonny Dawkes, Tommie Rose, Jack Lewis, Athur Knotto |
| 12/12/1949 | | | Variety | Sam Costa, Maureen Riscoe, Sid Millward and the The Nitwits (m) |
| 19/12/1949 | First steps to Stardom | | Talent | |
| 26/12/1949 | Mother Goose | | Panto | Albert Grant, Edgar Sawyer, Rosamund Sawyer, Bert Crew, The Permanes (m) |
| 23/01/1950 | Aladdin | | Panto | Renee Beck, Ken Barnes, Al Lester |
| 20/02/1950 | Careless Rapture | l Christopher Hassall, m Ivor Novello | Musical | Barry Sinclair, Nicolette Roeg, Muriel Barron |
| 27/02/1950 | Skimpy goes to Paris | | Revue | Hal Monty |
| 06/03/1950 | Your Country Cousins | | Revue | Harry Lester and his Hayseeds |
| 13/03/1950 | Round the World on Ice | | Ice Show | Vic Templar, Della Sweetman |
| 20/03/1950 | What's Wrong | | Revue | Will Hay Junior |
| 27/03/1950 | Carmen | | Opera | Swindon Musical Society |
| 03/04/1950 | You Lucky People | | Variety | Jean Melville, Bob Andrews, Vincent Tildsley's Mastersingers, Olga Varona |
| 10/04/1950 | Charley's Aunt | Brandon Thomas | Play | Martin Tiffen, Mary Hignett, Dawn Addams |
| 17/04/1950 | | | Variety | Max Miller, Percy Edwards |
| 24/04/1950 | The Lady of the Rose | | Musical | Margaret Burton, Frederick Bentley, Michael O'Connor |

| Date | Title/Event | Playwright/Author<br>l= lyrics; m= music | Category | Performers |
|------|-------------|------------------------------------------|----------|------------|
| 01/05/1950 | Old Mother Riley and her daughter Kitty | | Revue | Arthur Lucan, Kitty McShane |
| 08/05/1950 | Tobacco Road | Jack Kirkland | Play | Eric Micklewood, Constance Fecher, Jean Holness |
| 15/05/1950 | No Trees in the Street | Ted Willis | Play | Hilda Fenemore, John Stratton |
| 22/05/1950 | The Student Prince | l Dorothy Donnelly, m Sigmund Romberg | Musical | Harry Welchman, |
| 29/05/1950 | Rhythm on the range | | Revue | Tex McLeod and his horse Araby |
| 05/06/1950 | Please Teacher | | Musical | Eddie Molloy, Helen Ford |
| 12/06/1950 | The Forces Showboat | | Revue | Bartlett and Ross |
| 19/06/1950 | A Woman Desired | Gustav Salou | Play | Edwina Walton, Cyril James, David Johnson, Van Boolen |
| 26/06/1950 | Hollywood Way | | Revue | Eddie Henderson, June Thackeray, Viki Emra |
| 03/07/1950 | Starlight Rhapsody | | Revue | Eddie Connor, Eric Corrie |
| 10/07/1950 | "Air" We Are Again | | Revue | Stanelli, Renee Houston and Donald Stewart |
| 17/10/1950 | White Cargo | Leon Gordon | Play | |
| 24/07/1950 | Midget Town Marvels | | Midgets | |
| 31/07/1950 | Garden of Eden | | Revue | Bunny Doyle, Marion Gordon |
| 07/08/1950 | Lilac Time | l Adrian Ross, m Franz Schubert | Musical | John Torney, Phylllis Adrian |
| 14/08/1950 | Variety | | Variety | Kitty Bluett, Terry, the Irish Minstral |
| 21/08/1950 | Dear Miss Phoebe | l Christopher Hassall, m Harry Parr Davies | Musical | Peter Graves, Carol Raye |
| 28/08/1950 | Piccadilly Hayride | | Revue | Vic Gordon, & Peter Colville, Norman Vaughan |
| 04/09/1950 | Hollywood Lovelies | | Revue | Dump Harris and Stan as Laurel and Hardy |
| 11/09/1950 | Seeing is Believing | | Revue | Fredel, Ladd West, Prince Kari-Kari, Reggie Dennis, Alan Alan |
| 18/09/1950 | | | Variety | Lee Lawrence, Neville Bishop |
| 25/09/1950 | Annie Get Your Gun | Irving Berlin | Musical | Ann Doonan, Seamus Locke |
| 09/10/1950 | The Mikado | l W S Gilbert, m Arthur Sullivan | Opera | Swindon Musical Society |
| 16/10/1950 | | | Variety | Sonny Jenks & Rene Williams, Carroll Levis |
| 23/10/1950 | Prince's International Circus | | Circus | |
| 30/10/1950 | Bless the Bride | l A P Herbert, m Vivian Ellis | Musical | Valerie Lawson, Edmond Goffron |
| 13/11/1950 | Big Bill's Prairie Roundup | | Variety | Big Bill Campbell |
| 20/11/1950 | We'll Keep a Welcome | | Variety | Ossie Morris, Dan Donovan |
| 27/11/1950 | Radio Roundabout | | Variety | Elsie Carlisle, Harry Mooney |

| Date | Title/Event | Playwright/Author<br>l= lyrics; m= music | Category | Performers |
|---|---|---|---|---|
| 04/12/1950 | Smash Hits of 1950 | | Variety | |
| 11/12/1950 | | | Variety | Sam Browne, Joan Winters with Guy Fielding |
| 17/12/1950 | Ted Heath and his Music | | Big Band | Jack Parnell, Lita Roza, Dickie Valentine, Denis Lotis |
| 24/12/1950 | Cinderella | | Panto | Terry O'Neill, Pat Siddons |
| 22/01/1951 | Jack and the Beanstalk | | Panto | Hal Miller, Mary Genn, Dick Ray |
| 19/02/1951 | | | Variety | Bill Kerr, Robert Moreton |
| 26/02/1951 | | | Variety | Koringa, Four Ramblers, Peter Sinclair |
| 05/03/1951 | French Follies | | Revue | Carl and Roger Yale |
| 12/03/1951 | Down Lambeth Way | | Revue | Laurie Lupino Lane, Ken Wilson |
| 19/03/1951 | Ambassador Ballet | | Ballet | Antony Burke, Patricia Bentley |
| 26/03/1951 | 1001 Follies | | Revue | Arthur White, Karina |
| 02/04/1951 | Something Doing | | Revue | George Beck |
| 09/04/1951 | | | Variety | Reg Dixon, Victor Seaforth |
| 16/04/1951 | No, No, Nanette | l Irving Caesar, Otto Harbach, m Vincent Youmans | Musical | Peter Grant, Mignon Jarrold |
| 23/04/1951 | Come to see the Show | | Revue | Albert Grant, Renee Beck |
| 30/04/1951 | | | Variety | G H Elliott, "the chocolate coloured coon" |
| 07/05/1951 | The New French Capers | | Revue | |
| 14/05/1951 | Charley's Aunt | Brandon Thomas | Play | Leslie Phillips |
| 21/05/1951 | The Beggars Opera | John Gay | Ballet | Ballet Montmartre |
| 28/05/1951 | Together Again | | Revue | De Haven and Pace |
| 04/06/1951 | We'll keep a Welcome | | Variety | Ossie Morris, Stan Stennett |
| 11/06/1951 | Pardon my French | | Revue | Dresser and Dale, Con Stuart, Marie Joy |
| 18/06/1951 | Gold Digger Scandals of 1951 | | Revue | Harry Rowson, Phil Rivers, Ian Hynes (M) |
| 25/06/1951 | (K)nights with Beauties | | Revue | Low and Webster |
| 02/07/1951 | Strike a Nude Note | | Revue | Cyril Dowler, Rhoda Rogers |
| 09/07/1951 | Eve Comes to Town | | Revue | Jimmy Gay, Tommy Godfrey |
| 16/07/1951 | Festival Showboat of 1951 | | Revue | Jimmy Lee with Marion Rivers |
| 23/07/1951 | Ladies be Good | | Revue | Curly Jay, Sylvia Ross |
| 30/07/1951 | Gun Smoke | | Musical | James List, Peggy Brown |
| 06/08/1951 | Cocacabana | | Revue | Terry Cantor |
| 13/08/1951 | Snow White and the Seven Dwarfs | | Musical | Anne Rogers |
| 20/08/1951 | Mesdamoiselles from Armentierres | | Revue | Len Howe, Bernie Winters |
| 27/08/1951 | Why go to Paris | | Revue | |

| Date | Title/Event | Playwright/Author<br>l= lyrics; m= music | Category | Performers |
|------|-------------|------------------------------------------|----------|------------|
| 03/09/1951 | Dutch Serenade | | Variety | Macari and his Dutch Serenadors |
| 10/09/1951 | Sky High | | Revue | Reg Varney, Jacqueline Farrell |
| 17/09/1951 | Night life in Havana | | Revue | |
| 24/09/1951 | Soir de Paris | | Revue | |
| 01/10/1951 | Piccadilly Hayride | | Revue | Vic Gordon, Peter Colville |
| 08/10/1951 | Fred Karno's Army | | Revue | Four Graham Brothers |
| 15/10/1951 | Windmill Follies | | Revue | Billy Whittaker and Mimi Law |
| 22/10/1951 | Cinderella on Ice | | Ice Show | Paddy Woods, Vic Templar |
| 29/10/0951 | | | Variety | Arthur English, Dave Kaye, Ivor Moreton |
| 05/11/1951 | Stand Easy | | Revue | Charlie Chester |
| 12/11/1951 | Krazy Knights | | Revue | Johnny Lockwood |
| 19/11/1951 | Bob's Your Uncle | l Frank Eyton, m Noel Gay | Musical | Charles Heslop, Robert Dorning |
| 26/11/1951 | London, Paris and New York | | Revue | Sandy Powell |
| 03/12/1951 | Variety | | Variety | "Monsewer" Eddie Gray, Bunny Doyle |
| 10/12/1951 | Luckens Continental Circus | | Circus | |
| 17/12/1951 | Closed | | | |
| 24/12/1951 | Red Riding Hood | | Panto | Harry Lester and his Hayseeds. Also Mollie Tanner Dancers -1st pro panto |
| 21/01/1952 | Dick Whittington | | Panto | Betty Lotinga |
| 18/02/1952 | Wakey Wakey | | Variety | Billy Cotton and his band |
| 25/02/1952 | Going Gay | | Variety | Arthur Lucan as Old Mother Riley |
| 03/03/1952 | Stars of Radio Times | | Variety | Max Wall, Beryl Reid |
| 10/03/1952 | | | Variety | The Nitwits, Suzette Tarry |
| 17/03/1952 | Look In | | Variety | Naunton Wayne, Alfred Marks, Julie Andrews |
| 24/03/1952 | Exotic Nights | | Revue | Eddie Davies & Max Lee |
| 31/03/1952 | Goyescas and Down in the Valley | | Opera | Swindon Musical Society |
| 07/04/1952 | | | Variety | Bob & Alf Pearson |
| 14/04/1952 | | | Variety | Elsie & Doris Walters, Jack Watson |
| 21/04/1952 | Music and Madness | | Revue | Ken Morris, Joan Savage |
| 28/04/1952 | | | Variety | Gwen Liddle |
| 05/05/1952 | | | Variety | Carroll Levis (Discoveries) (m) |
| 12/05/1952 | | | Variety | Five Smith Brothers, Bill Waddington |
| 19/05/1952 | Isnt it Wonderful | | Revue | Reggie Dennis, Valita with Aldions (m) |
| 26/05/1952 | | | Variety | Anne Shelton, Terry O'Neil |
| 02/06/1952 | | | Variety | Frankie Howerd, Max Geldray Marcia Owen |
| 09/06/1952 | This was the Army | | Revue | Jack Lewis |

| Date | Title/Event | Playwright/Author<br>l= lyrics; m= music | Category | Performers |
|------|-------------|------------------------------------------|----------|------------|
| 16/06/1952 | | | Revue | Tom Moss (m) |
| 30/06/1952 | My Wife's Lodger | Dominic Roche | Play | Dominic Roche, Patricia Davies, Edna Hopcraft (m) |
| 07/06/1952 | It's Foolish But | | Revue | Billy Rhodes, Chika Lane (m) |
| 14/07/1952 | | | Variety | Burton Lester's Midgets |
| 21/07/1952 | | | | |
| 28/07/1952 | | | | |
| 04/08/1952 | Take a Peep | | Revue | Eddie Hart, Miriam Pearse, Joe Black (m) |
| 11/08/1952 | A Strip from Broadway | | Revue | Wally Brennan, Michael Cobb |
| 18/08/1952 | Une Nuit de Varietes | | | Warden Holt, Dennis Lawes |
| 01/09/1952 | Godiva Goes Gay | | Revue | Cyril Dowler, Rhoda Rogers |
| 08/09/1952 | Crazy Variety Nights | | Variety | Mastersingers, Doreen Harris |
| 15/09/1952 | Snow White and the Seven Dwarfs | | Panto | |
| 22/09/1952 | | | Variety | Macari and his Dutch Serenadors |
| 29/09/1952 | | | Variety | Maudie Edwards, Gladys Hay |
| 06/10/1952 | Let's Sing it Together | | Revue | Dorothy Squires, Joyce Golding |
| 13/10/1952 | Maid of the Mountains | l Harry Graham, m Harold Fraser-Simpson | Musical | Margaret Burton, Sonny Jenks |
| 20/10/1952 | Dick Whittington and his Cat on Ice | | Ice show | Joyce Marsh |
| 27/10/1952 | The Arcadians | l Arthur Wimperis, m Lionel Monckton, Howard Talbot | Musical | SALOS |
| 03/11/0952 | John Calvert | | Magic | Assisted by Ann Cornell |
| 10/11/1952 | Hip-Zoo-Ray Circus | | Circus | Roberts Brothers |
| 17/11/1952 | Why Worky | | Revue | Johnny Lockwood |
| 24/11/1952 | Record Roundup | | Variety | Eddie Calvert, Malcolm Mitchell Trio |
| 01/12/1952 | Paris to Paradise | | Revue | Davy Kaye |
| 08/12/1952 | Radio Highlights | | Variety | Peter Cavanagh |
| 15/12/1952 | His Grand Christmas Carnival | | Variety | Patricia Rossborough |
| 26/12/1952 | Babes in the Wood | | Panto | Dickie Arnold, Vera Christie |
| 02/02/1953 | Goldiocks and the Three Bears | | Panto | Nick Franks, Roma Derry |
| 23/02/1953 | Star Parade | | Variety | Nat Gonella, Billy Rhodes & Chika Lane |
| 02/03/1952 | Radio Pie | | Variety | Western Brothers, Leslie Sarony, Stanelli (m) |

| Date | Title/Event | Playwright/Author<br>l= lyrics; m= music | Category | Performers |
|---|---|---|---|---|
| 09/03/1953 | | | Variety | Morton Fraser's Harmonica Gang, Dick Emery, Dave King, Hylda Heath (m) |
| 16/03/1953 | Sleeping Beauty on Ice | | Ice Show | |
| 23/03/1953 | One for the Road | | Revue | Freddie Sales |
| 30/03/1952 | You Will Remember | | Variety | Georgie Wood, Hetty King. Dick Henderson |
| 06/04/1953 | | | Variety | Robin Richmond, Fayne and Evans, Radio Revellers |
| 13/04/1953 | Fred Karno's Army | | Revue | |
| 20/04/1953 | The Snow Maiden | | Opera | Swindon Musical Society |
| 27/04/1953 | Florodora | l Ernest Boyd-Jones, m Leslie Stuart | Musical | Valerie Lawson, Albert Grant |
| 04/05/1953 | | | Variety | Jack Hilliard |
| 11/05/1953 | Mystery Box Revue | | Revue | The Great Lyle |
| 18/05/1953 | The Spice of Life | | Variety | Jack Haig, Diana Dors |
| 25/05/1953 | Hollywood Party | | Revue | Reub Silver & Marion Day, Charlie Clapham, Stig Harris & Stan, Bernard Landy |
| 08/06/1953 | Piccadilly Hayride | | Revue | Bill Maynard, Terry Scott |
| 15/06/1953 | | | Variety | Jill Manners, Harry Mooney & Victor King |
| 22/06/1953 | | | Variety | Merry Macs |
| 29/06/1953 | Variety | | Variety | Rose Murphy, Nat Hope, Al & Victor Farrell |
| 06/07/1953 | Harem Scarem | | Revue | Ali Bey plus nudes |
| 13/07/1953 | Mighty Fine | | Revue | |
| 20/07/1953 | The Sauciest Girls of 1953 | | Revue | |
| 27/07/1953 | Oklahoma | l Oscar Hammerstein, m Richard Rodgers | Musical | Ray Buckingham, Barbara Ann Rogers |
| 04/08/1953 | Pack up your Troubles | | Revue | Sandy Lane |
| 10/08/1953 | King's Rhapsody | l Christopher Hassall, m Ivor Novello | Musical | Sylvia Cecil, Aileen Cochrane |
| 17/08/1953 | Blue for a Boy | l Harold Purcell, m Harry Parr Davies | Musical | Beryl Seton, Joan Emery |
| 24/08/1953 | Front Page lovelies of 1953 | | Revue | Collinson and Green |
| 31/08/1953 | Naughty, Naughty | | Revue | Kim Kean, Susan King |
| 07/09/1953 | Four Winds | Alex Atkinson | Play | William Kendall, Betty-Ann Davies, Frank Lawton, Raymond Francis |
| 14/09/1653 | Ambassador's Folly | Alan Melville | Play | Hugh Wakefield. Tom Gill |
| 21/09/0953 | The Man with Expensive Tastes | Edward Percy, Lilian Denham | Play | George Curzon, Peter Bull, Ruth Trouncer, Maurice Kaufmann |

| Date | Title/Event | Playwright/Author<br>l= lyrics; m= music | Category | Performers |
|---|---|---|---|---|
| 28/09/1953 | A Chance of Happiness | James Liggatt | Play | Rosamund John, Henry Oscar, Andrew Crawford, Vivien Merchant |
| 05/10/1953 | Not a Clue | | Play | Sonny Hale, Claude Hulbert |
| 12/10/1953 | Worms Eye View | R F Delderfield | Play | Fred McNaughton, Dorothy Freer, Paul Walters |
| 19/10/1953 | The Archers | Edward J Mason, Geoffrey Webb | Play | Edward Higgins, Marjorie Wilde |
| 26/10/1953 | Desert Song | l O Harbach, Oscar Hammer-stein, m Sigmund Romberg | Musical | SALOS |
| 02/11/1953 | The Housemaster | Ian Hay | Play | Jack Hulbert, Mary Glynne |
| 09/11/1953 | Nine Day's Wonder | Constance Cox | Play | Guy Rolfe, Sonia Dresdell |
| 16/11/1953 | Walter Gore's Ballet | | Ballet | |
| 23/11/1953 | Vice in the Streets | Ian Stuart | Play | Tony Doonan |
| 30/11/1953 | The Dominent Sex | Michael Egan | Play | Jimmy Hanley, Josephine Stuart |
| 07/12/1953 | | | Variety | Harry Dawson, Michael Moore |
| 14/12/1953 | | | Variety | Leon Cortez |
| 24/12/1953 | Mother Goose | | Panto | Sandy Powell, Charles Cardiff |
| 25/01/1954 | Old Mother Hubbard | | Panto | Arthur Lucan, Shirley Gordon, Roy Rolland |
| 01/03/1954 | Soldiers in Skirts | | Revue | Max Carole, Eric Lloyd |
| 08/03/1954 | We Couldn't Wear Less | | Revue | |
| 15/03/1954 | Mother Goose on ice | | Ice show | Dick Montague, Joyce Mendoza |
| 22/03/1954 | Reefer Girl | Lorraine Tier | Play | Adele Strong, Martin Lane |
| 29/03/1954 | | | Variety | Stan Stennett, Sid Millward and the Nitwits, Joan Hinde |
| 05/04/1954 | Cinderella | Massanet | Opera | Swindon Musical Society |
| 12/05/1954 | Honky Tonk | | Revue | Bob Grey, Geo E Beck |
| 19/04/1954 | Carroll Levis and his Discoveries | | Talent | Barry Took, Violet Pretty (Ann Heywood) |
| 26/04/1954 | Why Cover Girls | | Revue | Coral Grey, Jimmy French |
| 03/05/1954 | Paris after Dark | | Revue | Nick Franks |
| 10/05/1954 | Follies Montmartre | | Revue | Charlie Ellis |
| 17/05/1954 | Kiss me Goodnight Sergeant Major | | Revue | Margot Gaye, Jock Glen, Johnny Firpo |
| 24/05/1954 | Seagulls Over Sorrento | Hugh Hastings | Play | Ronald Radd, Wallas Eaton |
| 31/05/1954 | | | Variety | Four Ramblers |
| 07/06/1954 | The Girl Show | | Revue | Jill Summers, Danny O'Dare |
| 14/06/1954 | Call us Mister | | Revue | Alan Haynes, Tommy Osborne |
| 21/06/1954 | Shapes and Surprises | | Revue | Cingalee & Co, Roy Lester, Marion Lane |
| 28/06/1954 | Fluff and Nonsense | | Revue | Barry Pidduck,, Pauline Penny, Fluffettes, Erroll Avery |

| Date | Title/Event | Playwright/Author<br>l= lyrics; m= music | Category | Performers |
|---|---|---|---|---|
| 05/07/1954 | Lilac Time | l Adrian Ross, m Franz Schubert | Musical | Charles Gillespie, Peggie Allen, David Allen |
| 12/07/1954 | Peek-a-Boo | | Revue | Phyllis Dixey |
| 11/10/1954 | Affairs of State | Louis Verneuil | Play | Pauline Yates, Michael Hitchman, Dinah Rogers |
| 18/10/1954 | The Little Hut | Andre Roussin | Play | Pauline Yates, Michael Hitchman, Cyril Wheeler |
| 25/10/1954 | Vagabond King | l Brian Hooker, m Rudolf Friml | Musical | SALOS |
| 01/11/1954 | Dial M for Murder | Frederick Knott | Play | Irene Sunters, Leonard Kingston |
| 08/11/1954 | The Facts of Life | Roger McDougall | Play | Beau Daniels, Pamela Jackson, Gerald Sim |
| 15/11/1954 | Someone Waiting | Emlyn Williams | Play | |
| 22/11/1954 | A Question of Fact | Wynyard Browne | Play | |
| 27/12/1954 | Robinson Crusoe | | Panto | |

# Index